THE POLITICAL ECONOMY
OF GROWTH

THE
POLITICAL
ECONOMY
OF
GROWTH

Paul A. Baran

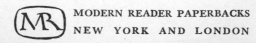

MODERN READER PAPERBACKS
NEW YORK AND LONDON

Library of Congress Catalog Card Number: 57-7953
Standard Book Number: 85345-076-5

First Modern Reader Paperback Edition 1968
Fourth Printing

Monthly Review Press
116 West 14th Street, New York, N.Y. 10011
33/37 Moreland Street, London, E.C. 1

Manufactured in the United States of America

*For
my son
Nicky*

Preface to the First Edition

The manuscript of the present volume was completed in the autumn of 1955. Much that has since happened in the world bears a direct relation to a number of themes dealt with here. Resisting for obvious reasons the strong temptation to insert some of the relevant considerations into the galley proofs, I decided to attempt to summarize them briefly in this preface.

The events in the Near East which culminated in the Anglo-French military action against Egypt provide corroboration of one of the main theses of this book: the "unreformed" nature of contemporary imperialism and its inherent animosity towards all genuine initiative at economic development on the part of the underdeveloped countries. The role played in this conflict by the United States demonstrates the unabated rivalry among the imperialist countries as well as the growing inability of the old imperialist nations to hold their own in face of the American quest for expanded influence and power. In the bitter words of the London *Economist*: "We must learn that we are not the Americans' equals now, and cannot be. We have a right to state our minimum national interests and expect the Americans to respect them. But this done, we must look for their lead." (November 17, 1956.)

While the assertion of American supremacy in the "free" world implies the reduction of Britain and France (not to speak of Belgium, Holland, and Portugal) to the status of junior partners of American imperialism, this shift may well have certain favorable consequences for the underdeveloped countries. Transferring as it were from service in an impoverished business to employment in a prosperous enterprise, the colonial and dependent countries may expect their new principal to be less rapacious, more generous, and more forward-looking. Although it is most doubtful whether this change will make any serious difference in the basic issues of economic and social development in the backward areas, some improvement in their fate is not unlikely.

Recent developments in the socialist countries of Europe are even

more germane to the propositions advanced in (and underlying) this
study. Khrushchev's revelations concerning some aspects of Stalin's
rule and the subsequent events in Poland and Hungary have brought
into the open with renewed force the steepness of the backward countries' ascent to a better and richer society. But it is merely the "cult
of personality" in reverse to ascribe all the crimes and errors committed in the Soviet Union before the Second World War and in all
of Eastern and Southeastern Europe after it to the evil personalities
of Stalin, Beria, and their associates. Matters are not so simple; and
the general feeling is wholly understandable that it is indeed the
"entire system" that must be held responsible for what was perpetrated
by the leadership. Yet it is a grievous fallacy to conclude from this
that *socialism* is the "entire system" that needs to be repudiated. For
it is not *socialism* that can be fairly charged with the misdeeds of
Stalin and his puppets—it is the *political system* that evolved from the
drive to develop at breakneck speed a backward country threatened
by foreign aggression and in face of internal resistance. The emergence
of such a political system under the unique circumstances prevailing
in Russia after Hitler's seizure of power and in the countries of Eastern
and Southeastern Europe during the frightening years of the cold war
does not "prove" that socialism is inherently a system of terror and
repression. What it does mean—and this is a historical lesson of paramount importance—is that socialism in backward and underdeveloped
countries has a powerful tendency to become a backward and underdeveloped socialism. What has happened in the Soviet Union and the
socialist countries of Eastern Europe confirms the fundamental Marxian
proposition that it is the degree of maturity of society's productive
resources that determines "the general character of social, political
and intellectual life." It casts no reflection on the fundamental rationality, desirability, and potentialities of a socialist transformation in
the West. Indeed, it accentuates its desperate urgency. For a socialist
society in the advanced countries would not be compelled to engage
in "forced marches" towards industrialization, or bound to withdraw
from popular consumption large parts of miserably low incomes, or
constrained to devote to military purposes significant shares of small
aggregate outputs. Such a socialist society would not only attack head-on
the waste, irrationality, and cultural and moral degradation of the
West, it would also throw its weight into helping to solve the entire
problem of want, disease, and starvation in the underdeveloped parts
of the world. Socialism in the West, once firmly established, would
destroy for all time the bases and the need for any reappearance of the
political and social repression that marked the early stages of socialism
in the East. Hence for socialists in the West the time is now—as never
before—to renew our dedication to the cause of reason, progress, and

freedom, to redouble our efforts to advance the cause of socialism. For it is on the ultimate success of these efforts that the fate of humanity depends—both in the West and in the East. It is only these efforts that can restore to the economically most advanced countries the moral, ideological, and political leadership of the world that at the present time is no longer theirs. Only the advanced countries' progress and guidance on the road to a socialist democracy will terminate the untold suffering to which mankind has been condemned thus far.

The contents of this book were presented in the barest outline in a course of lectures delivered at Oxford during the Michaelmas Term in 1953. In the interval of reworking the lectures with a view to their publication, I have made many changes both of a formal and of a substantive nature. The process of writing is a process of learning; and much has become clearer to me in the attempt to transform my original rough notes into what I hope is an intelligible presentation. Not that I suffer from any illusion of having now even approximately "covered the ground." The terrain is vast, and the complications and implications encountered at every step are numerous and baffling; the most I can aspire to is to have sketched its general contours and thus to submit a tentative map the chief function of which, I hope, will be to encourage further travel and to stimulate deeper exploration.

Throughout this work I have been fortunate enough to be in contact with a number of good friends working and thinking on similar problems. I am particularly grateful to Charles Bettelheim, Maurice Dobb, Leo Huberman, Michal Kalecki, Oskar Lange, and Joan Robinson for the time and attention which they have devoted to discussing matters related to the theme of this book or to reading all or parts of the manuscript. Their suggestions and criticisms were invaluable. I wish to thank also John Rackliffe who made a valiant effort to turn my style into comprehensible and readable English; if his success remained only partial, it is difficult to imagine what the book might have been without his help. I am obliged to Elizabeth Huberman who prepared the index, and to Sybil May and Catherine Winston who saw the book through press. My debt is largest to Paul M. Sweezy, whose generous friendship I have enjoyed for nearly two decades. The courage, lucidity, and unwavering devotion to reason that render his work one of the bright spots in America's postwar intellectual history have been to me all that time a never-failing source of stimulation and encouragement. There is hardly an issue considered in this book that we have not on one occasion or another touched upon in our discussions. It is impossible for me to say which of the thoughts expressed here belong to him, and which are my own. I hasten to add that neither he nor anyone else is responsible for whatever errors and confusions may still mar my argument. These are due wholly to my own failings and occasionally to my stubbornness.

In quoting foreign authors I have either referred to English translations, or in some cases I have cited from the original but have given the quotation in English; in these instances I have translated the relevant passages myself.

Los Altos, California   P. A. B.
December 1956

Foreword to 1962 Printing

On looking over this book again with a view to writing a foreword for the French and German translations as well as for a new American printing, I have a strong feeling of ambivalence. There is first the thought that it may be not too immodest on my part to submit this work once more to the reader in its original form. Neither historical events which have taken place since it was written, nor subsequent reflection and study, partly stimulated by the criticism to which it has been subjected, have changed my conviction that *taken as a whole* the view which it presents and the argument which it advances are still entirely valid. But then there are other considerations—referring not to the whole but to the parts—which are less comforting. For were I at this time to write the book afresh, I would try to eliminate what strike me now as weaknesses and to develop several of its themes in a more comprehensive and convincing manner. However, since the pressure of other, not unrelated, work renders such a major undertaking impossible, I must reluctantly adopt the principle of "letting bygones be bygones," and attempt to resolve the conflict between the whole and the parts by means of this prefatory note dealing briefly with those aspects of the book which are most in need of reconsideration and supplementation. The order in which the topics are taken up is determined not so much by their general importance as by the sequence in which they appear in the book itself.

I

Hard as I tried to clarify the prevailing confusion about a central concept of economic theory, that of *consumer sovereignty,* the success attained was anything but spectacular. There are few other areas where the limitations of the conventional economist are as obvious and as damaging to insight as in the treatment of this subject. Irrevocably committed to taking the existing economic and social order for granted, and thinking exclusively in categories reflecting capitalist relations of production, even the ablest academic economist is inexorably trapped by the basic predicament of all bourgeois thought: the compulsion to choose continually between equally pernicious alternatives. Like the man condemned to death who was granted "freedom of choice" between being hanged and being shot, bourgeois economics is eternally plagued by the problem whether the irrationality of monopoly is better than the anarchy of competition; whether the cumulation of means of destruction is better than unemployment; whether inequality of income and wealth leading to saving and investment on the part of the rich is better than fair shares and greatly reduced saving and investment. In the same way the problem of consumers' sovereignty is viewed as the question whether the consumer—however much exposed to the barrage of advertising and high-pressure salesmanship—should be left free to spend his income in any way he pleases or be forced to accept a basket of goods which a "commissar" would judge to be best for him. It can be readily seen that placed before *this* dilemma, the economist is indeed confronted by a Hobson's choice. Kneeling awe-stricken before the absolute truth of the consumer's "revealed preferences" places him in the disturbing position of having to refuse to make any judgments on the resulting composition of output and hence on all the waste and cultural degradation which so obviously characterize our society. On the other hand, rejecting the consumer's revealed preferences as the *ultima ratio* in favor of a set of decisions imposed by government would be equally distressing, implying as it would the repudiation of all the teachings of welfare economics and—more importantly—of all the principles of individual freedom which the economist rightly strives to uphold.

The conservative reaction to this perplexity appears in two variants. One school of thought deals with the problem by denying its existence. This school holds that the molding of consumers' tastes and preferences by the advertising and high-pressure sales efforts of corporate business is nothing but a bogey, because in the long run no amount of persuasion and no ingenuity of salesmanship can change "human nature," can force upon the consumer what he does not want.[1] Furthermore—so the argument runs—the revealed preferences of consumers yield

---

[1] *"The consumer is king today. . . .* Business has no choice but to discover what he wants and to serve his wishes, even his whims." Steuart Henderson Britt, *The Spenders*, (New York, Toronto, London, 1960), p. 36. Italics in the original. Also: *"If the product does not meet some existing desire or need of the consumer, the advertising will ultimately fail."* Rosser Reeves, *Reality in Advertising* (New York, 1961), p. 141. Italics in the original.

results which are quite adequate and call for no particular improvements.[2]

Another conservative current of thought takes a different tack. It freely acknowledges that the consumer's revealed preferences have nothing in common with the traditional notion of consumer *sovereignty*, that the power of the giant corporations is such as to mold consumers' tastes and preferences for the benefit of corporate interests, and that all of this has a deleterious effect on both our economy and our society. As Professor Carl Kaysen puts it:

> One aspect of [its] broad power . . . is the position that corporate management occupies as taste setter or style leader for the society as a whole. Business influence on taste ranges from the direct effects through the design of material goods to the indirect and more subtle effects of the style of language and thought purveyed through the mass media—the school of style at which all of us are in attendance every day. . . . This, more shortly stated, is the familiar proposition that we are a business society, and that the giant corporation is the "characteristic," if not the statistically typical, institution of our society. . . .[3]

Yet skeptical and realistic as the writers of this orientation are, they place the utmost emphasis on the fact that these irrationalities and calamities are *inherent* in the order of things, which they identify with the economic and social system of monopoly capitalism. "To touch the corporation deeply," remarks Professor Mason, "is to touch much else."[4] And in our day touching "much else" is definitely not on the economist's agenda.

This is not the stance of the so-called liberal. Considering the consumer's revealed preferences to be the source of our society's irrational allocation of resources, of its distressing moral and cultural condition, the liberal is exercised about the pernicious impact of advertising, about fraudulent product differentiation and artificial product obsolescence; he inveighs against the quality of culture purveyed by the educational system, Hollywood, the newspapers, the radio and TV networks; and, driven by this indignation, he arrives at the conclusion that "the choice is not whether consumers or a central planner should exercise sovereignty but whether and how the producer's power to ignore some con-

[2] "The so-called waste in our private economy happens to be the way people make a living and in so doing spread well-being among all. It happens to be the way we get our gleaming schools and hospitals and highways and other 'public' facilities." *The Wall Street Journal*, October 7, 1960, p. 16.

[3] "The Corporation: How Much Power? What Scope?" in Edward S. Mason, ed., *The Corporation in Modern Society* (Cambridge, Massachusetts, 1959), p. 101.

[4] *Ibid.*, p. 2.

sumers and influence the preferences of others should be curbed, modified, or shared in some ways."[5] To accomplish this curbing, modifying, and sharing, he recommends a list of "remedies and policies" ranging from regulatory measures such as those taken by the Food and Drug Administration, through government support for opera houses and theaters, to the formation of Distinguished Citizens Committees the task of which would be to influence public opinion in the direction of rational choices and better taste.

Disappointing as it may be to many, there can be little doubt that at the present stage of capitalist development the conservative "realist" often comes nearer the truth than the liberal meliorist. Just as it makes no sense to deplore war casualties without attacking their cause, war, so it is meaningless to sound the alarm about advertising and all that accompanies it without clearly identifying the *locus* from which the pestilence emanates: the monopolistic and oligopolistic corporation and the non-price-competitive business practices which constitute an integral component of its *modus operandi*. Since this *locus* itself is never approached, is indeed treated as strictly out of bounds by Galbraith, Scitovsky, and other liberal critics, since nothing is further from their minds (or at least their public utterances) than "touching deeply" the giant corporation, what can be expected from their recommending various regulatory boards and even their possible appointment to Distinguished Citizens Committees? One would think that the record of already existing regulatory agencies is sufficiently eloquent in showing that it is Big Business that does the regulating rather than *vice versa*. And is more evidence needed on the ineffectuality of the Food and Drug Administration, the Federal Trade Commission, and the Federal Communications Commission than has already been assembled thus far?[6] Nor is there any need to elaborate on the profound impact on society exercised by the recent activities and reports of the President's most distinguished Commission on National Goals.[7] But the liberal meliorists ignore all this. Treating the state as an entity which presides over society but does not form a part of it, which sets society's goals and reshuffles its output and income but remains unaffected by the prevailing relations of production and impervious to the dominant interests, they fall prey to a naive rationalism which, by nurturing

[5] Tibor Scitovsky, "On the Principle of Consumers' Sovereignty," *American Economic Review*, May, 1962. I am indebted to Professor Scitovsky for letting me see a copy of this paper prior to publication.

[6] Cf. for example, James Cook, *Remedies and Rackets* (New York, 1958), *passim*; and "Behind the FCC Scandal," *Monthly Review*, April, 1958.

[7] Cf. *Goals for Americans*, The Report of the President's Commission on National Goals (New York, 1960), *passim*.

illusions, merely contributes to the maintenance of the *status quo*.[8]
Compared with this, the "contracting out" dictum—"we have . . . reached
the frontier between economic and political theory; and we shall not
cross it"—with which Professor Scitovsky a decade ago concluded his
magnum opus,[9] formulates a relatively tenable position.

For the crux of the problem is not even approached by the liberal
critic. In the first place, he of all people, being a good Keynesian, cannot
avoid inconsistency when he recommends the interference with or curtailment of corporate advertising and other sales activities. In this
regard *The Wall Street Journal* and the "realistic" economists who share
its views are surely on firmer ground. For all these "undesirable"
business practices *do* in fact promote and increase sales, and *do* actually
directly and indirectly help in propping up the level of income and
employment.[10] So also does the sale of ever more motor cars, even if
they do strangle our cities and poison our atmosphere; and the production of armaments and the digging of shelters. None of these activities
can be regarded as promoting the progress and happiness of the human
race, although all of them constitute remedies against sagging production and increasing unemployment.[11] And yet such is the dialectic of the
historical process that *within the framework of monopoly capitalism*
the most abominable, the most destructive features of the capitalist
order become the very foundations of its continuing existence—just as
slavery was the *conditio sine qua non* of its emergence.

The "realistic" conservative scores also over the liberal "do-gooder"
in his general comprehension of the problem of consumer sovereignty.
For in warning against exaggerating the impact of advertising, high-
pressure salesmanship, and the like, on the preferences and choices of
consumers, they occupy a position of formidable strength. Their statements that consumers like only what they care for and buy only what

[8] For a lucid exposition of the Marxist theory of the state, cf. Stanley
W. Moore, *The Critique of Capitalist Democracy; An Introduction to the
Theory of the State in Marx, Engels, and Lenin* (New York, 1957).

[9] *Walfare and Competition: The Economics of a Fully Employed Economy* (Chicago, 1951), p. 450.

[10] This point was made for the first time to my knowledge in the excellent paper by K. W. Rothschild, "A Note on Advertising," *Economic
Journal*, 1942.

[11] "Right now, officials incline toward a new round of military ordering
in preference to either massive public works or a cut in taxes, if they decide
the economy needs another push." *Business Week*, December 9, 1961. And
it is not only "right now" that this is the "official inclination." For "some
advisers like the idea of shelters, but want to push it at a time when
the economy needs a stimulant." *Ibid.*, November 4, 1961. Thus the shelters
are not to protect the people against radioactive fallout but against depression and unemployment.

they wish to spend money on are obviously tautologies, but, being tautologies, they are equally obviously correct. From this, to be sure, it does not follow, as some business economists like to assert, that the barrage of advertising and salesmanship to which the consumer is continually exposed has *no* influence on the formation of his wants. But neither is it true that these business practices constitute *the* decisive factor in making the consumer want what he wants. Professor Henry C. Wallich comes closest to the spot where the dog is buried in his shrewd observation that "to argue that wants created by advertising are synthetic, are not genuine consumer wants is beside the point—it could be argued of all aspects of civilized existence."[12] This, to be sure, is overstating the case. Human wants are not *all* wholly "synthetic," created by an almighty Madison Avenue (or "purified" and "ennobled" by a Madison Avenue "in reverse": government regulatory boards and/or Distinguished Citizens Committees for the Promotion of Good Taste) : that view reflects the spirit of limitless manipulability of man which is so characteristic of the "men in gray flannel suits" who dominate the executive offices of corporations and the important bureaus of the government. But neither do *all* wants stem from man's biotic urges or from a mythical eternally unchanging "human nature": that concept is metaphysical obscurantism which flies in the face of all historical knowledge and experience. The truth is that wants of people are complex historical phenomena reflecting the dialectic interaction of their physiological requirements on the one hand, and the prevailing social and economic order on the other.[13] The physiological requirements sometimes must be abstracted from for analytical purposes because they are *relatively constant.* And once this abstraction is explicitly made and firmly borne in mind, the make-up of human wants can (and must) be legitimately thought of as being "synthetic," i.e., determined by the nature of the economic and social order under which people live. What Professor Wallich apparently fails to see is that the issue is *not* whether the prevailing social and economic order plays a prominent part in molding people's "values," volitions, and preferences. On this—Robinson Crusoe having finally departed from economics textbooks to his proper insular habitat—there is a nearly unanimous consensus among serious students of the problem. The issue is rather *the kind of social and economic order* that does the molding, the kind of "values," volitions, and preferences which it instills into the people under its sway. What renders the social and economic order of monopoly capitalism so irra-

[12] Quoted in Steuart Henderson Britt, *op cit.*, p. 31.
[13] For a more extended discussion of this, cf. my *Marxism and Psychoanalysis* (New York, 1960), containing a lecture on the subject, observations by critics, and a reply.

tional and destructive, so crippling to the individual's growth and happiness, is *not* that it influences, shapes, "synthesizes" the individual —as Professor Wallich suggests, every social and economic order does this—but rather *the kind* of influencing, shaping, and "synthesizing" which it perpetrates on its victims.

A clear understanding of this permits a further insight. The cancerous malaise of monopoly capitalism is not that it "happens" to squander a large part of its resources on the production of means of destruction, that it "happens" to allow corporations to engage in liminal and subliminal advertising, in peddling adulterated products, and in inundating human life with moronizing entertainment, commercialized religion, and debased "culture." The cancerous malaise of the system which renders it a formidable obstacle to human advancement, is that all this is not an assortment of fortuitously appearing attributes of the capitalist order, but the very basis of its existence and viability. And such being the case, bigger and better Food and Drug Administrations, a comprehensive network of Distinguished Citizens Committees, and the like can merely spread a veil over the existing mess rather than clean up the mess itself. To use an earlier comparison once more: building sumptuous cemeteries and expensive monuments for the victims of war does not reduce their number. The best—and the worst—that such seemingly humanitarian efforts can accomplish is to dull people's sensitivity to brutality and cruelty, to reduce their horror of war.

But to return to the starting point of this argument. Neither I nor any other Marxist writers with whose works I am familiar, have ever advocated the abolition of consumer sovereignty and its replacement by the orders of a commissar. The attribution of such an advocacy to socialists is simply one aspect of the ignorance and misrepresentation of Marxian thought that are studiously cultivated by the powers that be. The real problem is an entirely different one, namely, whether an economic and social order should be tolerated in which the individual, from the very cradle on, is so shaped, molded, and "adjusted" as to become an easy prey of profit-greedy capitalist enterprise and a smoothly functioning object of capitalist exploitation and degradation. The Marxian socialist is in no doubt about the answer. Holding that mankind has now reached a level of productivity and knowledge which make it possible to transcend this system and replace it by a better one, he believes that a society can be developed in which the individual would be formed, influenced, and educated not by a profit- and market-determined economy, not by the "values" of corporate presidents and the outpourings of their hired scribes, but by a system of rationally planned production for use, by a universe of human relations determined by and oriented toward solidarity, cooperation, and freedom. Indeed,

who does the "rational planning"?

only in such a society can there be sovereignty of the individual *human being*—not of the "consumer" or the "producer," terms which in themselves reflect the lethal fragmentation of the human personality under capitalism. Only in such a society can the individual freely co-determine the amount of work done, the composition of output consumed, the nature of leisure activities engaged in—free from all the open and hidden persuaders whose motives are preservation of their privileges and maximization of their profits.

And to those of my critics who skeptically or "realistically" sneer and condescendingly remark that the image of such a society is nothing but a utopia, all I can answer is that if they are right, all of us—my critics and myself—are utopians. They because they believe that a social and economic order which they wish to preserve can be made to last forever by means of manipulative tricks and superficial reforms that fail even to touch its increasingly manifest irrationality, destructiveness, and inhumanity; I because I trust that mankind, which has already managed to sweep capitalism off the face of one third of the globe, will in the fullness of time complete this Herculean task and succeed in establishing a genuinely human society. Having to choose between these two utopias, I prefer the second, subscribing to the beautiful words of Simone de Beauvoir: "Socialist Europe, there are moments when I ask myself whether it is not a utopia. But each idea not yet realized curiously resembles a utopia; one would never do anything if one thought that nothing is possible except that which exists already."[14]

II

Chapters Three and Four, dealing with monopoly capitalism, call for a clarification of the argument. The required modifications are not far-reaching, but may add—I hope—to its consistency and persuasiveness. My views on this vast subject have crystallized in the course of extensive work undertaken jointly with Paul M. Sweezy; the results of our studies and discussions will be presented in a book which we hope to complete in the near future. What follows in this section is confined therefore to only two points which the reader should bear in mind when turning to the relevant part of this volume.

I have argued above that it is necessary to probe deeper than the readily observable surface with regard to the problem of consumer sovereignty. This is at least equally true when it comes to what I consider to be the key to the understanding of the general working principles of capitalism: the concept of the "economic surplus." That I

[14] *Les Mandarins* (Paris, 1954), p. 193. I have translated this passage from French.

the key: economic surplus

was unable to explain it sufficiently well is apparent from the fact that a critic as eminent as Nicholas Kaldor failed to grasp its meaning and significance.[15]

The root of the trouble is that Mr. Kaldor, like all other economists spellbound by the surface appearances of the capitalist economy, *insists on identifying the economic surplus with statistically observable profits.* If such an identification were legitimate, there would be no need to introduce the term "economic surplus," and—what is obviously more important—there might be no justification for speaking about *rising* surplus. The crux of the matter is, however, that profits are *not* identical with the economic surplus, but constitute—to use what has become now a hackneyed metaphor—merely the visible part of the iceberg with the rest of it hidden from the naked eye. Let us recall that at an early stage of the development of political economy (and capitalism) the relevant relations were seen much more clearly than they are at the present time. An intense theoretical struggle was fought, in fact, to establish that the rent of land (and interest on money capital) are not necessary costs of production but components of the economic surplus. At a later phase, however, when the feudal landlord and moneylender were replaced by the capitalist entrepreneur and banker, *their* returns were "purged" of the surplus "stigma" and became promoted to the status of necessary prices of scarce resources or of indispensable rewards for "waiting," "abstinence," or "risk-taking." In fact, the very notion "economic surplus," still prominent in the writings of John Stuart Mill, was declared *non grata* by the new economic science which proclaimed any and every outlay as "necessary" as long as it received the stamp of approval from the revealed preferences of consumers operating in a competitive market.

The situation became more complicated with the proliferation of monopoly; and a number of economists—beginning with Marshall but later on inspired primarily by the work of Pigou—who conducted their investigations from the vantage point of competitive capitalism found it impossible to treat *monopoly* profits as necessary costs of production.[16] This was undoubtedly an important step forward; it constitutes, how-

[15] Cf. his review of the present book, *The American Economic Review*, March, 1958, pp. 164 ff.

[16] It was reserved for Schumpeter (to be followed eventually by Berle, Galbraith, and others) to make an effort to save the "honor" of monopoly profits by proclaiming even them to be "necessary costs of production." This *tour de force* was accomplished by pointing out that technological innovations were predicated upon monopoly gains on the part of the innovators, that it is monopoly profit that enables corporations to maintain costly research laboratories, etc. Thus static vice was made into dynamic virtue and the last attempt of economic theory to retain some minimum standards for the rational appraisal of the functioning of the capitalist system was swept aside by the comprehensive endorsement of the *status quo*.

ever, only the beginning of what needs to be understood. For monopoly capitalism generates not only profits, rent, and interest as elements of the economic surplus, but conceals an important share of the surplus under the rubric of costs. This is due to the ever-widening gap between the productivity of the *necessary productive workers* and the share of national income accruing to them as wages.

A simple numerical illustration may be helpful here. Assume that in period I, 100 bakers produce 200 loaves of bread, with 100 loaves constituting their wages (one loaf per man), and 100 loaves being appropriated by the capitalist as surplus (the source of his profit and his payment of rent and interest). The productivity of the baker is two loaves per man; the share of surplus in national income is 50 percent, and so is the share of labor. Now consider period II in which the productivity of the baker has increased by 525 percent to 12.5 loaves and his wage has risen by 400 percent to five loaves per man. Assume further that now only 80 bakers are employed in baking, producing altogether 1,000 loaves while the remaining 20 are engaged as follows: five men are commissioned to change continually the shapes of the loaves; one man is given the task of admixing with the dough a chemical substance that accelerates the perishability of bread; four men are hired to make up new wrappers for the bread; five men are employed in composing advertising copy for bread and broadcasting same over the available mass media; one man is appointed to watch carefully the activities of other baking companies; two men are to keep abreast of legal developments in the antitrust field; and finally two men are placed in charge of the baking corporation's public relations. All of these individuals receive also a wage of five loaves per man. Under these new circumstances, the total output of 80 bakers is 1,000 loaves, the aggregate wage of the 100 members of the corporation's labor force is 500 loaves, and profit plus rent plus interest are 500 loaves.[17] It might seem at first that nothing has changed between period I and period II except for the increase of the total volume of output. The share of labor in national income has remained constant at 50 percent, and the share of surplus does not appear to have varied either. Yet such a conclusion, though self-evident from the inspection of customary statistics, would be wholly unwarranted and in fact would merely serve to demonstrate how misleading such statistical inferences can be. For the statistical

[17] Clearly, if the wage of the 20 unproductive workers is higher than five loaves per man—as it would be realistic to assume it would be—then either the real wage of the bakers would have to be lower or the profits would be encroached upon, or both. In the former case, the surplus is larger; in the case of reduced profits, it remains the same; and if both the productive workers' wages *and* profits are lower, the surplus is increased by the amount of the wage reduction.

fact that the shares of labor and capital have not changed from period
I to period II is irrelevant so far as our problem is concerned. What has
happened, as can be readily seen, is that a share of the economic surplus, all of which in the earlier period was available to the capitalist as
profit and for payment of land rent and interest, is now used to support
the costs of a non-price-competitive sales effort, is—in other words—
wasted.[18]

In the light of this, it should be clear that Mr. Kaldor's and other
critics' contention that my admission of the validity of the thesis that
the share of wages in income remained more or less constant over a
number of decades is wholly incompatible with my maintaining the
theory of the *rising surplus*—that this contention reflects merely their
own failure to understand the surplus concept. A constant, and indeed
a rising, share of labor in national income can coexist with rising surplus
simply because the increment of surplus assumes the form of an increment of *waste*. And since the "production" of waste involves labor,
the share of labor may well grow if the share of waste in national output
is increasing. Treating productive and unproductive labor indiscriminately as *labor* and equating profits with surplus obviously obscure
this very simple proposition.

Several objections to the above could be raised. In the first place, it
could be (and is being) asserted that there is no point in distinguishing
between productive and unproductive labor or between socially desirable output and waste since there is no possibility of making these
distinctions "objective" and precise. The correctness of the latter asser-

---

[18] Incidentally, a couple of other interesting things can be learned from
this very simple illustration: first, customary statistics would usually tend
to suggest that the productivity per man engaged in the bakery business has
increased less than it actually did: with 100 men employed in the bakery
concern in period I as well as in period II, and with output rising from
200 loaves to 1,000 loaves, productivity would appear to have gone up by
400 percent rather than by 525 percent as was actually the case. To be
sure, a careful "sorting out" of the labor force denominator used for the
computation, with a view to limiting it to *productive workers* only, could
remedy this deficiency, but the statistical information which is usually supplied renders such an adjustment impossible. Secondly, statistics commonly
compiled would show that wages have increased in exactly the same proportion as productivity (from one to five loaves), while in reality the wages
of the *productive workers* lagged considerably behind the rise of *their* productivity. That the official statistics convey such garbled impressions is
obviously not fortuitous; it is due to the concepts which govern their
organization. With the notion "economic surplus" denied official recognition,
and with the all but meaningless distinction between "production" and
"non-production" workers substituted for the all-important difference between *productive* and *unproductive* workers, available statistics hide rather
than illuminate a most important aspect of capitalist reality.

tion can be readily granted. But that brandy and water mixed in a bottle cannot be separated, and that it may be impossible to establish accurately the proportions in which the two liquids are combined, does not alter the *fact* that the bottle contains both brandy and water and that the two beverages are present in the bottle in some definite quantities. What is more, to whatever extent the bottle may be filled, it can be safely asserted that in the absence of one or the other ingredient of the mix, it would be less full than in its presence. That we cannot at the present time neatly separate the wheat from the chaff, i.e., identify unequivocally the dimensions of the socially desirable output and of the economic surplus in our economy, is in itself an important aspect of the economic and social order of monopoly capitalism. Just as the problem of consumer sovereignty is *not* whether a commissar should screen existing consumers' wants and *impose* on them standards of good taste, but rather how to attain a social and economic order which will lead to the emergence of a differently oriented individual with different wants and different tastes, so it reflects a complete misunderstanding of the issue to demand from the critical economist that he present a comprehensive compilation of the existing number of unproductive workers and the existing volume and forms of waste. Apart from the, by no means trivial, fact that under prevailing conditions there is not (and cannot be) available the amount and kind of information and knowledge that would permit the drawing up of such a "catalogue," no economist, however ingenious, could presume to set himself up as a sort of tsar empowered to lay down the criteria by which the "sorting out" process should be carried out. For it can only be a socialist society itself—in which people are not governed by the profit motive and in which the individual is steeped not in the "values" and mores of the market place but in the consciousness emerging from the new, socialist relations of production—which will give rise to a new structure of individual preferences and to a new pattern of allocation of human and material resources. All that the social scientist can do in this regard is to serve as Hegel's "owl of Minerva which commences its flight in the onset of dusk," and signal *orbi et urbi* that a social order is fatally ill and dying. The concrete forms and working principles of what is moving to take its place and the exact specifications of the changes which the new society will carry in its train, can be broadly visualized but not precisely established by economists and statisticians, however skillful they may be. This must be left to the social *practice* of those who will struggle for and succeed in achieving a socialist order.

Of a different nature is another argument advanced against the theory of the rising surplus. Its burden is that the distinction between socially desirable output and economic surplus is irrelevant, even if it could be made with all the required exactness. For since a satisfactory level of income and employment depends on an adequate amount of aggregate spending *regardless of what the spending is on,* the question whether it evokes useful output or waste, employs productive or unproductive labor is brushed aside as having no bearing on "business conditions," and on the extent to which the society of monopoly capitalism provides for "fullness" of employment. This reasoning, cogent as it is, resembles all Keynesian short-run analysis in being desperately myopic. It is undoubtedly true that investment in productive equipment and investment in submarines, consumption of books and "consumption" of advertising, incomes of physicians and incomes of drug peddlers, all enter aggregate effective demand and help to maintain income and employment. It is equally clear, however, that the resulting structure of output, consumption, and investment exercises a profound impact not merely on the quality of society and the welfare of its members but also on its further growth and developmental possibilities. Moreover, while a few decades ago it might have been possible to argue that, given a shortage of *rational* employment, any employment—as irrational as digging holes in the ground, for example—is better than *no* employment, even this cold comfort is no longer available in our day when the alternative to unemployment is no longer relatively innocent digging but the all but innocent stockpiling of means of destruction.[19]

A further objection has been voiced that while all the above may be correct, it should not be forgotten that it is precisely owing to all the irrationality and waste that characterize monopoly capitalism that high levels of income and employment are maintained, considerable amounts of rational investment are induced, and certain—if admittedly low—rates of economic growth are achieved. This argument is very much akin to the counsel to burn the house in order to roast the pig. But the worst of it is that it is not even true that in the process "the pig gets roasted," that—to paraphrase J. K. Galbraith[20]—such increases in wealth as have taken place under monopoly capitalism in the United States go far to render the irrationality of the system "inconsequential." It surely is not "inconsequential" that even after World War II— during what C. Wright Mills has so aptly called the years of the

[19] An extension of this discussion can be found in Paul A. Baran, "Reflections on Underconsumption" in Moses Abramovitz and others, *The Allocation of Economic Resources* (Stanford, California, 1959); reprinted also in Shigeto Tsuru, ed., *Has Capitalism Changed? An International Symposium on the Nature of Contemporary Capitalism* (Tokyo, 1961).

[20] *American Capitalism: the Concept of Countervailing Power* (Boston, 1952), p. 103.

"Great American Celebration"—in at least one half of the period (1948-1949, 1953-1954, 1957-1958, 1960 to date) government-reported unemployment has been in the neighborhood of 5 million, and according to trade union sources no less (and probably more) than 6 million.

Nor can it be shrugged off as "inconsequential" that in what has come to be referred to as the affluent society, approximately one third of the people live under conditions of abject poverty, and at least one fifth of all American families (and twice as large a proportion of non-white American families) subsist in miserable substandard and slum dwellings. And if cold statistical aggregates are left aside and concrete conditions are examined in specific areas, the human tragedy encountered defies description. "In a slum section composed almost entirely of Negroes in one of our largest cities," writes a former president of Harvard University, James Bryant Conant, "the following situation was found: A total of 59 percent of the male youth between the ages of sixteen and twenty-one were out of school and unemployed. They were roaming the streets. . . ."[21]

All that can be said for the objection now under discussion is that the development of capitalism in general and of its last phase—monopoly capitalism—in particular, while nowhere near creating anything resembling a good society,[22] has produced the objective potentialities for the emergence of such a society. The prodigious expansion of the forces of production which has taken place during the period of imperialism, although a by-product of war, exploitation, and waste, has indeed laid the foundations for the truly affluent society of the future. But such a society cannot evolve under the rule of an oligarchy administering society's vast resources for the benefit of a few hundred giant corporations and with the all-controlling purpose of the preservation of the *status quo*. Such a society can become reality only when its abundant resources will be administered by a human "association in which the free development of each is the condition for the free development of all."

This brings me to the second comment which I should like to make in connection with the monopoly capitalism chapters of this book. This comment refers to the view of innovation and technological progress under monopoly capitalism which is there advanced. Although I still believe in the basic soundness of Steindl's contention, to which I subscribed, that technological progress and innovation are a function of

[21] *Slums and Suburbs: a Commentary on Schools in Metropolitan Areas* (New York, Toronto, London, 1961), pp. 33 f.

[22] This is not the place to go into a more detailed description and analysis of the quality of the monopoly capitalist society; for this the interested reader is referred to Sweezy's and my forthcoming book, and in the meanwhile to *Monthly Review*, July-August, 1962, where some parts of that book are scheduled to be published in advance.

investment rather than *vice versa*, I have devoted insufficient space to
the undeniable dialectical interaction of the two processes. Not only do
the institutionalized research and development staffs of giant corporations operate, to some extent at least, with a momentum of their own
and grind out inventions and technical improvements as a matter of
normal routine,[23] but what is perhaps even more important, the military
establishment which has become a permanent and vast component of
the economy of monopoly capitalism, has turned into a continuously
operating "external stimulus" to both investment *and* scientific and
technological progress. As the demand of the military has to a considerable extent replaced the demand of the would-be investor, so the
sequence of Soviet Sputniks and Luniks has taken over some of the
functions of the "perennial gale" of competition. This does not call
for regressing to the position of Schumpeter to whom technological
progress was a *deus cum machina*—autonomous and inexplicable. Nor
does it imply that technological progress *determines* investment, so that
forthcoming increments to knowledge tend to be regularly translated
into additional productive facilities. What it does suggest, however, is
that the consolidation of research and development activities within the
framework of giant corporations *combined with a steady flow of military
demand* creates certain investment opportunities when there otherwise
would be fewer or none. And the importance of the military nature of
demand as well as of the monopolistic and oligopolistic nature of supply
expresses itself most precisely in the *selection* of the technological potentialities which are made use of as well as in the rejection of those which
remain in the files of scientists and engineers. Both the slow progress
made in the economic application of atomic energy as well as the very
uneven advances in automation would seem to justify the proposition
that only that technical progress is acceptable to monopolistic and
oligopolistic business which is either required by the military or sharply
reduces costs without at the same time unduly expanding output.

III

We turn now to the underdeveloped countries. To Chapters Five,
Six, and Seven, dealing with one of the three dominant themes of our
age (the other two being the vicissitudes of monopoly capitalism during
its current period of decline and fall, and the outlook for the nascent
socialist societies in Europe and Asia),[24] I would like to add a qualification and a reaffirmation. The former has to do with the applicability of

[23] Cf. Paul M. Sweezy, "Has Capitalism Changed?" in Shigeto Tsuru,
ed., *op. cit.*, pp. 83 ff.
[24] Since this book was first published, Latin America has joined the
regions of socialist beginnings.

surplus & gov't. extraction

the general theory advanced in this book to some highly populated areas with what Marx called the "Asiatic mode of production"—notably India and Pakistan. In such parts of the underdeveloped world, several critics have contended, it might well be feasible to ascertain with some degree of accuracy the *magnitude* of the economic surplus appropriated by landowners, usurers, and commercial intermediaries of all kinds, but it would be wholly impossible to channel that segment of the surplus into productive investment even after these parasitic strata had been swept aside by a social revolution. This view is based on two sets of considerations. First, it is argued, a revolutionary government which would carry out the necessary expropriation measures could not possibly substitute itself for the blood-sucking rent collectors, money lenders, and greedy traders who were eliminated by the very revolution that put it into power. With such a switch in the destination of the surplus thus politically precluded, the nationalization and confiscation measures would not lead to an accumulation of an investible surplus in the hands of the revolutionary government but to its lapsing into the peasants' desperately skimpy consumption basket. The second point is that in an underdeveloped country in which the economic surplus accrues to a numerically insignificant group of exploiters (as was and is the case in countries with a "classic" feudal system and/or those dominated by a handful of domestic and foreign monopolists) the situation is quite different from that prevailing in a society in which a multi-million-strong stratum of *kulaks*, village bosses lending money on the side, small traders, dealers, and brokers, appropriate altogether an amount of economic surplus constituting a large slice of total national income but providing only low per capita incomes to its recipients. In the former case the expropriators can be relatively easily expropriated, and their fate after the expropriation does not present a major social problem; their number being small, they either find alternative employment, emigrate, or retire to live on some remnants of their fortunes. In the latter case, however, the surplus recipients, being many, constitute an important social and political force; and, once deprived of their revenues, present a serious problem in social welfare. In fact, supporting them on even a minimum level by means of relief or artificially created jobs could annul much of the advantage derived from the expropriation itself.

These are serious problems, and although I was by no means oblivious of their existence when writing this book,[25] they may not have received sufficient attention and emphasis. I do not believe, however, that recognizing their importance vitiates the basic approach to the issues confronting the underdeveloped countries which is outlined here. It undoubtedly implies that in some countries the breakthrough to the

[25] Cf. pp. 167 ff. as well as pp. 262 ff.

open road of economic and social growth is more difficult than in
others, and that the obstacles that need to be overcome are in some
places more formidable than elsewhere. It may well be, indeed, that in
countries which are particularly plagued by the structural malaise just
described, the strategy of development may have to be different from
the one suitable to societies more favorably structured. Lenin's famous
law of uneven development suggests obviously not only that the historical *process* is different in different societies, but also that the stage
reached at any given time differs from country to country. There is
thus no general formula applicable to all situations regardless of time
and place, and nothing was ever further from my mind than an intention
to assert the existence of such a magic wand.

Consider for instance a country in which there exists a certain
nucleus of an industrial economy and where the peasantry, whether
exploited by *kulaks,* or held in servitude by feudal landlords, is intensely
land-hungry, and longs for nothing but individually owned plots of
land. In such a country it may be possible to generate a sizable amount
of economic surplus *via* the economy's industrial sector. If, in addition,
the country is relatively small so that whatever aid it may receive from
abroad can materially influence the volume of its capital accumulation,
it may well be able to afford to allow its peasants to "sit it out" for a
while, and to learn by observation and experience the advantages of a
rational and modern organization of agricultural production. Such has
apparently been the broad perspective of some socialist countries in
Eastern and Southeastern Europe.   *Chinese model*

Take, on the other hand, a large country with a small industrial
oasis in a vast sea of subsistence farming. Here the industrially generated surplus is of necessity small, and the practically accessible foreign
assistance can constitute at best only a drop in the bucket of development requirements. If in such a country, the peasants' craving for
individually owned plots is for any number of economic or cultural
reasons not urgent or even absent, its agricultural economy can be
shifted onto new tracks based on cooperative farming or even on a
system of state-operated, large-scale, and increasingly productive "factories in the field." The gentry, rich peasants, village storekeepers, and
moneylenders displaced in the process may either be integrated into the
new agricultural economy or find employment in the expanding industrial and distributive sectors. And the surplus which they used to
appropriate may become available for purposes of economic development. This would seem to be—in a nutshell—the model of the Chinese
strategy of economic development.

And visualize finally a banana or sugar republic—if that flattering
designation is considered applicable to the semi-colonial dictatorships

involved—where the bulk of agricultural output is produced in plantations, and where the agricultural population consists predominantly
or in large part not of peasants but of agricultural workers. In such
countries the expropriation of the peasant was so thoroughly completed
by the domestic and foreign plantation owners that even the image of
individual land holdings has all but evaporated from the mentality of
the rural proletariat. There mass parcelling of land is not on the agenda
at all, and the nationalization of the plantations places immediately at
the disposal of society as a whole the surplus that was previously appropriated by foreign and domestic corporations. This is not to say that
all of the surplus so released can be turned to investment; much of it
may have to be used to raise immediately the wretched living conditions of the working population. Also complications and frictions in the
process of the reorganization of the economy, difficulties in securing
new sources of essential supplies, as well as in finding new markets for
customary exports—all largely due to the sabotage and obstruction on
the part of the former ruling class at home and its allies and protectors
abroad—may temporarily reduce aggregate output and accordingly
also the volume of available surplus. In such a situation the possibility
of overcoming all these hurdles is to such an extent dependent on various
economic and political factors at home and abroad that there can
hardly be a generalization that would fit the individual case. The obvious
example of what I mean is the dramatic experience of Cuba since its
great Revolution.[26]

Thus each and every one of the underdeveloped countries presents
a wide spectrum of economic, social, cultural, and political configurations; and nothing could be more futile than to seek to force them into
a rigid mold of a "universal prescription." But as the intellectual gratification derived from the discovery of a broad generalization should not
be permitted to deflect attention from the specificity of concrete reality,
so fixation on detail must not be allowed to bar the insights which can
only be gained through generalizing—i.e. theoretical—thought. And
this brings me to what I referred to earlier as a reaffirmation of my
views on the basic problem confronting the underdeveloped countries.
The principal insights which must not be obscured by matters of secondary or tertiary importance, are two.

The first is that, if what is sought is *rapid* economic development,
comprehensive economic planning is indispensable. Small and gradual
changes taking place, as it were, on the margin may well be expected

----

[26] A comprehensive account of the developments in Cuba will be found
in Leo Huberman and Paul M. Sweezy, *Cuba: Anatomy of a Revolution*
(2nd ed., New York, 1961), and an elaboration of the remarks above in
my *Reflections on the Cuban Revolution* (2nd ed., New York, 1961).

to come about by a spontaneous process of trial and error. A few percent increase of output of any product already being produced can usually be obtained without any major planning effort, by raising somewhat its price and by letting the necessary adjustments "work themselves out." However, if the increase in a country's aggregate output is to attain the magnitude of, say, 8 to 10 percent per annum; if in order to achieve it, the mode of utilization of a nation's human and material resources is to be radically changed, with certain less productive lines of economic activity abandoned and other more rewarding ones taken up; then only a deliberate, long-range planning effort can assure the attainment of the goal. On this there is actually hardly any disagreement among serious students of the subject.[27] What is perhaps even more important, on this there is no ambiguity in the historical record. While the most conservatively estimated per capita rates of economic growth in the socialist countries have been in the order of 10 percent per annum, in capitalist countries—advanced and underdeveloped alike—they rarely exceed 3 percent, except for extraordinary circumstances of war booms and postwar reconstruction.

The second insight of crucial importance is that no planning worth the name is possible in a society in which the means of production remain under the control of private interests which administer them with a view to their owners' maximum profits (or security or other private advantage). For it is of the very essence of comprehensive planning for economic development—what renders it, indeed, indispensable—that the pattern of allocation and utilization of resources which it must impose if it is to accomplish its purpose, is *necessarily* different from the pattern prevailing under the *status quo*. Since, however, the prevailing pattern of resource allocation and utilization corresponds, at least approximately, to the best interests of the dominant class, it is inevitable that any serious planning endeavor should come into sharp conflict with that dominant class and its allies at home and abroad. This conflict can be resolved in one of three ways: the Planning Board, if one is created by a capitalist government, can be taken over —like the government itself—by the dominant interests, its activities turned into a sham, and its existence used to nurture the illusion in the underlying population that "something constructive is being done" about economic development. The second possibility is that the Planning

[27] This is not the place for a survey of the relevant literature; suffice it to mention the writings of H. B. Chenery, E. S. Mason, T. Scitovsky, and J. Tinbergen, the principal burden of which is the demonstration of the necessity of coordination and synchronization of investment if the rapid economic development of underdeveloped (or, for that matter, developed) countries is to be effectively advanced.

Board established by a reform government remains more or less impervious to the influences, pressures, and bribes of powerful interests, is staffed by honest reformers who believe in the independence and omnipotence of the state in the capitalist society and set out to introduce far-reaching changes in the national economy. In that case the Board is bound to run into tenacious resistance and sabotage on the part of the ruling class, achieves very little if anything, and ends up in a state of frustration and impotence with the fatal by-product of discrediting the very idea of planning in the eyes of large strata of the population. The third alternative is that planning becomes the battle cry of a broad popular movement, is fought for relentlessly against the entrenched beneficiaries of the *ancien régime,* and is turned into the basic organizational principle of the economy by a victorious social revolution sweeping aside the former ruling class together with the institution of private property in the means of production on which its very existence rests.

It may be objected that all this may well be true if the fundamental premise is granted: that what is needed is *rapid* economic development. But why the hurry? Why this "obsession" with economic growth, to use an expression of a recent writer on the Soviet economy? The mere asking of these questions reflects the intellectual distance of Western observers from the living conditions in the underdeveloped countries and the mood of the people who have to endure them. Ours is an age in which misery, starvation, and disease are no longer accepted as ineluctable fate, and ours is the century in which socialist construction has moved from the realm of theory into the realm of practice. The peoples of the backward areas now *know* that economic and social progress *can* be organized, given the will, determination, and courage to declare a war against underdevelopment and given the unbreakable resolution to wage that war in the face of the most ruthless resistance on the part of domestic and foreign exploiters.

IV

From such historical experience as we have, it is abundantly clear that the struggle is protracted, hard, and cruel. The victory of the social revolution, although decisive, is merely a success "in the first round." The establishment of the capitalist mode of production and of bourgeois rule, where it was fully attained, took centuries of cataclysmic developments. It can hardly be expected, even in our much faster moving time, that the greatest social transformation of all—the abolition of private property in the means of production and therefore of exploitation of man by man—should be fully achieved within a few short decades.

It is quite understandable that to many the ascent appears sometimes to be prohibitively steep and the uphill movement hopelessly difficult. Since it is impossible to attempt here a comprehensive analysis of the hurdles and problems encountered in the process of socialist construction, I shall limit myself to a few brief remarks on some areas where the roadblocks have been particularly conspicuous in the recent past.

First and foremost among them is the international arena where social revolutions, regardless of where and how they unfold, meet with the implacable hostility of the ruling class of the United States—the most powerful citadel of reaction in the world today. No regime is too corrupt, no government too criminally negligent of the vital interests of its people, no dictatorship too retrograde and cruel to be denied the economic, military, and moral support of the leading power of the "free world"—as long as it proves its allegiance to the anti-socialist Holy Alliance. At the same time, no popular movement, however inclusive and however heroic, no socialist government, however democratically elected and however dedicated to the advancement of its people, can count on as much as non-intervention on the part of those who never tire of hypocritical professions of their devotion to social progress and to the democratic process. The unabating aggressiveness of the imperialist powers—large and small—immeasurably obstructs the economic and social progress in the countries which have entered the road of socialist construction.[28] Looking at the matter in purely economic terms and considering the burden of defense expenditures imposed on the socialist countries by the ever-present threat of imperialist aggression, it is obvious how large the costs are that the nascent socialist societies are forced by their class enemy to bear.[29]

The massive diversion of resources from investment, residential construction, and production of consumer goods that is necessitated by the maintenance of the indispensable defense establishment, slows down the rates of economic growth of the socialist countries, prevents a more

---

[28] The grave harm done to the magnificent revolutionary effort of the Cuban people by the "starving out" strategy of American imperialism is the most striking and the most distressing case in point.

[29] Those who are so influenced by the mendacious propaganda of imperialism as to believe that the vast armaments buildup in the United States is governed by the fear of aggression on the part of the socialist countries *must* read the monumental work of Professor D. F. Fleming, *The Cold War and Its Origins*, 2 vols. (New York, 1961), as well as the revealing account of the *actual* course of disarmament negotiations in recent years by Professor J. P. Morray, *From Yalta to Disarmament: Cold War Debate* (New York, 1961). It is hard to believe that anyone who is *willing* to recognize the truth can fail to be impressed by the incontrovertible evidence assembled in these extraordinary studies.

rapid increase in the living standards of their peoples, and creates and recreates frictions and bottlenecks in their economies. This heavy load will have to be carried by the socialist societies as long as the threat of imperialism exists; its burden will not decline until the socialist economies have grown—in spite of it—so strong as to greatly reduce its *relative* weight.

The second area in which the difficulties of the socialist countries have been most marked is that of agricultural production. There the sources of trouble are manifold. The process of industrialization, accompanied of necessity by a population shift from rural to urban areas, and the maintenance of a military establishment which eats but does not produce, have significantly raised the aggregate demand for food and other products of agriculture. This increase of demand has been, on the whole, nowhere accompanied by a sufficient expansion of supply. This is primarily due to the fact that while in countries with considerable underemployment in the villages, the productivity *per man at work* could be raised *relatively* fast, the increase of productivity *per acre* has proved to be an extremely slow process. Thus what might be called the mechanical revolution in agriculture brought about by the introduction of electricity, tractors, combines, and the like accomplished its purpose by freeing millions of peasants for nonagricultural employment; it did not lead to the spectacular increases of agricultural output per acre of land that was expected by many economic theorists—Marxist and non-Marxist alike. The increase of productivity per acre depends apparently much more than was anticipated on the *chemical* revolution in agriculture: on the application of synthetic and other fertilizers, on seed selection, the adoption of improved methods of livestock breeding, and so forth. This is, inevitably, a slow process: 2 to 3 percent increases of output per acre per year are considered by agronomists to constitute a respectable performance. The achievement of such a rate of growth is predicated on the availability of the necessary supplies (fertilizers, choice seeds, breeding animals, etc.), but also on the skill, diligence, and patience of the cultivators.[30]

This in turn points to another complication which has arisen in the Soviet Union as well as in other industrializing socialist countries. It stems from the fact that the industrialization of an agricultural country, particularly in its early phases, involves quite naturally the "glamorization" of industrial work, its acquiring greatly enhanced prestige and

[30] The situation is obviously somewhat different in parts of the world where the underemployment of manpower in agriculture is matched by underutilization of arable land—as in the case of Cuba. Under such circumstances, aggregate agricultural output can be, at any rate in the early stages, rapidly increased by taking into cultivation previously uncultivated areas, although even in such cases major difficulties are caused by lack of agricultural implements, fertilizers, and livestock.

attractiveness. Large new industrial plants, tremendous power developments revolutionizing the lives of entire regions, thrilling technological
achievements move into the center of national (and international) attention, become objects of intense—and justified—pride, and are allotted
a preponderant proportion of publicity, of the government's political
and organizational effort, and of scarce administrative and scientific
talent. By comparison, the plodding day-to-day drudgery of agricultural
work recedes into the gray and dull background of social existence. A
young man or woman of ambition, ability, and energy no longer wishes
to remain "stuck in the mud" of the agricultural backwaters, to stay confined to the "idiocy of rural life" and be limited in his or her growth
and development to what can be achieved even in the most progressive
agricultural community. The lure of the city, of its opportunities for
material and social advancement, education, participation in cultural
activities and plain fun, as well as the desire to become a member of the
industrial working class—the most respected stratum of society—exercise an all but irresistible pull on the younger generation. The result is
that agriculture becomes increasingly abandoned by its best potential
workers, and left to elderly people or to those who do not have the
imagination, the enterprise, and the drive to move into the "big, wide
world."[31]

This in turn contributes seriously to the persistent lag in the
growth of productivity in agriculture. Nor is it easy to compensate
for the relative weakness of the agricultural labor force by the employment of technical devices. Work in industry gives rise to discipline
and standards of performance by a specific momentum of its own.
The collective nature of the activity involved, its structuring and
timing by conveyor belts and similar arrangements, the interdependence and indispensability of specific operations—all impose on
the industrial worker a certain rhythm of work which sets its tone,
determines its tempo, and largely acounts for its outcome. The situation in agriculture is quite different—such modernization of agricultural methods of production as has taken place notwithstanding. Apart
from certain collective functions, the individual worker is to a large
extent on his own. Whether in plowing a field or in tending to an
animal, it is his (or her) initiative, conscientiousness, and exertion
which markedly influence the degree of success attained. And where
hide-bound conservatism, irresponsibility, and aversion to hard work
characterize those working in agriculture, aggregate agricultural output
is bound to be seriously affected.

[31] After World War II, the situation in the Soviet Union in particular
was seriously aggravated by the casualties suffered by the agricultural male
population to a larger extent than by the industrial proletariat who were
more frequently exempted from military service.

Under capitalist conditions the tendency of the cream of agricultural manpower to migrate to the cities has usually been kept in check by the slowness of the capital accumulation process and by the more or less chronic shortage of urban jobs resulting therefrom. Accordingly, agriculture remained overcrowded, competition in it fierce, and productivity and real income per man increased much more slowly than productivity per acre. In the socialist society matters had to take a different course. The collective, large-scale organization of agriculture which, by doing away with the unviable dwarfholdings of the peasantry, creates the indispensable conditions for the long-term, sustained growth of agricultural production, transforms the peasant into an industrial worker working in agriculture. In this way it insulates him from the ruinous impact of the capitalist market, immunizes him against the sticks and carrots of the competitive struggle, *without putting him at the same time into the framework of integration, coordination, and discipline characteristic of a large-scale modern industrial enterprise.* And what is even more paradoxical and economically serious: by advancing him to the status of a full-fledged working member of a socialist society, it accords him automatically a claim to a share of aggregate social output, to real income, which is at least approximately equal to the shares of other, more productive workers.

This amounts in effect to a reversal of the earlier relation: agriculture becomes subsidized by industry. This is exactly as it should be, except that these subsidies do not lead to an adequate expansion of agricultural output. In the longer run this problem can, and undoubtedly will, be solved. Once a considerably higher stage of economic development is reached, the living and working conditions in city and countryside will be more nearly equalized and it will become possible to provide for the movement of skilled, educated, and socially conscious and responsible workers not only from the village to the city but also from the city to the village, with both of these movements turning into a general means of enhancing the variety, stimulation, and gratification derived from productive work in industry as well as in agriculture. Before that situation is reached, however, there is still a long way to go. In the meantime, in different socialist countries reliance is placed on different palliatives. In some countries the collectivization of agriculture was halted (or even reversed) with a regulated exchange between city and village taking the place of an immediate socialization of agriculture. In another socialist country, China, a solution has been sought in the opposite direction, through a more rapid transformation of the peasant economy into a system of socially operated, disciplined, large-scale agricultural enterprises. In the Soviet Union an in-between course has been followed: agricultural work is being "re-glamorized," investment in agriculture is being increased as much as possible, and incentives to collective farmers raised by shifting relative prices in favor of agriculture. Much of this puts an additional strain on the industrial economy, cuts into real wages of industrial workers, and reduces the volume of surplus investible outside of agriculture, thus slowing down the overall rate of economic growth. Even so, the agricultural difficulties, not insuperable but seriously hampering and retarding the development of the socialist societies, represent only a fraction of the tremendous price which the socialist societies have to pay for having first emerged in underdeveloped countries.

It is against the background of this economic stringency—the insufficiency of agricultural output to keep pace with the rising living standards of the people, and the shortage of industrial output in the face of rapidly growing demands from within and without the individual socialist countries—as well as of the intensified class struggle in the international arena that one must consider the *political* troubles within the socialist camp. Under this heading, there is in the first place the all-important problem of retention of popular support by the socialist government during the most trying effort to initiate the "steep ascent." What has come to be called the "revolution of rising expectations" which is sweeping the world's underdeveloped countries confronts not only reactionary and corrupt regimes seeking to stem it by all available means, but also revolutionary governments dedicated to economic development and socialism. Since a rational plan of economic advancement calls not for the shot-in-the-arm policy of an immediate increase of popular consumption, but for a well-considered strategy of assuring maximum possible rates of growth over a planning horizon of, say 10-20 years, it is not only possible but most likely that during the early phase of the effort mass consumption should rise very slowly, if at all. Only after the foundations of a progressive economy have been laid, and the "hump" overcome, can the system begin to yield fruits in the form of an expanding supply of consumer goods, housing, and the like.

Yet the masses who have just been through a revolution, who have fought and suffered in the bitter struggles against their class enemies and exploiters at home and abroad, seek and feel entitled to immediate improvements in the daily lives of their cities and villages. The fledgling socialist government cannot conjure such improvements out of the ground. Still engaged in the "uninterrupted revolution," it must demand "blood, sweat, and toil" without being able to offer commensurable rewards *hic et nunc*. Only the most class-conscious and insightful groups in society recognize and comprehend the momentous issues involved.

Broad strata of the population, unaccustomed to thinking in terms of economic necessities and longer-run perspectives can easily become disaffected, can fall prey to enemy propaganda which seeks to capitalize on their age-old superstitions and ignorance, can lose their faith in the revolution. They do not grasp that the suffering under the *ancien régime* was suffering for the benefit of their domestic overlords and their imperialist exploiters, that the misery which they had to endure in the past was misery without hope and prospect—while the privations accompanying the revolution are the birth-pangs of a new and better society. And ignoring this fundamental difference, they frequently became apathetic or even hostile to the revolution itself. This inevitably gives rise to a more or less acute conflict between socialism and democracy, between people's long-run *needs* and their short-run *wants*. Under such circumstances the socialist government's unwavering and uncompromising commitment to the overriding interests of society as a whole, its unquestionable duty to defend these interests against their foreign and domestic enemies no less than against opportunists and traitors among its adherents, creates the need for political repression, for curtailment of civil liberties, for limitation of individual freedom. This need can only recede and eventually disappear when the objective hurdles are at least approximately mastered, when the most burning economic problems are at least approximately solved, and when the socialist government has attained a measure of stability and equilibrium.[32]

Stemming from the same basic cause, in one word poverty, is the second category of troubles besetting the socialist camp: the relations among socialist countries. These relations have obviously not been as harmonious as a socialist would have liked them to be; but while giving rise to legitimate concern, they must be subjected to a dispassionate analysis and put into a proper historical perspective. Although nothing that might resemble adequate information is at my disposal, from what little I have been able to learn it would seem that the causes of the existing tensions relate to several closely interdependent issues.

One has to do with the allocation of economic resources within the socialist camp, and stems essentially from the vast differences in the degree of economic development attained by the individual socialist countries. To put it in its simplest terms, the question is, how much aid should the economically most advanced members of the socialist camp—primarily the Soviet Union but also Czechoslovakia, the German Democratic Republic, and Poland—give other less (and very much less) developed socialist countries? Clearly, no such problem would exist, if all socialist societies were about equally rich or if all were about equally poor. It should also be clear that at the present time an even proximate

[32] The Soviet experience during the last decade provides an excellent illustration of this development.

really ?

equalization of per capita incomes between the haves and the have-nots in the socialist camp is entirely impossible. It would drastically reduce the living standards of the, say, 250 million people living in the better-off parts of the socialist world, and even if such a move could substantially accelerate the growth of the worse-off parts inhabited by over 700 million people, it would be politically and socially wholly unfeasible, would be, indeed, suicidal to socialism in the more fortunate nations.

This issue was obviously not on the agenda as long as the Soviet Union and other European socialist countries were in the throes of reconstruction from the economic catastrophe caused by the war, and could furnish no more than symbolic assistance to the worst situated arrivals in the socialist camp. It became more urgent in the middle 1950's by which time the Soviet Union had made major strides in its economic reconstruction and advancement, and embarked—after the death of Stalin—on a course of a far-reaching economic and political liberalization. In the economic realm this implied a shift from the earlier policy of austerity and limitation of current consumption for the sake of the highest attainable rates of investment and growth, to a marked increase in the supply of housing, manufactured consumer goods, and food to the Soviet people who had suffered grievous privations during the prewar era of industrialization and were forced to make even more enormous sacrifices during the shattering years of the war. In the area of politics it meant a drastic change in the general atmosphere prevailing in Soviet society, the elimination of political repressions, and a break with the rigid dogmatism which affected all aspects of Soviet life during the rule of Stalin. As far as international relations are concerned, the new course involved a major effort to arrive at some accommodation with the United States with a view to the preservation of peace, to a reduction of the burden of armaments, and to securing a relaxation of international tensions necessary for the consolidation and progress of socialist societies in the Soviet Union as well as in the countries which entered the road to socialism after World War II. Indeed, the advancement and increasing welfare of these socialist societies were pronounced to be one of the most important leverages for the further expansion of socialism in the world. In what appeared to be a repudiation or at least an important modification of the conventional theory of imperialism, the new Soviet leadership declared such an accommodation to be not impossible in view of the radical shift in the world's balance of power caused by the rapidly mounting strength of the socialist bloc and the progressive disintegration of the imperialist control over colonial and dependent countries. In fact, the latter process was to be accelerated by the extension of economic and political aid to the newly emerging nations.

Various aspects of this new course were met with skepticism in China and other socialist countries still struggling desperately with the initial, most formidable, hurdles on the road to economic development. The disagreement involved the timeliness and wisdom of the liberalization program in the Soviet Union in the light of the needs of the *entire* socialist camp, the appraisal of the "appeasability" of the imperialist powers, and the judgment on what constitutes the best strategy in the struggle against imperialism and for peace and socialism.[33]

But while increasingly pronounced in the course of the last few years, it was not until the 22nd Congress of the Communist Party of the Soviet Union in the autumn of 1961 that the controversy erupted into a publicly acknowledged major conflict. Although still retaining its original roots, the dispute became acerbated by a number of developments. In the last couple of years, for reasons which it would take us too far afield to discuss, the economic development of China has suffered a serious setback,[34] and accordingly its need for large-scale economic assistance from the Soviet Union has greatly increased. Soviet policy at the same time remains committed to continuing on the road to further liberalization. This was solemnly proclaimed in the program of socialist construction in the Soviet Union adopted by the Congress, which provides for spectacular increases not only of the gross national product of the USSR in the next twenty years, but also for a significant reduction of the number of working hours of Soviet workers and for a vast improvement of the general living standard of the Soviet people. The question naturally arises whether it is necessary to set the Soviet welfare targets as high as they are fixed in the new Program, whether the policy adopted with regard to the rates of growth of the entire economy combined with somewhat less ambitious goals in terms of *consumption* would not leave more room for a program of large-scale assistance to other socialist countries. In other words,

[33] In Albania, and possibly elsewhere, it was apparently also held that Soviet grants and credits to nonsocialist underdeveloped countries reflect nothing but an illusion that the nonsocialist governments of those countries could be genuinely won over to the cause of peace and socialism. In a decisive moment, regardless of what benefits they may derive from the Soviet Union and other socialist countries, these governments would betray their benefactors and join the imperialist camp. Therefore—it was argued—all resources allocated to such uncertain friends are wasted and could and should be more usefully employed in helping socialist countries. This is reported in an article by F. Konstantinov, the editor-in-chief of the official theoretical organ of the Central Committee of the Communist Party of the Soviet Union *Kommunist:* "Raskolnicheskaya, antimarksistskaya deyatelnost albanskikh rukovoditeley." ("The divisive, anti-Marxian activity of the Albanian leaders.") *Kommunist,* November, 1961, p. 48.

[34] Albania has apparently fared even worse, although there, according to some reports, the fault lies chiefly with highly inefficient management on the part of the party leadership.

does not the Soviet Party leadership take a too narrow, "nationalist" view of the needs and requirements of the *entire* socialist camp and focus too much on the rapid betterment of the economic situation of the Soviet people? And would not more rapid progress of the Chinese, North Korean, North Vietnamese, and other underdeveloped socialist economies have a larger impact on the world as a whole, and on the peoples in the non-socialist underdeveloped countries in particular, than the Soviet Union's "attaining and surpassing American standards of living" in twenty years, as envisaged by the new Program, rather than in, say, the thirty years that it would take if a larger slice of its national product were devoted to the advancement of other socialist societies?

These questions translate themselves into political terms. As mentioned earlier, the Soviet Union's departure from the policies of austerity and curtailment of consumption for the sake of rapid growth goes hand in hand with the accelerated drive of "de-Stalinization," with the reduction and progressive abolition of the system of political repression which was largely due to the earlier regime of belt-tightening and maximal exertion. It goes without saying that nothing could be more welcome to a socialist than the evolution of the Soviet Union into a socialist democracy with the highest attainable levels of welfare and enjoying an ever wider degree of individual freedom. Neither the Chinese, who remained remarkably free of Stalin's abuses of power, nor any other socialists to my knowledge, have objected to the elimination and drastic suppression of all the aberrations and crimes committed by Stalin and his henchmen. What is at issue therefore is not "de-Stalinization" *per se*, but the abandonment of the policy of "forced marches" which is so prominently associated with the name of Stalin. Neither China nor some other socialist countries are as yet *economically ready* for the "thaw"; and, not being economically ready, they cannot afford the liberalization, the relaxation of the pressures on consumption, and all that goes with them which in the Soviet Union are at the present time not only feasible but constitute major steps towards the economic, political, and cultural advancement of Soviet society. In explaining to their peoples their policy of rapid industrialization, collectivization of agriculture, and ineluctable limitation of consumption, the socialist governments of China and some other socialist countries made extensive use of the Soviet example and of the authority of Stalin who was universally considered to be the chief architect of the Soviet successes. The dramatic overthrow of that image of Stalin at a time when the policies which he symbolized cannot yet be discarded, constitutes undoubtedly a severe political shock to those socialist governments which are still confronted with the kind of obstacles which the Soviet Union by now has been able to overcome.

Similarly, in their international relations, China and other socialist countries of Asia find themselves in a position quite different from that of the Soviet Union and the European socialist countries. With important parts of their countries still under the control of the enemy, politically discriminated against, militarily threatened and economically blockaded by the imperialist powers, the socialist countries of Asia are much less able and willing to accept a *détente* on the basis of the prevailing *status quo* than the socialist countries of Europe. While in Europe the settlement of the German question is the only major issue standing in the way of an at least temporary accommodation, the issues in Asia are many and complex and their solution appears even less likely than an acceptable compromise over Germany. This difference in the objective situation obviously contributes to the crystallization in the Soviet Union and in China of different appraisals of the international situation.

And yet, taking the risks which always attach to prophecy, I would venture the opinion that in spite of all the heat generated in the current debate and all the sharp arrows flying back and forth between the protagonists, the conflict will not inflict irreparable harm on the cause of socialism. In the longer run the fundamental identity of the relations of production prevailing in the socialist countries will prove to be a more powerful factor than the temporary divergencies among their leaderships on short-run strategy and tactics. Just as the socialist mode of production survived all the abhorrent doings of Stalin, so the socialist revolutions in China and elsewhere remain irreversible historical facts which cannot be altered, let alone annulled, by whatever frictions and disagreements may temporarily shake their political superstructures. Compromises are possible and will probably be arrived at. But even should the socialist governments of the countries involved fail to arrive at a mutually acceptable *modus vivendi*, the resulting estrangement need neither prevent the continuous progress of the individual countries on the road to socialism, nor preclude their cohesion and solidarity in the fullness of time.

To conclude: the dominant fact of our time is that the institution of private property in the means of production—once a powerful engine of progress—has now come into irreconcilable contradiction with the economic and social advancement of the people in the underdeveloped countries and with the growth, development, and liberation of people in advanced countries. That the existence and nature of this conflict have not yet everywhere been recognized and fully understood by the majority of people is one of the most important, if not the decisive, aspect of this conflict itself. It reflects the powerful hold on the minds of men exercised by a set of creeds, superstitions, and fetishes stemming from the very institution of private property in the means of production which now desperately needs to be overthrown. The argument, now most prominent in bourgeois thought, that the "adjustment" of people to a pernicious social order and their inability and unwillingness to rise up against it *prove* that this social order caters adequately to human needs, demonstrates merely that bourgeois thought is guilty of rank betrayal of all its finest traditions of humanism and reason. One may well wonder what would have been the reaction of the great philosophers of the Enlightenment if they were told that the existence of God is adequately *proved* by the fact that many people believe in it? Substituting ignorance and "revealed preferences" for truth and reason, gloating over all manifestations of irrationality and backwardness, whether in advanced or underdeveloped countries, as proving the impossibility of a more rational social order, bourgeois thought in our day has negated itself and has returned to the condition which in its glorious youth it set out to conquer: agnosticism and obscurantism. Thus it exchanges the great commitments of all intellectual endeavor—the search for and the clarification of truth, the guidance and support of man in his struggle for a better society—for the contemptible functions of rationalizing irrationality, inventing arguments in defense of madness, serving as a source of an ideology of vested interests, and recognizing as a genuine human *need* merely the interests of those whose sole concern is the preservation of the *status quo*.

Palo Alto, California   P. A. B.
March, 1962

Contents

What social science needs is less use of elaborate techniques and more courage to tackle, rather than dodge, the central issues. But to demand that is to ignore the social reasons that have made social science what it is.

J. D. Bernal, *Science in History*

ONE

A General View

THE question why social and economic development has recently moved into the forefront of economic discussion—particularly in the United States—may appear to be a recondite and tedious issue in the history of knowledge only tenuously related to the subject matter itself. This is not quite the case. The history of thought reveals also here the thought of history, and an examination of the circumstances that have brought about the present burst of interest in social and economic change may shed valuable light on the nature and significance of the current debate, as well as on the substance of the problem itself.

It will be recalled that a strong interest in economic development is by no means an unprecedented novelty in the realm of political economy. In fact, economic growth was the central theme of classical economics. This much is indicated by the title and contents of Adam Smith's pathbreaking work, and many a generation of economic thinkers, regardless of the names that they gave their writings, were concerned with analyzing the forces that made for economic progress. Their concern with the conditions necessary for economic development grew out of their keen observation and study of the society in which they lived, and resulted in their firm conviction that the political, social, and economic relations prevailing at the time greatly impeded and retarded the development of productive resources. Whether they referred to the fallacies of the mercantilist foreign trade theory or to the rigidities of the guild system, or whether the issue was related to the functions of the state in economic life or to the role played by

1

the landowning class, the classical economists had no trouble in showing that economic progress was predicated upon the removal of out-
dated political, social, and economic institutions, upon the creation of
conditions of free competition under which individual enterprise and
initiative would be given ample opportunity for unhampered performance.

Not that they confined themselves to a critique of the then existing
society without making an attempt to provide a *positive* analysis of the
working principles of the rising capitalist order. On the contrary, it
was precisely this positive effort that furnished us with much of what
we know today about the functioning of the capitalist system. What
matters in the present context, however, is that the chief impetus to
their prodigious scientific and publicistic endeavors was supplied by
the strongly felt necessity to convince the public of the urgency of
liberation from feudal and semi-feudal shackles. In this sense, if in
no other, it is wholly appropriate to relate the classical school of
economics to the rise and development of capitalism, to the triumph
of the modern bourgeoisie. In the words of Professor Lionel Robbins:

The System of Economic Freedom was not just a detached recom-
mendation not to interfere: It was an urgent demand that what were
thought to be hampering and anti-social impediments should be removed
and that the immense potential of free pioneering individual initiative
should be released. And, of course, it was in this spirit that in the world
of practice its proponents addressed themselves to agitation against the
main forms of these impediments: against the privileges of regulated
companies and corporations, against the law of apprenticeship, against
restriction on movement, against restraints on importation. The sense of a
crusade which emerged in the free trade movement is typical of the
atmosphere of the general movement for freeing spontaneous enterprise
and energies, of which, without doubt, the classical economists were the
intellectual spear-head.[1]

[1] Lionel Robbins, *The Theory of Economic Policy in English Classical
Political Economy* (London, 1952), p. 19. It is strange, therefore, to
read on the next page of Professor Robbins' book: ". . . I find it hard to
understand how anyone who has given serious attention to the actual
works of these men . . . can question their integrity and their transparent
devotion to the general good. . . . It has become fashionable to dismiss
them and their ideas not on grounds of logic and assumptions, but on the
grounds of alleged class interest. On this view the classical economists
are the spokesmen of business, and *consciously or unconsciously* the
apologists of the dominant class." (Italics added.) Yet "consciously or
unconsciously" is precisely the issue. No serious writer to my knowledge
has asserted that the classical economists—at least the great and important
ones—were *consciously* servile scribes of a dominant or rising bourgeois

Yet, as soon as capitalism became fully established, and the bourgeois social and economic order firmly entrenched, this order was "consciously or unconsciously" accepted as history's "terminal station," and the discussion of social and economic change all but ceased. Like the Boston lady who, in reply to an inquiry whether she had traveled much, observed that she had no need to travel since she had been fortunate enough to be born right in Boston, the neoclassical economists, in contrast to their classical predecessors, were much less concerned with problems of traveling and much more with the question how best to explore and to furnish the house in which they were born. To be sure, to some of them that house did not appear altogether perfect. They all thought of it, however, as sufficiently comfortable and sufficiently spacious to permit of various improvements. But such improvements—desirable as they may have seemed—were to be undertaken slowly, cautiously, and circumspectly, lest harm be done to the foundations and the pillars of the structure. Merely marginal adjustments were deemed practicable and advisable—nothing drastic, nothing radical could hope for approval on the part of economic science.[2] *Natura non facit saltum* suggests clearly that no moving was contemplated; it is certainly not the motto of economic development.

For economic development implies precisely the opposite of what Marshall placed on the title page of his *Principles*. It implies the crude but crucial fact—often, if not always, overlooked—that economic development has historically always meant a far-reaching transformation of society's economic, social, and political structure, of the dominant organization of production, distribution, and consumption. Economic development has always been propelled by classes and groups interested in a new economic and social order, has always been opposed

---

class. In that case they would have hardly been worth the paper they were printed on, let alone the paper they are being constantly reprinted on. The crux of the matter is that they were—*probably most unconsciously*—the spokesmen of a rising bourgeoisie whose interests they *objectively* served. Professor Robbins himself has clearly seen the distinction between subjective awareness of interests and their objective contents in his *The Economic Basis of Class Conflict* (London, 1939) (p. 4). In general it may well be said that for the appraisal of a group's or an individual's role in the historical process, subjective motivations (conscious or unconscious) are much less important than objective performances. In case of doubt, it is always useful to ask in all such matters: *cui bono?* The answer may not always be conclusive—it is never irrelevant.

[2] Thus it is by no means fortuitous that the marginal utility theory, the static character of which is one of its outstanding features, has become the heart of neoclassical economics.

and obstructed by those interested in the preservation of the *status quo,* rooted in and deriving innumerable benefits and habits of thought from the existing fabric of society, the prevailing mores, customs, and institutions. It has always been marked by more or less violent clashes, has proceeded by starts and spurts, suffered setbacks and gained new terrain—it has never been a smooth, harmonious process unfolding placidly over time and space.

However, this historical generalization—probably one of the best established that we have—was quickly lost sight of in bourgeois economics. In fact, having started as advocacy of capitalism, having grown to be its most sophisticated and perhaps most influential rationalization, it had to share the fate of all the other branches of bourgeois thought. As long as reason and the lessons to be learned from history were manifestly on the side of the bourgeoisie in its struggle against the obscurantist ideologies and institutions of feudalism, both reason and history were confidently invoked as the supreme arbiters in the fateful contest. There are no more magnificent witnesses to this grand alliance of the ascending bourgeoisie with reason and historical thinking than the great Encyclopedists of the eighteenth century, than the great realists of the nascent bourgeois literature.

But when reason and the study of history began revealing the irrationality, the limitations, and the merely transitory nature of the capitalist order, bourgeois ideology as a whole and with it bourgeois economics began abandoning both reason and history. Whether this abandonment assumed the form of a rationalism driven to its own self-destruction and turning into the agnosticism of modern positivism, or whether it appeared frankly in the form of some existentialist philosophy contemptuously rejecting all search for and all reliance upon a rational comprehension of history, the result was that bourgeois thought (and economics as a part of it) turned ever more into a neatly packed kit of assorted ideological gadgets required for the functioning and the preservation of the existing social order.

In its beginnings, economics was a revolutionary intellectual effort to seek out and to establish the working principles of an economic system best able to advance the cause of mankind. In its later days it has turned upon its own past, becoming a mere attempt at an explanation and justification of the *status quo*—condemning and suppressing at the same time all endeavors to judge the existing economic order by standards of reason, or to comprehend the origins of the prevailing conditions and the developmental potentialities that they contain. As Marx remarked: "The economists explain to us the process of production under given conditions; what they do not explain to us, however, is how these conditions themselves are being produced, i.e., the historical movement that brings them into being."[3]

Thus the concern with economic and social change was left to a "heretical" school of economics and social science. Marx and Engels accepted in essence the insistence of the classical economists on capitalism's giant contribution to economic development. Yet, not wedded to the now dominant capitalist class, and neither "consciously nor unconsciously" compelled to regard capitalism as the "natural" form of society and as the ultimate fulfillment of human aspirations, they were able to perceive the limits and barriers to progress inherent in the capitalist system. Indeed, their approach to the matter was radically different from that of bourgeois economics. While the latter was (and is) interested in economic development only to the extent that it has led to the establishment, and is conducive to the stabilization, of the capitalist order, Marx and Engels considered the capitalist order itself as likely to survive only as long as it did not become a fetter on further economic and social progress. Overcoming the limitations of bourgeois thought, they were able to comprehend the era of capitalism as merely creating the prerequisites for a development of humanity that would lead far beyond the confines of the capitalist order. Once more: the *critical* efforts of Marx and his followers yielded most important *positive* results. They destroyed the veil of harmony with which bourgeois economics obscured the view of the capitalist system, and laid bare the conflict-laden, irrational nature of the capitalist order. Much if not all that we know about the complex mechanism responsible for the development (and stagnation) of productive forces, and for the rise and decay of social organizations, is the result of the analytical work undertaken by Marx and by those whom he inspired.

Such might have remained the situation, with economic development relegated to the "underworld" of economic and social thought, were it not for historical processes that in the course of a few decades have drastically changed our entire social, political, and intellectual landscape. Indeed, while the neoclassical economists were busy with further refinements of static equilibrium analysis and with the elaboration of additional arguments proving the viability and intrinsic harmony of the capitalist system, capitalism itself was going through far-reaching transformations.

Towards the end of the nineteenth century, the first phase of the industrialization of the Western world was nearing its completion.

[3] Marx, *The Poverty of Philosophy* (Stuttgart-Berlin, 1921), p. 86.

The economic consequence of the thorough exploitation of the then available technology—based primarily on coal and steam—was not merely a tremendous expansion of heavy industry, a vast increase of output, and a revolution in the means of transportation and communication; it was also a momentous change in the structure of the capitalist economies. Concentration and centralization of capital made giant strides, and large-scale enterprise moved into the center of the economic scene, displacing and absorbing the small firm. Shattering the competitive mechanism which regulated, for better or worse, the functioning of the economic system, large-scale enterprise became the basis of monopoly and oligopoly—the characteristic features of modern capitalism. The world of neoclassical economics was rapidly disintegrating. Neither the slow (but steady) growth, nor relatively painless continuous adjustments on the margin were to be expected under conditions of ubiquitous indivisibilities and discontinuities, of increasing returns to scale, and of narrowing investment opportunites. The harmonious movement of capital from the advanced to the less developed countries that was expected to be propelled by the profit motive assumed in reality the form of embittered struggles for investment outlets, markets, and sources of raw materials. Western penetration of backward and colonial areas, that was supposed to spread the blessings of Western civilization into every nook and corner of the globe, spelled in actual fact ruthless oppression and exploitation of the subjugated nations.

The powerful tendencies towards stagnation, imperialist conflagrations, and severe political crises discerned by Marx as early as the middle of the nineteenth century, and later observed and analyzed by Hobson, Lenin, Hilferding, Rosa Luxemburg, and others, expressed themselves so manifestly as to give cause for alarm to all but the most complacent. A frantic armaments race among the Great Powers began absorbing growing parts of their national outputs and became the most important single factor in determining the level of their economic activity. In quick succession the Sino-Japanese War, the Spanish-American War, the Boer War, the bloody suppression of the Boxer Rebellion, the Russo-Japanese War, the Russian Revolution in 1905, the Chinese Revolution in 1911–1912, and finally the First World War ushered in the present epoch in the development of capitalism—the epoch of imperialism, wars, national and social revolutions.[4]

[4] "The record of the main European wars . . . is shown by the following index series (combining size of the fighting force, number of casualties,

The Marxian theoretic challenge has become eminently practical. The "Indian summer" of stability, prosperity, and confidence in the future of capitalism—following the First World War—lasted less than one decade. The dream of "organized capitalism," of a "Ford-versus-Marx" solution of all economic and social ills, and of "economic democracy" assuring justice and welfare to all became the shortest-lived utopia on the historical record. The Great Depression with its manifold and protracted repercussions rendered the continuation of the "conspiracy of optimism" about economic growth and social progress under capitalism increasingly difficult to maintain. The time-honored "scientific" and "objective" finding of economics that socialism is impossible was dramatically refuted by the success of the industrialization effort in the USSR.

Tardily and reluctantly, economics began taking cognizance of the new situation. Although inspired by the immediate problem of counteracting depression and unemployment, and consequently addressing itself primarily to the issues of the short run, the "New Economics" of John Maynard Keynes carried implications that transcended by far its original scope. In an attempt at clarification of the determinants of short-run changes in the levels of output, employment, and income, Keynesian economics found itself face to face with the entire irrationality, the glaring discrepancy between the productive potentialities and the productive performance characteristic of the capitalist order. At the risk of grossly exaggerating the intellectual performance of Keynes, it might be said that what Hegel accomplished with respect to German classical philosophy, Keynes achieved with regard to neoclassical economics. Operating with the customary tools of conventional theory, remaining well within the confines of "pure economics," faithfully refraining from considering the socioeconomic process as a whole, the Keynesian analysis advanced to the very limits of bourgeois economic theorizing, and exploded its entire structure. Indeed, it amounted to an "official" admission on the part of the "Holy See" of conventional economics that instability, a strong tendency towards stagnation,

---

number of countries involved, and proportion of combatants to total population):

Century:	12th	13th	14th	15th	16th	17th	18th	19th	20th
Index:	18	24	60	100	180	500	370	120	3080

For details see Pitirim Sorokin, *Social and Cultural Dynamics*, Vol. 3, 1937, and Quincy Wright, *A Study of War*, Vol. 1, Chap. 9 and Appendixes, 1942"; cited in Harold D. Lasswell, *World Politics Faces Economics* (New York and London, 1945), p. 7.

chronic underutilization of human and material resources, are inherent in the capitalist system. It implicitly repudiated the zealously guarded "purity" of academic economics by revealing the paramount importance for the comprehension of the economic process of the structure of society, the relations of classes, the distribution of income, the role of the state, and other "exogenous" factors.

Yet this unintentionally undertaken revival of the inquiry into the "nature and causes of the wealth of nations" had nothing in common with the youthful, revolutionary enthusiasm of the early crusade for *laissez faire*. Although contributing greatly to the understanding of the mechanics of the capitalist economy, the New Economics was unable to rise to a full theoretic grasp of the general crisis of capitalism, and remained merely a supreme effort on the part of bourgeois economic thought to discover a way of saving the capitalist system in spite of the manifest symptoms of its disintegration and decay. Thus the "Keynesian Revolution" has never become associated with a vigorous movement for the abolition of an outlived and destructive social order, for economic development and social progress. Again, not unlike the philosophy of Hegel, in its "Leftist" interpretation, it supplied intellectual ammunition to a reform movement which expected once more to solve the contradictions of capitalism by changing the prevailing distribution of income, and by having a benevolent state provide henceforth for steady economic expansion and increasing standards of living. But the logic of monopoly capitalism proved to be much stronger than ever realized by Keynes and his radical followers. It turned their theoretic accomplishments to purposes quite alien to their intentions. The "Welfare State," guided by the canons of Keynesian economics and the precepts of "functional finance," has remained essentially on paper. It was fascist Germany that thus far has made the most extensive use of Keynesian insights in building an economic machine that enabled it to unleash the Second World War.

The war and the years of the postwar boom suspended all Keynesian concern with the excess accumulation of capital, with the shortage of effective demand. The requirements for the reconstruction of war damage in some countries, the satisfaction of postponed demand on the part of businesses and consumers in others, the urge to turn to productive purposes the technological innovations developed during (and frequently in connection with) the war—all combined to create a huge market for the output of capitalist enterprise.

Economists who only unwillingly and only under irresistible pressure of incontrovertible facts had "swallowed" the anti-capitalist implications of the Keynesian doctrine returned with conspicuous alacrity to the customary panegyrics of capitalist harmony. Remaining "close to observable facts," they cheerfully began to discuss inflation as the main threat to the continuous equilibrium of capitalist economies, and declared once more that oversaving, excess capacity, and depressions were relics of a remote and backward past. Extolling the virtues of the market mechanism, glorifying monopoly and "big business," economics all but canceled whatever advance was reached as a result of the Keynesian Revolution, and returned to the complacency of the "merry twenties."

To be sure, this regression will probably be no more than short-lived; it has in fact not even affected the entire profession. Not only behind some recent writings on problems of economic growth, but even behind the more down-to-earth discussions of current business conditions and short-run economic prospects, lurks a gnawing uncertainty about the future of capitalism and a painful awareness that the impediments to economic progress that are inherent in the capitalist system are bound to reappear with renewed force and increased obstinacy as soon as the extraordinary hothouse situation of the postwar period has ceased to exist.

II

But if the lability of the economy of the United States (and of other highly developed capitalist countries) is giving rise to much concern and provides a stimulus to thinking about the basic problems of economic growth and development, the processes unfolding in the world at large cannot fail to lend these meditations the utmost urgency.

For the Second World War and the events that constituted its sequel were a major earthquake that shattered the structure of the capitalist world even more violently than the First World War and the Russian Revolution. Indeed, the First World War led "merely" to the loss of Russia to the capitalist system. The Second World War, however, has been followed not only by the Chinese Revolution, but by a nearly universal awakening of the vast multitudes inhabiting the world's dependent and colonial areas. Aroused by the staggering irrationality and oppressiveness of their social and economic order, weary of the continuous exploitation by their foreign and domestic masters, the peoples of the underdeveloped countries have begun to manifest a mounting determination to overthrow a social and political system that is perpetuating their squalor, misery, and stagnation.

The momentous movement to do away with the entire edifice of imperialism, to put an end to the backwardness and prostration of the overwhelming majority of the human race, would by itself have created considerable consternation in the ruling class of the United States and other capitalist countries sitting on top of the imperialist pyramid. What has transformed this consternation into a state of near-panic, however, is the historic confluence of the restiveness in the underdeveloped countries with the spectacular advance and expansion of the world's socialist camp. The military performance of the Soviet Union during the war and the rapid recovery of its war-ravaged economy provided the final proof of the strength and viability of a socialist society. There can no longer remain any doubt that a socioeconomic system based on comprehensive economic planning can function, grow, and withstand the most trying historical tests—without the benefits of private enterprise and without the institution of private property in the means of production. What is more, a large number of dependent countries went through a social revolution after the war, and thus entered the road to rapid economic and social progress. Eastern and Southeastern Europe, and even more importantly China, dropped out of the orbit of world capitalism and became sources of encouragement and inspiration to all other colonial and dependent countries.

As a result of these developments, the issue of economic and social progress not merely returns to the center of the historical stage but relates—as two or three centuries ago—to the very essence of the widening and sharpening struggle between two antagonistic social orders. What has changed is perhaps not so much the nature and the plot of the drama as the leading dramatis personae. If in the seventeenth and eighteenth centuries the struggle for progress was tantamount to the struggle against the outlived institutions of the feudal age, similarly current efforts to bring about conditions indispensable for economic development in advanced and backward capitalist countries alike cóme continuously into conflict with the economic and political order of capitalism and imperialism. Thus to ruling opinion in the United States (but also in some other parts of the capitalist world), the world-wide drive for economic progress inevitably appears as profoundly subversive of the existing social order and of the prevailing system of international domination—as a revolutionary movement that has to be bribed, blocked, and, if possible, broken, if the capitalist system is at all to be preserved.

It is needless to say that approaching economic development from this standpoint amounts to its repudiation. As far as *advanced* capitalist countries are concerned, the incompatibility of sustained economic growth with the capitalist system has been brought into sharp relief by some of the recent writings on economic growth. The mere specification of the conditions that need to be fulfilled for output to increase at rates that would be attainable with the available human and material resources—presented in different forms by Domar, Harrod, Colm, and others—shows with utmost clarity that such rates of increase are impossible under capitalism. Indeed, both consumption and private investment are rather narrowly circumscribed by the requirements of profit maximization under conditions of monopoly and oligopoly, and the nature and volume of government spending are no less rigidly determined by the social basis and function of the state in a capitalist society. Consequently neither maximum output, rationally allocated as between investment and consumption, nor some predetermined level of output combined with a lessening of the burden of work, are to be expected in the capitalist system. What appears to be more probable is the continuous re-emergence of the grim dilemma between war-induced bursts of output and depression-induced floods of unemployment.

Yet, although demonstrating, and indeed greatly clarifying, the vicious and portentous nature of this impasse, none of the writers just mentioned has stated what is an inescapable conclusion of their own investigations—that socialist economic planning represents the only rational solution of the problem. To be sure, it may be held that there is no need for explicit statements of what necessarily emerges from the logic of a rigorous argument. However, even self-evident truths must be communicated if they are to be recognized as such by those whom they may otherwise escape. Nothing is perhaps more characteristic of the intellectual atmosphere surrounding the present discussion of economic growth—a discussion in which truisms and trivia abound—than that it is *this* self-evident truth that is strictly taboo even to the most enlightened writers on the subject.

Matters are still worse when it comes to economic development in *underdeveloped* countries. There a maze of pretense, hypocrisy, and make-believe confuse the discussion, and a major effort is required to penetrate the smoke screen obscuring the main issue. What is decisive

is that economic development in underdeveloped countries is profoundly inimical to the dominant interests in the advanced capitalist
countries. Supplying many important raw materials to the industrialized countries, providing their corporations with vast profits and
investment outlets, the backward world has always represented the
indispensable hinterland of the highly developed capitalist West. Thus
the ruling class in the United States (and elsewhere) is bitterly opposed to the industrialization of the so-called "source countries" and
to the emergence of integrated processing economies in the colonial
and semi-colonial areas. This opposition appears regardless of the
nature of the regime in the underdeveloped country that seeks to reduce the foreign grip on its economy and to provide for a measure of
independent development. Whether it is a democratically elected government in Venezuela, in Guatemala, or in British Guiana, an indigenous popular movement (as in Kenya, in the Philippines, or in Indo-
China), a nationalist administration (as in Iran, Egypt, or Argentina)
that undertakes to oppose the foreign domination of its country—all
leverages of diplomatic intrigue, economic pressure, and political subversion are set into motion to overthrow the recalcitrant national government and to replace it with politicians who are willing to serve
the interests of the capitalist countries.

The resistance of imperialist powers to economic and social development in colonial and dependent territories becomes even more desperate when the popular aspirations to national and social liberation
express themselves in a revolutionary movement that, internationally
connected and supported, threatens to overthrow the entire economic
and social order of capitalism and imperialism. Under such circumstances, the resistance hardens into a counter-revolutionary alliance of
all imperialist countries (and their reliable retainers) and assumes
the form of a systematic crusade against national and social revolutions.

The requirements of this crusade have molded decisively the attitude toward the development of underdeveloped countries prevailing
at the present time in the Western world. As the Prussian Junkers presented the continuation of serfdom on their estates as indispensable for
the defense of Christianity against the onslaught of liberal godlessness,
so the drive of the Western ruling classes to maintain the economic,
social, and political *status quo* in underdeveloped countries is proclaimed as the defense of democracy and freedom. As the Prussian Junkers' interest in high tariffs on grains was announced to be dictated

solely by their deep concern with the preservation of German food supplies under conditions of war, so the anxiety of dominant Western corporations to safeguard their investments abroad and to remain assured of the accustomed flow of raw materials from the backward world is publicized as patriotic solicitude for the "free world's" supply of indispensable strategic materials.

The arsenal of "united action" against the independent development of underdeveloped countries comprises an entire gamut of political and ideological stratagems. There are in the first place the widely broadcast statements of Western statesmen that appear to *favor* economic development in the underdeveloped world. Indeed, much is being made at the present time of the advanced countries' aid and support for the economic advancement of the backward areas. This advancement is conceived of as a slow, gradual improvement of the living standards of the native populations, and it is expected to *lessen* popular pressure for industrialization, to *weaken* the movement for economic and social progress.

However, this scheme of "bribing" the peoples of the underdeveloped countries to refrain from overthrowing the existing system and from entering the road to rapid economic growth is beset by a host of insuperable contradictions. The logic of economic growth is such that a slow and gradual improvement of living standards in little-developed countries is an extremely difficult if not altogether impossible project. Whatever small increases in national output might be attained with the help of such Western investment and charity as may be forthcoming are swamped by the rapid growth of the population, by the corruption of the local governments, by squandering of resources by the underdeveloped countries' ruling classes, and by profit withdrawals on the part of foreign investors.

For, where far-reaching structural changes in the economy are required if the economic development of a country is to shift into high gear and is to outstrip the growth of population, where technological indivisibilities render growth dependent on large investments and long-run planning, where tradition-bound patterns of thought and work obstruct the introduction of new methods and means of production—then only a sweeping reorganization of society, only an all-out mobilization of all its creative potentialities, can move the economy off dead center. As mentioned before, the mere notions of "development" and "growth" suggest a transition to something that is new from something that is old, that has outlived itself. It can only be

achieved through a determined struggle against the conservative, retrograde forces, through a change in the social, political, and economic
structure of a backward, stagnant society. Since a social organization,
however inadequate, never disappears by itself, since a ruling class,
however parasitic, never yields power unless compelled to do so by
overwhelming pressure, development and progress can only be attained if all the energies and abilities of a people that was politically,
socially, and economically disfranchised under the old system are
thrown into battle against the fortresses of the *ancien régime*.

But the crusade against national and social revolutions conducted
at the present time by the Western powers relies upon a mobilization of
altogether different social strata. It cements an international entente
of precisely those social groups and economic interests that are, and
are bound to be, bitterly antagonistic to genuine economic and social
progress, and it subordinates considerations of economic development
to the purpose of strengthening this alliance. It provides economic and
military aid to regimes in underdeveloped countries that are manifestly inimical to economic development, and it maintains in power
governments that would have been otherwise swept aside by the popular drive for a more rational and more progressive economic and social
order.

It is as part of the same effort to bribe the peoples of the underdeveloped countries while avoiding the appearance of old-fashioned
imperialism that political independence has been recently granted to
a number of dependent nations and that native politicians have been
allowed to rise to high offices. There is hardly any need to stress that
such independence and autonomy are little more than sham as long
as the countries in question remain economic appendages of the advanced capitalist countries and as long as their governments depend
for survival on the pleasure of their foreign patrons.

What is more, the attainment of political independence by colonial
peoples yields results under the conditions of imperialism that are frequently quite different from those hoped for by these peoples themselves.
Their newly won political independence often precipitates merely a
change in their Western masters, with the younger, more enterprising,
more resourceful imperialist power seizing the controls that have slipped
out of the hands of the old, now weakened imperialist countries. Thus
where it is politically no longer possible to operate through the medium
of the old-fashioned and compromised colonial administrations and to
impose its control merely by means of economic infiltration, American

imperialism sponsors (or tolerates) political independence of colonial countries, becoming subsequently the dominant power in the newly "liberated" regions. Both methods of expansion of American influence can be studied in Africa, Southeast Asia, and the Near East.

III

A considerable ideological campaign is being undertaken in order to "sell" to the public this modern, more subtle and less transparent policy of imperialism. As an astute economist recently remarked, "'development' as compared with 'civilization' . . . [has become] an intellectual *quid pro quo* for international domination by a major country."[5] And social sciences provide, as usual, the requisite rationalization for the systematic effort of the ruling class of the advanced capitalist countries to prevent, or at least to retard, the political and economic liberation of the colonial and dependent nations. Stimulated by lavish support on the part of various government agencies and private foundations, economists, anthropologists, social psychologists, and other social scientists in the West have been directing an ever-increasing amount of attention to the development of underdeveloped countries.

In the field of economic research, much energy is now given to an attempt to demonstrate that the advanced capitalist countries themselves have reached their present level of development by a process of spontaneous, slow growth—within the framework of the capitalist order and without major shocks and revolutionary upheavals. It is argued that it was, in fact, the relative absence of political disturbance and the continuity and stability of social institutions that provided the "climate" essential for the emergence and prosperity of the capitalist entrepreneur, who in turn is credited with having played a decisive role in promoting economic progress. Accordingly, large resources are being devoted to an extensive campaign of rewriting the history of capitalism. Its purpose is the rehabilitation of the "robber baron" and his glorification as the hero and prime mover of economic and social progress, and its related task is the minimization of the suffering and privations that were associated with the beginning and the growth of capitalist enterprise.

Thus the historically minded members of the economics profession

[5] H. G. Johnson, *Economic Journal* (June 1955), p. 303.

seek to prove that by relying on the forces of the free market and of private initiative economic development was achieved in the past without excessive sacrifices—with the obvious moral that this method still represents the most commendable avenue to economic progress. Little mention, if any, is accorded by these historians to the role that the exploitation of the now underdeveloped countries has played in the evolution of Western capitalism; little attention, if any, is given to the fact that the colonial and dependent countries today have no recourse to such sources of primary accumulation of capital as were available to the now advanced capitalist countries, that economic development in the age of monopoly capitalism and imperialism faces obstacles that have little in common with those encountered two or three hundred years ago, and that what was possible in a certain historical setting is unrealistic in another.

The more theoretically inclined economists follow a different tack. Dwelling on the technical aspects of economic development, they discover a host of insuperable difficulties preventing the formulation of a coherent theory of economic and social change. They list with obvious relish all and sundry matters more or less germane to the problem of economic development about which "we do not know enough," they stress the lack of unambiguous criteria for a rational allocation of resources under dynamic conditions, they elaborate on the obstacles to industrialization stemming from the character of the labor force in underdeveloped countries, from the scarcity of native managerial talent, from likely balances of payments disequilibria—with the result that all efforts at rapid development appear as adventures on uncharted seas, as gross violations of all accepted economic reasoning.

These endeavors to discredit implicitly or explicitly the drive for rapid development of underdeveloped countries, to present it as the manifestation of a deplorable impatience and irrationality of unenlightened mobs devilishly manipulated by sinister, power-greedy politicians—these are assisted by the neo-Malthusians who explain the backwardness of the backward countries as the inevitable result of their "excessive" population growth, and who therefore denounce all attempts at economic development in these areas as utopian so long as the population increase has not been brought to a halt. However, since a reduction of the population growth—assuming for the sake of argument that such a reduction is necessary—can only be achieved as a *result* of an all-round development of the backward societies, the neo-Malthusian position renders economic development a hopeless task, made insolvable by the very nature of the human animal.

A similar impact on opinion is exercised by most anthropological and quasi-philosophical writing related to the problem of economic development of underdeveloped countries. Here it has become fashionable to question the "absolute desirability" of economic development, to deride as unscientific its identification with progress, to accuse its protagonists in the West of "ethnocentrism," of hypostatization of their own culture, and of insufficient respect for the mores and values of more primitive peoples. In keeping with the general relativism and agnosticism of contemporary bourgeois thought, this strand of social science denies the possibility of a rational judgment on the usefulness, let alone urgency, of economic and social change in colonial and dependent areas, and counsels utmost caution in disturbing the continuity of the backward societies. While not explicitly endorsing the "white man's burden" concept of imperialist domination, this approach comes very close to it by pointing to the "cultural heterogeneity" of backward nations, by stressing the incomparability of value systems, and by suggesting that colonial and dependent peoples may actually "prefer" their present state to economic development and to national and social liberation. Small wonder that such a doctrine provides a poor background for the comprehension of the unprecedented popular movements that are at the present time revolutionizing and rejuvenating the greater part of the human race; small wonder that it supplies aid and comfort not to the peoples in the colonial and dependent countries struggling for freedom but to their masters seeking to preserve the *status quo.*

This political and ideological setting of the current discussion of economic development explains the highly unsatisfactory nature of what has been accomplished thus far. Robert Lynd's challenging question, "Knowledge for What?" bears not only on the fruitfulness of an intellectual effort in terms of the ends that it is designed to serve; it also necessarily relates to the conduct and the contents of the effort itself. Thus, motivated by the overriding preoccupation with the requirements of the counter-revolutionary crusade, muzzled by the fear of antagonizing the dominant interests determined to obstruct at all cost economic and social progress in the colonial and dependent countries, research and writing on economic development eschew as much as possible reference to what is in the very center of the problem. They make no reference to the irrationalities of monopoly capitalism and imperialism that block economic development in advanced capitalist countries, and they give no attention to the system of internal and foreign domination that prevents or distorts economic growth in the underdeveloped world. Correspondingly little emphasis is placed on the study of the unique experience in rapid development gathered in the USSR and in other countries of the socialist sector of the world—as if that experience was of interest only to Military Intelligence. And yet there can be no doubt that efforts at economic development could all derive immeasurable profit from fully comprehending the process of economic growth that has taken place in the Soviet Union and in other socialist countries.

IV

In speaking thus far about economic development, I have confined myself to rather broad allusions to this complex term. It is time to buckle down to a somewhat more detailed examination of this process, and it may be convenient to begin by deciding on a definition of economic growth. Not that it is my objective to present here a formula that would exclude any other, nor do I wish to suggest that other definitions might not be superior for other purposes. All I propose to do is to organize my categories in such a way as to be able to approach the subject matter by what appears to me to be a simple and useful method—a method which I plan to explore further in the course of subsequent chapters.

Let economic growth (or development) be defined as increase over time in *per capita* output of material goods.[6] It may be permissible

---

[6] Colin Clark suggests a different definition: "Economic progress can be defined simply as an improvement in economic welfare. Economic welfare, following Pigou, can be defined in the first instance as an abundance of all those goods and services which are customarily exchanged for money. Leisure is an element in economic welfare, and more precisely we can define economic progress as the attaining of an increasing output of those goods and services for a minimum expenditure of effort, and of other scarce resources, both natural and artificial." *The Conditions of Economic Progress* (London, 1940), p. 1. This definition appears to me unsatisfactory for a number of reasons: (1) the identification of economic growth with increase in welfare leaves out of account a considerable share of total output that bears no relation to welfare, however the latter may be conceived: currently produced investment goods, armaments, net exports, and the like belong in this group. (2) Regarding an increase of output of "all these goods and services which are customarily exchanged for money" as identical with "improvement in economic welfare" is untenable. Economic welfare may be greatly improved by an increased supply of goods and services that are customarily *not* exchanged for money (schools, hospitals, roads, or bridges) while on the other hand a great number of

in the present context to neglect the difficulty of comparing outputs over time, a difficulty arising whenever the outputs to be compared consist of more than one product, whenever, therefore, changes in output may affect its components unequally, and whenever certain products appear in the output of one period without appearing in the output of the other. This familiar index number problem, disturbing as it is even with regard to slow, gradual growth, becomes particularly vexing when what is considered is more or less rapid economic growth, the outstanding characteristic of which is profound change not only in the magnitude but also in the composition of output. Indeed, inter-temporal comparisons threaten to be outright misleading when the periods to be compared are separated by changes in economic and social organization, by big spurts in urbanization, by decreases or increases of the "marketed share" of output, and so forth. Especially troublesome is the services sector, the expansion of which would cause an increase in Gross National Product (as conventionally defined) suggesting thus "economic growth"—although in most countries it would be considered to be a retrograde step rather than one in the direction of economic progress.[7] Pigou's famous gentleman marrying his cook and thus reducing national income comes readily to mind. Equally easily can one imagine a tremendous expansion of national income caused by the introduction of compulsory payments to wives for services rendered.

---

goods and services that *are* customarily exchanged for money make no contribution whatever to human welfare (patent medicines and beauty parlors, narcotics, and items of conspicuous display, etc.) (3) Economic welfare can be improved without any *increase* of output—by a change in its *structure* and *distribution*. (4) While it is obviously *desirable* to secure any given output with a minimum of input, even an inefficiently secured increase in output might still constitute economic growth. It would seem to be preferable, therefore, to consider economic growth as an increase in output of goods regardless of whether they make a contribution to welfare, to the available stock of producers' goods, or to armaments—leaving to a related but nevertheless separate examination the factors determining the composition of this output and the purposes to which it is put.

[7] This was noted in the United Nations' *Economic Survey of Europe Since the War* (1953): "In the eastern European countries services not directly connected with the production and transport of goods are not regarded as productive and their value is thus excluded from national income. For a poor country which is trying to develop its industry and to reduce the underemployment common in service trades, the Marxist defi-nition of national income has some obvious advantages over the more inclusive concept suited to wealthy industrialized economies and now com-monly adopted in under-developed countries." (p. 25.)

But we shall assume that increases of aggregate output over time can somehow be measured, and shall ask ourselves how such increases come about. They can be the result of one of the following developments (or of a combination of them): (1) The aggregate resource utilization may expand *without changes in organization and/or technology,* i.e. previously unutilized resources (manpower, land) may be brought into the productive process. (2) The productivity per unit of resources at work may rise as a result of *organizational measures,* i.e. by a transfer of workers from less productive or unproductive occupations to more productive pursuits, by a lengthening of the working day, by an improvement in nutrition and strengthening of incentives available to workers, by rationalization of methods of production and more economic utilization of fuel, raw materials, and so forth. (3) *Society's "technical arm" may become stronger,* i.e. (a) worn-out or obsolete plant and equipment may be replaced by more efficient facilities, and/or (b) new (technologically improved or unchanged) productive facilities may be added to the previously existing stock.

The first three routes to expansion of output—(1), (2) and (3)(a) —are typically not associated with *net* investment. Although it is probably impossible to impute to each of these four processes a proper share of the increase of output that has actually taken place, there can be little doubt that the economic application of increasing technical knowledge and net investment in additional productive facilities have been the most important sources of economic growth.

To be sure, in actual fact some net investment may be needed for all of them: previously unused resources may be unusable without some outlays on equipment, soil improvements, and the like; organizational changes may be predicated upon the installation of conveyor belts or similar devices; technological progress yielding improved machinery to be added to or substituted for worn-out equipment may be forthcoming only under conditions of large net investment. "If . . . technique largely depends on the state of science, science depends far more still on the *state* and the requirements of technique. If society has a technical need, that helps science forward more than ten universities. The whole of hydrostatics (Torricelli, etc.) was called forth by the necessity for regulating the mountain streams of Italy in the sixteenth and seventeenth centuries. We have only known anything reasonable about electricity since its technical applicability was discovered."[8]

[8] F. Engels, Letter to H. Starkenburg, in Marx and Engels, *Selected Works* (Moscow, 1949-1950), Vol. II, p. 457. On the interesting relation

On the other hand, plowing back amortization allowances—without any *net* investment—*on a higher technological plane* may per se support a significant expansion of output. Therefore where the capital intensity of the productive process is already large—in other words, where depreciation allowance constitutes an important part of the cost of the product—there is continuously available a source of capital for financing technological improvements without any need for *net* investment. While this aggravates the instability of the advanced capitalist economies by increasing the amount of currently generated surplus that has to be disposed of by investment, it also gives the advanced countries a major advantage over the underdeveloped countries where the annual amortization allowances necessarily amount to little.[9]

Net investment in any case can take place only if society's total output *exceeds* what is used for its current consumption and for making good the wear and tear on its productive facilities employed during the period in question. The volume and the nature of net investment taking place in a society at any given time depends, therefore, on the size and the *mode of utilization* of the currently generated *economic surplus*.

Both, as we shall see later, are essentially determined by the degree to which society's productive resources have been developed, and by the social structure within which the productive process unfolds. The understanding of the factors responsible for the size and the mode of utilization of the economic surplus is one of the foremost tasks of a theory of economic development. It is not even approached in the realm of "pure" economics. We have to look for it in the political economy of growth.

---

between economic development on one hand and the progress of science and technology on the other, cf. B. Hessen, *The Social and Economic Roots of Newton's Principia* (Sydney, 1946), as well as J. D. Bernal, *Science in History* (London, 1954).

[9] Cf. Marx, *Theories of Surplus Value* (London, 1951), pp. 354 ff., where this point is stressed.

TWO

The Concept of the Economic Surplus

THE concept of economic surplus is undoubtedly somewhat tricky, and in clarifying and employing it for the understanding of the process of economic development neither simple definitions nor refined measurements can be substituted for analytical effort and rational judgment. Yet it would certainly seem desirable to break with the time-honored tradition of academic economics of sacrificing the relevance of subject matter to the elegance of analytical method; it is better to deal imperfectly with what is important than to attain virtuoso skill in the treatment of what does not matter.

In order to facilitate the discussion as much as possible, I shall be speaking now in terms of "comparative statics": that is, I shall ignore the paths of transition from one economic situation to another, and shall consider these situations, as it were, *ex post*. Proceeding in this way, we can distinguish three variants of the concept of economic surplus.

Actual economic surplus, i.e. the difference between society's *actual* current output and its *actual* current consumption.[1] It is thus identical

---

[1] It comprises obviously a lesser share of total output than that encompassed by Marx's notion of surplus value. The latter, it will be recalled, consists of the entire difference between aggregate net output and the real income of labor. The "actual economic surplus" as defined above is merely that part of surplus value that is being *accumulated*; it does not include, in other words, the consumption of the capitalist class, the government's spending on administration, military establishment, and the like.

with current saving or accumulation, and finds its embodiment in assets of various kinds added to society's wealth during the period in question: productive facilities and equipment, inventories, foreign balances, and gold hoards. It would seem to be merely a matter of definition whether durable consumer goods (residential dwellings, automobiles, etc.) should be treated as representing saving rather than consumption, and it is undoubtedly quite arbitrary to treat houses as investment while treating, say, grand pianos as consumption. If the length of useful life be the criterion, where should one place the benchmark? In actual fact, it is essential for the comprehension of the economic process to make the distinction *not* on the basis of the physical properties of the assets involved, but in the light of their economic function, i.e. depending on whether they enter consumption as "final goods" or serve as means of production contributing thus to an increase of output in the subsequent period. Hence an automobile purchased for pleasure is an object of consumption, while an identical car added to a taxi-fleet is an investment good.[2]

Actual economic surplus has been generated in all socioeconomic formations, and while its size and structure have markedly differed from one phase of development to another, its existence has characterized nearly all of recorded history. The magnitude of the actual economic surplus—saving or capital formation—is at least conceptually readily established, and today is regularly estimated by statistical agencies in most countries. Such difficulties as are encountered in its measurement are technical, and caused by the absence or inadequacy of statistical information.

(2) *Potential* economic surplus, i.e. the difference between the output that *could* be produced in a given natural and technological environment with the help of employable productive resources, and what might be regarded as essential consumption.[3] Its realization presup-

----

[2] While it need not detain us at this point, it is worth bearing in mind that from the standpoint of economic development it is most important whether the actual economic surplus assumes the form of capital goods increasing productivity, or appears as additions to inventories or gold hoards only tenuously, if at all, related to the "strengthening of society's technical arm."

[3] This also refers to a different quantity of output than what would represent surplus value in Marx's sense. On one hand, it *excludes* such elements of surplus value as what was called above *essential* consumption of capitalists, what could be considered *essential* outlays on government administration and the like; on the other hand, it comprises what is not covered by the concept of surplus value—the output lost in view of underemployment or misemployment of productive resources.

poses a more or less drastic reorganization of the production and distribution of social output, and implies far-reaching changes in the structure of society. It appears under four headings. *One* is society's excess consumption (predominantly on the part of the upper income groups, but in some countries such as the United States also on the part of the so-called middle classes), the *second* is the output lost to society through the existence of unproductive workers, the *third* is the output lost because of the irrational and wasteful organization of the existing productive apparatus, and the *fourth* is the output foregone owing to the existence of unemployment caused primarily by the anarchy of capitalist production and the deficiency of effective demand.

The identification and measurement of these four forms of the potential economic surplus runs into some obstacles. These are essentially reducible to the fact that the category of the potential economic surplus itself transcends the horizon of the existing social order, relating as it does not merely to the easily observable performance of the given socioeconomic organization, but also to the less readily visualized image of a more rationally ordered society.

II

This requires a short digression. Indeed, if looked at from the vantage point of feudalism, essential, productive, and rational was all that was compatible with and conducive to the continuity and stability of the feudal system. Nonessential, unproductive, and wasteful was all that interfered with or was unnecessary for the preservation and the normal functioning of the prevailing social order. Accordingly Malthus staunchly defended the excess consumption of the landed aristocracy, pointing to the employment-stimulating effects of such outlays. On the other hand, the economists of the rising bourgeoisie had no compunctions about castigating the *ancien régime* for the wastefulness of its socioeconomic organization, and about pointing out the parasitic character of many of its most cherished functionaries and institutions.[4]

---

[4] "The labor of some of the most respectable orders in the society, is like that of menial servants, unproductive of any value. . . . The sovereign, for example, with all the officers both of justice and war who serve under him, the whole army and navy, are unproductive laborers. They are the servants of the .public, and are maintained by a part òf the annual produce of the industry of other people. . . . In the same class must be ranked . . . churchmen, lawyers, physicians, men of letters of all kinds:

But as soon as the critique of pre-capitalist society lost its urgency, and the agenda of economics became dominated by the task of rationalizing and justifying the victorious capitalist order, the mere question as to the productivity or essentiality of any type of activity taking place in capitalist society was ruled out of court. By elevating the dictum of the market to the role of the sole criterion of rationality and efficiency, economics denies even all "respectability" to the distinction between essential and nonessential consumption, between productive and unproductive labor, between actual and potential surplus. Nonessential consumption is justified as providing indispensable incentives, unproductive labor is glorified as indirectly contributing to production, depressions and unemployment are defended as the costs of progress, and waste is condoned as a prerequisite of freedom. In the words of Marx, "as the dominion of capital extended, and in fact even those spheres of production not directly related to the production of material wealth became more and more dependent on it, and especially the positive sciences (natural sciences) were subordinated to it as means towards material production—second rate sycophants of political economy thought it their duty to glorify and justify every sphere of activity by demonstrating that it was 'linked' with the production of material wealth, that it was a means towards it; and they honoured everyone by making him a 'productive worker' in the 'narrowest' sense—that is a worker who works in the service of capital, is useful in one way or another to its increase."[5]

Yet "capitalism creates a critical frame of mind which after having destroyed the moral authority of so many other institutions, in the end turns against its own: the bourgeois finds to his amazement that the rationalist attitude does not stop at the credentials of kings and popes but goes on to attack private property and the whole system of bourgeois values."[6] Thus from a standpoint located outside and beyond

---

players, musicians, opera singers, opera dancers, etc. . . ." Adam Smith, *Wealth of Nations* (Modern Library ed.), p. 295.

"When the annual productions of a country more than replace its annual consumption, it is said to increase its capital; when its annual consumption is not at least replaced by its annual production, it is said to diminish its capital. Capital may, therefore, be increased by an increased production or by a diminished unproductive consumption." Ricardo, *Principles of Political Economy and Taxation* (Everyman's Library ed.), p. 150.

[5] Marx, *Theories of Surplus Value* (London, 1951), p. 177.

[6] J. A. Schumpeter, *Capitalism, Socialism and Democracy* (New York, 1950), p. 143.

the capitalist frame of reference, from the standpoint of a socialist society, much of what appears to be essential, productive, rational to bourgeois economic and social thought turns out to be nonessential, unproductive, and wasteful. It may be said in general that it is only the standpoint which is intellectually outside the prevailing social order, which is unencumbered by its "values," its "practical intelligence," and its "self-evident truths," that permits critical insight into that social order's contradictions and hidden potentialities. The exercise of self-criticism is just as onerous to a ruling class as it is to a single individual.

As can be readily seen, the decision on what constitutes potential economic surplus, on the nature of nonessential consumption, waste, and unproductive labor, relates to the very foundations of bourgeois economics and in particular to what has come to be called the economics of welfare. Indeed, the purpose of this—perhaps most ideological and apologetic—branch of economic theorizing is to organize our knowledge of the conditions that determine the economic welfare of people. Needless to say, the first and foremost prerequisite for such an effort to be meaningful is a clear notion of what is meant by economic welfare and of the criteria by which states of economic welfare may be distinguished. The welfare economists meet the issue (or, rather, believe they meet it) by referring to the utility or satisfaction experienced by individuals. The individual himself, with his habits, tastes, and preferences, is taken as given. Yet it should be obvious that such a view of the individual is altogether metaphysical, in fact misses the most essential aspect of human history. As Marx remarked in a passage devoted to Bentham: "To know what is useful for a dog, we must study dog nature. This nature itself is not to be deduced from the principle of utility. Applying this to man, he that would criticize all human acts, movements, relations, etc. by the principle of utility, must first deal with human nature in general, and then with human nature as modified in each historical epoch. Bentham makes short work of it. With the driest naiveté he takes the modern shopkeeper, especially the English shopkeeper, as the normal man. What is useful to this queer normal man and to his world is absolutely useful. This yardmeasure then he applies to past, present and future."[7]

Indeed, in the course of history the individual with his physical and psychic requirements, with his values and his aspirations, has been changing with the society of which he is a part. Changes in the

[7] *Capital* (Kerr ed.), Vol. I, p. 668.

"objective interests"

structure of society have changed him, changes in his nature have changed society. How are we then to employ the utility or satisfaction accruing to an individual at any given time as a criterion by which the conduciveness to welfare of economic institutions and relationships is to be judged? If we refer to the observable behavior of an individual, we are obviously moving in a circle. His behavior is determined by the social order in which he lives, in which he was brought up, which has molded and determined his character structure, his categories of thought, his hopes and his fears. In fact, it is this ability of a social constellation to produce the mechanism of such personality-molding, to provide the material and psychic framework for a specific type of human existence, that makes this social constellation a social *order*.

Economists, nevertheless, try to appraise that social order, its so-called efficiency, its contribution to human welfare, by criteria that it has itself evolved.[8] What would we think of judging the welfare contribution of homicide by the code of behavior established in a cannibalistic society? The best that can be attained in that way is a judgment on the *consistency* of the cannibals' behavior with their own cannibalistic rules and regulations. This kind of inquiry may be useful to an effort to devise arrangements needed for the preservation and better functioning of the cannibalistic society—but what is there to be deduced from such an investigation in terms of human welfare? Assuming, indeed, that the life of the cannibals fully conforms to the precepts of their society, that their headman gets exactly as many scalps a year as are called for by his wealth, his status, and his connections, and that all the other cannibals consume exactly the number of foreigners that corresponds to their marginal productivity and never in any other way but through a free purchase in a free market: do we then have a state of an optimum, can we then say that the cannibals' welfare is well looked after? It should be obvious that nothing of the sort follows. All we have established is that the practice of the cannibalistic society corresponds more or less fully to the principles evolved by that society. We have said nothing at all about the validity or rationality of those principles themselves or about their relation to human welfare.

Thus welfare economics engages in what comes very close to com-

[8] "The function of economic institutions is to organize economic life in conformity with the community's wishes . . . the efficiency of economic organization will . . . be judged by its conformity to the community's preferences." T. Scitovsky, *Welfare and Competition* (Chicago, 1951), p. 5.

objective interest but

pulsive brooding on the extent to which the existing economic organization satisfies the rules of the game laid down by the existing economic organization, on the degree to which the productive apparatus
of a capitalist society is "efficiently" organized for the production of
an output the size and composition of which are determined by the
structure of that productive apparatus. Furthermore, it laboriously
inquires into the degree to which the existing socioeconomic organization allocates resources in such a manner as to correspond to consumers' demand which in turn is determined by the distribution of
wealth and income, by the tastes and values of people which are themselves shaped by the existing socioeconomic organization. All this has
absolutely nothing to do with the exploration of the conditions that
are conducive to welfare or with the study of the measure to which
the economic and social institutions and relationships of capitalist
society further or impede the well-being of people.

But a conventional practitioner of welfare economics will stop us
here, and ask what other criteria of welfare do we have.[9] If the actual,
observable performance of the individual in the market is not to be
accepted as the ultimate test of what constitutes his welfare, what
other test are we to use?

The mere fact that this question is raised indicates how far we
have traveled along the road to irrationality and obscurantism since
the days of classical philosophy and classical economics. In truth, the
answer to this question is simpler than one may think—at once simpler
and more complicated. The answer is that the sole criterion by which
it is possible to judge the nature of a socioeconomic organization, its
ability to contribute to the general unfolding and growth of human
potentialities, is *objective reason*. It was objective reason that underlay
the criticism of the then existing society undertaken by men like
Machiavelli and Hobbes, and it was objective reason that inspired
Smith and Ricardo to call feudal lords, courtiers, and the established
clergy of their time parasites because they not only did not contribute to the advancement of their societies, but drained them of
all possibilities of growth.

Not that the substance of objective reason is fixed immutably in

[9] For instance Professor Scitovsky—one of the most authoritative
writers in the field—observes: ". . . if we begin questioning the consumer's ability to decide what is good for him, we embark on a road on
which it is difficult to stop, and we may end up by throwing overboard
the whole concept of consumers' sovereignty." *Op. cit.*, p. 184. In actual
fact, what is at issue is not the "concept of consumers' sovereignty" but
merely the unhistorical, apologetic version of that concept that underlies
bourgeois economics.

time and space. On the contrary, objective reason itself is embedded in the never-resting flow of history, and its contours and contents are no less subject to the dynamics of the historical process than nature and society in general. "One cannot step twice into the same stream," and what is objective reason on one historical stage is unreason, reaction on another. This dialectic of objective reason has nothing in common with the relativistic cynicism of pragmatism or with the opportunistic indeterminateness of the sundry philosophies of the *élan vital;* it is firmly anchored in man's expanding and deepening scientific understanding of both nature and society, in the concrete exploration and practical exploitation of the natural and social conditions of progress.

The historically shifting and ambivalent attitude toward progress and objective reason that has been characteristic of bourgeois thought ever since the bourgeoisie began to be continuously torn between opposition to feudalism and fear of nascent socialism accounts for the fact that the socialist critique of prevailing social and economic institutions used occasionally to find a relatively sympathetic reception on the part of bourgeois economics as long as it was directed at the residues of the feudal order. The squandering of wealth by the landlords in backward countries was no less an admissible target of attack than their prodigality under the *ancien régime* in the more advanced countries. There has always been much less tolerance when it came to the critique of capitalist institutions *sensu stricto.* And at the present imperialist stage of capitalist development, to emphasize for instance the sociopolitical structure of backward countries as the main obstacle to their progress is considered almost as suspect as to insist on the role of imperialism in the advanced capitalist countries in retarding development at home and in perpetuating stagnation in underdeveloped areas.

Similarly economists socially and mentally anchored in the competitive, petty-bourgeois phase (and stratum) of capitalist society have developed a certain degree of clairvoyance with respect to the irrationality, wastefulness, and cultural consequences of monopoly capitalism. Oblivious of the fact that it is liberal, competitive capitalism that inescapably breeds monopoly, they recognize some of the economic, social, and human costs of capitalism's monopolistic phase, discern some of the most obvious manifestations of excess consumption, unproductive activities, the irrationality and brutality of "economic royalism." At the same time the writers who have either liberated themselves from the shackles of an earlier age, or who have grown directly into the "new era," are at times impressively perspicacious when debunking the competitive order of the past—the sacrosanct virtues of capitalism's competitive adolescence.

While this tension within bourgeois thought accords a certain amount of insight (and information) that permits at least a proximate assessment of the nature (and magnitude) of potential economic surplus, the always latent and sporadically erupting conflict between the interests of the capitalist class as a whole and those of its individual members offers another opportunity for the comprehension of the issues involved. Thus in times of war, when victory becomes the dominant interest of the dominant class, what under the circumstances constitutes objective reason is permitted to ride roughshod over particular interests and subjective utilities. Whether it is compulsory service in the armed forces, war economic controls, or requisition and confiscation of necessary supplies, objective needs become recognized as fully ascertainable and are assigned a significance vastly superior to that of individual preferences revealed by market behavior. Yet as soon as the emergency passes, and further admission of the existence and identifiability of objective reason threatens to become a source of dangerous social criticism, bourgeois thought hastily retreats from whatever advanced positions it may have temporarily reached and lapses once more into its customary state of agnosticism and "practical intelligence."

What constitutes "excess consumption" in a society could be readily established if this question received but a fraction of the attention that is accorded to problems as urgent and as important as for instance the measurability of marginal utility. With regard not only to underdeveloped countries but to advanced ones as well, what represents "essential consumption" is far from being a mystery. Where living standards are in general low, and the basket of goods available to people little variegated, essential consumption can be circumscribed in terms of calories, other nutrients, quantities of clothing, fuel, dwelling space, and the like. Even where the level of consumption is relatively high, and involves a large variety of consumer goods and services, a judgment on the amount and composition of real income necessary for what is socially considered to be "decent livelihood" can be made.[10]

[10] The Bureau of Labor Statistics of the United States Department of Labor works with some notion of "essential consumption" in compiling its cost of living index. The Heller Committee for Research in Social Economics at the University of California employs similar concepts. Food,

As mentioned before, this is precisely what has been done in all countries in emergency situations such as war, postwar distress, and the like. What an agnostic apologist of the *status quo* and the worshipper of "consumers' sovereignty" treat as an unsurmountable obstacle, or as a manifestation of reprehensible arbitrariness, is wholly accessible to scientific inquiry and to rational judgment.

III

More complicated and quantitatively less easily encompassed is the identification of unproductive workers. As pointed out earlier, the mere distinction between productive and unproductive labor encounters a determined opposition on the part of bourgeois economics. From the experience of its own youth it knows this distinction to be a powerful tool of social critique, easily turned against the capitalist order itself. Attempting to do away with it altogether, it seeks to quench the entire issue by judging the productivity, essentiality, usefulness of any performance in terms of its ability to fetch a price in the market. In this way, indeed, all differences between various types of labor disappear—all except one: the magnitude of the remuneration that any given activity commands. As long as a performance rates any monetary reward, it is treated as useful and productive *by definition*.[11]

---

housing, and medical requirements for various countries have been studied by the United Nations, by the Food and Agriculture Organization and other agencies, and represent a most important field for further investigations. Cf. Food and Agriculture Organization, FAO Nutritional Studies No. 5, *Caloric Requirements* (Washington, June 1950); National Research Council, Reprint and Circular Series, *Recommended Dietary Allowances* (Washington, 1948); United Nations, *Housing and Town and Country Planning* (1949-1950), as well as the material referred to in these sources.

[11] It may be interesting to note that this drive to glorify the capitalist order by eliminating the distinction between productive and unproductive labor has seriously contributed to the self-emasculation of modern economics. Committing its protagonists to treat as productive *all* activities in capitalist society that earn a monetary reward, the criterion of market approval and market valuation that might have at least a claim to consistency under conditions of *pure* capitalism becomes a source of serious troubles when what has to be dealt with is a society permeated with feudal remnants. Adherence to the market valuation principle under such circumstances forces economists either into the somewhat ludicrous position of having to criticize the existing state of affairs from the unhistorical and unrealistic standpoint of Mises, Hayek, Knight, and others of that school, or into the uncomfortable necessity to twist and bend the "principle" by claiming usefulness and essentiality for various non-

From the preceding discussion it should be clear, however, that market valuation cannot be considered a rational test for the appraisal of the "adequacy" or "efficiency" of a socioeconomic organization. Indeed, as stressed above, the acceptance of this test would involve circular reasoning: judging a given socioeconomic structure by a yardstick that itself represents an important aspect of that very socioeconomic structure. Thus what is productive and what is unproductive labor in a capitalist society cannot be decided by reference to the daily practice of capitalism. Here again, the decision has to be made concretely, from the standpoint of the requirements and potentialities of the historical process, in the light of objective reason.

Considered in this way a not insignificant part of the output of goods and services marketed and therefore accounted for in the national income statistics of capitalist countries represents unproductive labor. To be clear about it: all of it is altogether productive or useful *within the framework of the capitalist order,* indeed may be indispensable for its existence. And needless to say, the individuals engaged in this type of labor may be, and in most cases are, "upstanding citizens," hardworking, conscientious men doing a day's work for a day's wage. Therefore their classification as "unproductive laborers" involves neither moral opprobrium nor any other stigmatization. As very frequently, men of good will may not only not achieve what they strive to achieve but may accomplish its very opposite if constrained to live and to work within a system the direction of movement of which is beyond their control.

As can be easily seen, the isolation and measurement of this unproductive share of a nation's total economic effort cannot be undertaken by the application of a simple formula. *Most generally speaking, it consists of all labor resulting in the output of goods and services the demand for which is attributable to the specific conditions and relationships of the capitalist system, and which would be absent in a rationally ordered society.* Thus a good many of these unproductive workers are engaged in manufacturing armaments, luxury articles of all kinds, objects of conspicuous display and marks of social distinction. Others are government officials, members of the military establishment, clergymen, lawyers, tax evasion specialists, public relations experts, and so forth. Still further groups of unproductive workers are

---

marketed activities in view of their "indirect" contribution to marketable output or in view of their essentiality for the preservation and functioning of the capitalist system as a whole.

advertising agents, brokers, merchants, speculators, and the like. A particularly good example is given by Schumpeter—one of the very few contemporary economists who was not content to dwell on the level of "practical intelligence" but attempted to rise to some understanding of the historical process:

A considerable part of the total work done by lawyers goes into the struggle of business with the state and its organs . . . in socialist society there would be neither need nor room for this part of legal activity. The resulting saving is not satisfactorily measured by the fees of the lawyers who are thus engaged. That is inconsiderable. But not inconsiderable is the social loss from such unproductive employment of many of the best brains. Considering how terribly rare good brains are, their shifting to other employment might be of more than infinitesimal importance.[12]

What is crucial to remember is that unproductive labor as just defined is not directly related to the process of essential production and is maintained by a part of society's economic surplus. This characteristic it shares, however, with another group of workers that would not fall under our definition of unproductive labor. Scientists, physicians, artists, teachers, and similarly occupied people live off the economic surplus but engage in labor the demand for which in a rationally ordered society, far from disappearing, would become multiplied and intensified to an unprecedented degree. Thus while it is perfectly appropriate from the standpoint of the measurement of the *total* surplus currently generated by society to include these workers in the class of individuals supported by the economic surplus, it would seem advisable to treat them separately if what is at issue is the assessment of the magnitude of the surplus *potentially* available for rational utilization. "Labor may be necessary without being productive."[13]

This distinction becomes particularly useful when not only the possibilities of economic growth but also the transition from capitalism to socialism is considered. For what is defined above as unproductive labor is bound gradually to disappear as a socialist society advances in the direction of communism. In fact, certain classes of unproductive workers are immediately eliminated with the introduction of a planned economy, while others remain for considerable periods of time in systems transitional from capitalism to communism such as, for instance, the USSR. It may well be said that the degree to which unproductive

---

[12] J. A. Schumpeter, *Capitalism, Socialism and Democracy* (New York, 1950), p. 198.

[13] Marx, *Grundrisse der Kritik der Politischen Ökonomie* (Rohentwurf) (Berlin, 1953), p. 432.

labor in our definition has been abolished, and institutions such as the army, the church, and the like have been dispensed with, and the human and material resources thus freed have been directed to the advancement of human welfare, represents the most important single index of a socialist society's progress towards communism.

The group of workers, on the other hand, that is supported by the economic surplus and that is *not* covered by our definition of unproductive labor expands greatly with the development of a socialist society. As Marx predicted, the part of the total product ". . . which is destined for the communal satisfaction of needs such as schools, health services, etc. . . . is . . . from the outset . . . considerably increased in comparison with present-day society and it increases in proportion as the new society develops . . . [while] the general costs of administration not belonging to production . . . will from the outset, be very considerably restricted in comparison with present-day society and it diminishes in proportion as the new society develops."[14] Thus the resources used for the maintenance of the individuals who draw on society's economic surplus, but are not included in unproductive labor as I defined it, cannot be considered to represent a fund potentially available for purposes of economic growth.

Once more: regardless of the difficulties that may be encountered in attempting to gauge accurately the volume of unproductive work performed in a capitalist economy, in times of emergency the nature of *this* task is no less clear than the need for curtailment, if not elimination, of nonessential consumption. Unproductive workers are drafted into the army while productive workers are deferred. Labor exchanges try to move people from unproductive to productive employment. Rationing boards issue different ration cards to individuals in different occupations, with productive workers receiving preferential treatment.

Conceptually no more complex, although perhaps still more difficult to measure, is the *third* form in which potential economic surplus is hidden in the capitalist economy. The waste and irrationality in the productive organization that fall under this category can be observed in a great number of instances, and result in a reduction of output markedly below what could be obtained with the same input of human and material resources. There is first the existence (and continuous reproduction) of excess capacity unproductively absorbing a significant share of current investment. We do not refer here to manpower,

[14] Marx, *Critique of the Gotha Program*, in Marx and Engels, *Selected Works* (Moscow, 1949-1950), Vol. II. pp. 20 ff.

plant, and equipment that are reduced to idleness in times of depressions. To that we shall come later. What we have in mind now is the physical capacity that remains unused even in years of prosperity, and not merely in declining but also in expanding industries.[15]

An investigation of excess capacity in the United States in 1925-1929 was made by the Brookings Institution.[16] "Capacity" of an industry is there defined as the output which it would turn out with the length of the working day and number of shifts ordinarily in use in the industry, and with a proper standard of plant maintenance (i.e. taking account of necessary shutdowns for repairs, etc.). Plants which are shut down have been excluded, so that they do not count as excess capacity. The capacity so (conservatively) defined is thus lower than the "rated capacity" usually given by trade statistics and based on technical estimates. The Brookings Institution found that "in general . . . in the years from 1925 to 1929 available plant was used between 80 and 83 percent of capacity."[17] The study cautions that "probably not all the additional productivity indicated as possible by the above figures could have been realized, for there were striking differences in the potential capacity of the different branches of industry, and if each industry would run to its full capacity, huge surpluses of some goods would no doubt soon pile up."[18] Yet as the authors of the study realize, "if new productive effort were directed toward coordinating the various industries," this disproportionality could be markedly reduced, if not altogether eliminated. They do not estimate the volume of output that could have been produced given such coordination. Even in its absence, however, "an output of 19 percent greater than was realized would have been possible. Stated in terms of money, this increased productivity would have approximated 15 billion dollars"—i.e. nearly 20 percent of the national income in 1929.

No excess capacity studies of a similar scope have been undertaken

[15] Incidentally, in a rationally planned economy there is no need for excess capacity to exist for any length of time even in declining industries, that is, in industries facing a shrinkage of demand for their products. Timely conversions of such capacities to the production of other outputs could reduce such excess capacity to a minimum.

[16] *America's Capacity to Produce and America's Capacity to Consume* (Washington, 1934). For an excellent summary of this study, cf. J. Steindl, *Maturity and Stagnation in American Capitalism* (Oxford, 1952), pp. 4 ff., from which some sentences in the text above have been borrowed.

[17] *America's Capacity to Produce and America's Capacity to Consume* (Washington, 1934), p. 31.

[18] *Ibid.*

during the postwar period. From such scattered data as are available it would seem, however, that even in the unprecedentedly prosperous years following the end of the Second World War excess capacity in American industry assumed tremendous proportions. Calculations by one investigator suggest that merely 55 percent of capacity (conservatively estimated) was in use in the boom year 1952.[19] This does not include the prodigious quantities of food, the production of which is prevented by various control schemes, or which is allowed to spoil, to be destroyed, or fed to animals.

All estimates of capacity (and excess capacity) are highly tenuous. Apart from suffering from the inadequacy of the underlying statistical information, they depend on what definition of capacity is adopted, on the degree of utilization that is assumed as "normal," and on the extent to which market, demand, and profit considerations are taken into account in deciding on the magnitude of the excess. Yet difficulties encountered in the measurement of a phenomenon should not be permitted to obscure the existence of the phenomenon itself; in any case, they do not matter in the present context where our purpose is not to assess the magnitude of the potential economic surplus in any particular country at any particular time, but merely to outline the forms in which it exists.

Equally clearly discernible is the waste of resources caused by various aspects of monopoly and monopolistic competition. The potential economic surplus under this heading has never been analyzed in its entirety, although its components have been frequently referred to in the literature. There is first and probably foremost the output foregone in view of underutilization of economies of scale stemming from irrational product differentiation. No one, to my knowledge, has undertaken to calculate the aggregate saving that would be realized if a great number of purely nominally different articles were to be standardized, and if their production were concentrated in technically the most efficient and economic plants. Whether we look at automobiles and other consumers' durable goods such as refrigerators, stoves, electrical appliances, and the like, or whether we think of products such as soaps, toothpastes, textiles, shoes, or breakfast foods, there can be little doubt that standardization and mass production could appreciably lower the unit costs of output. To be sure, instances can be found where even under monopolistic conditions firms are operating technologically optimal-size plants, where, in other words, no further

[19] Lewis H. Robb, "Industrial Capacity and Its Utilization," *Science & Society* (Fall 1953), pp. 318-325.

economies of scale can be realized in the present state of technology. There is ample reason to believe, however, that such cases are relatively rare, and that limitations of the market for individual trademarks, and of capital available to individual firms, account for plant sizes that are less (and frequently considerably less) than what would be rational. The continuous existence and proliferation of small, inefficient, and redundant firms—not merely in industry but in particular in agriculture, distribution, and service trades—result in an amount of waste of human and material resources the magnitude of which can hardly be fully assessed.[20]

The multiplication of facilities and the squandering of resources called forth by irrational smallness of enterprises have their counterpart in the waste on the part of monopolistic giants who, shielded by their monopolistic positions, need not bother with minimizing costs or with maximizing efficiency. We have to consider in this connection the large so-called overhead costs of corporate business with their skyrocketing expense accounts, their exorbitant salaries paid to executives making no contribution to the firms' output but drawing revenues on the strength of their financial connections, personal influence, or character traits making them particularly adapted to corporate politics.

Nor should one overlook the imponderable but perhaps most valuable potential asset that is being systematically despoiled by monopolistic business: the human material ground up in the degrading, corrupting, and stultifying mill of vast corporate empires, and the ordinary man and woman whose entire upbringing and development are being warped and crippled by continuous exposure to the output, the propaganda, and the sales efforts of big business.[21]

[20] While even under emergency conditions only a relatively small part of this type of potential economic surplus is actually tapped, what has been accomplished on occasions suffices to indicate at least the dimensions of the problem involved. The wartime increase in output that resulted merely from concentration of production in large-scale plants, from the elimination of the most flagrant cases of duplication, cross-hauling, and inefficiency, was most impressive in the United States as well as in Great Britain and Germany.

[21] Not that Babbitt—the fittest participant in the "rugged" competitive struggle for survival—who is idolized by some liberal economists and some old-fashioned Chambers of Commerce is a more attractive human specimen than the "modern" man described in David Riesman's *The Lonely Crowd*, in C. Wright Mills' *White Collar: The American Middle Classes*, in T. K. Quinn's *Giant Business*. There indeed would be little room for confidence in the future of the human race if these two types were the only ones to choose from.

Even more elusive is the benefit to society that could be derived from scientific research if its conduct and exploitation were not subject to profit-oriented business control or armaments-oriented government control.[22]

This kind of support and administration of scientific work heavily influences its general outlook, its choice of subjects, and the methods that it employs. Demoralizing and disorienting scientists, depriving them of genuine stimuli for creative work, it hampers and distorts the development of science. Determining at the same time the mode of utilization of scientific achievements, it limits severely the benefits resulting from scientific progress. Whether in reference to atomic energy and to public utilities, to substitutions among materials or to manufacturing processes, evidence abounds that the productive employment of technical possibilities is frequently and seriously stymied by the interests of the sponsors of technological research.

This myriad of more or less readily identifiable forms in which the potential economic surplus hides in the complex spiderweb of the capitalist economy has never been subjected to a systematic investigation, let alone a statistical assessment. Not that economists have not in the past attempted to expose the waste and irrationality permeating the capitalist order. They treated them, however, as imperfections and frictions of the system that could be overcome by suitable reforms, or as anachronistic residues from pre-capitalist times that could be expected to disappear in the course of capitalist development. Lately,

[22] "We know that under international cartel agreements, patents frequently served not as an incentive to investment but rather as a device for limiting production, establishing restricted market areas, limiting the rate of technical advancement, fixing prices, etc. We know that the pre-war Standard Oil–I.G. Farben marriage seriously retarded the development of a synthetic rubber industry in the United States. We know that Standard's concessions to Farben were, in large part, motivated by a desire to suppress the synthetic gasoline patents outside of Germany. We know that Du Pont's arrangements with I.C.I. resulted in a division of world markets rather than a dynamic, competitive development of these markets. . . . Investigations revealed . . . that when Du Pont developed a pigment which could be utilized either in paints or as a textile dye, the director of one of its research laboratories wrote: 'Further work may be necessary on adding contaminants to "Monastral" colors to make them unsatisfactory on textiles but satisfactory for paints.' The investigations described the Rohm & Haas research effort to discover a contaminant which would make methyl methacrylate suitable for use as a commercial molding powder but unfit as an ingredient for dentures. The investigations told of the heroic effort by the General Electric research organization to shorten the life of flashlight batteries, etc." Walter Adams, *American Economic Review* (May 1954), p. 191.

as it has grown increasingly obvious that waste and irrationality, far from being fortuitous blemishes of capitalism, relate to its very essence, it has become fashionable to minimize the importance of the entire problem, to refer to it as a "minor matter" which is of no concern to our age of plenty.[23]

The last but by no means least important is the *fourth* heading in our catalogue of the forms in which potential economic surplus is hidden in the capitalist economy. This is the output lost to society through unemployment of human and material resources caused partly by the inadequacy of coordination of productive facilities, but mainly by insufficiency of effective demand. Although it is very difficult, if not impossible, to disentangle those two causes of unemployment, imputing to each the share for which it is responsible, it is most useful for analytical purposes to keep them clearly apart. The former, usually referred to in economics as "frictional" unemployment, was alluded to above. It appears as displacement of workers occasioned either by shifts in the composition of market demand or by the introduction of labor-saving devices of various kinds, accompanied by discarding of productive plant and equipment. While both the manpower and the facilities involved are capable of being converted to useful employment and thus of being reintegrated into the productive process, in the capitalist economy such conversion, if it takes place at all, proceeds even under the most favorable circumstances with a great deal of delay and waste. Under conditions of rational planning such losses may not be entirely avoidable; they could, however, be greatly reduced.

More important still, in fact next to military spending the most important single cause for the continuous existence of a large gap between potential and actual surplus, is the unemployment resulting from insufficiency of effective demand. It affects both fully employable manpower and fully usable productive facilities, and, while varying in intensity from period to period, immobilizes a large proportion of the available human and material resources. The impact of this continuously present unemployment of productive potentialities is not adequately gauged by assessing and aggregating the differences between output in times of prosperity and times of depression. This procedure overlooks in the first place that even in most periods of so-

[23] This approach, suggested originally by Schumpeter, has been given wide currency by J. K. Galbraith's *American Capitalism* (Boston, 1952), where we read: ". . . the social inefficiency of a wealthy community grows with the growth of wealth that goes far to make this inefficiency inconsequential." (P. 103.)

called full employment there is not inconsiderable unemployment of labor and productive capacity, and secondly that even boom outputs are lower than what they could be if businesses were not constrained to reckon with bad years as well as with good years and to adjust accordingly their plans for production and investment. Thus calculations based merely on comparisons between outputs in different phases of the business cycle necessarily understate the volume of output lost through fluctuations in the level of employment.

Yet even such calculations, conservative as they are, present a picture sufficiently illustrative of the volume of potential economic surplus attributable to mass unemployment. For instance, Isador Lubin, then Commissioner of Labor Statistics, United States Department of Labor, stated in his testimony at the Hearings of the Temporary National Economic Committee (December 1, 1938): "Assuming a working population of the size of 1929, you will note that if you add the employment lost in '30, '31, '32, up to 1938, the total number of man-years lost during that period of time was 43,435,000. Or, to put it in other words, if everybody who had worked in 1929 continued their employment during the past 9 years, all of us who were working could take a vacation for a year and 2 months and the loss in national income would be no greater than it has actually been."[24] In terms of national income valued in 1929 prices the total loss amounted to $133 billion (as compared with the national income in 1929 of $81 billion).[25] This unemployment of manpower was accompanied by surplus capacity of productive facilities amounting in the aggregate to about 20 percent "at the peak," that is, in 1929, and to "more than a third" at the time of the hearings, that is, in 1938.[26]

It should be remembered that Lubin's calculations were based on the assumptions that the working population remained constant from 1929 to 1938 and that its productivity also stayed unchanged during the entire period. In actual fact, as he himself realized, the working population had grown by 6 million, and output per capita would have grown at usual rates given more or less prosperous economic conditions. Taking this increase of employable manpower into account, and considering the rates of growth of productivity that were observed in the '20s and that could have been expected to prevail in the '30s,

[24] TNEC Investigation of Concentration of Economic Power, Hearings, Part 1 (Washington 1939), p. 12.
[25] Ibid., p. 16.
[26] Ibid., p. 77.

"Dr. L. H. Bean of the Department of Agriculture has estimated that the loss in national income has been $293 billion since 1929."[27]

These calculations were carried to 1938 because that was the time the hearings were held. The conditions of underemployment there depicted prevailed until the outbreak of the Second World War. The war mobilization demonstrated even more convincingly than all statistical computations how large a productive potential had been dormant in the American economy. As is well known, in the years of the war the United States was not merely able to raise a military establishment comprising over 12 million people, to produce a prodigious quantity of armaments, to supply its allies with large quantities of food and other goods, but to *increase* simultaneously the consumption of its civilian population. The entire war, in other words—the largest and most costly war in its history—was supported by the United States by the mobilization of a *part* of its potential economic surplus.

It hardly needs stressing that the waste resulting from unemployment is neither an exclusively American phenomenon nor of merely historical interest. It can be readily observed at the present time, and it has been characteristic of the entire history of capitalism everywhere. While its magnitude has been different in different countries at different times, it always depressed total output considerably below what it could have been in a rationally organized society. Nor is the impact of unemployment adequately expressed in any measure of output foregone. No one can estimate the benefits to society that might have been realized, if the energy, the ability to work, the creative genius of the millions of unemployed had been harnessed for productive ends.

IV

If the potential economic surplus is a category of considerable scientific interest for the understanding of the irrationality of the capitalist order, and of major practical significance to a capitalist society under emergency conditions or facing the necessity of economic development, the *planned* economic surplus is relevant only to comprehensive economic planning under socialism. It is the difference between society's "optimum" output attainable in a historically given natural and technological environment under conditions of planned

[27] *Ibid.*, testimony of Leon Henderson, p. 159.

"optimal" utilization of all available productive resources, and some chosen "optimal" volume of consumption. The meaning and contents of the "optimum" involved are essentially different from those attached to this notion in bourgeois economics. They do not reflect a configuration of production and consumption determined by profit considerations of individual firms, by the income distribution, tastes, and social pressures of a capitalist order; they represent a considered judgment of a socialist community guided by reason and science. Thus as far as resource utilization is concerned, it implies a far-reaching rationalization of society's productive apparatus (liquidation of inefficient units of production, maximal economies of scale, etc.), elimination of redundant product differentiation, abolition of unproductive labor (as previously defined), a scientific policy of conservation of human and natural resources, and the like.

Nor does this "optimum" presuppose the maximization of output that might be attainable in a country at any given time. It may well be associated with a less than maximum output in view of a voluntarily shortened labor day, of an increase in the amount of time devoted to education, or of conscious discarding of certain noxious types of production (coal mining, for example). What is crucial is that the volume of output would not be determined by the fortuitous outcome of a number of uncoordinated decisions on the part of individual businessmen and corporations, but by a rational plan expressing what society would wish to produce, to consume, to save, and to invest at any given time.[28]

Furthermore the "optimum" husbandry of resources in a socialist

[28] That a planned economy could easily dispose of the most striking irrationality of the capitalist system—unemployment caused by insufficient demand—is most succinctly shown by M. Kalecki: "It is useful to consider what the effect of a reduction in investment in a socialist system would be. The workers released from the production of investment goods would be employed in consumption goods industries. The increased supply of these goods would be absorbed by means of a reduction in their prices. Since profits of the socialist industries would be equal to investment, prices would have to be reduced to the point where the decline in profits would be equal to the fall in the value of investment. In other words, full employment would be maintained through the reduction of prices in relation to costs. In the capitalist system, however, the price-cost relationship . . . is maintained and profits fall by the same amount as investment plus capitalists' consumption through the reduction in output and employment. It is indeed paradoxical that, while the apologists of capitalism usually consider the 'price mechanism' to be the great advantage of the capitalist system, price flexibility proves to be a characteristic feature of the socialist economy." *Theory of Economic Dynamics* (London, 1954), pp. 62 ff.

economy does not call by any means for reduction of consumption to merely what is essential. It can and will go together with a level of consumption that is considerably higher than what the criterion of essentiality might suggest. Again, what is decisive is that the level of consumption and therefore also the volume of the actually generated surplus would not be determined by the mechanism of profit maximization but by a rational plan reflecting the society's preference as to current consumption versus future consumption. Therefore the economic surplus under socialism may be smaller or larger than the actual economic surplus under capitalism, or may even be equal to zero if society should choose to refrain from net investment. It would depend on the stage that has been reached in the historical process, on the degree of development of productive resources, on the structure and growth of human needs.

So much about our primitive tools. Now let us try to use them on some historical material.

THREE

Standstill and Movement
Under Monopoly Capitalism, I

THE rate and direction of economic development
in a country at a given time, as suggested earlier, depend on both the
size and the *mode of utilization* of the economic surplus. These in turn
are determined by (and themselves determine) the degree of development of productive forces, the corresponding structure of socioeconomic relations, and the system of appropriation of the economic surplus that those relations entail. Indeed, as Marx has pointed out:

> . . . the specific economic form, in which unpaid surplus labor is
> pumped out of the direct producers, determines the relation of rulers and
> ruled, as it grows immediately out of production itself and in turn reacts
> upon it as a determining element. . . . It is always the direct relation of
> the owners of the means of production to the direct producers which
> reveals the innermost secret, the hidden foundation of the entire social
> structure. . . . The form of this relation between rulers and ruled naturally
> corresponds always to a definite stage in the development of labor and
> of its social productivity. This does not prevent the same economic basis
> from showing infinite variations and gradations in its appearance even
> though its principal conditions are everywhere the same.[1]

It would be a fascinating task to follow up the evolution of the
volume and the employment of the economic surplus in the course of

---

[1] *Capital* (Kerr ed.), Vol. III, p. 919. (A few words have been changed
by this writer where the translation appeared inadequate.)

44

pre-capitalist development. The necessary material could be pieced together from available anthropological and historical writing, and its systematic survey would go far toward providing the urgently needed organizational principle for a meaningful analysis of economic and social history. It goes without saying that such an undertaking cannot even be attempted within the limits of the present essay. Suffice it to stress that the transition from feudalism to capitalism represented a radical change in the method of extraction, the mode of utilization, and consequently the size of the economic surplus.[2] The classical econo- mists were fully aware of this crucially important implication of the rising capitalist order; in fact they saw its principal *raison d'être* in the ability to provide for rapid economic progress not merely by the maximization of the economic surplus on the basis of a given level of productivity and output—after all, this problem was being solved also under feudalism—but primarily by its rational, productive utiliza- tion.

For in the economic order emerging from the decay of feudalism and already visible in its most essential contours to the great classical writers, there appeared tremendous possibilities for large-scale invest- ment in productive facilities. The striving of individual entrepreneurs —now operating in a different socioeconomic environment, freed of earlier restraints and enabled to give full play to their relentless drive for profits—to "get ahead," to accumulate and to enlarge their enter- prises, would necessarily serve as a powerful engine of expansion of aggregate output. Competition among businessmen would continuously force them to improve their methods of production, to promote tech- nological progress and to make full use of its results, as well as to increase and to diversify their output. As all available productive re- sources would tend to be drawn into useful employment, and as cost reduction would become the dominant concern of profit-maximizing capitalists, waste and irrationality would be eliminated from the pro- ductive process. The operation of Say's Law would see to it that aggre- gate output would normally encounter adequate demand, while such "frictional disproportionalities" as might result from technological change or shifts in tastes would be merely "diseases of growth," in- considerable in scope and not very dangerous in repercussions. In fact, by adjusting the productive apparatus to society's changing re-

[2] Just as the advance from slavery to serfdom—the basis of the feudal order—which took place at the end of antiquity constituted an important benchmark in economic and social development.

quirements, and by purging it from time to time of backward and inefficient units, such short crises would indeed be beneficent in their effects: promoting general progress and facilitating the survival of the fittest.

Of this maximum output a maximal share would constitute economic surplus. Competition among workers would prevent wages from rising above the subsistence minimum and from eating into profits— the characteristic form in which the economic surplus would appear in capitalist society.[3] Nor would there be any danger of the demand for labor—capital accumulation—outstripping the supply of labor. The increase of the population could be relied upon to keep the labor market under pressure and to prevent any expansion of the share of output absorbed by the "wage fund."

Nor should there be in a competitive capitalist order any room for "unproductive" workers not contributing to capital accumulation. The large retinue and extravagant style of life at the feudal courts should no more be allowed to encroach upon the economic surplus than the luxuries and comforts indulged in by medieval town patricians.[4] And worship of God should be made less expensive: simple and modest rites performed by humble clergy frugally maintained by their congregations would be substituted for the pomp and circumstance organized by the elaborate and richly appointed hierarchy of the Roman Catholic or the Established Church.

Similarly, large selling costs, major advertising expenses, excess capacities, legal or public relations departments did not enter the model of an economy thought of as composed of relatively small firms producing more or less homogeneous, interchangeable products. True,

[3] "The natural price of labour is that price which is necessary to enable the labourers, one with another, to subsist and to perpetuate their race, without either increase or diminution." Ricardo, *Principles of Political Economy and Taxation* (Everyman's Library ed.), p. 53. Also: "If wages continued the same, the profits of manufacturers would remain the same, but if . . . wages should rise . . . then their profits would necessarily fall." *Ibid.*, p. 64.

[4] "The expense of a great lord feeds generally more idle than industrious people. The rich merchant, though with his capital he maintains industrious people only, yet by his expenses, that is by the employment of his revenues he feeds commonly the very same sort as the great lord." Adam Smith, *Wealth of Nations* (Modern Library ed.), p. 317. It is interesting to note that to Adam Smith the "rich merchant" is still a figure of the feudal past and not the hero of the rising capitalist order. That role is reserved for the industrial and agricultural entrepreneur to whom accumulation of capital and its profitable employment rather than lavish living represent the content and the meaning of existence.

some unproductive workers would necessarily remain—bankers, brokers, merchants—but, once integrated in the capitalist system, they would play an altogether different role as compared with feudal society. Not only would they *aid* in the generation of the economic surplus, but the share of surplus accruing to them as reward for services rendered would also be in its bulk accumulated rather than consumed. In fact by encroaching upon the real income of the masses onto whom they would shift some of the costs of their operations, they would make an independent contribution to capital formation rather than detract from it.[5]

Yet even more important was the envisaged curtailment if not disappearance of what was then considered to be one of the most gluttonous claimants to the economic surplus: the sprawling, corrupt, and inefficient network of government dating back to the feudal age. Probably on nothing were the classical economists so outspoken and insistent as on this point. "It is the highest impertinence and presumption . . . in kings and ministers, to pretend to watch over the economy of private people, and to restrain their expence. . . . They are themselves always, and without any exception, the greatest spendthrifts in society. Let them look well after their own expence, and they may safely trust private people with theirs."[6] In a society dedicated to the maximization and rational utilization of the economic surplus all the state had to do was to abstain from interfering with the formation of capital by refraining from collecting excessive taxes, by foregoing meddling in social affairs and subsidizing the poor, and by markedly reducing the number of unproductive workers maintained by resources that otherwise would form a part of the actual economic surplus.[7] It would be incumbent upon the state to safeguard law and order, and possibly it might be invoked to protect foreign markets, sources of supplies, and outlets for investment abroad, but the government activi-

---

[5] Operating in a capitalist rather than feudal milieu bankers would facilitate capital formation partly by centralizing smaller savings, partly by extracting additional economic surplus from the population via inflation.

[6] Adam Smith, *op. cit.*, p. 329.

[7] "The clear and direct tendency of the poor laws . . . is not, as the legislature benevolently intended, to amend the condition of the poor, but to deteriorate the condition of both poor and rich; instead of making the poor rich, they are calculated to make the rich poor; and whilst the present laws are in force, it is quite in the natural order of things that the fund for the maintenance of the poor should progressively increase till it has absorbed all the net revenue of this country." Ricardo, *op. cit.*, p. 81. The classical bourgeoisie's distaste for militarism and military spending was stressed by Schumpeter, *Capitalism, Socialism and Democracy* (New York, 1950), p. 122.

ties involved were expected neither to assume major proportions nor to be associated with major expenses.

However, one more condition would need to be satisfied if the maximum obtainable economic surplus were to provide for the largest possible rates of growth. That condition is <u>frugality</u> and <u>will to invest</u> on the part of the new recipient of the economic surplus: the capitalist businessman.

There were good reasons to expect this condition to be fulfilled. In the first place, the competitive mechanism would compel businessmen to accumulate, since only by continuously reinvesting their earnings in cost-reducing innovations could they hope to maintain themselves in the competitive struggle. That there would be no dearth of such and other technological discoveries could well be taken for granted. Not only were the vistas of potential scientific advance well-nigh infinite, but business interest in lower costs, in new products, in possibilities of using new materials could be safely relied upon to call forth scientific ingenuity and technological inventiveness.

Secondly, the rise of the members of the business class from humble origins to affluence and power was explained by their propensity to work hard and to save. It was judged as probable—on sociological and characterological grounds—that they would retain a way of life that had led them to spectacular successes and that assured them a social status never enjoyed before by them.

Thirdly, the advent of what Weber and Sombart called the "capitalist spirit"—to which in fact they ascribed the genesis of modern capitalism[8]—accompanied by the prevalence of puritan ethics established a system of social values in which thriftiness and the drive to accumulate were elevated to the position of supreme merit and paramount virtue.[9] The intimate relation between the rise of Protestantism

---

[8] Incidentally, the development of rational calculation and accountancy so much stressed by Weber and Sombart had been pointed out as an important factor in the growth of bourgeois culture by Marx as early as 1847. "The bourgeoisie is too enlightened, it calculates too well, to share the prejudices of the feudal lord who makes a display of the brilliance of his retinue. *The conditions of existence of the bourgeoisie compel it to calculate.*" *Wage Labor and Capital,* in Marx and Engels, *Selected Works* (Moscow, 1949-1950), Vol. I, p. 91. (Italics supplied.)

[9] "Is it merely a coincidence or is it a consequence that the lofty profession of spirituality made by the Friends has gone hand in hand with shrewdness and tact in the transaction of mundane affairs? Real piety favours the success of a trader by insuring his integrity and fostering habits of prudence and forethought, important items in obtaining that standing and credit in the commercial world which are requisite for the

and puritanism on one hand and the genesis and development of capitalism on the other—a relation expressing itself not merely in profound changes in the dominant ideology, but also in the drastic reduction of the share of the economic surplus absorbed by the church—the discovery of which is usually ascribed to Weber, was clearly pointed out by Marx. "The money cult implies its own asceticism, its own self-denial, its own self-sacrifice—parsimony and frugality, a contempt for worldly, temporal, and transient satisfactions: it implies the striving for *everlasting* treasure. Hence the connection of English puritanism, but also of Dutch Protestantism, with money making."[10]

The only dark cloud hanging over the otherwise clear prospect of economic progress was the fear of "diminishing returns" in agriculture, which, raising the costs of food, would force up the cost of the basket of goods constituting the laborers' subsistence minimum. The result would be a steady increase of the revenues of the landowning class and correspondingly a continual pressure upon profits, the principal source of capital accumulation. "The interest of the landlord is always opposed to that of the consumer and manufacturer," warned Ricardo.[11] And the struggle against the feudal lord who, as parasitic owner of the land, while contributing nothing to the process of production would seize a rising share of the economic surplus and squander it on unproductive purposes, was the foremost interest of the capitalist class of which Ricardo was one of the outstanding spokesmen.

It was not until a generation after the publication of Ricardo's *Principles* that technological progress in agriculture and the opening up of the vast agricultural resources across the seas allayed this concern over the tardiness and inadequacy of the growth of productivity in agriculture. By that time the aristocratic landowner of old was

---

steady accumulation of wealth." G. A. Rowntree, *Quakerism, Past and Present* (London, 1859), p. 95. Or: "In short, the way to wealth, if you desire it, is as plain as the way to market. It depends chiefly on two words, *industry* and *frugality*; that is, waste neither *time* nor *money*, but make the best use of both. Without industry and frugality nothing will do, and with them everything. He that gets all he can honestly, and saves all he gets (necessary expenses excepted), will certainly become *rich*, if that Being who governs the world, to whom all should look for a blessing on their honest endeavours, doth not, in his wise providence, otherwise determine." Benjamin Franklin, *Works* (Jared Sparks ed., Boston, 1840), Vol. II, pp. 87 ff.

[10] Marx, *Grundrisse der Kritik der Politischen Ökonomie* (Rohentwurf) (Berlin, 1953), p. 143. (Italics in the original.)

[11] *Principles of Political Economy and Taxation* (Everyman's Library ed.), p. 225.

either driven from his estate by his inability to make ends meet and to pay his debts, or himself became transformed into a capitalist businessman operating his agricultural enterprise in the same way in which urban capitalists conducted their industrial undertakings.[12] And it was at this time that the anti-feudal fervor of the rising bourgeoisie came to inspire merely its lunatic fringe—social reformers and single taxers —while the main body of the ruling class closed ranks with what by that time had become largely capitalist landed interests in a common front against the growing socialist menace. From that point on, after the Paris Commune was drowned in blood by the "united action" of all the property-owning classes in Europe, and the international labor movement had suffered one of its most grievous setbacks, nothing appeared to stand in the way of sustained and rapid economic progress within the framework of the capitalist order. The only issue that faced society was the creation and preservation of political and social institutions that would permit the capitalist mechanism to function smoothly, without outside disturbance and interference. God's invisible hand would then guide society along the path of increasing output, rising welfare, and ever more equitable distribution of worldly goods.

II

There is hardly any need to point out that this picture of the *modus operandi* of a capitalist economy—so hastily sketched—is at best a rather apologetic, and in some important respects inaccurate, portrayal even of the earlier, competitive phase of capitalist development. Nevertheless, the picture may be well worth keeping before our eyes; it indicates, at least approximately, the essential principles of the mechanism that has actually provided for a vast volume of productive investment, for an unprecedented development of productive forces, for a gigantic advance in technology, and for a momentous increase in output and consumption. What is more, it suggests, if only obliquely, the nature of the process that has led to the growth of large-scale enterprise—the principal vehicle of expanding productivity—and to

[12] "The Commons in England, the Tiers-Etat in France, the bourgeoisie of the Continent generally . . . were a saving class, while the posterity of the feudal aristocracy were a squandering class. . . . Therefore the former by degrees substituted themselves for the latter as the owners of a great proportion of the land." John Stuart Mill, *Principles of Political Economy* (New York, 1888), p. 38.

the evolution of monopoly and oligopoly—the dominant forms of economic organization in today's capitalism.[13] Thus it may serve as a convenient point of departure for the understanding of the salient features of the advanced, monopolistic phase of capitalist development —the topic of the present chapter and the next.

Indeed, I find it illuminating to consider to what extent our "classical conditions" for economic growth are satisfied in the current, monopolistic phase of capitalism. Are the changes that have occurred sufficiently significant to render the competitive model obsolete, to result in an economic, social, and political development under advanced capitalism that is in important respects different from what it was in capitalism's competitive youth? Are there some regularities about the economic, social, and political functioning of monopolistic capitalism that could be visualized better with the help of a different frame of reference?

To begin with the beginning: it will be recalled that the first and perhaps the most important of our previously formulated four conditions—to which everything else is intimately related—is full utilization of all available productive resources. With competition reigning supreme, real costs and waste were supposed to be kept near the bottom, and factors to be so allocated as to assure maximum output. While there was never sufficient reason to expect such maximization of output even under competitive capitalism, not even the most zealous apologists of capitalism would probably wish to maintain that this condition is being fulfilled in the capitalist economy of the present time. What has been said earlier—in the course of our discussion of the potential economic surplus—about unemployment, excess capacity, curtailment of agricultural production, and so on, suffices to show that with the possible exception of war years the capitalist system of our

---

[13] This is not to say that there was no monopoly during the "golden age" of competition. On the contrary, monopoly was ubiquitous from the very beginning of the capitalist order. It is, however, the fallacy of "modernism" frequently encountered in the writing of history (political as well as economic and social) indiscriminately to equate earlier institutions with those existing under the altogether different conditions of the present time. The basis and nature of monopoly in the seventeenth and eighteenth centuries rendered it a phenomenon quite distinct from what it is now. Then it dated back to the restrictive institutions of the feudal guilds; it was generated by continuously recurring local and temporary scarcities, immobilities of resources, poor systems of communication and transportation, and assumed the form of cornering thin and narrow markets rather than the modern form of large enterprises controlling decisive shares of vast outputs.

days has been generating an output smaller, and frequently considerably smaller, than what would have been possible with the available equipment, natural resources, and manpower—allowing for the prevailing division of people's time as between work and leisure. Pursuit of individual advantage, competition among businessmen, the working of the market mechanism, and what other factors were usually counted on by bourgeois economists to furnish the necessary engines of economic progress, resulted in a great deal of economic advance, but by no means succeeded in securing rates of growth that would correspond to the development of technology, to the growth and the creative potentialities of the population.

Available information does not permit a calculation of the magnitude of the gap between the actual and the potential output throughout the history of capitalism in different countries. It is therefore impossible to obtain a precise measure of the extent to which this gap has increased under monopolistic capitalism as compared with competitive capitalism. All we can study—and even that only with great difficulties —is the actual performance, i.e. the rates of growth that were attained in some countries. We have very little to go on in deciding what *could* have been accomplished under conditions of full employment and efficient allocation of available resources.

Thus while it would seem that the rates of growth of per capita output in the United States before the Civil War were lower than thereafter,[14] it is to be considered that the demographic, economic, and technological *potentialities* of growth were also at that time smaller than in the subsequent decades. With a much larger share of total output generated in the non-capitalist sectors of the economy (agriculture, handicrafts, etc.), the gap between the actual and the potential output was in all probability much narrower than later on, when the non-capitalist parts of the economy began their rapid contraction. What applies to the United States applies even more strongly to the Western European countries, where the non-capitalist sectors of the economy were larger to begin with, and where the process of their shrinkage was considerably slower.

On the other hand there is apparently no doubt among the experts that the rates of growth have been declining markedly since the Civil War, that is, during the period that is commonly associated with ad-

[14] Cf. S. Kuznets, *National Income, A Summary of Findings* (New York, 1946), p. 33, where R. F. Martin, *National Income in the United States, 1799-1938,* is cited as the source of this statement.

vanced or monopolistic capitalism. The increase of total national income in the United States fell from about 27 percent per quinquennium in the first part of the period to about 9 percent in the last part.[15] To be sure, a part of this drop in the rate of growth is associated with a slowing down of the growth of the population. In the United States the rate of increase of population changed from about 12 percent to about 6.5 percent per quinquennium from the earlier to the later part of the post-Civil War period; still, the decline of the rate of growth of income per capita was from 13.5 percent per quinquennium to less than 3 percent.[16] Moreover, as Kuznets notes, the rate of change in the population may be itself the result of the change in the rate of economic growth.

A factor which has to be assigned some independent responsibility for the slowing down of the growth of output is the considerable reduction of the number of hours worked per week that took place during the period in question. This reduction offset a part of the increase in productivity per man-hour, with the result that some of the potential increase of output was actually taken out in the form of additional leisure.[17]

Yet the principal reasons for the decline in the rate of growth that took place in the United States, and for the very slow expansion that has been characteristic of a number of other advanced countries during the current century, have to be sought elsewhere. These were primarily the violent fluctuations in economic activity and employment that have marked particularly the latter part of the period, and the greatly diminished rate of capital formation representing both the cause and the effect of these fluctuations.[18]

Once more: although there is no satisfactory basis for comparing the magnitude of the gap between actual and potential output in the nineteenth century and in the twentieth, it would seem that this gap has grown considerably larger. Ups and downs in economic activity were possibly more frequent during the competitive period, their appearance and disappearance possibly more dramatic; there is much

[15] S. Kuznets, *op. cit.*, p. 34; Colin Clark presents estimates for a number of other advanced countries all of which point in the same direction. Cf. his *Conditions of Economic Progress* (2nd ed., London, 1951), Chapter III.

[16] S. Kuznets, *op, cit.*, p. 54.

[17] United States Department of Commerce, Bureau of the Census, *Historical Statistics of the United States, 1789-1945* (Washington, 1949), Section D.

[18] Cf. S. Kuznets, *op. cit.*, p. 58, and pp. 61 ff.

evidence, however, to support the view that the aggregate loss in output, as a proportion of total possible output, caused by unemployment, unutilized capacity, production curtailment, and the like has been much larger in the current century than during the preceding one.[19] If calculations similar to those made by Dr. Louis Bean for the '30s in the United States were made for the entire lifespan of monopolistic capitalism, the resulting estimate of the total gap between what *could* have been produced and the actually realized output would yield astronomic magnitudes. Thus our first condition has hardly been lived up to in the course of capitalist development. It was not fulfilled during its competitive stage, and it has been still further from fulfillment in its advanced monopolistic phase.

III

The situation is somewhat different, and more complex, when it comes to our second condition. It demanded, as may be remembered, a wage level (and, related to it, a level of mass consumption) such as to permit the largest possible share of aggregate full employment income to go into economic surplus and thus to become available for capital accumulation. In attempting to establish, at least approximately, the extent to which this condition has been fulfilled in different phases of capitalist development, we must continue to bear in mind what has just been said about the realization of the first condition. Indeed, as maximum *output* only sporadically materialized in the course of capitalist development, with underproduction more pronounced under advanced than under competitive capitalism, the economic surplus was accordingly markedly below what it would have been under full employment conditions. Furthermore, we have to be clear as to the specific meaning of the notions "largest *possible*" economic surplus, and conversely "lowest *possible*" level of wages (and mass consumption), giving way to the generation of *maximum* surplus out of maximum output. In the general framework of classical eco-

[19] While all such generalizations are obviously risky, it may well be said that if in the nineteenth century economic fluctuations assumed *primarily* the form of price movements, in the twentieth century their *main* expression was variation in the level of output. This is clearly related also to the increase of the proportion of industrial output in aggregate output, with the response of industrial production to changes in demand being quite different from the responses typical of agricultural production.

nomics these problems hardly arise: full employment output was taken for granted, and wages (and mass consumption) were thought to tend toward the "subsistence minimum"; the subsistence minimum then represented a firm floor below which wages could not fall for any length of time, and constituted an effective limit to the magnitude of the possible economic surplus.

As a matter of historical fact, however, the subsistence minimum is anything but such a firm floor. It is rather a continually moving escalator, and there can be no doubt that what was considered to be the "subsistence minimum" at any given time—at least in the advanced capitalist countries—has been a *rising* quantity of goods and services. Under such circumstances, the hypothesis that wages under capitalism oscillate around the subsistence minimum does not get us very far. It could be maintained in the face of *any* level of wages and consumption—that is, even if living standards were markedly improving and if the economic surplus were declining. In other words, the validity of this hypothesis can be neither proved nor disproved by reference to the historical record. Whatever the wage and mass consumption level may have been in any given period may be held to coincide with the "subsistence minimum" for that period—by definition.[20]

That the subsistence minimum approach does not provide us with an easy definition of the maximum *possible* economic surplus or the lowest *possible* level of wages (and mass consumption) does not imply, however, that we are left entirely at sea, and that there is no solution to our problem. In actual fact we need not be at all concerned with the factors determining the *absolute* size of the economic surplus or the *absolute* volume of wages (and mass consumption).[21] What is

[20] It is for this reason that the subsistence minimum theory of wages cannot be substantiated by comparisons between the actually earned wages and various "subsistence minima" or "minimum budgets" such as those computed by the Heller Committee for Research in Social Economics of the University of California and other organizations. While such comparisons are most important and illuminating if what is sought is a picture of the prevailing standard of living and of the level of economic welfare attained by the mass of the people, they cannot be used as arguments supporting the view that wages are below, above, or at the subsistence minimum. A quick glance at the Heller Committee budget, for instance, would readily show that what is depicted there is certainly not the subsistence minimum envisaged, say, by Ricardo or, for that matter, "enjoyed" by British and American workers a century or even fifty years ago.

[21] These depend on a multitude of historical, geographical, and

essential for our purposes is whether there is any determinateness about the *relative* shares of income going into economic surplus and mass consumption respectively. Such is undoubtedly the case; while there are considerable divergencies in the *explanation* of the phenomenon, there is far-reaching agreement among economists on the *existence* of limits to the share of output that is available for wages (and mass consumption) as well as to the proportion constituting economic surplus. The presence of such limits is, however, all that is required to impart concrete, historical meaning to the notions "largest *possible*" economic surplus and "lowest *possible*" amount of wages (and mass consumption) out of any given volume of total output.

We may return then to our original question: how did our second condition of growth fare in the history of capitalism? Although such statistical studies of the class distribution of income as have been undertaken differ somewhat so far as specific estimates are concerned, there is considerable evidence that it has displayed a remarkable stability during the entire period for which information is available. Thus Kalecki has assembled data showing a striking constancy of the share of labor in the United Kingdom for the period 1889-1938: a constancy that, according to other students of the problem, was not disturbed even in the postwar years under a Labor government.[22]

For the United States the conclusions arrived at by various investigators are less uniform. While some of them hold that "a slight but definite upward trend is noticeable in labor's share in product in the USA,"[23] others feel that no such improvement has actually been taking

demographical circumstances influencing the economic development and the state of productivity of a country at any given time.

[22] Even such a staunch believer in the possibilities of a "welfare state" as John Strachey states that "in the last 15 years [the wage earners' share in the national income] may have risen again but not, probably, by more than enough to bring it back to the 1860 level." "Marxism Revisited," *New Statesman and Nation* (1953), p. 537. Contrary to frequently held views, such redistribution of income as has taken place in Great Britain after the war as a result of the economic policies of the Labor government has had no impact on labor's share in national income. "Social expenditures for food and health . . . have been largely offset by higher taxes on beer, tobacco and other purchases; so that the wage earners have made no net gain from these subsidies." Clark Kerr, "Trade Unionism and Distributive Shares," *American Economic Review* (May 1954), p. 291, where Findlay Weaver, "Taxation and Redistribution in the United Kingdom," *Review of Economics and Statistics* (May 1950), is cited as the source of this statement. Cf. also A. A. Rogow, "Taxation and 'Fair Shares' Under the Labour Governments," *Canadian Journal of Economics and Political Science* (May 1955).

[23] Colin Clark, *Conditions of Economic Progress* (2nd ed., London, 1951), p. 524.

place or even that the share of labor has had a tendency to decline. According to Kuznets' calculations the workers' share was in 1949 one-fifth lower than in 1939.[24] The *Economic Report of the President to Congress* (January 1953) states: "The increases in real disposable personal income in the postwar period have been relatively small. . . . In this connection it is interesting to note . . . that during the period over-all, contrary to the common impression, average hourly earnings in manufacturing, adjusted for consumers' price changes, have not risen faster than the economy's real productivity gains, but instead apparently have lagged significantly." (P. 111.)

To be sure, these discrepancies in findings may be due to differences in the frames of reference. In one case, it is the longer trend that is an issue; in the other, attention is focused upon shorter-run variations related to changes in the level of prices, income, and employment. It is important to bear in mind, moreover, that whatever slight gains may have been made by the wage earners' share in the course of the last fifty years were for the most part achieved not by an enhancement of the relative position of the working class but by its expansion through the absorption of formerly independent small businessmen, craftsmen, and the like.[25] The share of income going to profits remained unaffected. The situation is probably best depicted in a recent study: ". . . extensive wage increases have been introduced over the past quarter-century, in many industries having many differing characteristics, and in periods of depression as well as overemployment, without yielding any significant reduction in the profit share. . . . The potentialities of redistribution out of profits are very slight so long as producers remain free to adjust their prices, techniques and employment so as to protect their profit position."[26]

Yet the fact that in the course of the last five to seven decades— the period commonly associated with monopoly capitalism—the relative share of aggregate income going to labor has remained generally stable (or showed merely short-term fluctuations) leaves the question open whether there was any change by comparison with competitive

[24] Referred to in Victor Perlo, *The Income Revolution* (New York, 1954), p. 54.

[25] "Self-employed enterprisers constituted 36.9 percent of the gainful workers in 1880, but only 18.8 percent in 1939. Of most importance to the subject is the decline of the independent businessman. Non-farm business enterprisers declined from 8 percent in 1880 to 6 percent in 1939." House of Representatives, Committee on Small Business, *United States vs. Economic Concentration and Monopoly* (Washington, 1949), p. 96.

[26] Harold M. Levinson, "Collective Bargaining and Income Distribution," *American Economic Review* (May 1954), pp. 314, 316.

capitalism. To my limited knowledge there is no statistical answer to this question; no studies comparable to those mentioned above seem to have been feasible for the second half of the eighteenth and the first three quarters of the nineteenth century. If speculation is in order, however, it may be permissible to suppose that there has been no significant change in the relative share of wages (and mass consumption) in national income. For the evolution of large-scale enterprise, monopoly, and oligopoly that began in the fourth quarter of the last century has been gaining momentum ever since and affecting an ever larger segment of the economic system. As this deepening and broadening of the impact of monopoly that has taken place during the last fifty to eighty years does not seem to have markedly depressed the relative share going to labor, it may be supposed that no such decline was caused by the earlier emergence of monopolistic enterprise. This reasoning is reinforced by theoretical considerations. They were formulated clearly by Marx: "The monopoly price of certain commodities would merely transfer a portion of the profit of the other producers of commodities to the commodities with a monopoly price. What would take place would be a local distortion in the distribution of surplus value among the various spheres of production; it would leave, however, the boundaries of the surplus value itself unaffected."[27] What this suggests is that the spreading of large-scale enterprise and monopoly should be expected to affect primarily the *distribution* of profits among capitalist enterprises, rather than the relative share of aggregate profits in national income. In the words of Kalecki, ". . . the rise in the degree of monopoly caused by the growth of big corporations results in a relative shift of income to industries dominated by such corporations from other industries. In this way income is redistributed from small to big business."[28] For this there is ample factual evidence.

Since it is legitimate to assume that the concentration of profits is closely related to the concentration of assets (as well as of sales and employment), the basic tendency is beyond dispute. "It is apparent . . . that there has been a more or less steady upward trend in the concentration of control exercised by the corporate giants. Thus, the 200 largest non-financial corporations increased their relative impor-

[27] *Capital* (Kerr ed.), Vol. III, p. 1003. As Marx notes on the same page, this is not to say that there may be no tendency for monopoly to depress the income of workers qua consumers. If nevertheless the share of income going to labor displays considerable stability, this stability may well be due to the efforts of the trade unions to offset the pressures of monopoly and to maintain wages in some relation to prices and profits.

[28] *Theory of Economic Dynamics* (London, 1954), p. 18.

tance from ownership of one-third of the assets in 1909 to 48 percent in 1929 and to 55 percent in the early thirties."[29] Although no studies comparable to those for the prewar years have been made for the postwar period, there can be no doubt that the massive merger movement that has been taking place since the end of the Second World War has further advanced the position of the small top group of corporate enterprises.[30] Looking at what little direct information there is on the distribution of profits, one gets exactly the same impression. Thus in 1923 the largest 1,026 corporations—0.26 percent of all corporations reporting to the Bureau of Internal Revenue—received 47.9 percent of all corporate net profits. In 1951, the latest year for which information is published, 1,373 corporations (0.23 percent of all corporations) accounted for 54 percent of all corporate net profits, and 747 corporations (0.12 percent of all corporations) for 46.5 percent of all corporate net profits.[31] In actual fact, the ratios of concentration of both assets and profits increasingly understate the share of the total controlled by very few interests. Many corporations reporting independently are in reality closely linked by holding companies, common stockholders, interlocking directorates, and so on.[32]

Yet it is frequently believed—a belief diligently nurtured by various publications emanating from obvious sources—that the concentration of profits in the hands of a small number of firms is of little significance, since these giant firms themselves may be owned by a very large number of individuals. This picture of a shareholders' democracy is, however, but a myth. As a number of investigations have shown, the control of the few corporations that hold the lion's share of the assets and earn a correspondingly large share of the aggregate profits is vested in a small number of individuals who in turn receive the bulk of distributed profits.[33] That this reflects itself fully in the

[29] Smaller War Plants Corporation, *Economic Concentration and World War II* (Washington, 1946), p. 6.

[30] Federal Trade Commission, *Report on the Merger Movement* (Washington, 1948).

[31] For 1923, United States Treasury Department, Bureau of Internal Revenue, *Statistics of Income*, p. 118; for 1951, *Statistics of Income, Preliminary Report*, p. 41.

[32] For the prewar situation see the excellent study by Paul M. Sweezy, "Interest Groups in the American Economy," originally published as Appendix 13 to Part I of the National Resources Committee's *Structure of the American Economy* and recently reprinted in the author's *The Present as History* (New York, 1953), pp. 158 ff.

[33] Cf. The Brookings Institution, *Share Ownership in the United States* (Washington, 1952), where much is made of the finding that nearly 6.5 million Americans own shares in publicly owned stocks with an average

distribution of personal income and savings can be seen from recent
studies undertaken by the Federal Reserve Board, the Michigan Survey
Research Center, and a group of economists at the Harvard Graduate
School of Business. Surveying this material, Victor Perlo comes to the
conclusion that "averaging their share in undistributed profits and
their share in individual savings, it turns out that the top 1% own
between 50 and 55% of all savings, individual and corporate combined."[34]

Let us now try to sum up this brief discussion of the second "classical" condition for growth. Although under monopolistic capitalism
the economic surplus is much larger in absolute terms than under
competitive capitalism, it is markedly lower than the largest *possible*
surplus, if the latter were to be defined as the difference between full
employment output and some physiological subsistence minimum level
of mass consumption. The economic surplus generated under monopolistic capitalism is, however, as large as possible in the only relevant
sense of the notion, that is, taking into account the prevailing level
of output, the market mechanism responsible for the distribution of
income under capitalism, as well as the more or less steady rise of
conventional standards of subsistence.[35] Where in this area the outstanding difference between monopolistic and competitive capitalism
is to be found is in the *distribution* of the economic surplus among
those to whom it accrues. As the transition from feudalism to competitive capitalism led not only to a vast expansion of the economic surplus but also to the transfer of a large share of it from the feudal
landlord to the capitalist businessman, the transition from competitive
to monopolistic capitalism has resulted likewise in a tremendous in-

---

holding of approximately 4 shares per stockholder, where, however, the
information is also conveyed—although much less conspicuously—that
2.3 percent of all stockholders in manufacturing corporations account for
57 percent of the total number of those corporations' shares. In the field
of public utilities 1 percent of shareholders own 46 percent of all shares.
In finance and investment 3 percent of shareholders control 53 percent
of the number of shares, and in transportation 1.5 percent of shareholders
hold 56 percent of stock. A similar story for the prewar period is presented
in M. Taitel, *Profits, Productive Activities and New Investment*, TNEC
Monograph No. 12 (Washington, 1941).
   [34] *The Income Revolution* (New York, 1954), p. 58.
   [35] It is in promoting this rise of what is socially considered to be the
minimum standard of living that the trade unions have played their
largest role. The unions have had much to do with the growth of
productivity and aggregate output. By raising the price of labor they
stimulated the introduction of labor-saving devices and the spreading
of technical progress.

crease of the absolute volume of the economic surplus and in the shift of the control over it from the relatively small capitalist to a few giant corporations.

IV

Thus with the growth and propagation of large-scale enterprise, monopoly, and oligopoly, the distribution of the economic surplus has become incomparably more uneven than in the age of small competitive business; the resulting concentration of assets and profits in the hands of a small group of giant concerns (and a small circle of the capitalists who control them) assumes, however, major significance when we consider our remaining "classical" conditions for growth. These are, first, the maximization not merely of the economic surplus, but of the share of it available for plowing back into business—in other words, thrifty and abstemious husbandry of it on the part of its recipients; and secondly, the availability of sufficient outlets for its profitable investment. Only passing acquaintance with recent economic developments (and the literature) is required to see that it is here that monopolistic capitalism has departed furthest from the competitive period.

With regard to the first of the two requirements, matters have taken a somewhat paradoxical turn. The individual capitalist today has gone a long way from living up to the image of his puritan ancestors—thrift, frugality, and relentless self-denial can hardly be considered at the present time to be his (and his spouse's) outstanding characteristics. Yet the essence of what was to be the result of the individual capitalist's thrift is still being attained under monopolistic capitalism—if in a significantly different way. The strikingly uneven distribution of profits causes only a relatively small share of the aggregate economic surplus to go into the capitalists' consumption. Under conditions of full employment and large aggregate output and surplus, the smallness of that share becomes even more pronounced. The proportion of the economic surplus that is being retained by corporations, and that is available for investment, is thus not merely large but increases markedly in periods of prosperity.[36]

The situation is much more complex when it comes, as it were, to

[36] This is an important tenet of the so-called underconsumption theory. For a qualification, see p. 90 below.

the other side of the issue: not to the volume of the economic surplus, and the need for investment opportunities, but to the demand for accumulated capital and the availability of profitable investment outlets. Indeed, on this part of the story we shall have to dwell somewhat longer.

For a considerable time economics has hardly related the development of large-scale enterprise, of monopoly and oligopoly, to the problem of investment opportunities, of sufficiency of the demand for investible funds to absorb the economic surplus generated under conditions of full employment. As our "classical" conditions were assumed to prevail, i.e. as Say's Law was thought to be valid, the utilization of the economic surplus appeared to present hardly any problem. It was taken for granted that such surplus as accrues to the capitalist entrepreneur—monopolistic or otherwise—is plowed back into business, with this investment propelling economic progress. Indeed, the larger that surplus, the faster would be the growth of productivity and output. Thus, while it was considered to be possible that too big a surplus would unduly reduce *current* consumption in favor of *future* consumption, yet little wisdom was seen in trying to tamper with the size of that surplus. Reducing it could render investment less attractive to those who were in a position to invest, and cause in this way a fall in investment (and a slowing down of economic progress) entirely out of proportion to the temporary benefit secured by the original increase of consumption. Consequently, the concern of some writers with what they considered to be too large a volume of the economic surplus, their insistence on curbing an "excessive" accumulation of capital, their complaints about "underconsumption," were regarded as somewhat myopic overvaluation of the present as compared with the future —reflecting a commendable compassion for their underprivileged fellow men but hardly sufficient appreciation of the canons of sound economics.

Not that the proliferation of monopoly and the size of monopoly profits were of no concern to the economics profession. On the contrary, in the last quarter of the nineteenth and in the first quarter of the twentieth century economists in advanced capitalist countries displayed a great deal of preoccupation with the growing importance of monopolistic and oligopolistic enterprise. Yet academic economics, reflecting its middle-class background and environment, expressing the mounting frustration and anxieties of the small, willy-nilly competitive businessman helplessly watching the portentous rise of his large-scale monopolistic rival—academic economics was incapable of taking a forward-looking historical view of the growth of big business. Thus all the ammunition that was fired at monopoly was drawn from the arsenal of the theory of perfect competition—the perfect ideology of petty business—and the evil effects of large-scale enterprise were seen primarily in the distortion of the "optimal" arrangements that were expected to emerge from the reign of free markets. Identifying the interests of the small businessman with the interests of society as a whole,[37] this denunciation of monopoly blamed it for distorting the "optimal" distribution of income, although what was actually at issue was the monopolies' effect on the distribution of *profits*. Ambivalently motivated by fear and envy, the critics of monopoly castigated the monopolists' price and output policies as depressing consumers' welfare, although what was frequently, if not always, at issue was the competitive superiority of large-scale enterprise. Faced with a spectacular rise of big business to social influence and power, the foes of monopoly decried the monopolists' position in the body politic as a danger to democracy and freedom, although what was at issue was the threat to the small businessman's earlier ascendancy in capitalist society. Concerned with the preservation of the *status quo*, trying to hang on to the best of all possible worlds, never thinking in terms of historical change and development, this petty-bourgeois hostility to large-scale enterprise and big business left no room for a rational understanding of the impact of monopoly on the process of investment and economic growth.[38]

Even after the so-called Keynesian Revolution repudiated Say's Law and placed the determination of the level of income and employment at the center of economic discussion, the relation between the process of investment (and economic development) and the growing role of large-scale enterprise and monopoly has received only spotty

[37] Cf. Lee Benson, *Merchants, Farmers, and Railroads* (Cambridge, Massachusetts, 1955).

[38] A notable exception is Schumpeter, who made no secret of his contempt for the "shopkeeper" approach to the monopoly problem, and in whose work the significance of monopoly was considered primarily from the viewpoint of the long-run development of capitalism. However, it took as long as forty years for Schumpeter's anticipation of the economics of monopoly capitalism to attract the attention (and acclaim) of the economics profession. Only in Marxist literature was the growth of monopoly treated as a crucially important aspect of the general development of capitalism. Hilferding's *Finanzkapital* (1910) was the classical Marxist contribution to this theme—followed by Lenin's famous *Imperialism: The Highest Stage of Capitalism* (1917), and other works.

and sporadic attention. Following in the footsteps of Keynes, treating investment (or rather the bulk of it) as an exogenously determined "autonomous" datum, and little concerned with its composition, the discussion of the theory of income and employment bypassed, so to speak, the problem of the impact of monopoly and oligopoly on the volume and the long-run effect of investment. What is more, this orientation of economic thought has pushed into the background the earlier type of "welfare"-oriented monopoly critique, and intellectually cleared the ground for the present tendency toward wholesale acceptance, if not glorification, of monopoly.

To be sure, the "New Economics" suggested an anti-monopoly attitude in its concern with overaccumulation. Yet the emphasis of that reasoning has been on the necessity for a rise in the share of consumption in national income rather than on the role of monopoly in the process of investment. In this view the economic surplus, whether appropriated by monopolists or by competitive businessmen, was considered to be too large not so much because it encroached upon current consumption to an extent undesirable in terms of welfare but because it did not find sufficient utilization via private investment. In the words of Professor Alvin H. Hansen, "The problem of our generation is, above all, the problem of inadequate investment outlets."[39]

This inadequacy of investment outlets has been attributed in most contemporary economics—as Schumpeter would have said—not to causes inherent in the working of the economic engine, but to the action of factors external to it. Most representative of this approach is the so-called "theory of vanishing investment opportunities" that has received its best-known formulation in the writings of Professor Hansen. But while the economists associated with this concept have correctly registered the phenomenon of a growing inadequacy of the volume of private investment outlets in relation to the size of the economic surplus under conditions of full employment, it can hardly be said that they have satisfactorily *explained* this inadequacy. Neither the slowing down of population growth, nor the disappearance of the so-called frontier, nor the alleged changes in the tempo and nature of technological progress, which all play a major part in this argument, can be considered to provide such an explanation.

Apart from the probability that such decline of population growth

[39] "Economic Progress and Declining Population Growth," *American Economic Review* (March 1939), reprinted in *Readings in Business Cycle Theory* (Philadelphia-Toronto, 1944), p. 379.

as has taken place in advanced capitalist countries may itself be a phenomenon to be explained in terms of insufficient investment, employment, and income, there is no reason to expect population changes per se to exercise a major influence on the volume of investment. As far as the relation of population changes to effective demand is concerned, Kalecki points out: ". . . what is important . . . is not an increase in population but an increase in purchasing power. An increase in the number of paupers does not broaden the market. For instance, increased population does not necessarily mean a higher demand for houses; for without an increase in purchasing power the result may well be the crowding of more people into existing dwelling space."[40]

This is not to deny that population increases may have *some* bearing on aggregate demand. A growing population may generate a structure of consumption different from what might be characteristic of a stagnant population. It may buy more milk and less whiskey, more diapers and less neckties, more houses and less automobiles—and these differences in the composition of the consumers' baskets may have some significance for the volume and profitability of investment.[41] However, whether a growing population would on balance save more or less is a moot problem, and not enormously important. It could be argued that larger spending on the support of big families would reduce personal saving; it could be held equally strongly that the responsibility for the upbringing of larger families would call for larger reserves and for reduced current spending. Since the overwhelming majority of people even in the wealthiest countries of the world hardly save in any case, the difference would not amount to much regardless of which hypotheses might be borne out.

Somewhat more relevant may appear the argument that businessmen in making investment decisions are strongly influenced by population statistics. If this were indeed true, and if all capitalists invested heavily when population growth is rapid (while curtailing investment when it is slow or absent), their profit expectations might be temporarily borne out by experience: not by the anticipated population increases but by the volume of aggregate investment and the resulting volume of aggregate income and demand. In reality, however, only a

[40] *Theory of Economic Dynamics* (London, 1954), p. 161.
[41] "Thus a deflection of demand from things in general to housing has the same effect as a bout of innovations 'favorable to capital' and tends to promote investment in the same way." Joan Robinson, *The Rate of Interest and Other Essays* (London, 1952), p. 109.

few firms—primarily those in the fields of public utilities and communications—are likely to be guided in their investment planning by
population statistics; and, even so, the relevant statistics are not those
reflecting *overall* changes in population but rather those depicting internal migration, and rise and decline of individual regions or locali-
ties.

A certain significance may also attach to the appropriations on the
part of government authorities on all levels for poor relief, for schools,
hospitals, parks, and the like. These appropriations may be determined
in the main by the social structure and size of the population (and
their changes). It is most important to note, however, that such outlays
would constitute net additions to aggregate spending and exercise a
stimulating effect on the economy as a whole *only if they are not offset
by a contraction of spending elsewhere.* Yet, if undertaken by munici-
palities—as they freqeuntly would be—these expenditures are likely
to be made possible either by saving on some other positions of the
budget or by additional local taxes.[42] Whenever this is the case, the
impact of these "population-related" expenditures will be inappre-
ciable.

However, population changes are frequently considered to affect
investment not so much by augmenting effective demand as through
their impact on the supply of labor. It is argued in this connection
that a rapid increase of the population exercises pressure on the wage
level, and leads to higher profits, thus promoting capital accumulation
and rendering investment at the same time more attractive to the capitalist entrepreneur. Yet the implications of this reasoning are by no
means unambiguous.[43] In the first place, it should be borne in mind
that the changes that are relevant in this connection are not changes
over time in *population* totals, but changes in the number of people
entering the labor market.[44] These depend, however, as much (or less)
on overall population developments as on the extent to which *internal
migration* from the non-capitalist sectors of the economy (subsistence
agriculture, handicrafts, and the like) adds to the pool of manpower at
the disposal of capitalist enterprise.[45]

Moreover, unless it is assumed that the elasticity of capitalists'

[42] Cf. Joan Robinson, *op. cit.*, p. 107.
[43] Cf. Kalecki, *op. cit.*, p. 160.
[44] This very important, but frequently overlooked, point is stressed in
Paul M. Sweezy, *Theory of Capitalist Development* (New York, 1942), pp.
222 ff.
[45] This internal migration is typically caused by economic or technological displacement of manpower in the non-capitalist sectors of the economy,

demand for labor is at least unity—and there surely is no obvious reason for making such an assumption—the lowering of wages resulting from an intensified competition for jobs among workers would by reducing the income of wage earners cause a drop in aggregate consumers' demand without this drop being offset by a corresponding increase in investment. In fact, investment would be discouraged by the reduction of consumers' purchases, and furthermore the availability of cheap labor would tend to weaken the incentives to introduce labor-saving machinery the development and production of which themselves represent an important investment opportunity. Thus the increase of the labor supply and the cheapening of labor might lead not to growth of investment and output but rather to growth of unemployment—open or disguised.[46] That such is a highly likely outcome is strongly sug-

---

although in a number of cases it was the result of "extra-economic" coercion (enclosures in Britain, *Bauernlegen* in Germany), the background of which was, however, industrial development in the cities. In new, originally thinly populated countries such as the United States, Canada, Australia, and New Zealand, the non-capitalist sectors from which the additions to the industrial manpower pool were drawn were located not only *within* the countries but also in the Old World. Immigration was therefore the form in which much of this influx appeared.

[46] This is not in conflict with the important consideration that the cheapening of labor and the discouragement of technological progress resulting from rapid population growth are favorable to the *long-run* stability of capitalism: they retard its development and thus postpone the crises arising in its maturity. (Cf. Paul M. Sweezy, *loc. cit.*) As Hans Neisser puts it: "Economic stability does not imply a high level of per capita income and does not even exclude so-called structural unemployment; on the contrary, poor economies are likely to display a greater economic stability than rich ones." "Stability in Late Capitalism," *Social Research* (Spring 1954), p. 85. Indeed by keeping down capital equipment per worker, productivity, and aggregate output, the rapid growth of the population reduces the volume of the currently generated economic surplus. What is more, in the case of an aggregate output produced with the help of little capital, capital consumption allowances account necessarily for only a small share of its value, with the *gross* surplus correspondingly smaller than in a case in which depreciation of capital equipment constitutes a large component of the total product. Since under such circumstances the amount of economic surplus available for investment is small—after allowance is made for the capitalists' consumption—the number of workers that can be added to the employed labor force is also small, notwithstanding the smallness of the amount of capital needed to equip a new worker. Thus even if the capitalists invest all of the investible surplus in productive plant and equipment—which is by no means to be taken for granted—the result is likely to be slow expansion and full employment (of the existing capital equipment) in the industrial sector of the economy, while the non-capitalist sectors (agriculture, handicrafts, distributive trades, etc.) turn into slums filled with rapidly growing "surplus population." This brings into sharp relief one of the most striking contradictions

gested by the experience of the old underdeveloped countries that cannot complain about insufficient growth of the population. At the same time a strong case could be made for the view that it was precisely the relative scarcity of labor throughout earlier American history that accounted for the large volume of investment, the rapid progress of technology, and the resulting increase in productivity in the United States.

To be sure, a growing *population* represents an indispensable condition for investment and economic expansion if technological progress is absent—both in industry and agriculture—if no new, previously unexplored natural resources are taken into exploitation, and if displacement of manpower in agriculture by extra-economic coercion fails to materialize. Yet under such circumstances the problem would hardly arise: the impossibility of investment would be matched by the absence of all incentives to invest. Needless to say, a constellation of this kind bears no resemblance to reality. It is even too static to apply to a feudal society. Where there is at least some technological progress, at least some opening up of new natural resources, at least some internal migration out of agriculture, investment can take place and productivity can advance, regardless of whether the population is increasing, stagnant, or even declining. It may well be said that investment projects, just as they force their own financing, likewise call forth the labor supply that is needed for their realization. This applies not merely to old countries where agriculture, handicrafts, retail trade, and so forth provide permanent manpower reserves; it applies also to new, thinly populated countries where immigration supplies the necessary labor if capitalist accumulation creates a sufficiently strong demand for it.

The conclusion that emerges is that, far from determining the volume of investment, the demographic situation itself assumes a different complexion at different stages of economic development—depending on the extent of capital accumulation, on the nature of technological changes, on the speed and intensity of shifts in the occupational structure of society, and so forth.

---

of the capitalist order: rapid expansion of productivity and output results in instability, depressions, and unemployment in the industrial sector of the economy with all their repercussions for society as a whole. A slight increase of productivity and output causes disguised unemployment, poverty, and stagnation in the vast non-industrial sectors of society, continuously pulling down the relatively advanced industrial islands in the sea of backwardness.

Similarly it is by no means obvious what significance, if any, is to be attached to the so-called passing of the frontier. First of all, frontiers of economic expansion and development do not coincide with geographic frontiers: there is ample room for growth within almost any geographic boundaries. No one would deny, for instance, that there has been a great deal more development in Belgium than in Spain. Secondly, large underdeveloped areas exist within most advanced capitalist countries; there are plenty of investment opportunities in the American South, in the so-called depressed areas in Great Britain, in large parts of France, Italy, or Scandinavia. What is more, the less developed territories beyond the advanced countries' national borders could provide as good as or better investment outlets than those seized upon at home. It would seem therefore that when conditions are propitious to investment, investment opportunities are found; and that when investment is flagging, what would have been considered at other times excellent investment opportunities are left unutilized.

Nor would the situation appear to be very different when it comes to technological innovations. It is highly questionable whether the intensity or the nature of technological discoveries in recent decades have been such as to require for their realization a lesser investment of capital than, say, a century earlier. Kalecki may be right in drawing attention to the fact of the diminishing importance of opening up new sources of raw materials as well as of the growing significance of "scientific organization" of the assembly process which does not involve heavy investment.[47] Sweezy may have a point in stressing the extraordinary importance of railroads in providing an outlet for investment in the second half of the nineteenth century.[48] Some significance may also attach to the argument that the relative cheapening of capital goods that has taken place in the course of the last hundred years has reduced capital requirements in relation to the intended physical output, although physical output is not what matters to a capitalist investor.

On the other hand, it could be held—with what would seem to me considerable force—that all of the above considerations are hardly relevant to the issue, that in fact they put the cart before the horse. In the ancient world as well as in the Middle Ages there were many ingenious technical devices that were not utilized because socioeconomic conditions for their realization were lacking. One could list a

[47] *Theory of Economic Dynamics* (London, 1954), p. 159.
[48] *Econometrica* (October 1954), p. 532.

vast number of more or less recently evolved technical discoveries the utilization of which would call for large capital outlays—as large, indeed, as any ever undertaken in history. Whether in the area of atomic energy or "automation," of transportation or land improvement, of consumer goods or agricultural equipment, of housing or food —projects exist that are technically as feasible and economically as rational as any undertaken in the past. The difference is "merely" that the earlier technical innovations attracted sufficient investment to be translated into reality, while more recent technological possibilities are less readily (and more selectively) seized upon by capitalist enterprise. Therefore it is more plausible that technological innovations no less than underdeveloped or little developed areas inside and outside of advanced capitalist countries offer a steadily available pool of investment opportunities—with other factors determining how much of its contents is being made use of at any given time. In the words of J. Steindl, "innovations . . . affect only the *form* which net investment takes. . . . Technological innovations accompany the process of investment like a shadow, they do not act on it as a propelling force."[49]

To be sure, the foregoing is not intended to be an endorsement of the frequently encountered response to the "prophets of doom and gloom"—a response that points to the great number of useful projects that "could" be undertaken, and the completion of which would contribute to human welfare. Indeed, this response fully shares the fundamental fallacy underlying the very argument that it attempts to refute. Although an elementary textbook in economics usually begins its exposition by stressing that what matters in a capitalist economy are not human *wants* at large but only those backed up by sufficient purchasing power ("effective demand"), as soon as the discussion is carried to an "advanced" level even most sophisticated economists tend to forget this basic principle. Whether they blame insufficient or ill-directed technological progress for the inadequacy of investment opportunities, or whether they pronounce those investment opportunities to be practically unlimited in view of a host of consumers' wants that are as yet unsatisfied[50]—the error in the reasoning is the same. Both parties to the argument would seem to evade the central issue. There is indeed a continuous and growing inadequacy of private investment in relation

---

[49] *Maturity and Stagnation in American Capitalism* (Oxford, 1952), p. 133, and p. 235 *n*. (Italics in the original.)

[50] Perhaps the best examples of this type of building castles in the air are to be found in the article of J. K. Galbraith, "We Can Prosper Without War Orders," *New York Times* Magazine (June 22, 1952), and in David Lilienthal, *Big Business, A New Era* (New York, 1953), pp. 8 ff.

to the volume of economic surplus under conditions of full employment. There is, moreover—visible to all—a plethora of technically
possible and socially urgent undertakings that could readily absorb
all such economic surplus, and· a great deal more. The problem that
has to be solved, therefore, is what it is in the structure of advanced
capitalism, and in such changes in the investment process as have
occurred in the course of the last five to eight decades, that renders
the employment of the economic surplus in the realization of these
projects difficult, if not downright impossible.

Not that only so-called endogenous factors should be taken into
account in an attempt to answer this question. The distinction between
endogenous and exogenous elements of what constitutes a socioeconomic totality is in any case most tenuous and arbitrary. As Lenin
remarked, "the question as to whether these changes [in the structure
of the capitalist system] . . . are 'purely' economic or *non*-economic
(e.g. military) is a secondary one, which does not in the least affect
the fundamental view on the latest epoch of capitalism."[51] What *is* of
prime importance, however, is whether the far-reaching changes in the
mode of functioning of the capitalist system that have taken place
during the first half of our century are due to more or less accidental
fortuitous configurations of events, or whether these transformations
represent the natural result of capitalist development, indeed, are
necessitated by this development's intrinsic logic. To ascribe them to
factors encompassed by the theory of vanishing investment opportunities or by the philosophy attributing all the mishaps that befell capitalism during the last fifty years to untoward chance occurrences is
not only analytically inconclusive—as was indicated above. It also
amounts to an implicit acceptance of the agnostic (and apologetic)
view that relates all the contradictions and irrationalities of the capitalist system not to its inherent laws of motion but to random "disturbances"—economic, political, and others—in the absence of which
capitalism supposedly could operate in a harmonious fashion.

V

In actual fact, however, to explain the inadequacy of private investment in relation to the volume of economic surplus under full

[51] E. Varga and L. Mendelsohn (eds.), *New Data for Lenin's Imperialism—The Highest Stage of Capitalism* (New York, 1940), p. 168.
(Italics in the original.)

employment, there is no need to seek refuge in factors "external" to
the working principles of the capitalist economy, in errors of government or in unforeseeable adversities of fate. It can be adequately accounted for by a process that is deeply rooted in the basic structure
of capitalism and promoted by its entire development: the growth of
large-scale enterprise, of monopoly and oligopoly, and their ever-
increasing sway over all sectors and branches of the capitalist system.[52]

One of the most conspicuous results of this development has already
been mentioned: the concentration of profits in the hands of a small
number of capitalists. It is to this point that we must return from our
extensive detour. For in the competitive world approximately reflected
in our "classical" model, there was no room for such a distribution of
profits. Accruing to a plethora of various-sized enterprises, each accounting for no more than a small fraction of its respective markets,
aggregate profits would be necessarily split up into a vast number of
small, albeit unequal, morsels. What is more, not only would the
differences between the absolute amounts of profit earned by individual
firms be comparatively small, the rates of return on invested capital
would tend to be approximately equal in all lines of business. This
equalization of the rates of profit was assigned, in fact, paramount
importance. It was charged with the responsibility for the allocation
of resources and for the maintenance of the equilibrium of the competitive system. The mechanism relied upon can be briefly sketched.
Suppose a state of equilibrium in which the rates of profit of individual firms are equalized. In this situation let some firm come upon
a technological device that lowers its cost of production. A slight reduction of price made possible by the lowering of costs will enable
this firm to sell a larger output and to realize extra-profits. The higher-
than-usual rate of profit will not only stimulate a further increase of
output on the part of the pathbreaking firm but will attract capital
from other branches of the economy where the rate of profit is merely
normal. Yet the extra-profits accruing to the innovating firm are bound
to be transitory. Other firms in the industry are confronted with the
alternatives of being squeezed out of the market by their low-cost
competitor or of themselves adopting the new method of production.
The financially weaker (or otherwise inflexible) may have no choice
and will tend to be eliminated from the industry. The rest will intro-

[52] It is the adoption and most interesting exploration of this approach
by J. Steindl in his *Maturity and Stagnation in American Capitalism*
(Oxford, 1952) that renders his book singularly valuable and important.
In much of what follows I have drawn heavily on Steindl's work.

duce the new methods of production, lower their costs and prices, thus retaining their shares of the market. In this way the extra-profits of the pioneers will be wiped out and the normal rate of profit once more be restored.

What is most important to note is that under these conditions the transition to the new, technologically improved method of production is not a matter of discretion for the competitive firm. Only at the peril of its extinction can it disregard the available possibilities of cost reduction. Thus, in addition to offering the carrot of extra-profits, the competitive system brandishes the stick of bankruptcy to promote and to enforce investment and technological progress. That in this competitive race "the devil catches the hindmost," and that the less efficient, less viable firms fall by the wayside, plays in itself a major role in the working of the mechanism. In this way excessive productive capacity, developing at the early stages of the nexus sketched above, tends to become eliminated.[53] This in turn clears the ground for the repetition of the entire sequence of events, when new technological improvements once more create extra-profits which are used for and attract additional investment, for the presence of much excess capacity would retard and obstruct new investment in the industry by rendering the breakthrough of new, cost-reducing methods of production more difficult.[54]

Thus the process never comes to a rest. The cheapening of the output of one industry would create "pecuniary external economies" everywhere where that output serves as input.[55] In this way extra-profits would be created in various branches of the economy, investment would be stimulated now in one, now in another industry, with this "perennial gale"—to use Schumpeter's favorite expression—incessantly propelling economic growth. "We see how in this way the mode of production and the means of production are continually trans-

[53] It is by no means unimportant whether this liquidation of excess capacity takes the form of scrapping the old-fashioned equipment, or whether the old-fashioned equipment lingers on in an industry that becomes thus quasi-permanently "sick" because of the difficulty of getting rid of the redundant capacity. American economic history is full of this phenomenon (coal, textiles, agriculture) and it has been one of the most important causes of the monopolization or of government regulation of those industries.

[54] This is stressed by Steindl, who also mentions the necessary qualifications resulting from the existence of what might be called "normal" excess capacity.

[55] J. Viner, "Cost Curves and Supply Curves," *Zeitschrift für Nationalökonomie* (1931), Vol. III, No. 1, p. 98.

formed, revolutionized, how the division of labor is necessarily followed by greater division of labor, the application of machinery by
still greater application of machinery, work on large scale by work
on still larger scale. That is the law which again and again throws
bourgeois production out of its course and which compels capital to
intensify the productive forces of labor *because* it *has* intensified them
[already], the law which gives capital no rest and continually whis-
pers in its ear: Go on! Go on!"[56]

However, for this "going on" to take place, a number of conditions
would have to be fulfilled that were explicitly or implicitly referred
to above. First and foremost, the number of firms in the economy (and
in each industry) has to be large, and the individual firms' output
has to be small in relation to the total output of their industry. Moreover the products of firms comprising an industry should be more or
less perfect substitutes for each other, so that a slight difference in
price would shift market demand from one firm to another. Only under
such circumstances would the individual firm be unable to influence
significantly by its own production and price policies the price prevailing in the market; only under such circumstances would the individual firm be in a position to make decisions concerning investments,
expansion of output, and the like, without regard to possible retaliation on the part of its competitors. For since all of them are small,
none of them is able to affect significantly the market situation underlying the firm's decisions to invest and to increase its production. At
the same time, the number of firms being large, there is little possibility for the individual firm to assess accurately what the rest of the
industry is about to undertake. Thus the firm, in formulating its own
investment policy, will be guided by its own "intramural" considerations: the existing possibilities of lowering costs, its ability to raise
capital, its actual and anticipated rates of return. It will neither be in
a position, nor compelled, to take into account the future combined
effect on the market of the concurrent investment decisions of others
inside and outside the industry.

It is this anarchy of the capitalist markets, so strongly emphasized
by Marx, in conjunction with the continuous appearance, disappearance and reappearance of extra-profits that produced a strong tendency
towards large and, indeed, excessive volume of investment during the

[56] Marx, *Wage Labor and Capital*, in Marx and Engels, *Selected Works*
(Moscow, 1949-1950), Vol. I, p. 93. (Italics in the original; the bracketed
word added by this writer on the basis of the German original.)

competitive phase of capitalism.[57] The result was a wasteful utilization of the economic surplus, premature destruction of capital assets, with both investment decisions and capital losses caused by the vagaries of technological developments, by sporadic and fortuitous emerging of extra-profits. Yet on the other side of the ledger, the competitive organization of the capitalist economy could be "credited" with providing sufficient (or nearly sufficient) outlets to absorb the economic surplus under conditions of fairly full employment—although much of this investment constituted a loss to society which in turn depressed the rates of growth markedly below their potential magnitude. The loss has found its expression not merely in an output much lower than attainable but also in employment much smaller than possible. This is in no contradiction to what was just said about the sufficiency of investment to absorb the economic surplus under conditions of full employment. Underemployment under competitive capitalism tended to be of a type quite different from what in our days has come to be called Keynesian unemployment. It was not so much due to inadequacy of investment in relation to the potential economic surplus but rather to the inadequacy of investment (both in volume and composition) in relation to the number of people available for work. With the minimum amount of capital required to equip a worker more or less rigidly fixed by the prevailing level of technology—determined in turn by competition—and with much capital wasted in the competitive process, the number of individuals that were enabled to find gainful employment was necessarily lower than would have been possible if capital had been utilized in a rational way.

VI

Yet whatever the (absolute) faults and (relative) merits of the investment process in the competitive system, only moderate reflection is needed to realize that very little is left of its essential characteristics in the current, monopolistic stage of capitalist development. The most

[57] Cf. Joan Robinson, "The Impossibility of Competition," in E. H. Chamberlin (ed.), *Monopoly and Competition and Their Regulation* (New York, 1955). It was this specific nature of the investment process under competitive capitalism, its frequent excessiveness and irrationality, that accounted for the particular pattern of economic crises that characterized the nineteenth century: waves of insolvencies, panics resulting from the snowballing effects of business failures, acute but relatively short-lived gluts in individual markets, etc.

drastic difference relates to the conditions of entry into an industry. Indeed, in an economy consisting of industries comprising multitudes of small firms each responsible for an insignificant part of the industry's more or less homogeneous output, the entry of a new firm into an industry presents no problem. Any capitalist in possession of the requisite amount of capital can become an entrepreneur and start a new business. With the structure of the market fairly simple, with the industry's product fairly homogeneous, the prerequisites for undertaking the venture are not many, and the obstacles to overcome relatively small.

This obviously is a far cry from the structure of the monopolistic and oligopolistic industry. Here the number of firms in an industry is small, the size of the typical firm is large, the market faced by it complex, and the product that it sells—while in many cases not notably distinct as far as its physical characteristics are concerned—strongly identified by trademarks, intense advertising, etc. Under such circumstances, the conditions of entry into an industry are of an altogether new nature. Leaving aside legal obstacles such as patents, government concessions, and the like that may be held by the existing large-scale concerns, the amount of capital required for the establishment of a new firm assumes prodigious proportions.[58]

Not only are the present standards of technology such as to render the erection of a modern, scientifically adequate plant very expensive, but the initial outlays on advertising, sales promotion campaigns, and so forth, that have to be met by a new firm call for large amounts of investment. What is more, the largely ephemeral nature of the initially acquired "asset" (good will, market connections, etc.) greatly increases the riskiness of the new product. It becomes thus entirely inaccessible to small businessmen or even to groups of businessmen (corporations) neither themselves endowed with the requisite funds nor able to obtain sufficient support from the capital market.[59] Schum-

[58] Needless to say, what is at issue is not the absolute amount of money that might be involved, but the volume of wealth measured either in wage units, as a proportion of national income, or in some other real terms. The capital requirements for the founding of new plants of the technologically most desirable size were studied by J. S. Bain. Cf. his "Economies of Scale, Concentration and Entry," *American Economic Review* (March 1954), where some of his findings are summarized.

[59] "Thus the limited credit of many firms which does not permit any one of them to obtain more than a limited amount of capital at the current rate of interest, is often a direct consequence of its being known that a given firm is unable to increase its sales outside its own particular market

peter's daring and dashing entrepreneur is now a legendary figure from a distant past—if not from the mythology of capitalism—or is to be found only in the demimonde of business, founding new ice-cream parlors or "deep freeze subscription clubs."[60]

The extraordinary difficulty, if not impossibility, of entry of new firms into monopolistic and oligopolistic industries endows the established monopolies and oligopolies with what might be called "privileged sanctuaries." The rules of behavior in the relative tranquillity and security of these retreats are, however, quite different from those applicable to industries exposed to the sharp winds of competition. Although, as mentioned before, the relation between the process of investment and this far-reaching transformation in the basic structure of capitalism has received much less attention in economic literature than the subject matter would obviously deserve, a number of propositions can be considered to be pretty well established. The most significant of these can be stated with the utmost simplicity. *In any given situation* an expansion of output is likely to be contrary to the monopolists' profit-maximization policy. Depending on the prevailing elasticity of demand for his product (and the shape of his marginal revenue curve derived therefrom), an increase in output may fail to increase his total profits or may even reduce them below their pre-output-expansion level. In the words of Paul M. Sweezy: ". . . the monopolist's investment policy cannot be dominated by his overall profit rate or by the rate obtainable on the additional investment taken by itself. He must rather be guided by what we may call the marginal profit rate, that is to say the rate on the additional investment after

without incurring heavy marketing expenses." P. Sraffa, "Law of Return Under Competitive Conditions," *Economic Journal* (December 1926), p. 550. What holds true for an existing firm holds so a fortiori for a "would-be" firm. Nor should it be overlooked that the intimate connection between the capital market and the powerful, old-established corporations greatly reduces the newcomer's chances of securing financial support on reasonable terms.

[60] "There is no more cherished view of the American economy than that which regards it as a biological process in which the old and the senile are continuously being replaced by the young and vigorous. It is a pleasant but almost certainly a far-fetched fiction. In fact, the present generation of Americans, if it survives, will buy its steel, copper, brass, automobiles, tires, soap, shortening, breakfast food, bacon, cigarettes, whiskey, cash registers and caskets from one or another of the handful of firms that now supply these staples. As a moment's reflection will establish, there hasn't been much change in the firms supplying these products for several decades." J. K. Galbraith, *American Capitalism* (Boston, 1952), p. 39.

allowance has been made for the fact that the additional investment, since it will increase output and reduce price, will entail a reduction in profit on the old investment."[61]

To be sure, a monopolist like any other capitalist is always interested in reducing his costs of production. To the extent that the reduction of costs is predicated upon the introduction of new and improved machinery and equipment, it represents an important opportunity for new investment. Yet the drive to reduce costs may be (and frequently is) counteracted by other considerations. There is in the first place the desire to preserve the value of existing investment, and to postpone new investment until the available equipment is amortized.[62] This would seem to be at odds with the well-known rule that a new machine should be introduced to replace an old machine if the average *total* costs of a unit of output produced with the new machine promise to be lower than the average *prime* unit costs of output turned out with the old machine. The contradiction is, however, only apparent: the rule is much less unambiguous than it might seem at first sight. To begin with, for the substitution of new machinery for the old machinery to be rational in terms of this rule, the saving secured with the help of the new machine has to be of such a magnitude as not merely to pay the interest charges on the capital loss incurred in the process of the substitution but also to make good that capital loss in a relatively short period of time.[63] This means that only major technological improvements would have a chance of "breaking through," while others would have to wait until the existing equipment wears out. On the other hand, the applicability of the rule just mentioned clearly depends on the investor's or management's ability to foresee accurately the lifespan of the new machine. It is this lifespan that would determine the magnitude of the *average* total unit costs of output that would be produced with its help.[64] Needless to say, what matters in this connection is not the anticipated *physical* endurance of

[61] *Theory of Capitalist Development* (New York, 1942), p. 275.

[62] O. Lange, *On the Economic Theory of Socialism* (Minneapolis, 1938, 2nd printing, 1948), p. 114; cf. also E. D. Domar, "Investment, Losses and Monopolies," in Lloyd Metzler and others, *Income, Employment and Public Policy: Essays in Honor of Alvin H. Hansen* (New York, 1948), p. 39.

[63] This requirement is imposed not merely by the limitation of capital available to the firm, but also by considerations of risk that assumes larger proportions the longer the period involved.

[64] Cf. G. Terborgh, *Dynamic Equipment Policy* (Washington, 1949), Chapter 11.

the machine, but the time for which it can be counted on not to be superseded by a still better, still more efficient technological device. Therefore in times of rapid technological change the situation becomes particularly complex. Machine A would be replaced by a new, improved machine B when such a substitution would promise significant saving. Yet if there is reason to believe that machine C, which in turn could constitute a major improvement over machine B, is just around the corner, it would be foolish to scrap equipment A only to acquire equipment B—itself likely to be due for scrapping long before it is used up.[65] Thus while technological progress stimulates investment, under conditions of monopoly and oligopoly there may be a strong tendency to wait with outlays on new equipment until the technological conditions have become more or less settled, or to suppress technological advance until the existing equipment is written off.

Not that this tendency is peculiar to the monopolist, and that it would not be equally operative in competitive enterprise. The difference is merely—and this difference is very important—that the competitive firm will be *compelled* by competition to introduce the new machine regardless of the concomitant capital losses or be driven out of business by its old or newly arrived competitors now able to produce and to sell more cheaply, while the monopolist is exposed to no such pressure. As Professor Hansen puts it: "Under vigorous price competition new cost-reducing techniques were compulsorily introduced even though the scrapping of obsolete but undepreciated machinery entailed a capital loss. But under the monopoly principle of obsolescence new machines will not be introduced until the undepreciated value of the old machine will at least be covered by the economies of the new techniques. Thus progress is slowed down, and outlets for new capital formation available under a more ruthless competitive society are cut off."[66] What this means, however, is that under conditions of monopoly outlays on technological improvements as well as capital losses—both important forms of utilization of the economic surplus under capitalism—are significantly reduced.[67]

[65] This obviously applies to *new* investment no less than to replacement.

[66] "Economic Progress and Declining Population Growth," *American Economic Review* (March 1939), reprinted in *Readings in Business Cycle Theory* (Philadelphia-Toronto, 1944), p. 381.

[67] It is nevertheless misleading to say, as Schumpeter does, that the policy of a socialist planned economy would in this respect be the same as that of big business under monopolistic conditions. *Capitalism, Socialism and Democracy* (New York, 1950), pp. 96 ff. In terms of a rational husbandry of society's resources, the capital preservation policy of the

Intimately related to the foregoing is a further point. A great number, if not the bulk, of technological improvements and cost-reducing innovations are predicated upon expansion of the scale of operations. Indeed, "internal economies" or "increasing returns to scale" are primarily responsible for the growth of large-scale enterprise and for the development of mass production. Yet the phenomenon of increasing returns to scale enters the economic stage on two quite distinct occasions. It first eliminates the sweatshop, provides a powerful impetus to the development of productive forces and thus subverts competition by concentrating output in a relatively small number of large, technologically advanced monopolistic (and oligopolistic) enterprises—only to appear at a later phase as a brake on further technical progress by linking up technical improvements with what has become an undesirable expansion of output.[68] A device that would lower unit costs by, say, doubling the number of units produced may be of no interest to the monopolist (or oligopolist) whose profits would fall rather than increase as a result of such flooding the market. "Thus . . . oligopoly exerts a selective action against output-increasing, and in favor of factor-saving innovations."[69]

monopolistic firm may be frequently preferable to the excess investment and the destruction of capital that take place under competitive conditions. Yet, as is often the case under capitalism, such advance in rationality as is achieved is perverted into its opposite if the monopolistic capital preservation policy contributes to a shrinkage of investment opportunities and leads to a reduction of output, income, and employment. In a socialist planned economy the situation is altogether different insofar as the decision to postpone any given investment (in replacement or in new facilities) need not imply a reduction in *aggregate* investment or—if such a reduction is desired—can be accompanied by an appropriate increase in consumption. Neither output decline nor unemployment need result. What this means is that in allocating scarce capital (be it for new investment or for replacement) the socialist planning board will employ it so as to give priority to those branches of the economy and enterprises where the additional investment will be socially most desirable. In other words, some enterprises may go on for a while producing with outmoded equipment not because their capital values are to be preserved, but because the capital needed for the introduction of new machinery can be more productively employed elsewhere. It is plain that such allocation of capital according to social priorities is an entirely different matter from the monopolist's practice of maximization of returns on *his* capital or the preservation of the value of *his* assets.

[68] It appears for a third time in a socialist planned economy in which its productivity-promoting role is no longer curbed by profit maximization policies of monopolistic enterprise.

[69] O. Lange, "Note on Innovations," in *Readings in the Theory of Income Distribution* (W. Fellner, B. F. Haley, eds.) (Philadelphia and

The question might be raised, however, why an oligopolistic firm controlling only a share, albeit a large share, of the market for its product should not avail itself of existing technical possibilities of lowering unit costs by expanding output so as to be able to undersell its competitors and conquer the entire market (or a larger share of it). A number of elements enter the answer. Crucial among them is that price competition under conditions of oligopoly has a tendency to become increasingly odious to the businessmen involved.[70] Any moderate price reduction on the part of one oligopolist calculated to enlarge his share in the market would be immediately countered by corresponding price cuts on the part of his fellow oligopolists—all sufficiently large and sufficiently strong to be able to absorb the resulting loss of profits.[71] On the other hand, a price war to the finish among oligopolistic giants would call for such large amounts of capital and would involve such great risks that accommodation is preferred to ruinous warfare. More or less explicit agreements are concluded, or "price leadership" is established, the consequence of which is that cut-throat competition is eliminated, and that the contracting parties accept the principle of live and let live rather than attempting to destroy one another. This

Toronto, 1946), p. 194. A similar observation is contained in P. Sraffa's "Law of Return Under Competitive Conditions," *Economic Journal* (December 1926), p. 543. This relation between cost-reducing improvements and the *volume* of output goes far in explaining the frequently encountered technical backwardness of many monopolistic and oligopolistic enterprises in Great Britain and elsewhere in Western Europe. To refer to this situation as caused by the "narrowness of the markets" confronting the firms in question, which is quite often done in discussions of Western European economies, amounts to putting the cart before the horse, since it is the "narrowness of the market" *caused by monopoly* that is at issue.

[70] The following report on the appearance of Mr. Benjamin Fairless, Chairman of the Board of the United States Steel Corporation, before a Senate Committee was published in the *New York Times*, March 22, 1955: "There has been a change in our thinking—Mr. Fairless agreed—price is not the only form of competition. We also compete by quality and service. 'So that to talk about price competition may be unrealistic under our new conditions?'—the Senator asked. The witness said that was true, then noted that with its 'profit objective' in mind, United States Steel Corporation sometimes decided not to meet lower prices. 'You feel that we may have a false idea of the value of price competition as it existed fifty years ago, and that people who long for it may be completely wrong?'—'Yes'— Mr. Fairless replied." And Mr. Harlowe Curtice, President of the General Motors Corporation, said before the same committee: "The automobile industry is intensely competing, but mainly in the fields of design and quality." *New York Times*, March 19, 1955.

[71] Cf. Paul M. Sweezy, "Demand Under Conditions of Oligopoly," *Journal of Political Economy* (August 1939).

tendency is greatly reinforced by the fact that financial groups interested in more than one large enterprise in an industry usually exercise their influence to forestall major capital losses that are bound to result from aggressive expansiveness on the part of an oligopolistic firm, and the eventual recovery of which must be always more or less uncertain.[72]

Abstinence from price competition and adherence to the principle of live and let live exercise a significant influence on the structure of oligopolistic industry. High-cost firms are not thrown out of the market, but are enabled to carry on beside more productive and more profitable enterprises. Consequently excess capacity that has developed either as the result of earlier economies of scale or in order to meet fluctuating demand does not have a tendency to be squeezed out of the industry. It remains not merely in the form of productive potentials of low-cost firms that are larger than they need be for their ordinary operations, but also in the form of high-cost establishments that are protected from stormy weather by the umbrella of the oligopolistic industry. Excess capacity in turn discourages new investment, particularly in an industry where its existence is well known in view of the small number of the relevant firms.

Thus the monopolist and oligopolist grows necessarily more cautious and circumspect in his investment decisions and finds *in any given situation* little inducement to plow back his profits into his own enterprise. His high profits may provide such inducement to a would-be investor. The appetite of the outsider is, however, effectively frustrated by the obstacles to entry into a monopolistic and oligopolistic industry as well as by his awareness that his arrival into that industry's market could not fail to affect unfavorably the existing price level. In other words, the would-be oligopolist no less than the established one has to think not so much in terms of what are the *actually* earned rates of return on capital already invested in the industry, but rather in terms of the *prospective* rates of profit on new investment. Where the possible outsider is himself a member of some oligopolistic industry, what was said before about the limitations on the struggle among oligopolists applies also here *mutatis mutandis*. An oligopolist trespassing into another oligopolistic industry would not only run the risk of retaliation in his own market on the part of some members of

---

[72] For this point cf. Hilferding, *Das Finanzkapital*, where attention is drawn to the habitual cautiousness of large-scale financial institutions and to their reluctance to engage in too risky gambles.

the invaded industry, but would also be likely to run foul of powerful financial interests involved simultaneously in a number of such industries.

Both the threat and the difficulty of such invasions play important roles in the policies of large-scale enterprise. The former may exercise a restraining effect on its lust for profits and induce it to charge lower prices and be content with lesser returns than would be compatible with the demand elasticity prevailing in the market for its product. More frequently, however, it serves as a powerful stimulus to fortify a monopolistic or oligopolistic firm's position in the market, to lead it to spend increasing amounts on advertising (thus strengthening the identification of its products), to enter vertical mergers, to develop and to multiply its links with financial institutions, and the like. The more successful it is in building such defenses, the less it need be afraid that its profits would tempt an outsider to try his luck in the monopolist's or oligopolist's preserve.

On the other hand, the difficulty of breaking into a monopolistic or oligopolistic industry greatly influences the monopolistic or oligopolistic firm's investment policy. Unable to invest its profits remuneratively in its own firm, prevented from investing them in other highly concentrated industries, the monopolistic or oligopolistic firm "suffocating" in its profits seeks to employ them in competitive industries or in such where the degree of concentration is relatively low. There it need not fear strong resistances, there is no danger of retaliation, there it is unlikely to encounter the restraining hand of financial institutions. Upon entering such an industry, the monopolistic and oligopolistic enterprise tends to shape that industry to its own likeness. Production becomes concentrated in relatively few large firms, modern technical devices are introduced, price, profit, and investment policies are streamlined in keeping with the practices prevailing in monopolistic and oligopolistic markets. The result is that monopoly and oligopoly spread from one branch of the economy to another, that large-scale enterprise takes over where small, competitive business used to be in control, and that the economy as a whole increasingly tends to become a system of monopolistic and oligopolistic empires each composed of relatively few giant enterprises.

It goes without saying that there are a number of industries which for technical reasons do not lend themselves to being operated by large-scale enterprise, and thus remain inaccessible to investment on the part of monopolistic and oligopolistic firms. Agriculture is probably an outstanding example, although even here large-scale enterprise plays an ever-increasing role, either as direct producer or as processor and distributor. There are other businesses that are not readily concentrated—predominantly found in the area of services. But also many seemingly independent businessmen or craftsmen are more or less well paid retainers of larger corporations, such as the cobbler operating a United Shoe machine or an automobile dealer holding a license of the General Motors Corporation.[73]

As the process of concentration advances, as one industry after another becomes "oligopolized," the competitive sector of the economy tends to be reduced to the technically determined rock bottom. What remains in it can no longer serve as an investment outlet for the overflowing profits of monopolistic and oligopolistic enterprise.[74]

There is, however, another outlet for these profits, an outlet that has played historically a major role. This is founding new industries which, like most parts of Africa in the early nineteenth century, are not yet appropriated by any great power and represent a no-man's land that is free for all. As mentioned above, this mode of utilization of the economic surplus is not foreclosed by technical possibilities. Such possibilities have always existed to a sufficient extent, and are at present, if anything, more ample than ever before. What limits the founding of new industries at the present time is the structure of the investment process. Only large-scale firms are in a position to raise the capital that is needed for the establishment of a new industry. These firms either themselves operate in monopolistic or oligopolistic industries, or—if they are financial institutions—are closely connected with such industries. Thus in deciding on whether to undertake the development of a new industry, they have to consider first and foremost

[73] Cf. the instructive book by C. Wright Mills, *White Collar: The American Middle Classes* (New York, 1951), *passim*, but in particular Parts One and Two.

[74] To be sure, the competitive sector remains large in terms of the number of people finding livelihood in it. In fact, it becomes increasingly crowded by small capitalists having no access to large-scale business, and by employees and workers unsuited, unwilling, or unable to join the ranks of the corporate labor force. Thus the profits earned in the competitive sector tend to be small, the efficiency of the small firm low, and prices high. Cf. N. Kaldor, "Market Imperfection and Excess Capacity," *Economica, New Series* (1935). It is interesting to note that to the extent that large corporations relieve themselves of some of their uninvestible profits by paying large dividends, this situation may tend to become aggravated since the extra dividends, particularly those accruing to small capitalists, are likely to seek investment precisely in the competitive sector of the economy.

whether that new industry will not compete with their established businesses. Clearly, a firm in one oligopolistic industry could promote the development of a new industry that would compete not with its own product but with that of a third party. Yet for reasons referred to before, such operations are looked at askance in the world of giant business and finance, and tend to be undertaken only on rare occasions.

VII

What is the upshot of this discussion? It may be briefly telescoped as follows: In the monopolistic phase of capitalist development the mechanism of equalization of the rates of profit operates only in the greatly compressed competitive sector of the economic system. There the rates of profit are low, and the mass of profits available for investment relatively small. In the monopolistic and oligopolistic sphere of the economy the rates of profit on invested capital are unequal but predominantly high and the mass of profit available for investment prodigiously large. This tends to reduce the volume of aggregate investment, since the relatively few monopolistic and oligopolistic firms to which the bulk of the profits accrues find it both unprofitable to plow them back into their own enterprises and increasingly difficult to invest them elsewhere in the economy. The latter becomes progressively harder as more and more of the competitive sector becomes "oligopolized" and as the chances of founding new industries that would not compete with established oligopolistic enterprises become slimmer. Thus *in any given situation* the volume of investment tends to be smaller than the volume of the economic surplus that would be forthcoming under full employment. There is consequently a tendency towards underemployment and stagnation, a tendency towards overproduction that was precisely identified by Marx a hundred years ago: "*General overproduction* occurs not because there is relatively too *little* produced of the workers' or of the capitalists' consumption goods, but because there is too much produced of *both*—too much that is *not for consumption*, but too much to maintain *the right relation between consumption and accumulation; too much for accumulation.*"[75]

While most if not all of the preceding argument can be found in one context or another in the writings of many economists, it is usually

---

[75] *Grundrisse der Kritik der Politischen Ökonomie* (Rohentwurf) (Berlin, 1953), pp. 346-347. (Italics in the original.)

given a different interpretation. It is argued, for instance, that it is only with the presence of monopoly that technical progress is at all possible in a capitalist economy. Neither an established capitalist nor a would-be investor would dream of risking a major capital commitment were he not protected against incipient competition by some bars to entry into his field of business. Furthermore, only a large-scale enterprise would be in a position to finance the outlays called for by modern technology. Finally, only big business could afford to maintain the research facilities that are indispensable for the advance of technology. In the light of the earlier discussion it would seem, however, that this line of reasoning entirely overlooks the historical dialectic of the whole process. There can be very little doubt that at a certain stage of capitalist development (fifty to eighty years ago) the growth of large-scale enterprise, of monopoly and oligopoly, was a *progressive* phenomenon *furthering* the advance of productivity and science. The evidence is equally clear that today this very same phenomenon tends to turn economically, socially, culturally, and politically into a *retrograde* force hindering and perverting further development. The fact that competition is not compatible with modern, technologically advanced production is by no means tantamount to the proposition that monopoly is a rational framework for the development of productive forces. And, as Lenin points out, ". . . if monopolies have now begun to retard progress, it is not an argument in favour of free competition, which has become impossible since it gave rise to monopoly."[76]

[76] E. Varga and L. Mendelsohn (eds.), *New Data for Lenin's Imperialism—The Highest Stage of Capitalism* (New York, 1940), p. 236.

FOUR

Standstill and Movement
Under Monopoly Capitalism, II

THE insufficiency of investment under monopolistic capitalism has been discussed thus far in static terms. It was stressed that in *any given situation* there is a lack of opportunity for remunerative plowing back of profits accruing to the capitalist enterprise. While the resulting "underemployment equilibrium" may be quite profitable, it can hardly be considered a satisfactory or stable situation. In the first place, it is highly frustrating to the capitalist whose element is the accumulation of capital, and whose *raison d'être* is not to clip coupons but continuously to increase his profits.[1] Worse still, the mere continuation of the "given situation" does not represent a practical option that is available for any length of time to the

---

[1] The changes in the structure of business management, its "bureaucratization" and "impersonalization," of which much has been made in recent literature, while of interest in a different context, hardly call for a reappraisal of the fundamental objectives of a capitalist enterprise. They may be quite significant, however, in accentuating the cautiousness and circumspection of a monopolistic and oligopolistic firm as compared with one operating under former competitive conditions. A survey of some of the relevant writings may be found in A. G. Papandreou, "Some Basic Problems in the Theory of the Firm," in *A Survey of Contemporary Economics* (B. F. Haley ed.) (Homewood, Illinois, 1952), Vol. II. Cf. also the brilliant essay by Paul M. Sweezy, "The Illusion of the Managerial Revolution," *Science & Society* (Winter 1942), reprinted in his *The Present as History* (New York, 1953).

capitalist class. Stagnating output necessarily implies a steadily growing volume of unemployment. For the mere replacement of worn-out
equipment by new and more efficient machinery, with or without some
net investment, increases the productivity of labor, and more or less
steadily displaces a certain proportion of the employed workers, while
the normal growth of the population increases the available labor
force year in and year out. It has been estimated that even in the
absence of *net* investment, the mere substitution of modern machinery
for worn-out equipment in the United States would cause an annual
productivity increase of approximately 1.5 percent. Accompanied by
an annual expansion of the labor force by over 1 percent, this would
imply that a simple reproduction of any given output necessarily
leads to an annual swelling of unemployment by over 2.5 percent of
the labor force. Needless to say, such snowballing of unemployment
would seriously threaten the social and political equilibrium of the
capitalist order, and render the "given situation" highly precarious.

Yet under monopolistic capitalism there is no strong tendency for
the *automatic* development of conditions that would permit breaking
out of the "given situation," and that would provide additional incentives for the investment of the economic surplus. Two such automatically appearing fields of maneuver were mentioned earlier: investment in competitive industries subject to monopolization and oli-
gopolization,[2] and development of new industries that can be created
without harm to the established (and powerful) monopolistic and
oligopolistic interests. But as these internal, as it were, reserves of the
system become progressively exhausted, the possibility of escaping the
"given situation" depends to an increasing extent on impulses from
outside the immediate market relationships of monopolistic capitalism. There is no clear dividing line between the automatically emerging and deliberately created outlets for the overflowing economic surplus. It is nevertheless of utmost importance—for reasons that should
become subsequently clear—to be fully aware of this distinction.

An obvious and "simple" way of providing an outside stimulus to
monopolistic enterprise and to widen the market for its output would
be an increase in consumption (as a ratio to total output). This would
on the one hand reduce the proportion of output constituting actual

---

[2] It should be noted that the unevenness of development within the
monopolistic and oligopolistic sector itself will frequently place a "backward" monopolistic or oligopolistic industry in the position of a competitive industry that can be invaded and streamlined by another, more advanced, more concentrated monopolistic or oligopolistic industry.

economic surplus, and on the other hand create investment opportunities resulting from expanding aggregate demand. Such a solution
is not generated, however, by an economic system in which the distribution of income as between capital and labor is determined by profit
maximization on the part of individual firms. As we have seen earlier,
the share of income accruing to labor tends to be rather stable;
there is no reason to suppose that there are any tendencies at work
that would cause significant changes in this respect. Individual firms
cannot be expected to function as Santa Claus to their workers and
buyers in order to increase mass consumption. What might be wholly
rational from the standpoint of the capitalist system as a whole would
spell losses or even bankruptcy if undertaken by the individual capitalist.

To be sure, an increase in aggregate consumption could result also
from an expansion of personal consumption on the part of the capitalists themselves. Such indeed has been the case; the form in which
it has occurred merits particular attention. Although the modern capitalists' standards of living and spending have greatly risen compared
with those of their forebears, the resulting increase in consumption
has been certainly not more, and probably less, than proportionate to
the growth of the economic surplus. For this there are compelling reasons. In the first place, the concentration of profits and dividends in
the hands of a relatively small number of stockholders places an
effective curb on the amount of consumption expenditure that can
be expected from that source. Not even the most extravagant of the
contemporary Croesuses can spend a large part of his income for
personal purposes. Moreover, the paradox that we have just encountered with regard to mass consumption appears even more strikingly
when it comes to capitalists' consumption. While for the stability of
the capitalist economy an increase in his consumption would be altogether advantageous, this cannot be a guiding principle in the life of
the individual capitalist. The harmony between puritanism and the
requirements of capitalist development that so powerfully advanced
the former and so felicitously served the latter breaks down under
conditions of monopoly capitalism and of overflowing economic surplus. Under such circumstances the interests of the individual capitalist no longer correspond to the interests of his class or those of
capitalist society as a whole. For him, accumulation and thrift are
still indispensable means to success and advancement, and lavish living beyond whatever happens to be the conventional level for people

in his group can be not only destructive of his capital but also damaging to his credit-worthiness and standing in the community.[3]

This contradiction between what is rational for the individual capitalist and what is called for by capitalist society as a whole cannot be resolved by an individual acting for himself. It can be overcome only by changes in the socioeconomic structure which in turn result in shifts in mores and values that determine the volitions and the behavior of individuals. It is to such a transformation of society that the bulk of the increase of unproductive outlays under monopoly capitalism must properly be ascribed. Its cause lies not in changes of the *individual* capitalist's income disposal habits, in his larger or smaller "propensity to consume"; there are strong indications that this propensity has been conspicuously stable over a long period of time. Its roots are the far-reaching changes in the structure of capitalist enterprise and the closely related shifts in the distribution and mode of utilization of the economic surplus. Indeed, the expenditures pattern of a monopolistic or oligopolistic firm bears little resemblance to what it was (and still is) in a comparatively small competitive business. Lavish salaries and bonuses for corporate executives, generous retainers for lawyers, public relations experts, advertising specialists, market analysts and lobbyists, vast outlays on sprawling bureaucracies, on representation, and business expenses, all these were unknown in the age of competitive capitalism and are still beyond the reach of the small fry operating in the competitive back yards of the advanced capitalist economy. Nor could the competitive businessman of old even dream of the tremendous sums assigned by giant corporations to foundations of various kinds the more or less overt purpose of which is to influence the makers of "public opinion" in favor

[3] There is, however, an important element of general rationality that reinforces the subjective rationality of the individual capitalist's relative abstemiousness. Where the class struggle is intense and the political stability of the capitalist order precarious, "indecent" display of wealth and "riotous" living would antagonize the underlying population, and are therefore considered to be in "bad taste." The simplicity and functionality of the façade become essential, and such excessive indulgences, frivolous spending, and profligacy as are engaged in by the top of the capitalist income pyramid are carefully hidden from the public eye. They take place in foreign centers of entertainment, in exclusive country estates, or in sumptuous town residences with deceptively simple exteriors. In countries and in historical periods in which social tension is less pronounced, this need for hypocrisy and concealment correspondingly subsides and "conspicuous consumption" becomes more apparent. The result is a decline in the standards of "good taste"—so frequently lamented by Europeans observing the demeanor of the socially more secure American upper class.

of monopoly capital. All this has become an integral part of the lore of monopoly capitalism and absorbs a large fraction of the vast share of the aggregate economic surplus that accrues to big business.[4] The extent to which the still growing contingent of unproductive workers directly or indirectly supported by society's economic surplus has grown under monopoly capitalism is hardly ever fully realized. "In 1929 for every 100 engaged in commodity production in the United States, 74 were otherwise employed. In 1939, for every 100 in commodity production 87 were otherwise employed. And by 1949, for every 100 in commodity production 106 were otherwise employed."[5]

Yet, vast as it is, corporate spending on unproductive purposes does not come even near providing a sufficient outlet for the overflowing economic surplus or to furnishing an adequate stimulus to additional investment by expanding aggregate demand. For much of what the corporations disburse to unproductive workers has come to be considered "necessary expenses" in the conduct of large-scale business, and is treated as part of overhead costs that have to be covered (at least in the long run) by the price of the product.[6] To this extent the maintenance of the unproductive workers does not come out of the profits of big business but is shifted to the buyers of its products. It

[4] As Marx foresaw, "bourgeois society reproduces in its own form everything against which it has fought in feudal or absolutist form." *Theories of Surplus Value* (London, 1951), p. 176. This points to a truly tragic dilemma continually confronting an advanced capitalist society. A *reduction* of the wasteful utilization of the economic surplus spells depression and unemployment. The increasingly indispensable *intensification* of the dissipation of the economic surplus on unproductive purposes results in an ever larger volume of conspicuous consumption, in a mushroom growth of the "entertainment industries" marketing their wares to captive audiences, in an accelerated decline of all standards of culture. Cf. the interesting article by Russell Lynes, "What's So Good About Good Times?" *Harper's Magazine* (June 1956), where the problem is well stated without being analyzed.

[5] Victor Perlo, *American Imperialism* (New York, 1951), p. 226. A note on the same page explains that "engaged in commodity production" includes employees in agriculture, mining, construction, manufacturing, transportation, communication, and public utilities as well as farm operators. For differently constructed estimates revealing, however, the same tendency, cf. C. Wright Mills, *White Collar: The American Middle Classes* (New York, 1951), Chapter 4.

[6] The principles of fixed mark-ups on average prime costs of a standard output have come increasingly to be recognized in economic literature as general rules of pricing in monopolistic and oligopolistic business. Their significance for the problem of shifting of unproductive expenditures as well as of tax liabilities is obvious. Cf. Elmer D. Fagan, "Impôt sur le revenu net des sociétés et prix," *Revue de Science et de Législation Financières*, Vol. XLVI, No. 4 (1954), as well as William H. Anderson, *Taxation and the American Economy* (New York, 1951), Chapter 16.

is of no less importance that a significant part of the income received by the normally well-looked-after beneficiaries of corporate generosity —the "new middle class"—is not spent on consumption but saved. The saving of this group accounts in fact for a large fraction of the *individual* saving that is currently undertaken in an advanced capitalist country. Thus the net effect of the proliferation of unproductive workers on capital accumulation and aggregate demand is not even suggested by the sum total of their income receipts. Part of the increase in aggregate consumption due to the maintenance of the unproductive workers is matched by a *decrease* of consumption on the part of the rest of the population, and is thus canceled out. Another part of that consumption increase, however, causes a reduction of saving among the rest of the population and therefore leads to a genuine absorption of economic surplus. On the other hand, a part of the economic surplus absorbed in this way, or because some of the income paid to the unproductive workers could not be shifted by their employers and was actually paid out of profits, reappears once more as economic surplus in the form of the unproductive workers' personal saving.

In fine, while the automatically working mechanism of monopoly capitalism has undoubtedly increased the unproductively utilized share of total product, this increase is not large enough to reduce sufficiently the volume of economic surplus available for investment under conditions of full employment or to create an adequate expansion of investment opportunities. More deliberate "outside impulses" are needed for the economy of monopoly capitalism to be able to move off dead center, to find the requisite incentives for a profitable utilization of the currently generated economic surplus.

II

These can only be provided by the state. Not that the state has not played a major role in economic life throughout the entire history of capitalism. Whether directly or indirectly, whether by subsidizing the construction of railroads as in Germany and the United States, or by promoting with suitable means the native capitalists' economic interests abroad as in Britain and Holland, or by elaborate financial transactions and imposition of tariffs as in France and Russia, the state everywhere had an important hand in determining the course and

role of the State: (Marx)

speed of economic development in the capitalist age. Yet in the beginning, the economic activities of the state were essentially of a sporadic
nature, addressed to specific economic issues or responding to more
or less general requirements of the capitalist class as a whole. Serving,
in the words of Marx and Engels, as "a committee for managing the
common affairs of the whole bourgeoisie," the state performed energetically and unequivocally its basic function: the maintenance and
protection of the capitalist order. As to its role in the strictly economic
sphere, matters were somewhat more complex.

Indeed, the "whole bourgeoisie" on whose behalf the government
was acting as its "committee" was a composite of a vast multitude of
businessmen appearing as a conglomeration of many different and
divergent groups and interests. What is most important, however, is
that these businessmen were relatively small, of approximately equal
strength and scope, with their industrial or regional groupings also of
similar power and influence. Under such circumstances the state could
live up to their *common* mandate of protecting and strengthening the
capitalist order itself against attacks on the part of the exploited
classes. It was not supposed to interfere with the relations among
individual groups or factions of the bourgeoisie, it was not supposed
to cater to the needs of one of them in its competitive struggle against
another. The equality or at least similarity of the weights that each
component of the bourgeoisie could throw upon the social and political scales tended to create an equilibrium of forces *within* the bourgeoisie and to make the state an instrument of the *entire* class. While
the political expression of this basic socioeconomic constellation appears in the classical mechanism of bourgeois democracy, the ideological formula for this neutrality of the state in the competitive struggle within the capitalist class is the belief in economic automaticity,
the creed of non-intervention of the state in the free play of market
forces. As Thomas Jefferson succinctly put it, the state was to guaran-
tee "equal rights for all, special privileges for none." Clearly, as long
as the pulling power of the contestants in the competitive struggle was
nearly equal, as long as no one could exercise a larger influence upon
the state than anyone else, both the reliance upon the automaticity of
the market and the insistence on the neutrality of the government
could be readily accepted by the entire capitalist class and thus unani-
mously elevated to the status of supreme social values.[7]

[7] The political usefulness of these concepts was greatly enhanced by
the fact that the impartiality of the government as between different parts

the state: changes since Marx

The crumbling of this structure became conspicuous with the advent of large-scale enterprise. The participants in the *bellum omnium contra omnes* not only became increasingly unequal in economic and social power, but big business in its ascent progressively undermined all ability and will to resist its dominance in the remainder of the capitalist class. By taking over one segment of the economic system after another, it transformed rising numbers of previously independent small businessmen, artisans, and farmers into employees and commissionmen of giant corporations. Although leaving them frequently with the illusion of being still on their own, monopolistic business made them depend to a growing extent for their livelihood and social status on the good will of corporate management.[8] From a full member of the capitalist class—small but in importance and weight second to none—the competitive businessman came to be a retainer of giant business, the economic, political, and social leadership of which he was not in a position to challenge. What was perhaps even more portentous, he increasingly lost the will to dispute it. Identifying himself with the feudal lords of monopoly capitalism, looking up to them as to heroic figures worthy of respect and emulation, the new social yeoman of the leaders of big business developed rapidly into the most important claque of the monopolistic elite of the capitalist class. As German peasants whose interests were diametrically opposed to those of the Junker faithfully followed the leadership of the aristocratic squires in the ranks of the famous *Landbund*, competitive business in the age of monopoly capitalism rides obediently on the coattails of the "economic royalists."

At first, monopoly capital's ascent to economic and social power did not imply a renunciation of the hallowed principles of rugged individualism, market automaticity, and government neutrality. On

of the bourgeoisie could be readily presented to the people at large as impartiality of the state as between different classes of society as a whole. Occasional governmental departures, such as factory legislation, restrictions on child labor, and the like—impartial with regard to the entire bourgeoisie because affecting all of its members—appeared to corroborate the view of the state as taking care also of the "lower classes." The Russian peasant who considered the czar to be an objective umpire between the landlord and himself is no less striking an example of the impact of this ideology than the American shopkeeper expecting the government to shield him against his monopolistic competitors.

[8] "The power of large businesses is such that even though many small businesses remain independent, they become in reality agents of larger businesses." C. Wright Mills, *White Collar: The American Middle Classes* (New York, 1951), p. 26.

the contrary, with those principles serving admirably as a smoke screen behind which they were able to amass vast fortunes and to obtain a firm grip on the state, the captains of monopolistic business spared no effort to advance and to further the ideology of the unhampered survival of the fittest. As Max Horkheimer astutely observes, throughout history "the value of the individual has been extolled by those who had an opportunity of developing their individualities at the expense of others."[9] Indeed, having attained the summit of the social pyramid, big business could not possibly find an ideological formula better suited to its requirements than the principle of the individual's unfettered freedom to make the utmost of such opportunities as might be available to him. Combined with the injunction that social interference with the individual's efforts should be kept down to a minimum, this principle not only sanctions inequality, privileges, and exploitation, but gives the victims of inequality, privileges, and exploitation a deep sense of the inevitability or even appropriateness of their fate. While in advanced capitalist countries the working class itself has been profoundly affected by this ideology, competitive businessmen, farmers, and other petty bourgeois were unable to resist it anywhere. Although gradually devoured by big business, although losing both their profits and their independence, they everywhere continued to consider themselves members of the capitalist class, a privileged stratum markedly superior to any mere proletariat. This actual or illusory sharing in the privileges, in the fruits of exploitation—even if its share was perceptibly declining —robbed the petty bourgeoisie of all moral and political independence, rendered it a willing tool in the hands of its new monopolistic masters.

Not that there was no opposition to this development. Yet this opposition was never very strong; it appeared in two clearly distinguishable currents. One was the populist demand for determined government action against the economic power of the few who were usurping the government for their own advantage. This drive was carried primarily by non-capitalist elements in society—workers, artisans, some farmers—and it enjoyed a measure of support among some segments of small competitive business. It was strongly imbued with the notions of Jeffersonian democracy, with the ideology of the state's impartiality towards *all* social classes, and it took for granted that the government would suppress the abuses of monopolistic busi-

[9] *Eclipse of Reason* (New York, 1947), p. 178.

ness with the same vigor it displayed in dealing with the nascent labor organizations. The outstanding achievement of this movement in the United States was the anti-trust legislation commissioning the government—increasingly subservient to big business—to curb the powers of big business.

The other, no less naive, trend of opposition—adhered to mainly by the competitive business community as well as by intellectuals brought up on the traditional tenets of *laissez faire* economics and bourgeois democracy—clamored for a return to the "good old days," insisted on honest and consistent respect for the principles of automaticity and non-intervention, and directed its wrath not so much against monopolistic business as against the government which it blamed for all evils.[10] Since it refrained from seriously attacking big business, this type of "loyal opposition" was particularly attractive to big business itself. Providing a harmless outlet for discontent and endangering none of big business's important positions, fitting in perfectly well with its own phraseology, this ideology of anti-statism and free competition was not only wholly compatible with the increasing hegemony of monopoly capital, but could also be turned to good use in warding off the populist type of opposition as well as all other social reform movements.

All these ideological and political currents are still with us, though their role and their coloration have changed greatly together with the underlying socioeconomic situation. The breakdown of the capitalist economy in the '30s irretrievably compromised the concept of market automaticity. In view of the catastrophic decline of output and income, it has become impossible to maintain that the capitalist system, if left to itself, tends to generate the greatest welfare for the greatest number. Nor could it any longer be held that the market mechanism gave to all the "fit" an opportunity of getting ahead and of making good—in the face of the multitudes of men and women willing and able to work but without a chance of finding a job. The need for some action of the government to mitigate at least the most outrageous aspects of the situation became imperative. Whether through public works or through relief payments to the unemployed, whether through subsidies to the farmers or through doles to veterans, the government had to step in if the economic breakdown was not to lead to

[10] This anti-statism linked up with the entire tradition of the bourgeoisie's political struggle against feudalism, and was particularly near to the hearts of European immigrants to the United States whose hatred of their tyrannical governments at home was the outstanding feature of their ideological luggage.

a collapse of the capitalist order. The energies of the social forces
that were traditionally in favor of government intervention, the mounting despair of the non-capitalist strata least affected by the ideology
of automaticity and government neutrality (or most readily able to
shed it under the impact of the surrounding reality) had to be given
an outlet compatible with the preservation of the capitalist system.
The New Deal in the United States performed this function fully. At
the very low cost of government recognition and protection of labor
unions, institution of systematic supports for the farmers, and some
social security legislation and moderate supervision of financial markets, President Roosevelt's first administration was able to avert political and social upheavals that might have shaken the foundations of
capitalism itself.

So serious was the crisis, so thoroughgoing the bankruptcy of the
notions of automaticity and government non-intervention, that even
monopolistic business had to readjust its public philosophy. This
obviously did not happen overnight, and even now there is still a
sizable segment of the big business community that appears to have
remained unaffected by the earthquake of the '30s. In its leading
echelons, however, big business opinion shifted actually quite rapidly
to new ideological positions. The transition was greatly facilitated by
the remarkable fact that it hardly involved a genuine ideological
change.[11]

[11] It is in fact doubtful whether the term "ideology," as conventionally
used in the sociology of knowledge, is at all applicable under monopoly
capitalism. While denoting an inadequate, partial, biased conception of
reality, with this inadequacy, partiality, and bias imputable to the structure of society and to the place occupied in it by a class, "ideology" has
two important characteristics. Its inadequacy, partiality, and bias that
render it a half-truth make it partake at the same time of truth itself.
It encompasses in other words an aspect of truth by expressing certain
views of reality and certain interests in reality shared by a class or
stratum of society. For this very reason an "ideology" is firmly *believed*
in by those who espouse it; it is not something that they can shed, change,
or adjust at will. In that sense "ideology" is akin to Freud's "rationalization," except that the former is seen as emerging from the structure of
society, the latter from the psychic structure of the individual (in turn,
however, determined by the society in which he lives). An entirely
different entity is a set of inadequate, partial, biased notions that is
consciously implanted in the minds of men by a manipulative effort of a
class, bent on achieving certain ends by inducing its more or less general
acceptance. Thus in the age of monopoly capitalism, in which beliefs,
values, convictions are increasingly succumbing to the pragmatist attack,
ideology yields rapidly to mass-conditioning, adjustment, etc., with the
proper study of the subject moving away from the sociology of knowledge
into the realm of manipulative opinion research. As Engels brilliantly

Earlier monopolistic business extolled automaticity and government neutrality not because *it* firmly believed in them but because, accepted and cherished both by the capitalist class as a whole and by the majority of the underlying population, they offered the most convenient screen for ever-increasing penetration of the government by giant corporations. That philosophy had now outlived its usefulness. Its substantive inadequacy became manifest, its political serviceability for mass consumption accordingly all but vanished, while such sectors of competitive business as were still clinging to the old notions were rapidly becoming a negligible quantity. Indeed, the program of full employment to be assured by appropriate government action that took the place of rugged individualism and government neutrality had all the virtues of what it displaced and none of its obvious drawbacks. It removed the onus for the malfunctioning of the economy from the capitalist class and placed it upon society at large and its expendable political functionaries; it provided an attractive ideology for the newly arrived labor unions; it satisfied the requirements of the farmers; it beaconed high profits to monopoly capital and promised at the same time good incomes to the growing, politically and socially important "new middle class." What may look astonishing, in fact, is not the alacrity with which the most farsighted leaders of big business shifted their allegiance to the new course but rather the relative slowness with which many others dragged themselves over to the new positions.

The reason for this is, however, rather simple. Apart from the "cultural lag" inevitably arising when time-honored mental constructs have to yield to the changing realities of the historical process, there was an important objective justification for caution and circumspection in embracing the "new course." Being better historians and social scientists than many who are professionally so engaged, the leaders of monoply capital understood full well that what mattered was not the theory of the new course nor even the complex web of government agencies created to implement it but the basic question as to who would effectively control its execution.[12] What to some economists viewing reality through their blinkers appears to be a secondary side

perceived, "ideology is a process accomplished by the so-called thinker consciously, indeed, but with a false consciousness. The real motives impelling him remain unknown to him, otherwise it would not be an ideological process at all." Letter to Mehring, July 14, 1893, in Marx and Engels, *Selected Correspondence* (New York, 1934), p. 511.

[12] As Schumpeter saw clearly, "the personnel and methods by which and the spirit in which a measure or a set of measures is administered are much more important than anything contained in any enactment." *Business Cycles* (New York, 1939), Vol. II, p. 1045.

issue was astutely sensed by monopoly capital as the heart of the entire matter. It was the supreme manifestation of big business power and of Roosevelt's inability to resist it, as soon as the worst was over, that as early as in the beginning of his second term individuals enjoying the trust of big business began to displace the suspect elements swept into office by the populist wave of 1932. It was not, however, until the war and the subsequent administrations of Presidents Truman and Eisenhower that corporate control over the government was fully re-established, and that the government even in its personal composition became once more the "committee" no longer of "the bourgeoisie as a whole" but of its decisive element, monopolistic and oligopolistic business.

Once the dominance of monopoly capital over the way in which the new course was to be followed was unequivocally enforced, once the groups were eliminated from government that tried—essentially in vain—to promote social reform under the guise of full employment policies, once the conduct of the "full employment" policies was placed in hands wholly acceptable to big business, then even the laggard contingents in the monopolistic camp found their way to subscribing to the new line. And with this backing came a vigorous campaign to sink it into the consciousness of the masses, to make it an ideological structure tying the people to the capitalist system, to give it as much force and stability as was previously enjoyed by the notions of automaticity and government neutrality. It is this acceptance on the part of monopoly capital of the so-called full employment policy, together with the capacity of this program to satisfy at the present time the needs of the majority of the nation, that create the atmosphere of unanimity on the political scene, an atmosphere undisturbed by the continuing presence of the still underfed, underclad, and underhoused, and by the barely hidden instability of the prevailing prosperity. J. K. Galbraith is entirely right in observing that "much of our debate is loud and violent, not because the issues are close but because they are not. There is anger not because issues are being settled but because they are settled. The noise, nonetheless, leaves the impression that the matter is still in doubt. Although a vehement argument may mean that an important question is being decided, it far more frequently means only that a hopelessly outnumbered minority is making itself felt in the only way it can."[13]

He is right, however, only in one sense. Many issues are indeed

[13] *Economics and the Art of Controversy* (New Brunswick, New Jersey, 1955), p. 103.

settled insofar as the program of government intervention for full
employment is embraced by the dominant segment of the ruling class,
by the dominant trade union stratum of labor as well as by the new
middle class, by most farmers, intellectuals, and the like. In fact, as
Galbraith correctly notes, the choice "whether a government [faced
with the reality of a depression] shall be Keynesian or not . . . comes
to nothing more or less than a choice of whether or not to commit
political suicide."[14] This is only one aspect, however, and not even
the most important aspect of the story. Actually, the conspicuous
sound and fury generated in public debates of relatively minor matters,
as well as the underlying agreement on the more significant issue of
the necessity for a government full employment policy, both obscure
the really serious questions as to the meaning of full employment and
as to the ways and means by which government intervention is to
attain and to maintain it.

For one thing should be clearly realized: the drive of monopoly
capital to secure control over the state, to concentrate in its hands the
conduct of such government intervention in economic affairs as may
be required, to eliminate from the government all elements even
slightly tainted by inclination toward a reformist interpretation of
full employment policies—this drive does not stem from monopoly
capital's lust for power, or from its avidity for public office.[15] Actually, under different conditions, monopoly capital preferred to keep
itself out of the limelight of political life, to remain in the background pulling invisible wires behind its "powerful" puppets. It is
only when the operations of the government assume paramount importance, when what is involved can no longer be trusted to shifty
politicians and second-rate agents, that the leading echelon of monopoly capital moves openly into the center of the stage. Because what
is at stake is the most vital interests of monopoly capital, which
concern, indeed, its very existence.

[14] *Ibid.*, p. 100.
[15] Not to speak of the superficiality, if not outright meaninglessness,
of the currently fashionable explanation of historical events by "lust for
power" which is treated as if it were an inherent instinct of the species
man. Apart from the fact that such "lust for power" as may characterize
men is in itself a historical category calling for explanation rather than
invocation like a *deus ex machina*, the important question is, what
sociopolitical forces and economic interests underlie the drive for power
on the part of nations, classes, and even ambitious individuals.

III

The management of governmental intervention for the attainment and maintenance of full employment involves a number of distinct, if closely interrelated, problems. In most general terms: if aggregate demand, that is, the demand of consumers, investors, and the government, falls short of the aggregate output under conditions of full employment, the government is confronted with five different possibilities (or some combination of them). The first one is to admit of whatever unemployment may develop, and to allow output to correspond to such a volume of effective demand as may be forthcoming in the market. As we have seen before, the manifest irrationality and the social and political explosiveness of this course render it unacceptable not merely to society as a whole but to all the decisive parts and factions of the capitalist class. Yet the rejection of this alternative leaves the question entirely open as to what is to be meant by full employment. Far from being a semantic quibble, what is at issue is of far-reaching importance. Full employment has been defined in economic literature as a condition in which everybody who is able and willing to work at the going rate of pay should be in a position to secure employment. What this actually implies is that the number of vacancies should normally somewhat exceed the number of job seekers, that the labor market should be as a rule a seller's market.[16]

Once again, however: the leaders of monopoly capital have a much better instinct for the working principles of the capitalist economy than the professional economists who consider full employment, as just defined, to be a realistic goal under capitalism. The leaders of monopoly capital are fully aware of the fact that full employment of this kind is incompatible with the normal functioning of the capitalist system. For under conditions of permanent labor scarcity, capitalist

---

[16] This still leaves room for what is called "frictional unemployment," which may be due to seasonal factors, to the movement of people from one locality to another, to changes in technology or in industrial structure, and the like. Such unemployment, usually treated by economists as insignificant and inevitable, is actually quite sizable, and in a planned economy could be markedly reduced by facilitating the necessary reallocation and retraining of manpower, by anticipating technological developments, etc. Nor should the serious mistake be made of equating full employment, even as defined above, with *rational* employment, since the former is wholly compatible with the maintenance of unproductive activities of all kinds.

enterprise has to operate under severe pressure: marginal or even submarginal workers have to be kept on the payroll even when their contribution to the firm's output is relatively small; the task of supervision becomes more burdensome and costs tend to rise. What is worse still, in a seller's market for labor it becomes increasingly difficult to curb the aspirations of the trade unions, and to keep their demands for higher wages, better working conditions, and other fringe benefits within "reasonable" limits. The continuous existence of an industrial reserve army is indispensable to keep labor in its place, to assure the work discipline of the capitalist enterprise, to preserve the command position of the entrepreneur by safeguarding his fundamental source of power and profit: the ability to hire and fire.[17]

Thus a government controlled by monopoly capital will not conduct its full employment policies so as to maintain genuinely full employment.[18] Accordingly, in the United States, the Employment Act of 1946—widely acclaimed as the Magna Charta of full employment —declares it to be a continuous responsibility of the government "to use all practicable means . . . for the purpose of creating and maintaining in a manner calculated to foster and promote free competitive enterprise . . . maximum employment." The level of employment to be striven for is thus clearly no higher than what will "foster and promote free competitive enterprise," while "free competitive enterprise" has become the usual urbane and tactful designation for monopolistic and oligopolistic business.

What matters, however, are not statutes or pronouncements of business or government spokesmen. Deeds are more eloquent than words: at the first major occasion thus far for the philosophy of the new course to be applied in practice—the marked rise of unemployment in the summer of 1953—the government and the big business circles on whose behalf it acts made their understanding of the term

[17] "Unemployment remains too low for the work force to have flexibility. Anytime the jobless total is less than 2 million, even common labor is scarce. Many employers must tend to hoard skills. And certainly, the labor unions are in the driver's seat in wage negotiations. More workers can be had, to be sure. But only at considerable cost. And they probably wouldn't be of the skills most desired. There's no assurance against inflation like a pool of genuine unemployment. That's a blunt, hard-headed statement, but a fact." *Business Week*, May 17, 1952.

[18] "On an average of good and bad years (statistical) unemployment should be higher than five to six million—seven to eight perhaps. This is nothing to be horrified about . . . because adequate provision can be made for the unemployed." Schumpeter, *Capitalism, Socialism and Democracy* (New York, 1950), p. 383. Cf. also John Jewkes, *Ordeal by Planning* (New York, 1948), pp. 78 ff., for similar views and estimates.

"full employment" abundantly clear. They permitted the existence of unemployment numbering approximately 5 million people.[19] Nor is this by any means the result of unfortunate accidents or of "insufficient knowledge" on the methods of dealing with growing unemployment. That the maintenance of some such "healthy" amount of unemployment is deliberate policy can be seen with all clarity even through the fog of bombastic phraseology that fills the Council of Economic Advisers' *Economic Report for 1955:* "It is necessary to recognize that, at times, growth processes may falter . . . increased knowledge on the part of the public should, however, be accompanied by a realistic understanding of the practical difficulties in attaining increases in total production, employment, and personal income, entirely free from interruptions. . . . Statesmanship requires that we make every effort to harness the idealism of our generation to the practical end of minimizing economic fluctuations. . . ."[20] Meanwhile, however, "we should direct our program for 1955 principally to [fostering long-term economic growth] rather than seek to impart an immediate upward thrust to general economic activity." (P. 48.) And "fostering long-term economic growth" is to consist in promoting "free, competitive enterprise" and "a feeling of confidence in the economic future . . . widely shared by investors, workers, businessmen, farmers and consumers." (P. 2.)

Monopoly capital's embrace of "full employment" becomes thus a kiss of death. What it implies is not a government policy towards the attainment and maintenance of full employment as conceived of by well-meaning economists or as dreamt of by "starry-eyed" social reformers: its goal is avoidance of *major* catastrophes such as the crash in 1929-1933, its end is prevention of *major* depressions such as characterized all the '30s. It does not aim at the elimination of "normal" crises or at abolition of "normal" unemployment. These in fact are considered to be "healthy readjustments," desirable not merely for the preservation of the indispensable industrial reserve army but also as welcome conditions under which monopolistic and oligopolistic firms can pick up bargains, swallow up weaker competitors, and consolidate their market positions.[21]

To be sure, unemployment and decline of income must not be per-

[19] *Report of the Joint Committee on the Economic Report*, on the January 1955 Economic Report of the President (Washington, 1955), pp. 95 ff.

[20] Pp. 65 ff.

[21] The wave of mergers that swept the American economy during the 1953-1954 recession provides an excellent illustration of this point.

mitted to go too far lest the political repercussions become dangerous to the stability of the system. Public works, relief payments and doles of various kinds have to be kept in readiness to alleviate extreme distress and to bribe the victims of the "readjustment" so that "confidence" should not be lost in "an economic system that is at once strong and humane, a system that can provide both greater material abundance and a better quality of living."[22] The limits to unemployment and loss of output that have to be tolerated are drawn not by the vaunted "dignity of the individual" or by the no less intensely advertised solicitude for the starving people in the world's underdeveloped countries; those limits are dictated by the requirements and convenience of big business, and by the readiness of people to endure the hypocrisy and the irrationality of an economic order governed by the interests of monopoly capital.

Another possibility would be a reduction of output by a general shortening of the number of working hours. It should be obvious that this method of creating an equilibrium between aggregate demand and aggregate supply—that is, by reduction of total output together with the maintenance of full employment—would be rational only if the inability of the prevailing effective demand to absorb the full employment output produced with the *given* work week were to express a *genuine* satiety of people with regard to all goods and services, be it for consumption or for investment. That such a satiety would not yet exist—even with an equal distribution of income—requires no elaboration. What is more, if it did exist, the capitalist system would admit of a general shortening of the work week only very slowly, and only under severe pressure. For, as far as the individual capitalist enterprise is concerned, a reduction of the work week resulting in a curtailment of output would imply a reduction of profits. As a matter of historical fact, the reduction of working hours from the earlier 16 to 14 to 12 hours a day to the present 40 hours a week (in the United States) has been achieved only against tenacious opposition on the part of the capitalist class, and reflected an intensification of labor and increases in productivity that took place in the course of a century as well as the emergence of a powerful labor movement that could no longer be resisted.[23] There can be no doubt that at the present time

[22] Council of Economic Advisers, *Economic Report for 1955*, p. 3.
[23] Even so, only particularly felicitous political and economic constellations accounted for most victories won by social reform. These were in part temporary alliances between feudal elements in society and the rising labor movement cemented by common hostility towards the capitalist

further statutory reduction of the work week would be fought by
capitalist interests no less strenuously than before. Moreover, if such
a reduction of the number of working hours were not matched by at
least a corresponding increase in productivity, and therefore actually
resulted in an absolute curtailment of total output (the only case that
is relevant to this discussion), there is every probability that a large
share, if not all, of it would be shifted to aggregate wages, in other
words, would have to be absorbed by the working class. Under such
circumstances, a further shortening of the labor week would neither
solve the problem of the overflowing economic surplus nor be acceptable to labor. Thus, apart from the fact that there is still a long way
to go until productivity has reached the state in which in a rationally
ordered society there would be no want left that is more urgent than
the want for leisure, in which therefore curtailment of output would
be the appropriate procedure, it is impossible that under capitalism
the continuously present problem of potential overproduction could be
resolved—even partly—by a *voluntary* reduction of the work week.
An attempt to enforce such a reduction on the part of the government
—if such an attempt could be expected at all from a government
dominated by the capitalist class—would encounter bitter opposition
not merely on the part of business but also on the part of labor that
could ill afford a cut in real wages.

With the voluntary curtailment of output thus neither possible nor
desirable, a government-promoted equilibration of aggregate demand
with aggregate output (on a predetermined level of employment)
could assume the form of government spending on additional consumption, individual and/or collective. Indeed, government disburse-
ment of funds to people unable to satisfy their consumption requirements could not fail to increase aggregate effective demand. Such disbursements could take any number of forms, and be directed either
towards individuals enjoying less than a stipulated level of income or
towards special groups of the population such as farmers, industrial
workers, veterans, college students, or parents of many (or few) children. The only requirement, in order that this kind of spending result
in a relatively large increase in total income and employment, is that

---

class (as in Great Britain, Bismarck Germany, and some other European
countries), in part major crises of the capitalist order that furnished
opportunities for wresting major concessions from a weakened and
frightened bourgeoisie (as in the United States in the 1930s).

the initial beneficiaries be people with a high marginal propensity to spend, i.e. belong to the lower income groups of the population.

However, except under conditions of severe crisis, large-scale subsidies to individual consumption are altogether inconsistent with the spirit of capitalism and most unattractive to dominant interests. Such subsidies would entail a number of repercussions highly detrimental to the normal functioning of the capitalist order. Not only would unrequited government remittances to individuals tend to raise the floor under the wage level, providing the wage earner with a subsistence minimum regardless of employment and thereby changing his relative valuation of income and leisure, but, what is perhaps no less important, such unearned receipts would be wholly alien to the fundamental system of ethics and values associated with the capitalist system. The principle that the ordinary man has to earn his bread in the sweat of his brow is cement and mortar to a social order the cohesion and functioning of which are predicated upon monetary penalties and monetary rewards. Reducing the necessity to work for a living, the distribution of a large volume of free goods and services would inevitably undermine the social discipline of capitalist society and weaken the positions of social prestige and social control crowning its hierarchical pyramid.[24]

Since these considerations apply to a much less extent to government contributions to *collective* consumption, spending on such purposes is considered to be a more respectable method of priming the pump. Involving, as it usually does, construction, it adds more directly than contributions to individual consumption to the demand for the output of heavy industries and in many cases provides them with valuable "external economies." Building new roads in the right locations has clearly such favorable implications, and properly placed post offices, schools, hospitals, and the like may be of considerable usefulness to business enterprise. Whether rendering their services gratuitously, as is sometimes the case, or only against payment of fees, such collective-consumption establishments have neither the material

---

[24] It is for this reason that when subsidies to individual consumption are undertaken in situations requiring the alleviation of supreme distress, the receipt of such benefits is associated with serious social opprobrium. What was true about the notorious poorhouses in Britain one hundred years ago is equally true of modern conditions, even though the large increase in the number of people who have had at one time or another to draw on public relief has rendered the disgrace connected with it somewhat more bearable to the individuals involved.

nor the ideological drawbacks of subsidies to individual consumption. They neither affect negatively the willingness to work on the part of labor nor its price, and they do not interfere with the sovereign rule of the golden calf.

The amount of money that the government can spend for such purposes is, however, somewhat limited. There is in the first place serious resistance on the part of upper income strata to supporting with taxes the establishment of facilities of which they themselves will not make much use.[25] Some of the collective-consumption establishments interfere, moreover, with powerful vested interests: low-cost housing and slum clearance, for instance, are bitterly fought by the real estate lobby. Furthermore, the scope of such a program is narrowly circumscribed at any time by the potential of the construction industry. To be sure, that potential can be expanded, but such expansion may be difficult in the short run in view of the immobility of various resources and the temporary nature of the projects involved. Construction firms could not be easily induced to undertake major investments knowing that their business might fall off sharply within a few years. And, at the present time in most countries, if not everywhere, a large expansion of collective-consumption establishments is likely to be in any case highly irrational in terms of the existing social priorities. There is no justification for building additional roads or monuments when there is a crying need for slum clearance, for schools, or for food and clothing; nor is there any justification for transferring tailors to construction work if there is a long-run need for the development of the garment industry. While government spending on collective consumption is thus more sensible than outlays on mere "leaf-raking," i.e. on utterly useless enterprises which merely provide wages to individuals uselessly engaged, its rationality may be questionable. What may be even of larger "practical" significance, it can hardly attain magnitudes sufficient to absorb a major part of the economic surplus.

This brings us to the fourth possible method of government intervention: investment in productive facilities. For if neither a planned

[25] This applies obviously also to government subsidies to *individual* consumption. The vociferous opposition from these quarters to government support of education is an excellent example of this attitude. Interestingly enough, this opposition comes not so much from big business circles, where the value of a well-trained labor force is more or less clearly understood, as from smaller business which is much less given to thinking in such "global" terms.

curtailment of total output nor a sufficient increase of current consumption are feasible, expanded investment represents the only rational way in which aggregate utilization of output could be brought up to the level of aggregate supply under conditions of full employment. Yet it hardly needs stressing that of all conceivable ways of government spending, this is the one that is completely taboo under the regime of monopoly capital. Indeed, all the considerations that prevent monopolistic business from itself investing its overflowing profits preclude a fortiori its tolerating such investment on the part of the government. Whether such government investment should be directed towards the monopolistic or oligopolistic industries where it is being held down by the profit maximization policies of the firms involved, or whether it should aim at the development of new industries either themselves attractive to monopoly capital or the output of which might compete with that of existing big business—it is equally intolerable to the dominant interests.

Where the government is "permitted" to invest is in areas that are as yet so far removed from all commercial exploitation as to be of no relevance to big business interests. In fact, there the government's taking over the costs and risks of exploration and experimentation is encouraged by monopoly capital. Yet if and when the initial phases of such undertakings prove successful, their further development and the profits resulting therefrom have to be turned over promptly to private enterprise.[26]

What remains, then, is the fifth possibility of government action: exhaustive government expenditures neither on objects of individual

---

[26] "The opponents of giving free enterprise greater latitude in the atomic energy program point to the nearly 13 billions of dollars that will have been spent in the field of atomic energy by the American taxpayers, including this fiscal year. They cry aloud that it would be foolhardy to turn over such an investment to private enterprise. . . . We should not forget the billions of dollars of tax money spent in developing the airplane, the turbine and diesel engines, and in many other fields of industrial development, that were later turned over to free enterprise for further improvement and development for the benefit of mankind. . . . Because of the terrific cost in the beginning, private industry may not be able to shoulder the burden. This means that the government will have to share the initial costs during the experimental years. However, after acquiring the necessary knowledge and experience, the genius of our American free enterprise system will enable it to do as it has on other occasions when working with the government, and take over the industrial development program." Address by Representative James E. Van Zandt, member of the Joint Congressional Committee on Atomic Energy, at 18th Congress of American Industry, sponsored by the National Association of Manufacturers, December 4, 1953 (quoted in *Monthly Review*, May 1954).

or collective consumption nor on useful investment, but on unproductive purposes of all kinds. This avenue of government spending is, indeed, the widest of all, and in all respects the most significant. It overshadows by far all the other positions of the government budget taken together, and constitutes the main "outside impulse" preventing the economy of monopoly capitalism from lingering in the "given situation," and enabling it at times to generate conditions of prosperity and relatively high employment. This outlet for the overflowing economic surplus of an advanced capitalist country is associated with its international relations. In view of their paramount importance these call for a somewhat more detailed discussion.

IV

When speaking before of the possibilities of equating aggregate demand with aggregate output, the reference was to what in economic literature is usually conceived of as a "closed system." Yet once the international economic relations of an advanced capitalist country are taken into account, the situation presents itself in a somewhat different light. To be sure, foreign trade provides an outlet for the economic surplus only if exports are undertaken in exchange for monetary gold or if the proceeds are invested abroad. If the exports are compensated for by imports, there is prima facie no change in the size of the national income and correspondingly no change in the volume of the economic surplus. Nonetheless even the mere exchange of exports for imports is of vital importance to a number of countries. Indeed, in many countries the mere maintenance of the "given situation" is possible only if there is sufficient, albeit balanced, foreign trade. It is only via foreign trade that they can obtain the *physical assortment* of goods that is required by the structure of their production, consumption, and investment. What is more, by opening up sources of new, cheaper, or better raw materials, fuel, and so forth, even balanced foreign trade may give rise to new industries, new technology, or new products that may stimulate additional investment. Similarly, by expanding the market for the products of individual firms, foreign trade may cause increases in output and investment that otherwise would not take place.[27] Still, the significance of foreign trade as a dynamic

---

[27] Under conditions of *balanced trade*, the effect of this on the economy as a whole is, however, less certain, since the expansion in the exporting industries may well be offset by the contraction in the industries affected by the entry of imported goods into their markets.

factor, as the source of an impetus helping the capitalist economy to break out of the "given situation," lies primarily in its providing the mechanism for capital exports.[28]

This is, however, only a part, and not even the decisive part, of the story. In a capitalist country foreign trade, like any other trade, is carried on by individual firms, and individual firms cannot be guided in their activities by "global" considerations, by concern with the impact of their operations on the economy as a whole. If the effect of the individual firm's transactions on national income and employment is to be understood, the question that has to be answered is what are the results that may be expected from the interplay of these transactions under different historical circumstances.

Under competitive capitalism businessmen were anxious to sell their wares abroad. If prices on foreign markets were more tempting than those at home, and the expected returns higher, competitive firms made all efforts to enter those markets and thus to increase their average profits. They were similarly anxious to procure from foreign countries raw materials and products of any kind if such imports could be profitably sold on domestic or international markets. Under competitive conditions there was, however, a certain automatic mechanism at work that imposed a serious limitation on such foreign trade activity. That barrier was the balance of international payments. If capitalists of one country tended to export to another country more than they imported from that country, there was a more or less rapid and more or less automatic reaction to the developing balance of payments' disequilibrium. Either changes in the level of economic activity or the outflow of gold from the deficit country led to a lowering of its price level and thus discouraged imports (and encouraged exports), or a depreciation of its currency (and possibly suitable shifts in its tariff structure) accomplished the same end. The individual capitalists in both countries—the surplus as well as the deficit countries—were normally not in a position to influence this development, and had to accept it willy-nilly as a datum with which they had to reckon.

Similarly, such capital exports as took place under competitive capitalism were in the main outcomes of a multitude of relatively small capital movements. Indeed, competitive firms each endowed

---

[28] The importation of monetary gold differs in many respects from capital exports. Its volume is naturally limited, it constitutes no act of investment to an individual firm, yields accordingly no returns, etc. Nevertheless, in the present context it may be treated as equivalent to capital exports.

with relatively little capital could not typically engage in capital exports; whatever capital exports there were resulted primarily from more or less accidental historical constellations. Thus Britain's capital exports in the earlier part of the nineteenth century were closely related to the migration of British nationals to various parts of the Empire (where they settled with the help of moneys brought from home) and to activities of venturesome merchants employing their capital abroad as short-term revolving funds.[29] Of a not much different nature was the "portfolio" investment based upon the acquisition of stock in enterprises of one country by residents of another country. None of this attained major proportions and none of it represented a systematic effort at investment abroad.

Under monopolistic capitalism, in this as in many other respects, matters have assumed an altogether different complexion. The monopolistic and oligopolistic firm operating under conditions of rapidly decreasing costs is even more anxious than its competitive predecessor to expand its sales abroad. In fact, even if the prices prevailing in foreign markets are lower than those at home, it may find it profitable to push its exports and to engage in price discrimination since such discriminatory price reductions will not affect its domestic market position. At the same time, engaged in mass production, and being a large-scale buyer of raw materials, it must take more than incidental interest in the supply and the price of such imports as may be indispensable to the conduct of its business. It must seek to maintain and to develop foreign sources of supply and endeavor to secure as nearly as possible a monopsonistic position with the help of investments in the "source countries"—investments that it can readily afford in view of the large amounts of capital at its disposal.

Indeed, what confronted (and still confronts) a small competitive firm as an immutable datum is now subject to manipulation by a giant corporation. The more or less automatically functioning balance of payments mechanism, that equilibrated import and export activities of innumerable firms and short-term and long-term movements of a multitude of relatively small capital amounts, no longer represents an objective handicap to the efforts of a monopolistic or oligopolistic

[29]Cf. the interesting article by Ragnar Nurkse, "The Problem of International Investment Today in the Light of Nineteenth-century Experience," *Economic Journal* (December 1954). Needless to say, the discussion here does not refer to governmental borrowing from other governments or in private capital markets that was motivated for the most part by political and military considerations.

firm. If its export drive should run into the obstacle of the importing country's balance of payments deficits, it is capable of extending massive credits to its buyers, or of inducing powerful financial institutions, to which it is related, to help furnish the required financing. If the importing country's government should contemplate a devaluation of its currency or other import-restricting measures, the firm can exercise its own influence or organize joint pressure by a number of large-scale concerns to prevent such inimical departures. If the raw materials of which it may be in need should be in short supply in the source country or should gravitate towards some other export market, it can make large capital investments in that source country, thus securing those raw materials for itself.

Not that capital exports under monopolistic capitalism are plain sailing and can readily assume ever larger proportions. On the contrary, not only do some of the forces hampering investment at home also curtail it abroad, but many additional roadblocks stand in the way of private capital exports. For the drive of monopolistic and oligopolistic firms (and the financial groups related to them) to invest abroad is necessarily closely circumscribed by their general business policies. They are rarely inclined to sink their funds into the construction of plants and facilities abroad that would cater to the requirements of foreign markets. Quite naturally they prefer to export to those markets their own products the marginal costs of which tend to be very low. Nor is their interest in the development of foreign raw materials such as to induce them to promote their optimal output. The amount of investment that is undertaken in this area depends rather on the quantity of raw materials that the investing corporation can use in its own plants or profitably dispose of in its own country or elsewhere.

This implies, however, that the familiar principles of profit maximization under conditions of monopoly and oligopoly—not "spoiling the market," not engaging in cut-throat competition with powerful rivals, and the like—are as pertinent to foreign investment as they are to domestic investment. And it is evident that the larger the relevant firms, the greater their significance in their national economies or in any particular branch of the world economy, the more able they are to assess the structure of any particular market, and the more circumspect and cautious they will be in their investment decisions.

In addition to these "normal" handicaps to investment there are, however, in the case of foreign investment other impediments that are no less telling. Even where investment abroad appears promising to a corporation in an advanced capitalist country, it has to be considered in the light of the political and social uncertainties associated with foreign ventures. These uncertainties have markedly increased in the age of imperialism, wars, and national and social revolutions, and the resulting riskiness of capital exports greatly reduces their attractiveness to possible investors. Fears of military conflagration, of "riot, unrest and revolution," of nationalization measures, of foreign exchange or trade regulations in other countries, have necessarily a depressing effect on the volume of investment abroad.

But what is of far-reaching, indeed epoch-making, significance is that none of these obstacles to the expansion of foreign markets and to export of capital need be passively accepted by monopolistic and oligopolistic business. Accounting for a significant share of its industry's (or even its country's) aggregate output, controlling a large agglomeration of wealth, disposing over far-flung connections and widely spread influence, a giant corporation can alone or in conjunction with other similarly placed concerns play as large a part in determining its government's course in foreign economic and political affairs as it plays in determining its policies at home.[30] As a consequence in all of its operations in the international arena a large enterprise in an advanced capitalist country can throw upon the scales not merely its own prodigious financial power but also the enormous resources of its country's national government.

The availability of such government support markedly enhances the monopolistic and oligopolistic firm's ability to cope with the difficulties standing in the way of its foreign economic activities. As far as the limitations are concerned that are imposed upon it by the structure of international markets, the backing of its government greatly increases its competitive power. In any case the stability of any international market structure is bound to be more precarious than that of any market structure within a single country. The number of oligopolistic firms in the world economy is naturally larger than in one country, and common financial controls, interlocking directorates, and the like less frequent. Consequently the restraints on competition among oligopolistic firms of different nationalities are less pronounced and the considerations that militate against aggressive

[30] For a brilliant and comprehensive study of the dominant role played by big business in the foreign policies of the Great Powers prior to World War I, cf. G. W. F. Hallgarten, *Imperialismus vor 1914* (Munich, 1951).

tactics of oligopolistic firms in the economy of one country are less compelling in the case of the world economy.[31] But the fact that each oligopolistic Titan, in its competitive struggle in the world markets, can lean upon its national government reduces even further the influence of the factors that account for the stability of the market structures in individual countries. Able to rely upon its national government's economic, diplomatic, and military power, the oligopolistic firm operating in the world market is irresistibly tempted to try to conquer a larger share of the market or to seek additional outlets for investment. Where granting credits to buyers in an importing country suffering from balance of payments deficits appears to be commercially unsound, monopolistic business can cause its government to provide either the necessary loans and grants, or to assume the risks by the issuance of suitable guarantees. Where the outlays required to eliminate or to curtail the activities of a competitive firm from another country are too large, monopolistic business can more or less readily shift them to its country's national treasury. Where investment in development of raw materials in a source country does not attract a corporation or the financial group associated with it, be it because of too high costs of initial exploration or of insufficient expected profitability, their national government can be induced to carry all or a part of the financial burden.[32]

Government support of the giant corporation competing in the world economy influences the situation also in another way. Political, economic, and military pressure upon a smaller and weaker country brought to bear by the corporation's national government may exclude from the market of that country a competitor from another country. A loan granted to such a country on the part of one oligopolist's government may be tied to conditions that decisively shift the competitive balance in favor of that oligopolistic firm.[33]

[31] Members of an oligopolistic industry of *one* country rarely compete among themselves in the world markets. The considerations which curtail if not preclude their effective competition at home apply equally strongly to their foreign operations. In fact very frequently oligopolists of one country operate jointly in the world markets by founding common syndicates, purchasing agencies, etc. The United States anti-trust laws even provide specifically for such (Webb-Pomerane) combinations.

[32] Cf. my article "The Rich Got Richer," *The Nation* (January 17, 1953).

[33] "In certain parts of the world an American corporation must do its business frankly and openly with the foreign government, with or without assistance from the United States Department of State. American oil companies doing business in Venezuela, American copper companies

Similarly, the impediments to foreign investment stemming from political uncertainties, from the danger of social upheavals or from obstreperousness of the governments in the dependent countries, can frequently be successfully overcome with the help of the governments of the imperialist powers. A giant corporation not only often confronts a small and weak nation as the sole buyer of its exports or an important source of its imports (and/or credits): it is able alone or by making use of its own government's appropriate facilities to intervene actively in that country's internal politics, to buy, to install, or to depose its administration, to make or to break its politicians.[34] And when need be, the military potential of the imperialist country can be used to assure "freedom" to the activities of monopolistic business.

Thus the competition among oligopolists in the world arena becomes to an ever increasing extent a power contest among imperialist countries. Its outcome depends not merely on the strength of the contestant firms but on the political and military potentials of their countries. The limits to such expansion of foreign trade or foreign investment as may be attained by the government-backed monopolistic and oligopolistic business of one country are set by the resistance of government-backed monopolistic and oligopolistic business of other countries, by the recalcitrance of nations inhabiting the dependent countries, as well as by the extent to which domestic social and political conditions facilitate or hamper its government's subservience to the interests of big business.

---

doing business in Chile, American sugar companies doing business in the Dominican Republic, for example, deal directly with the competent authorities of these states. Though corporate practice is far from uniform, it would seem that most American corporations prefer to deal direct rather than through American Embassies or diplomatic officials, though the diplomats can be of help under some circumstances. Some of the larger corporations have continuous and careful reports made to them on the attitudes and aptitudes of the American diplomatic officials, rating them according to their probable usefulness in advancing or protecting the company's interest." A. A. Berle, Jr., *The Twentieth Century Capitalist Revolution* (New York, 1954), pp. 131 ff. It should be noted that Professor Berle's background lends exceptional weight to his testimony. He was Assistant Secretary of State from 1938 to 1944 and United States Ambassador to Brazil from 1945 to 1946.

[34] Examples of this are so ubiquitous that they can be picked at random. Whether we look at British or American practices with regard to Near Eastern countries, to Latin America, or to Southeast Asia, the pattern of imperialist manipulation of political conditions in smaller and weaker nations is invariant. We return to this point below.

This necessarily causes a considerable fluidity in the advantages derived from foreign trade and investment by individual capitalist countries. The unevenness in the development of their domestic politics and in the growth of their national power (and in the strength of their industrial and financial groups) accounts for continuous changes in their relative status in the world economy. Periods of precarious peace and stability are rapidly succeeded by conditions of turmoil and frictions. "Normal" coexistence under cartel and quota agreements yields to sharp conflicts and open warfare. The intensity of the impulse that an advanced capitalist economy receives from its foreign relations differs therefore not only from country to country, but from one historical period to the next—being at one time most pronounced for one country and at another time most tangible in the case of one or some of its rivals.

V

The amount of economic surplus that is being "automatically" absorbed through foreign economic relations proper is, however, far from giving even a proximate measure of their importance for the economies of the imperialist powers. What is of overriding significance is the impact of these relations on the scope and nature of government activities in advanced capitalist countries. Indeed, as mentioned before, the competitive status in the world economy of an imperialist country's monopolistic and oligopolistic business depends largely on systematic and comprehensive support on the part of its government. What did the trick a century or two ago is no longer sufficient at the present time. Neither an occasional angry *démarche* on the part of the Foreign Office nor even the deployment of a battleship to a suitable location—which in the good old days frequently sufficed to "normalize" the relations of an unreasonable country to the businessman of a great power—delineate nowadays the scope of the requisite government intervention. What is called for now in economic terms is large government loans, grants, and "technical assistance" appropriations to countries that are of interest to corporate foreign activities. What is called for now in political terms is the establishment of military bases wherever possible to assure political and social stability, pliable governments and appropriate economic and social policies in all accessible countries of the world. Whatever equilibrium is thus attained at any given time is, however, highly unstable. Minor and major wars mark the readjustment of world conditions to the changing potentials of the competing powers—only to result in precarious new balances of uncertain durability.

The socioeconomic constellation under monopoly capitalism is such as to condition the general public, the relevant officials, legislators, and intellectual leaders to the policies of imperialism. Writing more than fifty years ago, Hobson gave us a glimpse of the mechanism involved.[35] Yet, impressive as his insight was, it did not fully penetrate the intricacies of the subject. What has been decisive in promoting monopolistic business's spectacular success in rendering the body politic of advanced capitalist countries a willing tool of its foreign interests is the fact that these policies are not merely and not even primarily based upon obfuscation of the masses, upon corruption of officials, and upon treachery of politicians. That the policy of imperialism may be actually of benefit to the ordinary man in an imperialist country was clearly realized by Lenin, who drew attention to the existence of a "labor aristocracy" sharing in the extra-profits of monopolistic business.[36] It was perhaps even more broadly adumbrated by Engels who in a letter to Marx (October 7, 1858) prophetically wrote: "The English proletariat is becoming more and more bourgeois, so that this most bourgeois of all nations is apparently aiming ultimately at the possession of a bourgeois aristocracy and a bourgeois proletariat *as well as* a bourgeoisie. For a nation which exploits the whole world this is of course in a way understandable."[37] Indeed, the fruits of imperialist policies accrue not solely to the plutocratic summit of an advanced capitalist country

[35] "The controlling and directing agent of the whole process . . . is the pressure of financial and industrial motives, operated for the direct, short-range material interests of small, able and well-organized groups in a nation. These groups secure the active co-operation of statesmen and political cliques who wield the power of 'parties,' partly by associating them directly in their business schemes, partly by appealing to the conservative instincts of members of the possessing classes, whose vested interest and class dominance are best preserved by diverting the currents of political energy from domestic into foreign politics. The acquiescence, even the active and enthusiastic support, of the body of a nation in a course of policy fatal to its own true interests is secured partly by appeals to the mission of civilization but chiefly by playing upon the primitive instincts of the race." J. A. Hobson, *Imperialism* (London, 1902), p. 212.
[36] E. Varga and L. Mendelsohn (eds.), *New Data for Lenin's Imperialism—The Highest Stage of Capitalism* (New York, 1940), p. 224.
[37] Marx and Engels, *Selected Correspondence* (New York, 1934), p. 115. A minor change in the translation was made by this writer.

and its immediate dependents and retainers, they greatly affect the existence of the entire society under monopoly capitalism.

What matters here is not whatever increases in income and employment an imperialist country may derive from foreign trade and investment. These need not be very large, even if of vast importance to the individual corporations involved and the groups associated with them.[38] In fact, as long as the advantages *immediately* related to foreign economic activities represented the major consideration promoting imperialist policies, their political foundations as well as their ideological justification were inevitably somewhat shaky. It is impossible for more than relatively short periods to manipulate an advanced nation by sheer fraud and bribery, nor can the philosophy of the white man's burden and the doctrine of racial superiority stand up very long to the staggering contrast between the terrifying human and material costs of imperialism and its yields—lavish profits to a handful of large-scale businesses. This contrast could not but discredit the corrupt spokesmen of imperialism and explode their hypocritical and fraudulent fables, limiting the circulation of both to the jingoist fringes of imperialist politics and "culture."

The issue appears in an altogether different perspective when not merely the direct advantages of imperialist policies to the society of an advanced capitalist country are taken into account but when their effect is visualized in its entirety. The loans and grants to so-called friendly governments of dependent countries, the outlays on the military establishment needed to "protect" certain territories or to enforce certain policies abroad, the expenditures on a sprawling apparatus designed to organize propaganda, subversion, and espionage both in subject areas as well as in other competing or "uncertain" imperialist countries—all assume prodigious magnitudes. Although they account for a large share of the gross national product, in the United States in the average of the last decade nearly 20 percent, their importance is not fully reflected even by that ratio. It may become clearer when it is realized that the share of the *economic surplus* that is absorbed by these outlays is substantially larger. Thus the impact of this form of utilization of the economic surplus on the level of income and employment in an advanced capitalist country transcends by far the income- and employment-generating effect of foreign economic activities themselves. The latter assume actually only incidental significance

[38] A special case, however, is Britain, where foreign trade and investment have constituted per se major sources of national income.

compared with the former—an errant stone setting into motion a mighty rock.

That the means of imperialist policy overshadow almost entirely its original ends has tremendous implications. Providing a vast outlet for the overflowing economic surplus, this spending on the where-withal of imperialist policy becomes the main form of the government's "exhaustive expenditures," the central core of the government intervention on behalf of "full employment." Indeed, this form of government spending is the one form that is fully acceptable to monopoly capital. It favors large-scale enterprise, providing it with additional demand for its output without interfering with its normal markets; it has none of the drawbacks of all other types of government spending assuring at the same time high levels of profits and the required levels of employment. Thus the continuation or even expansion of imperialist policies and of military outlays related to them obtain the support not merely of their direct beneficiaries: the corporations collecting vast profits from their government-backed dealings abroad, the firms whose business it is to supply the government with military equipment, the generals and admirals anxious not to be relieved of their none-too-arduous responsibilities, the intellectuals who find ample application for their talents in various organizations that owe their existence to those policies, and the "labor aristocracy" gathering the crumbs from the monopolistic tables. Large-scale government spending on military purposes appears essential to society as a whole, to all its classes, groups, and strata whose jobs and incomes depend on the resulting maintenance of high levels of business activity.

Under such circumstances there evolves a far-reaching harmony between the interests of monopolistic business on one side and those of the underlying population on the other. The unifying formula of this "people's imperialism"—to use Oskar Lange's apt expression—is "full employment." With this formula on its banner, monopolistic business has little trouble in securing mass support for its undivided rule, in controlling the government openly and comprehensively, in determining undisputedly its external and internal policies. This formula appeals to the labor movement, satisfies the requirements of the farmers, gives contentment to the "general public," and nips in the bud all opposition to the regime of monopoly capital.

VI

This glittering façade of economic prosperity and social and political cohesion is, however, highly deceptive. It may readily convey the impression that monopoly capitalism's basic problem of overproduction and underemployment has been mastered and that the stability and functioning of the system are "in principle" assured. This view of capitalism, always contained in one form or another in bourgeois economics, receives at the present time its most sophisticated formulation in the hands of the Keynesian theorists of full employment. Confronted with persistent overaccumulation and insufficient outlets for the economic surplus, and having grasped the theory of income determination in the short run, Keynesians proclaim as economics' ultimate wisdom that *any* spending promotes prosperity, *any* utilization of the surplus advances general welfare, and they rest content with this profound insight.[39] If bothered by the manifest irrationality of a position that extols as an absolute good what might be at best considered a lesser evil—although in the case of spending on preparation for war even this is utterly untrue—these economists retreat to "previously prepared positions," and stress that a rise in income and employment, however obtained, causes an expansion of aggregate demand, and thus leads to increased consumption as well as to some additional investment induced by the widening of the market. There is probably no better example of the absurdity that can be reached by the exercise of "practical intelligence." For what is there to be said for a reasoning that justifies the waste of enormous quantities of human and material resources by pointing to the *by-product* of that waste—a certain increase of consumption and an (uncertain) increase of investment?[40]

The irrationality of the economists is, however, not merely a re-

[39] Commenting on Malthus, Ricardo notes that Malthus' view would imply that "a body of unproductive labourers are just as necessary and as useful with a view to future production, as a fire, which should consume in the manufacturers warehouse the goods which those unproductive labourers would otherwise consume," and adds, "I cannot express in language so strong as I feel it my astonishment at the various propositions advanced in this section." Ricardo, *Works* (P. Sraffa ed.) (Cambridge, 1951), Vol. II, pp. 421 and 423.

[40] In the presence of large excess capacity, the amount of "induced" investment resulting from a rise in consumers' demand may actually be very small, and may express itself primarily in an increase of inventories.

flection of the irrationality of the social and economic system that they are seeking to serve and to perpetuate.[41] It is an important component of the entire ideological apparatus continuously conditioning the people to the requirements of monopoly capitalism. Indeed, under the aegis of the principle that "any spending is good," all inquiry into the rationality of resource utilization becomes meaningless. All outlays on the part of monopolistic business, regardless of their nature, productivity, or conduciveness to human welfare, are now sanctified not merely by having passed the acid test of profitability. They become hallowed in addition as essential to the maintenance of income and employment.[42] Simultaneously, this principle puts to rest all concern with the nature and purposes of government spending by rationalizing it in any case as a welcome supplement to aggregate demand leading to the necessary expansion of economic activity.

To be sure, systematic wastage of a sufficiently large proportion of the economic surplus on military purposes, on piling up redundant inventories, on multiplying unproductive workers, can provide the necessary "outside impulse" to the economy of monopoly capitalism, can serve as an immediate remedy against depressions, can "kill the pain" of rampant unemployment. But as with many other narcotics, the applicability of this shot in the arm is limited, and its effect is short-lived. What is worse, it frequently aggravates the long-run condition of the patient.

A certain volume of government spending lifts income and employment to a new level. This boost is reinforced by a certain amount of private investment undertaken in direct response to the government demand for military supplies: the armaments business calls continuously for the construction of new productive facilities, for rapid technological change, for prompt introduction of the most up-to-date

[41] Thus a collection of essays on full employment and related matters by a group of leading Keynesians edited a few years ago by S. E. Harris was characteristically named *Saving American Capitalism.*

[42] Incidentally, Keynes himself, still essentially belonging to an age in which reason was not yet entirely banished from the temple of social sciences, was rather ambivalent on this issue. On one hand he remarked that "there is no clear evidence from experience that the investment policy which is socially advantageous coincides with that which is most profitable." *General Theory of Employment, Interest, and Money* (London, 1936), p. 157. On the other hand, he observed that there is "no reason to suppose that the existing system seriously misemploys the factors of production which are in use. . . . It is in determining the volume, not the direction of actual employment that the existing system has broken down." *Ibid.*, p. 379.

means and methods of production.[43] The resulting expansion of aggregate demand in turn widens the market confronting the capitalist enterprise. An increase in output that earlier would have led to lower prices and reduced profits can now be undertaken without such untoward repercussions. This stimulates investment in both the monopolistic and the competitive sectors of the economy—in improved machinery and in enlarged capacity in the former, primarily in founding new businesses in the latter.[44] Needless to say, this increase in the nation's aggregate productive establishment does not even approximate in volume and composition what it would have been if the wasted amount of economic surplus had originally been turned to rationally allocated investment. Still, in a country as wealthy as the United States, even this "induced" investment assumes tremendous significance. It causes an increase of productivity greatly surpassing what would have been attained in the absence of net investment. If it has been estimated that the mere replacement of worn-out machinery by more modern and more efficient equipment would cause an annual productivity increase of 1.5 percent per worker, in the presence of such net investment as has been taking place under the impact of the "outside impulses" this average productivity increase has been reaching approximately 3 percent per worker per year. What this implies is that the production of any given volume of output requires the employment of 3 percent less manpower every year. This in turn means that, taking into account the natural increase of the labor force by over 1 percent per year, the mere reproduction of any given physical output would be accompanied by an annual growth of unemployment of over 4 percent of the labor force. It is quite obvious that unemployment advancing at such a rate would rapidly assume major proportions considerably surpassing whatever might be considered to be the "desirable" size of the industrial reserve army. In other words, if "full employment" is to be maintained—even allowing for whatever

---

[43] The munitions industry becomes, as it were, a perennial "new industry" providing a vast outlet for investible funds—with the added advantage of the government's preparedness to assume all the risks and costs of the initial research, exploration, and experimentation.

[44] It should be noted that an increase in output of the monopolistic and oligopolistic part of the economy almost automatically calls forth a certain expansion in the number of quasi-independent businesses eking out a more or less adequate livelihood on the fringes of the big business empires: automobile repair shops and service stations, grocery stores and dry-cleaning establishments, insurance agencies and small loan companies.

volume of unemployment is thought of as necessary by the dominant interests—output has to increase continuously in keeping with the growth of productivity and the expansion of the labor force.

This brings us back, however, to the problem with which we started. Once the system has adapted itself to the new level of income and employment, that new level becomes once more the "given situation" the properties of which we earlier discussed. Aggregate demand becomes stabilized, monopolistic and oligopolistic firms reach again their optimal positions with regard to output and price, and the competitive sector of the economy returns to its state of overcrowding and low profits. Yet, the rise of income resulting from the injection of government spending, if sufficiently large, may generate a mood of optimism and "confidence" in which not only adventurous small businessmen but habitually prudent and cautious corporate managements consider the sky to be the only limit to further expansion. In this state of exhilaration, the increase of capacity is driven further than what would be warranted by the new level of aggregate demand. Although this additional investment itself causes an increase of income, the resulting widening of demand cannot keep pace with the expansion of capacity. Excess capacity becomes ever more pronounced not merely in the competitive branches of the economy but also in its monopolistic and oligopolistic industries. Thus what confronted the economic system before, now appears in a magnified and more acute form. For in the new "given situation" excess capacity is larger, inducements to invest accordingly weak, while the economic surplus of society is not only greater in absolute terms but constitutes a significantly increased proportion of aggregate output and income. The latter is primarily due to the method by which the government's spending has to be financed. This requires some elaboration.

VII

It will be recalled that a government policy aiming at any predetermined level of employment would have to rely in the main on spending large enough to fill the gap between the actual economic surplus forthcoming on that level of income and the volume of intended private investment that would take place under those conditions. Clearly, the larger that gap, and the higher the decided-upon level of employment, the larger the requisite spending. The simplest procedure for financing such spending would seem to be outright budgetary deficits incurred either by printing money or by borrowing from businesses, financial institutions, and individuals. While appearing most feasible and unproblematic, this method is, however, hardly practicable for any length of time. If the government expenditures involved were directed towards productive investment, the counterpart of the growing balances of cash or near-cash in the hands of the public would be a steadily and rapidly growing volume of output. But as the bulk of government spending does not call forth the construction of productive facilities but finds its embodiment in military supplies and similar "assets," deficit financing of government expenditures is bound to increase continuously the ratio of cash and near-cash in the hands of the public to currently produced marketable output. This in turn creates an ever-increasing threat of inflation. Under the impact of unforeseen circumstances (in particular threats of war and concomitant scarcities) the accumulated balances of cash and near-cash may suddenly start seeking transformation into tangible goods—with speculation reducing their supply—and cause an inflationary run on the economy. Although under the impact of inflation profits increase and the distribution of income shifts in favor of the capitalist class, the capitalist class itself is unwilling to risk the consequences of a major decline in the purchasing power of the currency. Undermining the possibility of rational calculation, depleting the liquid assets of firms and individual capitalists, inflation—and this is perhaps one of its worst features so far as business is concerned—endangers the entire elaborate credit structure of modern capitalism and constitutes a considerable threat to banks and financial institutions.[45] What is mo⁘, by causing the development of a cleavage between the interests of creditors and debtors, by dispossessing the new middle class and the rentiers, by depressing the real income of workers, it seriously weakens the authority of the government and disrupts the political and social cohesion of the capitalist order. Needless to say, the danger of inflation and of its consequences becomes progressively larger the more frequently the deficit medicine is applied. The Damocles sword of potentially spendable balances becomes ever heavier, and the risk of its falling down on the economy ever more formidable. Thus this device has to be used most sparingly, and its adoption saved only for exceptionally critical situations such as

---

[45] Schumpeter even regarded a well-functioning mechanism of credit to be the *conditio sine qua non* for the operation of the capitalist system.

war or a particularly sharp depression. It is precisely the purpose of government spending—armament—rendering budgetary deficits an unsuitable method of financing that heightens the danger of war when the inflationary pressures would become largest.

Therefore as a matter of longer-run policy, the government expenditures required for the maintenance of a decided-upon level of income and employment have to be at least approximately matched by tax revenues. This means, however, that government spending has to remain within more or less narrowly circumscribed limits. For it is in the nature of the tax mechanism normally employed under capitalism that while it siphons off some of the economic surplus (in the form of business profits and personal saving), it necessarily also cuts into consumption. Hence the paradox that the larger the amount of surplus that the government must spend in order to maintain the desired level of income and employment, the larger it tends to make the surplus itself by seizing parts of income that otherwise would have been spent on consumption. As long as the total amount of tax collection is at all "reasonable," matters are under control. As we have seen earlier, monopolistic and oligopolistic firms are able to shift all, or a good part, of their tax liabilities onto the buyers of their products. The additional economic surplus that is squeezed out of the system thus comes from the competitive sector of the economy that enjoys no such favorable position, as well as from the bulk of the population that consists of "price takers" rather than "price makers"—to use Professor Scitovsky's expression.[46] How large that burden may be permitted to grow can only be determined by trial and error. On one hand it obviously depends on its distribution as among different income groups. On the other hand, it must not be forgotten that the resulting reduction of real income among some parts of the population is accompanied by an expansion of employment favorably affecting the real income of others. It would seem on the whole that the resulting balance of interests is such that a fairly high level of taxation can be sustained for a long time, given a suitable political atmosphere.[47]

The picture would change considerably if the government spending required to attain a predetermined level of employment (let

[46] These are therefore characteristically the strata most energetically clamoring for lower taxes!

[47] The continuous production and reproduction of that atmosphere becomes in this way not merely a political desideratum but an utmost economic necessity for monopoly capitalism.

alone of genuine full employment!) were to become very large and were still to be financed within the framework of a balanced budget. While it has been shown that technically such an arrangement is not impossible,[48] its practical feasibility is entirely out of the question. The nature of government spending being what it is, it would divert an exorbitant share of total output to military spending and similar unproductive purposes—"nationalizing" and redistributing at the same time what would remain of the national product. Under such conditions the shifting of the tax liability on the part of monopolistic and oligopolistic business would become extremely difficult, if not impossible, and the tax load that would have to be borne by competitive business, by the new middle class, by farmers, workers, and other groups would become nothing short of prohibitive. The repercussions of such a policy for the social stability of the capitalist system, and the political dangers that it would entail, would be worse than those resulting from a continuous inflation.

We have not yet mentioned, however, one mode of government action to raise the level of income and employment, the procedure that is closest to the hearts of business as well as of the general public. This is an increase of aggregate spending by a *reduction* of taxes. With an unchanged volume of government spending, this method leads to what has been occasionally dubbed "deficit without spending." It is obviously open to the same objections as all other forms of deficit financing. What is even more serious is that its efficacy is very limited. This is caused by the asymmetry of the effects of an *increase* of tax revenue, and those of its *reduction*. Within limits drawn by the prevailing living standards, by the existing habit of tax discipline, and the like, in advanced capitalist countries, the *former* is always bound to increase the economic surplus, at least in the short run. As tax rates are raised, some economic surplus—part of profits and saving— is seized by the government. At the same time, however, additional income is "transferred" to economic surplus—part of what would have been otherwise spent on consumption. Indeed, it has always been the essence of taxation policy under capitalism to minimize the share of tax revenues which confiscate privately appropriated economic surplus and to increase simultaneously the proportion constituting additional economic surplus. This basic principle underlies

[48] For an excellent summary of the argument, cf. Paul A. Samuelson, "Simple Mathematics of Income Determination," in Lloyd Metzler and others, *Income, Employment and Public Policy: Essays in Honor of Alvin H. Hansen* (New York, 1948), as well as the literature referred to therein.

obviously also all *reductions* of taxes under capitalism. They are so calculated as to *maximize* the amounts returned to privately appropriated economic surplus and to *minimize* the sums that are released, as it were, from the economic surplus and made available for consumption.[49]

Consequently the tax reductions that are usually undertaken do not exercise a marked impact on the level of consumption. To accomplish that, they would have to apply primarily to the tax liabilities of the bulk of the consumers, that is, of the lower income groups. They would have to assume the form of higher tax exemptions, of removal of excise taxes on mass consumption goods, and the like. There is hardly any need to repeat that this kind of taxation policy is not held in high esteem by the capitalist class, and such tax reductions as have been undertaken in recent (and most recent) history have certainly not conformed to this pattern. A lowering of the tax burden of higher income brackets, however, will have a relatively small influence on aggregate consumers' spending. It will increase instead the volume of the economic surplus in the form of individual saving.[50]

Nor is there much reason to believe that a reduction of taxes on profits and the resulting boost in the privately appropriated economic surplus would seriously stimulate private investment. As we have seen earlier, the inadequacy of private investment under monopoly capitalism cannot possibly be attributed to insufficiency of investible capital or to an unsatisfactory level of profits (after taxes). To be sure, lavish profits and overflow of investible funds in an advanced capitalist economy are characteristic of the monopolistic and oligopolistic sectors of the economy, and go together with low profits and shortage of capital in its competitive part. Therefore, if there is no general expansion of demand, a reduction of taxes on profits will not stimulate investment on the part of monopolistic and oligopolistic firms; their reluctance to invest was not motivated in the first place by paucity of current earnings or by shortage of capital. All that a tax reduction is likely to accomplish in that case is either to permit a

[49] This is greatly facilitated by the fact that inequitable and regressive tax cuts are always politically easier to get away with than inequitable and regressive tax increases. The former impose no new burdens on anyone, and are therefore less noticed than the latter.

[50] Cf. R. A. Musgrave and M. S. Painter, "Impact of Alternative Tax Structures on Consumption and Saving," *American Economic Review* (June 1945), as well as R. A. Musgrave, "Alternative Budget Policies for Full Employment," *Quarterly Journal of Economics* (June 1945).

higher degree of internal financing—of such investment as was contemplated in any case—and thus to deprive some personal saving of the investment outlet that it might have otherwise found in the securities of the floating firms, or to provide for higher retained (and uninvested) earnings and/or higher dividend payments, if no additional investment had been planned. In both cases the tax reduction is likely to increase corporate and personal saving (combined) rather than lead to a larger volume of investment.

The effect might be quite different as far as the competitive sector of the economy is concerned. There a reduction of taxes may indeed cause an expansion of investment, to the extent that such investment has been actually stymied before either by unsatisfactory prospective profits or by lack of investible funds. Whether in the light of the relatively low capital intensity in the competitive part of the economy and its long-run relative contraction such expansion could assume proportions sufficient to exercise a marked impact on the economy as a whole is, however, rather doubtful. The rationality of a policy promoting investment in the crammed areas of distribution, service trades, and similar competitive activities is even more questionable.

Yet to return to the point at which we embarked upon this lengthy detour: in whichever way the government spending that had ignited the original expansion may have been financed, its result is not merely an increase of total output but also a rise of both the absolute size of the economic surplus and also of its share in national income.[51] Thus if growth of unemployment in the next period is to be avoided, the utilization of the economic surplus (on the part of business and/or government) must not merely remain on the given level but must increase. But nothing resembling the required increase can be expected from private investment. On the contrary, as we have seen, once the new plateau of income and demand has been reached, private investment tends to come to a standstill. What is worse, the increased volume of excess capacity renders the system less sensitive to the stimulus of further government spending. Once a large armaments

[51] An excellent illustration for this is provided by the postwar development in the United States. While Gross National Product (measured in 1954 prices) increased from 1946 to 1954 by about 11 percent per capita, consumption rose in the same period by about 5 percent per capita. *Economic Report of the President* (January 1955), pp. 138, 149. The actual increase of the economic surplus must have been even larger than this difference suggests, since in this period capitalists' consumption probably grew more than in proportion to the slight increase of mass consumption.

industry has been erected, once a major wave of increasing demand and "confidence" have led to large investment, the possibilities of further "induced" investment become very much smaller. At the same time, the possibility of increased government spending is predicated upon increased taxation. This in turn means further cuts in consumption, further expansion of the economic surplus, further dependence for economic stability on government outlays.[52]

VIII

Thus the stability of monopoly capitalism is highly precarious. Incapable of pursuing a policy of genuine full employment and of genuine economic progress, having to abstain from productive investment as well as from a systematic expansion of consumption, it has to rely in the main on military spending for preservation of the prosperity and high employment on which it depends both for profits and for popular support. Such a course, however, while creating the semblance of a "good time had by all," amounts to a continuous dissipation of the nation's economic surplus and leads to no improvement of people's real income. Worse still, it cannot be followed indefinitely. The common man, employed and hard-working but seeing no advances in his living conditions, is bound to get increasingly weary of paying taxes to maintain a military establishment the necessity of which becomes progressively doubtful. Although for quite a while he can be reconciled to this arrangement under conditions of high employment, in the long run this reconciliation is bound to run into mounting difficulties. What becomes ever more urgently required is systematic ideological "processing" of the population to assure its loyalty to monopoly capitalism. To secure popular acceptance of the armaments program, the existence of external danger has to be systematically hammered into the minds of the people. An incessant campaign of official and semi-official propaganda, financed by both government and big business, is designed to produce an almost complete uniformity of opinion on all important issues. An elaborate system of economic and social pressures is developed to silence independent thought and to stifle all "undesirable" scientific, artistic, or literary expression. A spiderweb of corruption is spun over the entire political and cultural

[52] For a masterful analysis of the relevant magnitudes, cf. the editors of *Monthly Review*, "The Economic Outlook" (December 1954).

life of the imperialist country and drives principles, honesty, humanity, and courage from political life.[53] The cynicism of vulgar empiricism destroys the moral fibre, the respect for reason, and the ability to discriminate between good and evil among wide strata of the population. The stress on crude pragmatism, on the "science" of control and manipulation kills any preoccupation with the purposes and goals of human activity, and elevates efficiency to an end in itself regardless of what is to be "efficiently" accomplished. Nonconformism and noncompliance with the "culture" of monopoly capitalism lead to loss of employment, to social ostracism, and to endless harassment from the authorities.

If and when propaganda, indoctrination, and social and administrative pressure fail to keep the people attuned to the requirements of imperialism, incidents are provoked to lend a basis to the cultivated fears, to give substance to the systematically sustained hysteria. Such incidents are easily produced. Surrounded by colonial and dependent nations, underdeveloped, starving, and seething with unrest, the imperialist powers are continuously faced with challenges to their authority and to their dominance. The supply of potential incidents is thus more than ample, and opportunities for major or minor police actions offer themselves all the time. And these police actions create and recreate the danger of war, kindle and rekindle the fire under the boiling pot of mass hysteria.

In the past, the inner tensions and frustrations of imperialism found their catastrophic release in war. Although the tendency of imperialism to escape from the impasse by means of war is today as strong as ever, there are a number of new factors that have to be taken into account in an analysis of the present situation. The overwhelming preponderance of one imperialist power over all other imperialist powers makes a war among them increasingly difficult. Even formerly proud imperialist empires tend to descend to the status of satellites of the dominant imperialist country, with the latter assuming more and more the role of supreme arbiter within the imperialist camp. While wars among lesser imperialist countries or among combinations

[53] Speaking at the fifty-ninth annual meeting of the American Academy of Political and Social Science, Adolf A. Berle, Jr., observed that "a series of influences had been building up that tend increasingly to push out men whose habits of mind, or whose honest research, or whose speculations, or whose artistic expressions tend to conflict with the even tenor of current operations, or are antagonistic to current business thought." *New York Times*, April 2, 1955.

of imperialist countries remain a possibility, the possibility is rather remote.

At the same time there arises an increasing danger of war in which all or some imperialist powers might seek to re-establish imperialist domination over the countries that constitute today the socialist part of the world. Yet this possibility also is probably less acute than is frequently assumed. Not only is the socialist part of the world—inhabited by one-third of the human race—growing stronger all the time, but a war against it would in all probability cause a complete collapse of the imperialist structure. There would be few if any colonial and dependent nations in Asia, Africa, and elsewhere to whom such a conflict would not be a signal for national and social revolution. It is this consideration, in conjunction with the more or less pronounced social and political instability at home, that accounts for the conspicuous lack of enthusiasm for new military adventures in the chancelleries of the imperialist powers.[54]

What serves, however, as probably the most important deterrent to excessive "trigger happiness" is the unprecedented destructive power of the newly developed and continuously perfected thermonuclear weapons. The fact that the imperialist world possesses no monopoly on these instruments of annihilation renders their employment a prohibitively risky undertaking. The prospect of atomic retaliation tends to chill even the most martial spirits in the councils of imperialist powers, indeed tends to reduce greatly the attractiveness of war even on purely economic grounds. For if in earlier wars the division of functions was such that it was the common man who undertook the fighting and dying while the ruling class attended to the political, administrative, and economic aspects of hostilities, in an atomic war there would be but little room for such an arrangement. Not only the lives but also the property of the capitalist class would have a poor chance of coming safely through an A-bomb and H-bomb holocaust. In a bit of grim if unintended humor two business economists have recently expressed a correct assessment of war in the present atomic age. "The march of science and invention, high-lighted by the harnessing of atomic energy in August 1945, emphasizes that capital assets are always on the way to the scrap heap. The creative destruction going on under dynamic capitalism opens up vast investment

---

[54] Needless to say, this in no way eliminates the threat of accidents in which "calculated risks" turn out to have incalculable consequences.

opportunities."[55] A serious trouble with this otherwise sound analysis is, however, that such harnessing of atomic energy as took place in August 1945 in Hiroshima and Nagasaki would, if repeated, not merely send the capital assets on the way to the scrap heap but also the would-be investors on the way to the cemetery.

The prospect of limitless destruction that is associated with atomic war not only exercises its influence on the leaders of monopoly capital but gives rise to serious doubts as to its political feasibility. It is one thing to mobilize popular support for imperialist policies and armaments with the help of high employment and psychological warfare, it is an altogether different thing to be assured of popular cooperation in the face of atomic retaliation. That the morale of people cannot be readily counted on to withstand a catastrophe of this kind is strongly suggested by various studies of the experience of the Second World War. Under such circumstances it becomes progressively more questionable whether the game is really worth the candle, whether a general war—far from solving, if only temporarily, the problems of monopoly capitalism—would not in actual fact destroy our civilization as a whole.

It thus appears not impossible that in world affairs the leadership of monopoly capital controlling the destinies of imperialist countries will try to develop some of the caution and circumspection that it has developed in its business affairs. Leaving it to the overzealous among its political retainers and to the overadventurous among its military servants to beat the drums of preventive war, monopoly capital's responsible statesmen would seem increasingly to prefer "cold" wars to "hot" wars, smaller police actions to general conflagrations, the atmosphere of danger to danger itself. Such an arrangement would assure them of the better part of both worlds: continuous prosperity based on large-scale expenditures on armaments, continuous dominance over a frightened and politically submissive population, as well as the avoidance of an atomic conflict that would bury under its debris the capitalist order itself.

It is quite clear that this possibility is far from being a certainty. Politics of imperialism have a dynamics of their own, interests and ideologies once cast loose tend to assume their own momentum, servile puppets suddenly become independent political factors, and what has been believed to be subject to complete manipulation and control

[55] E. W. Swanson and E. P. Schmidt, *Economic Stagnation or Progress* (New York, 1946), p. 197.

suddenly erupts with elemental force. The spirits once invoked are not readily banished, as many big business magnates in Germany discovered to their sorrow in the '30s. Worse still, the arrangement of *neither* war nor peace, the precarious balancing on the brink of the abyss, provides no long-run solution to the basic problem of monopoly capitalism. For its prosperity to last, for employment to stay high, the impulse of large armaments spending is not sufficient. This impulse has to grow continuously stronger, this spending has to keep increasing: the system has to run fast if it is to stay where it is. Yet the larger and more permanent the military establishment, the bigger and more elaborate the stockpile of military hardware, the stronger are the vested interests of those producing military supplies.[56] And the larger and the more permanent the military establishment, the greater the temptation to "negotiate from strength"—which means to serve ultimata to smaller and weaker nations and to back them, if need be, by force. Thus the danger of spontaneous ignition becomes ever present, the threat of an unplanned explosion paramount. "But if nations can learn to provide themselves with full employment by their domestic policy . . . there need be no important economic forces calculated to set the interest of one country against that of its neighbors."[57] This profound insight of Keynes encompasses one half of the problem. The other half that remained wholly obscure to him was clearly seen by one of his most brilliant students: "In the present age, any government which had both the power and the will to remedy the major defects of the capitalist system would have the will and the power to abolish it altogether, while governments which have the power to retain the system lack the will to remedy its defects."[58]

[56] "For the first time in its history the United States is getting a full-time, national-scale arms industry most companies of which now treat their war output as a permanent part of their business." *Business Week,* September 27, 1952. An example of the nature of this "full-time, national-scale arms industry" is given in *Pull Magazine,* March 1955, where it is stated that "years ago five concerns made ammunition. Today these companies have been absorbed by two companies—The Du Pont Company of Wilmington, Del., and the Olin-Mathieson Chemical Company in East Alton, Ill. These two gigantic corporations have complete control over ammunition and all its component parts in these United States."

[57] Keynes, *General Theory of Employment, Interest, and Money* (London, 1936), p. 382.

[58] Joan Robinson, *Economic Journal* (December 1936), p. 693.

FIVE

On the Roots of Backwardness

WE have been concerned thus far with highly developed capitalist societies overflowing with economic surplus and incapable of its rational utilization. They represent, however, only one aspect of the general landscape of contemporary capitalism. Its other and no less significant component is the large segment of the "free world" that is usually referred to as underdeveloped. Just as the advanced sector includes a multitude of areas as far apart in economic, social, political, and cultural characteristics as the United States and Japan, Germany and France, Britain and Switzerland, so the underdeveloped sector is composed of a wide variety of countries with tremendous differences between them. Nigeria and Greece, Brazil and Thailand, Egypt and Spain all belong in the group of the backward areas.

Nevertheless in attempting to comprehend the laws of motion of both the advanced and the backward parts of the capitalist world, it is possible, and indeed mandatory, to abstract from the peculiarities of the individual cases and to concentrate on their essential common characteristics. In fact, no scientific work is conceivable if this method is not to be applied; and whether it be Marx's "pure capitalism," Marshall's "representative firm," or Weber's "ideal type," abstraction from the secondary attributes of a phenomenon and concentration on its basic scaffolding have always been the primary tools of all ana-

134

lytical effort.[1] That the resulting "model" of whatever happens to be studied does not do full justice to any particular case, does not adequately accommodate all its peculiarities and specifications, matters very little, and does not represent a valid censure of the method itself or of its immediate results. If the model lives up to its aim, if it succeeds in capturing the dominant features of the real process, it will contribute more to its understanding than any quantity of detailed information, any amount of particular data. What is more, it is only with the help of such a model, only with the contours of the "ideal type" clearly in mind, that meaning can be attached to all the information and data continually assembled by organized research that more frequently serve as a substitute for insight than as an aid to it.

The relevance of this to the study of the conditions prevailing in the underdeveloped countries and to the comprehension of the problems confronting them was recognized in a recent United Nations report: ". . . while it may be true that no two countries face identical difficulties in their industrialization process, it is also true that countries at a similar developmental stage face difficulties of much the same kind and, being subjected to much the same economic forces, often find themselves in very similar situations."[2] Thus in what follows no attempt is made to present a photographic picture of any *particular* underdeveloped capitalist country nor to analyze the obstacles to industrialization under capitalism existing in *specific* geographic areas. It is rather the purpose of this and the subsequent chapters to identify what I consider to be the essential elements of the matter, and to assemble as it were the bare skeleton of the issue—without concern for the concrete setting and form in which it may appear in any individual case.

With this reservation in mind we may proceed *in medias res*.

[1] This is not to say that the knowledge of what *are* the essential characteristics of a phenomenon is given by God to "His own in their sleep." It cannot be attained except as the result of a thorough and detailed study of the subject matter, with this research forming the basis for the decision as to what is to be abstracted from and what is to be included in the theoretical model. In this sense social sciences no less than other sciences convey *cumulative* knowledge; not each and every investigator needs to start from scratch. There are available wholly adequate guideposts to what constitutes the essential elements of a socioeconomic process. As in all scientific work, the adequacy of these guideposts can be established in no other way than by practice, that is, in their theoretical and empirical application to concrete historical material.

[2] *Processes and Problems of Industrialization of Under-developed Countries* (1955), pp. 6 ff.

What characterizes all underdeveloped countries, indeed what accounts for their designation as underdeveloped, is the paucity of their per capita output. Although international comparisons of national income estimates are beset by a host of well-known difficulties, a notion of the situation existing in underdeveloped countries is adequately conveyed by the following table:

World Income Distribution in 1949[3]

	World income (percent)	World population (percent)	Income per capita
High-income countries	67	18	$915
Middle-income countries	18	15	310
Low-income countries	15	67	54

It can be seen that approximately two-thirds of the human race have an average per capita income equivalent to some 50 to 60 dollars a year; it needs no explanation that for nearly all areas to which this statistic applies it signifies chronic starvation, abysmal squalor, and rampant disease. Nor has there been any appreciable change in this condition for a century or two; in some underdeveloped countries matters may even have deteriorated in the course of the last hundred years. Since during this period living standards in the advanced countries have markedly improved, "the distribution of per capita income among the countries of the world has grown less rather than more equal."[4]

The question that immediately arises is, why is it that in the backward capitalist countries there has been no advance along the lines of capitalist development that are familiar from the history of other capitalist countries, and why is it that forward movement there has been either slow or altogether absent? A correct answer to this question is of foremost importance. It is indeed indispensable if one is to grasp what at the present time stands in the way of economic and social progress in underdeveloped countries, and if one is to understand the direction and the form which their future development is likely to assume.

The problem may best be approached by recalling the conditions

[3] Ragnar Nurkse, *Problems of Capital Formation in Underdeveloped Countries* (Oxford, 1953), p. 63, where the source for this calculation is indicated.

[4] E. S. Mason, *Promoting Economic Development* (Claremont, California, 1955), p. 16.

from which capitalism evolved in both the now advanced and the now underdeveloped parts of the world. These were everywhere a mode of production and a social and political order that are conveniently summarized under the name feudalism. Not that the structure of feudalism was everywhere the same. Quite on the contrary, just as "one would be right in talking, not of a single history of capitalism, and of the general shape which this has, but of a collection of histories of capitalism, all of them having a general similarity of shape, but each of them separately dated as regards its main stages,"[5] so one has to bear in mind the tremendous difference between the histories of the feudal systems in different parts of the world. Indeed, the far-reaching divergences between the pre-capitalist structure of China, the society founded upon the village communities of India, and the social order rooted in serfdom that was characteristic of much of the pre-capitalist development of Europe have led many historians to doubt the general applicability of the term "feudalism." Without having to enter this debate, we may confine ourselves to a proposition on which there would seem to be fairly wide consensus: that the pre-capitalist order, be it in Europe or be it in Asia, had entered at a certain state of its development a period of disintegration and decay. In different countries this decomposition was more or less violent, the period of decline was shorter or longer—the general *direction* of the movement was everywhere the same. At the risk of extreme oversimplification the following distinct, if closely interrelated, processes may be considered to have been its salient features. First, there was a slow but nevertheless appreciable increase in agricultural output accompanied by intensified feudal pressure upon the underlying agricultural population as well as ever more massive displacement and rebellion of peasants and consequently emergence of a potential industrial labor force. Secondly, there was a more or less far-reaching and more or less general propagation of division of labor and with it the evolution of the class of merchants and artisans accompanied by the growth of towns. And thirdly there was a more or less spectacular accumulation of capital in the hands of the more or less steadily expanding and rising class of merchants and wealthy peasants.

It is the confluence of all these processes (and of a number of other secondary developments) that forms the indispensable precondition for the emergence of capitalism. In the words of Marx, "what

[5] Maurice Dobb, *Studies in the Development of Capitalism* (London, 1946), p. 21.

enables money wealth to become capital is on one hand its meeting with free workers; is secondly its meeting with equally free and available for sale means of subsistence, materials etc. that were otherwise d'une manière ou d'une autre the property of the now dispossessed masses."[6] Yet it is the third—the primary accumulation of capital—to which, as the term "capitalism" clearly suggests, strategic significance must undoubtedly be assigned. To be sure, the mere accumulation of merchant capital does not per se lead to the development of capitalism.[7] What warrants nonetheless its being singled out for particular attention are two considerations. In the first place, other conditions determining the transition from feudalism to capitalism were maturing nearly everywhere—if at different times and with different speed—under the impact of the internal stresses and strains of the feudal order. Secondly, it was the scope and the speed of the accumulation of merchant capital and of the ascent of the merchant class that played itself a major part in corroding the structure of feudal society, in creating the prerequisites for its ultimate demise. To quote Marx again: "It is determined by the very nature of capital . . . by its genesis that it stems from *money* and therefore from wealth which exists in the form of money. For the same reasons it makes its appearance as emerging from circulation, as its *product*. Capital formation does not stem therefore from landed property (here at best from the *tenant* to the extent to which he is a trader in agricultural produce); nor from the guild (although there is a possibility)—but from merchant and usurer wealth."[8]

In Western Europe, mercantile accumulations were particularly large, and, what is of considerable significance, highly concentrated. This was partly due to the geographical location of the Western European countries which gave them the possibility for an early development of navigation, and with it of a rapid expansion of maritime and riparian commerce. It was caused secondly—paradoxically enough—by Western Europe's being in terms of natural resources poorer and in terms of its economic development at the relevant time in many respects more backward rather than more advanced than the

[6] *Grundrisse der Kritik der Politischen Ökonomie* (Rohentwurf) (Berlin, 1953), p. 404.

[7] As Dobb points out, "one feature of this new merchant bourgeoisie that is at first as surprising as it is universal, is the readiness with which this class compromised with feudal society once its privileges had been won." *Op. cit.*, p. 120.

[8] *Loc. cit.*

parts of the world which were the objects of its commercial penetration. Hence the drive to procure tropical produce of all kinds (spices, tea, ivory, indigo, etc.) that could not be obtained nearby, hence also the effort to import valuable products of Oriental skills (high quality cloth, ornaments, pottery, and the like), and hence finally the wild scramble to bring back precious metals and stones that were in short supply at home. The resulting far-flung trade, combined with piracy, outright plunder, slave traffic, and discovery of gold, led to a rapid formation of vast fortunes in the hands of Western European merchants.[9]

This wealth had the usual tendency to snowball. The requirements of navigation gave a strong stimulus to scientific discovery and technological progress. Shipbuilding, outfitting of overseas expeditions, the manufacturing of arms and other supplies required by them for protection as well as for the conduct of "negotiations" with their overseas trading partners—all provided a mighty impulse to the development of capitalist enterprise. The principle that "one thing gives another" came in full operation, external economies of various kinds became increasingly available, and further development could proceed at an accelerated rate. We need not trace here in any detail the varied ways by which the accumulated capital turned gradually to industrial pursuits. Wealthy merchants entered manufacturing to assure themselves of steady and cheap supplies. Artisans grown rich or in partnership with moneyed tradesmen expanded the scale of their operations. Not infrequently even rich landowners became involved in industry (particularly mining) and thus laid the foundation for large capitalist enterprises. But most important of all, the state, ever more under the control of capitalist interests, became increasingly active in aiding and advancing the budding entrepreneurs. "They all employ the power of the State, the concentrated and organized force of society, to hasten, hothouse fashion, the transformation of the feudal mode of production into the capitalist mode, and to shorten the transition."[10]

[9] Cf. Dobb. *op. cit.*, pp. 207 ff. On the role played by slavery and slave traffic in the primary accumulation of capital, cf. Eric Williams, *Capitalism and Slavery* (Chapel Hill, North Carolina, 1944).

[10] Marx, *Capital* (Kerr ed.), Vol. I, p. 823. Of the role played by the capitalist-dominated state in the early development of capitalism, even in a country with proverbially little government participation in economic affairs, there is a useful reminder by Professor E. S. Mason: "Most Americans are unaware of the extent to which the Federal and State governments promoted the early economic development of the United

Western Europe's large leap forward need not necessarily have prevented economic growth in other countries. Though they might not have been able to narrow down, let alone to eliminate, the gap between themselves and the Western European pioneers, they could nevertheless have entered a growth process of their own, attaining more or less advanced levels of productivity and output. Indeed, the expanding contact with the scientifically and technologically leading Western European nations might have been expected to facilitate the forward movement of the countries with which Western Europe came into contact. So it actually appeared during the latter seventeenth and the eighteenth centuries, in the beginnings of modern capitalism; and such developments as took place at that time in a number of now underdeveloped countries lent ample support to this expectation. The primary accumulation of capital was making rapid progress, crafts and manufacturing expanded, and mounting revolts of the peasantry combined with increasing pressure from the rising bourgeoisie everywhere shook the foundations of the pre-capitalist order. This can be seen whether we consider the early history of capitalism in Russia and in Eastern and Southeastern Europe or whether we retrace the beginning of capitalism in India, the Near East, or even China. Not that all these and other countries would necessarily have moved along a road identical to that traveled by Britain, Holland, Germany, or France. Differences not only in the natural prerequisites of economic development, in geographic location and climate, but also in political, cultural, and religious background were bound to create divergences in levels and rates of increase of productivity. Similarly these differences could not but cause wide variations in the amounts of capital accumulation in the hands of the capitalist classes of individual nations as well as in the degrees of cohesion and resilience of their respective pre-capitalist political and social structures. Still, whatever its speed and whatever its zigzags, the general direction of the historical movement seems to have been the same for the backward echelons as for the forward contingents. "The country that is more developed industrially only shows to the less developed the image of its own future."[11]

That in reality things have not developed in this way, that Western

States through the provision of social capital in the form of canals, river development, turnpikes, railways, port facilities and the like. The provision of public works of this sort by government was, of course, essential to the expansion of private investment." *Promoting Economic Development* (Claremont, California, 1955), p. 47.

[11] Marx, *Capital* (Kerr ed.), Vol. I, p. 13.

Europe left the rest of the world far behind was, however, by no means a matter of fortuitous accident or of some racial peculiarities of different peoples. It was actually determined by the nature of Western European development itself. For the effects of Western European capitalist penetration of the outside world were enormously complex. They depended on the exact nature of that penetration. They depended no less on the stage of development reached by the societies that were exposed to the foreign contacts. Therefore one cannot distinguish sharply enough between the impact of Western Europe's entrance into North America (and Australia and New Zealand) on one side, and the "opening up" by Western capitalism of Asia, Africa, or Eastern Europe. In the former case Western Europeans entered more or less complete societal vacua, and *settled* in those areas establishing themselves as their permanent residents. Whether such were their original intentions or not; whether they were merchant-adventurers seeking quick profits to take home and refugees from political and religious persecutions as in the case of North America, or deportees of all kinds as in the case of Australia; whether they brought with them some capital or merely aggressiveness, skills, and ingenuity—this matters very little. They came to the new lands with "capitalism in their bones" and meeting no resistance worth the name—the exploits of Davy Crockett notwithstanding—they succeeded in a short time in establishing on virtually virgin (and exceptionally fertile) soil an indigenous society of their own. From the outset capitalist in its structure, unencumbered by the fetters and barriers of feudalism, that society could single-mindedly devote itself to the development of its productive resources. Its social and political energies were neither sapped by a protracted struggle against feudal rule nor dissipated in overcoming the conventions and traditions of the feudal age. The only obstacle to accumulation and capitalist expansion was foreign domination. Yet, although by no means free of internal tensions and conflicts of considerable intensity—Benedict Arnold!—the newly emerging bourgeois societies were at an early stage cohesive and strong enough to overthrow that domination and to create a political framework conducive to the growth of capitalism.

This is a far cry from what occurred in other parts of the world. What is decisive is not so much that the Western European enterprisers breaking into India, China, the countries of Southeast Asia, the Near East, and Africa were in many respects different from those who had directed themselves to North America. Equally products of the capitalist development in the West, they nurtured aspirations that were nothing but self-seeking and engaged in activities that were nothing but predatory. Where the crucial difference lay was in what they found upon their arrival in Asia and Africa. That was indeed a world apart from what was encountered in America or in Australia.

Where climate and the natural environment were such as possibly to invite Western European settlers, they were faced by established societies with rich and ancient cultures, still pre-capitalist or in the embryonic state of capitalist development. Where the existing social organizations were primitive and tribal, the general conditions and in particular the climate were such as to preclude any mass settlement of Western European arrivals. Consequently in both cases the Western European visitors rapidly determined to extract the largest possible gains from the host countries, and to take their loot home. Thus they engaged in outright plunder or in plunder thinly veiled as trade, seizing and removing tremendous wealth from the places of their penetrations. "In the cruel rapacity of its exploitation colonial policy in the seventeenth and eighteenth centuries differed little from the methods by which in earlier centuries Crusaders and the armed merchants of Italian cities had robbed the Byzantine territories of the Levant."[12] And "the treasures captured outside Europe by undisguised looting, enslavement and murder flowed back to the mother-country and transformed themselves into capital."[13]

The importance of these "unilateral transfers" of wealth from the non-European countries to those of Western Europe is commonly obscured by focusing attention merely on their magnitude in terms of the *aggregate outputs* of the countries to which they accrued or of those from which they were taken. Not that they were not large even by that standard. However, what lent them their crucial significance to the development of Western Europe and to that of the now underdeveloped countries is the nature, so to speak, the economic *locus* of the resources involved. Indeed whatever may have been the fractional increase of Western Europe's *national income* derived from its overseas operations, they *multiplied the economic* surplus at its disposal. What is more: the increment of the economic surplus appeared immediately in a concentrated form and came largely into the hands of capitalists who could use it for investment purposes. The intensity of the boost to Western Europe's development resulting

---

[12] Dobb, *Studies in the Development of Capitalism* (London, 1946), p. 208.

[13] Marx, *Capital* (Kerr ed.), Vol. I, p. 826.

from this "exogenous" contribution to its capital accumulation can
hardly be exaggerated.[14]

This transfusion itself and in particular the methods by which
it was perpetrated had perhaps an even more telling impact on the
reluctant—to say the least—"donor" countries. They violently jolted
their entire development and affected drastically its subsequent course.
They burst with explosive force into the glacial movement of their
ancient societies and tremendously accelerated the process of decomposition of their pre-capitalist structures. By breaking up the age-old
patterns of their agricultural economy, and by forcing shifts to the
production of exportable crops, Western capitalism destroyed the
self-sufficiency of their rural society that formed the basis of the pre-
capitalist order in all countries of its penetration, and rapidly widened
and deepened the scope of commodity circulation. By outright—in
many countries, massive—seizure of peasant-occupied land for plantation purposes and other uses by foreign enterprise and by exposing
their rural handicrafts to the withering competition of its industrial
exports, it created a vast pool of pauperized labor.[15] Enlarging thus
the area of capitalist activities, it advanced the evolution of legal and
property relations attuned to the needs of a market economy and
established administrative institutions required for their enforcement.
If only in order to expand and to tighten the economic and political
grip on the areas of its domination, it forced the diversion of some of
their economic surplus to the improvement of their systems of communication, to the building of railroads, harbors, and highways, providing thereby as a by-product the facilities needed for profitable investment of capital.

This is, however, only one side of the ledger. Accelerating with
irresistible energy the maturing of *some* of the basic prerequisites for
the development of a capitalist system, the intrusion of Western capitalism in the now underdeveloped countries blocked with equal force
the ripening of others. The removal of a large share of the affected
countries' previously accumulated and currently generated surplus
could not but cause a serious setback to their primary accumulation
of capital. Their being exposed to ruinous competition from abroad

[14] This is not to say that on balance the effect on the "beneficiary"
countries was an unmixed blessing. The corruption of social and political
life in Western Europe, the growth of chauvinism and racism, the eventual
development of imperialism and jingoism, all owe much to the heinous
rape of non-European peoples that accompanied the early development of
Western capitalism.

[15] Cf. W. E. Moore, *Industrialization and Labor* (Ithaca and New
York, 1951), p. 52.

could not but smother their fledgling industries. Although the expansion of commodity circulation, the pauperization of large numbers of peasants and artisans, the contact with Western technology, provided a powerful impetus to the development of capitalism, this development was forcibly shunted off its normal course, distorted and crippled to suit the purposes of Western imperialism.

Thus the peoples who came into the orbit of Western capitalist expansion found themselves in the twilight of feudalism and capitalism enduring the worst features of both worlds, and the entire impact of imperialist subjugation to boot. To oppression by their feudal lords, ruthless but tempered by tradition, was added domination by foreign and domestic capitalists, callous and limited only by what the traffic would bear. The obscurantism and arbitrary violence inherited from their feudal past was combined with the rationality and sharply calculating rapacity of their capitalist present. Their exploitation was multiplied, yet its fruits were not to increase their productive wealth; these went abroad or served to support a parasitic bourgeoisie at home. They lived in abysmal misery, yet they had no prospect of a better tomorrow. They existed under capitalism, yet there was no accumulation of capital. They lost their time-honored means of livelihood, their arts and crafts, yet there was no modern industry to provide new ones in their place. They were thrust into extensive contact with the advanced science of the West, yet remained in a state of the darkest backwardness. *Asiatic mode*

II

The outstanding case in point is obviously India. The record of India from the days of the East India Company is well known and calls for no elaboration. On few historical subjects is there so much agreement among students of widely differing persuasions as on what happened to India after Western capitalism appended her to its chariot. It is well expressed by an authority surely not suspect of anti-British prejudice who summarizes her findings as follows: ". . . up to the eighteenth century, the economic condition of India was relatively advanced, and Indian methods of production and of industrial and commercial organization could stand comparison with those in vogue in any other part of the world. . . . A country which has manufactured and exported the finest muslins and other luxurious fabrics and articles, at a time when the ancestors of the British were living an extremely primitive life, has failed to take part in the economic revolution initiated by the descendants of those same wild barbarians."[16] Nor was that "failure" something accidental or due to some peculiar inaptitude of the Indian "race."[17] It was caused by the elaborate, ruthless, systematic despoliation of India by British capital from the very onset of British rule. So stupendous was the extent of plunder, so utterly fantastic the amount of what was extracted from India that in 1875 the Marquess of Salisbury—then Secretary of State for India —warned that "as India must be bled, the bleeding should be done judiciously."[18] The volume of wealth that Britain derived from India and that was added to Britain's capital accumulations has to my knowledge never been fully assessed. Digby notes that estimates had been made according to which between Plassey and Waterloo—a period of crucial importance for the development of British capitalism —between £500,000,000 and £1,000,000,000 worth of treasure was taken by Britain from India. The vastness of this sum can be visualized when it is considered that at the turn of the nineteenth century the aggregate capital of all joint stock companies operating in India amounted to £36,000,000. The authoritative Indian statisticians, K. T. Shah and K. J. Khambata, calculated that in the early decades of the current century Britain appropriated annually under one title or another over 10 percent of India's gross national income.[19] And it can be safely assumed that this drain was smaller in the twentieth century

[16] Vera Anstey, *The Economic Development of India* (London, New York, Toronto, 1929; cited from 4th edition, 1952), p. 5.

[17] As was noted by an earlier observer of India, "the great mass of the Indian people possesses a great *industrial energy*, is well fitted to accumulate capital, and remarkable for a mathematical clearness of head, and talent for figures and exact sciences. Their intellects are excellent." Quoted in Marx, "The Future Results of the British Rule in India," in Marx and Engels, *On Britain* (Moscow, 1953), p. 390. (Italics in the original.) That at the same time the British-organized-and-supervised educational system did all it could not to promote but to repress the growth of scientific and industrial aptitude among the Indians has been attested by a number of students of India. In the words of Vera Anstey: ". . . should we not inquire how far the system of education introduced by the British has helped to generate the scientific spirit and the spread of scientific knowledge? Do we not find that, instead of teaching the people to understand the world about them and how natural forces can best be utilized and controlled, they have been taught to write notes on archaic phrases in the works of sixteenth- and seventeenth-century Englishmen and to learn by rote the personal history of obscure rulers of a foreign land?" *Op. cit.,* p. 4.

[18] William Digby, *"Prosperous" British India* (London, 1901), p. xii.

[19] Referred to in R. Palme Dutt, *India Today* (Bombay, 1949), p. 32. This ratio should be considered in the light of the share of income that could be expected to constitute *economic surplus* in a country as poor as India.

than in the eighteenth and nineteenth centuries. It can moreover be considered as certain that this ratio understates the extent of Britain's encroachment on India's resources since it refers merely to *direct* transfers and does not include India's losses due to unfavorable terms of trade imposed upon her by the British.

Looking at the matter in terms of what it meant to Britain, Brooks Adams paints a vivid picture that is worth citing at some length:

Upon the plundering of India there can be no better authority than Macaulay, who held high office at Calcutta . . . and who less than any of the writers who have followed him was a mouth-piece of the official class. He has told how after Plassey "the shower of wealth" began to fall, and he has described Clive's own gains: "We may safely affirm that no Englishman who started with nothing has ever, in any line of life, created such a fortune at the early age of thirty-four! But the takings of Clive, either for himself or for the government, were trifling compared to the wholesale robbery and spoliation which followed his departure, when Bengal was surrendered a helpless prey to a myriad of greedy officials. These officials were absolute, irresponsible, and rapacious, and they emptied the private hoards. Their only thought was to wring some hundreds of thousands of pounds out of the natives as quickly as possible, and hurry home to display their wealth. Enormous fortunes were thus rapidly accumulated at Calcutta, while thirty millions of human beings were reduced to the extremity of wretchedness. . . . The misgovernment of the English was carried to a point such as seems hardly compatible with the very existence of society. The Roman proconsul, who, in a year or two, squeezed out of a province the means of rearing marble palaces and baths on the shore of Campania, of drinking from amber, of feasting on singing birds, of exhibiting armies of gladiators and flocks of camelopards; the Spanish viceroy, who, leaving behind him the curses of Mexico or Lima, entered Madrid with a long train of gilded coaches, and of sumpter-horses trapped and shod with silver, were now outdone."[20] . . . Very soon after Plassey the Bengal plunder began to arrive in London, and the effect appears to have been instantaneous, for all authorities agree that the "industrial revolution," the event which has divided the nineteenth century from all antecedent time, began with the year 1760. Prior to 1760 . . . the machinery used for spinning cotton in Lancashire was almost as simple as in India; while about 1750 the English iron industry was in full decline. . . . To the capitalist then, rather than to the inventor, civilization owes the steam-engine as a part of daily life."[21]

A comprehensive analysis of the impact of this frantic orgy of primary accumulation of capital upon the development of India is

---

[20] The above passage is from Macaulay's *Lord Clive*.
[21] *The Law of Civilization and Decay, An Essay on History* (New York, 1896; cited from 1943 reprint), pp. 294 ff.

presented in the standard work by Romesh Dutt, *The Economic History of India*,[22] and we can do no better than borrow his words:

It is, unfortunately, a fact, that in many ways, the sources of national wealth in India have been narrowed under the British rule. India in the eighteenth century was a great manufacturing as well as a great agricultural country, and the products of the Indian loom supplied the markets of Asia and of Europe. It is, unfortunately, true that the East Indian Company and the British Parliament, following the selfish commercial policy of a hundred years ago, discouraged Indian manufacturers in the early years of British rule in order to encourage the rising manufactures of England. Their fixed policy, pursued during the last decades of the eighteenth century and the first decades of the nineteenth, was to make India subservient to the industries of Great Britain, and to make the Indian people grow raw produce only, in order to supply material for the looms and manufactures of Great Britain. This policy was pursued with unwavering resolution and with fatal success; orders were sent out, to force Indian artisans to work in the Company's factories; commercial residents were legally vested with extensive powers over villages and communities of Indian weavers; prohibitive tariffs excluded Indian silk and cotton goods from England; English goods were admitted into India free of duty or on payment of a nominal duty. . . . The invention of the power-loom in Europe completed the decline of the Indian industries; and when in recent years the power-loom was set up in India, England once more acted towards India with unfair jealousy. An excise duty has been imposed on the production of cotton fabrics in India which . . . stifles the new steam-mills of India. Agriculture is now virtually the only remaining source of national wealth of India . . . but what the British Government . . . take as Land Tax at the present day sometimes approximates to the whole of the economic rent. . . . This . . . paralyses agriculture, prevents saving, and keeps the tiller of the soil in a state of poverty and indebtedness. . . . In India the State virtually interferes with the accumulation of wealth from the soil, intercepts the incomes and gains of the tillers . . . leaving the cultivators permanently poor. . . . In India, the State has fostered no new industries and revived no old industries for the people. . . . In one shape or another all that could be raised in India by an excessive taxation flowed to Europe, after paying for a starved administration. . . . Verily the moisture of India blesses and fertilizes other lands.

The catastrophe that was brought upon India by the invasion of British capitalism thus assumed staggering proportions. To be sure, the process of transition from feudalism to capitalism, and of the

[22] London, 1901; quoted from the 7th edition, 1950, pp. viii ff. This writer, a high-ranking civil servant in the British administration of India and Lecturer in Indian History at University College, London, is not to be confused with R. Palme Dutt, the author of the important book on India, *India Today* (London, 1940; 2nd edition, Bombay, 1949).

diversion of resources to capital formation that forms its integral part, has caused a vast amount of suffering, misery, and destitution wherever it has taken its inexorable course. Society's economic surplus was not only transferred from one use to another with all the attendant upheavals, struggles, and hardships; more of it was squeezed from the underfed, underclad, underhoused, and overworked masses. Yet this surplus—albeit only incompletely and irrationally—was used for productive investment, and served to lay the foundations for the eventual expansion of productivity and output. Indeed, there can be no doubt that had the amount of economic surplus that Britain has torn from India been *invested in India*, India's economic development to date would have borne little similarity to the actual somber record. It is idle to speculate whether India by now would have reached a level of economic advancement commensurate with its fabulous natural resources and with the potentialities of its people. In any case the fate of the successive Indian generations would not have resembled even remotely the chronic catastrophe of the last two centuries.

But the harm done to India's economic potential is exceeded only by the crippling, and perhaps even more lasting, damage inflicted upon its people. "All the civil wars, invasions, revolutions, conquests, famines strangely complex, rapid and destructive as the successive action in Hindustan may appear, did not go deeper than its surface. England has broken down the entire framework of Indian society, without any symptoms of reconstitution yet appearing. This loss of his old world, with no gain of a new one, imparts a particular kind of melancholy to the present misery of the Hindu and separates Hindustan, ruled by Britain, from all its ancient traditions, and from the whole of its past history."[22]

For British policy in India was patterned very closely upon the practice followed by some Indian tyrants eloquently described by Macaulay: "When they dreaded the capacity and spirit of some distinguished subject, and yet could not venture to murder him, [they used] . . . to administer to him a daily dose of the pousta, a preparation of opium, the effect of which was in a few months to destroy all the bodily and mental powers of the wretch who was drugged with it, and to turn him into a helpless idiot. The detestable artifice, more horrible than assassination itself, was worthy of those who employed

[23] Marx, "British Rule in India," in Marx and Engels, *Selected Works* (Moscow, 1949-1950), Vol. I, p. 313.

it."[24] Thus the British administration of India systematically destroyed all the fibres and foundations of Indian society. Its land and taxation policy ruined India's village economy and substituted for it the parasitic landowner and moneylender. Its commercial policy destroyed the Indian artisan and created the infamous slums of the Indian cities filled with millions of starving and diseased paupers. Its economic policy broke down whatever beginnings there were of an indigenous industrial development and promoted the proliferations of speculators, petty businessmen, agents, and sharks of all descriptions eking out a sterile and precarious livelihood in the meshes of a decaying society. "British rule thus consolidated itself by creating new classes and vested interests who were tied up with that rule and whose privileges depended on its continuance. There were the landowners and the princes, and there were a large number of subordinate members of the services in various departments of the government, from the patwari, the village headman, upward. . . . To all these methods must be added the deliberate policy, pursued throughout the period of British rule, of creating divisions among Indians, of encouraging one group at the cost of the other."[25] And reference has already been made to British policies with regard to education. In the chapter of Nehru's book from which the above passage was taken, the following is quoted from Kaye's *Life of Metcalfe:* ". . . this dread of the free diffusion of knowledge became a chronic disease . . . continually afflicting the members of Government with all sorts of hypochondriacal day-dreams and nightmares, in which visions of the Printing Press and the Bible were making their flesh creep, and their hair stand erect with horror. It was our policy in those days to keep the natives of India in the profoundest state of barbarism and darkness, and every attempt to diffuse the light of knowledge among the people, either of our own or of the independent states, was vehemently opposed and resented."

It is thus a fair assessment of the effects on India of two centuries of domination by Western capitalism as well as a correct analysis of the causes of India's present backwardness when Nehru says: ". . . nearly all our major problems today have grown up during British rule and as a direct result of British policy: the princes; the minority problem; various vested interests, foreign and Indian; the lack of industry and the neglect of agriculture; the extreme backward-

[24] *Speeches,* quoted in Digby, *"Prosperous" British India* (London, 1901), p. 63.

[25] Jawaharlal Nehru, *The Discovery of India* (New York, 1946), pp. 304 ff.

ness in the social services; and, above all, the tragic poverty of the people."[26]

It is hardly necessary to add that all this is not to idealize India's pre-British past and to portray it romantically as a Paradise Lost. As Marx stressed in "a magnificent passage" of one of his previously cited articles on India:

. . . we must not forget that these idyllic village communities, inoffensive though they may appear, had always been the solid foundation of Oriental despotism, that they restricted the human mind within the smallest possible compass, making it the unresisting tool of superstition, enslaving it beneath traditional rules, depriving it of all grandeur and historical energies. We must not forget the barbarian egotism which, concentrating on some miserable patch of land, had quietly witnessed the ruin of empires, the perpetration of unspeakable cruelties, the massacre of the population of large towns with no other consideration bestowed upon them than on natural events, itself the helpless prey of any aggressor who deigned to notice it at all. We must not forget that this undignified, stagnatory, and vegetative life, that this passive sort of existence evoked on the other part, in contradistinction, wild, aimless, unbounded forces of destruction and rendered murder itself a religious rite in Hindustan. We must not forget that these little communities were contaminated by a distinction of caste and by slavery, that they subjugated man to external circumstances, instead of elevating man the sovereign of circumstances, that they transformed a self-developing social state into never changing natural destiny, and thus brought about a brutalizing worship of nature.[27]

At the same time it should not be overlooked that India, if left to herself, might have found in the course of time a shorter and surely less tortuous road toward a better and richer society. That on that road she would have had to pass through the purgatory of a bourgeois revolution, that a long phase of capitalist development would have been the inevitable price that she would have had to pay for progress, can hardly be doubted. It would have been, however, an entirely different India (and an entirely different world), had she been allowed— as some more fortunate countries were—to realize her destiny in her own way, to employ her resources for her own benefit, and to harness her energies and abilities for the advancement of her own people.

[26] *Ibid.*, pp. 306 ff.
[27] "British Rule in India," *op. cit.*, p. 317.

III

This is speculation to be sure, but a legitimate one. For the alternative to the massive removal of their accumulated wealth and current output, to the ruthless suppression and distortion of all indigenous economic growth, to the systematic corruption of their social, political, and cultural life that were inflicted by Western capitalism upon all of the now underdeveloped countries is by no means purely hypothetical.[28]

This can be clearly seen in the history of the only Asian country that succeeded in escaping its neighbors' fate and in attaining a relatively high degree of economic advancement. For in the period under consideration—when Western capitalism was ruining India, establishing its grip over Africa, subjugating Latin America, and opening up China—conditions in Japan were as conducive, or rather as unfavorable, to economic development as anywhere else in Asia. Indeed, Japan "with its purely feudal organization of landed property and its developed small peasant economy" (Marx), while torn by all the internal tensions and conflicts of a feudal society, was perhaps even more tightly locked in the straitjacket of feudal constraints and restrictions than any other pre-capitalist country. "Every effort was made for over two hundred years to suppress growth and change. . . . society was frozen into a legally immutable class mold. . . . Maintenance of the warrior class continued to take the surplus of society, leaving little for investment. . . . the closed class system smothered creative

---

[28] We have treated India at some length, but what applies to India applies *mutatis mutandis* to all the other backward areas. For comprehensive surveys of the experience of Burma and the Dutch East Indies (as well as for an excellent discussion of the entire colonial policy of the Western powers), see the books by J. S. Furnivall, in particular *Netherlands Indies* (Cambridge, England, 1944) and *Colonial Policy and Practice* (Cambridge, England, 1948). Very useful is also J. H. Boeke, *The Evolution of the Netherlands Indies Economy* (New York, 1946). The literature on China is vast. In the context of the present discussion most illuminating are Michael Greenberg, *British Trade and the Opening of China 1800-1842* (Cambridge, England, 1951), and G. E. Efimov, *Ocherki po Novoy i Noveyshey Istorii Kitaya* (Essays on the Recent and Most Recent History of China) (Moscow, 1951). A good survey of what has happened to Africa will be found in Leonard Woolf, *Empire and Commerce in Africa* (London, N.D.), while of the truly unbelievable catastrophe that befell the Caribbean region the classic book by Bishop Bartolomeo de las Casas, *The Tears of the Indians* (reprint, Stanford, California, N.D.), is probably still the best account.

energies and tended to freeze labor and talent in traditional occupations. To sweep away these obstacles to industrial development was
unthinkable."[29]

At the same time, however, under the rigid crust of feudal rule,
there was a rapid accumulation of capital in the hands of urban and
rural merchants.[30] As a measure of the magnitude of the wealth that
was being amassed by the prosperous bourgeoisie, the following may
serve: "In 1760 the Bakufu 'borrowed' from members of the great
trading guilds as much as 1,781,000 *ryo*, a sum of the same order of
magnitude as the total ordinary expenditure of the government for one
year."[31] Since such "borrowing" was frequently not followed by re-
payment, this sum conveys not merely an indication of the affluence of
the mercantile class, but also a notion of the extent of the exactions
to which the government forced it to submit. Those exactions were
not merely financial.[32] "The authorities hedged [the merchant class]
. . . about with numerous restrictions; their style of clothing, use of
foot-gear, umbrellas, all these and a thousand other petty details were
regulated by law. The government would not even allow a merchant
to have a name which resembled a *daimyo* name, nor would it permit
tradesmen to live in the *samurai* district. In fact no feudal aristocracy
could express greater distaste for money-making and money-makers
than the Tokugawa moralists and legislators."[33]

While there seems to be some disagreement among the historians
of Japan on the share of "credit" due to different classes for their part
in overthrowing the Tokugawa rule, there is no doubt that the pressure
of the rapidly developing capitalist relations against the barriers of

[29] Thomas C. Smith, *Political Change and Industrial Development in
Japan: Government Enterprise, 1868-1880* (Stanford, California, 1955),
Chapter II. I am greatly indebted to Professor Smith for letting me see
the galley proofs of this excellent monograph.

[30] It is most important to note that already in the eighteenth century
powerful feudal clans, in particular that of Satsuma in southern Kyushu,
engaged in far-flung trading and accumulated large amounts of capital.
E. Herbert Norman, *Japan's Emergence as a Modern State* (New York,
1946), p. 15. The early orientation toward mercantile activities on the
part of some feudal lords had probably much to do with the fact that,
belonging to the 86 *tozama* or "outside" lords, they were excluded by
the ruling Tokugawa group from all participation in government and
were thus forced to seek outlets for their energies in other pursuits.

[31] G. B. Sansom, *The Western World and Japan* (New York, 1950),
p. 240.

[32] They are described in some detail by G. B. Sansom, *loc. cit.*

[33] E. Herbert Norman, *Japan's Emergence as a Modern State* (New
York, 1946), p. 17.

the feudal order was the basic force that brought about the Meiji Restoration. This is intended neither to belittle the tremendous *political* significance of the mounting opposition of the (lower) *samurai* or of the rising wave of peasant uprisings that during the first half of the nineteenth century shook the very foundations of the Tokugawa regime, nor to exaggerate the political role played by the merchant class as such in establishing the new order.[34] As in all revolutions, it was a combination of heterogeneous social groups that accomplished the overturn of the *ancien régime*. But while the most active and most conspicuous among them were the *déclassé* warriors and the frustrated intellectuals, the embittered feudal lords and the disgruntled courtiers who were left out by the Tokugawa ruling group, yet it was the rising bourgeoisie that determined both the direction and the outcome of the movement, and it was the capitalist class that reaped the political and

[34] It is in general rather questionable how much importance should be attached to the class background of *individuals* participating in revolutionary events. Too many random factors influencing the decisions and behavior of individual members of different classes are at work for a close relation to be found between the class content of a historical movement and the class origin of possibly even significant numbers of its participants and leaders. A bourgeois revolution is rendered no less bourgeois by the fact that it is joined by a great number of noblemen who, precisely because of their background and education, may have risen above the vantage point of their own class, and to a position of leadership in a progressive movement: nor is a proletarian revolution less proletarian because its leading echelons may contain, for similar reasons, many individuals of bourgeois or aristocratic background. Therefore, I would not give much weight to the information presented by Thomas C. Smith (*op. cit.*, Chapter II) on the class origins of the Restoration leaders given court rank posthumously, presumably in recognition of the part they played in the Restoration. The striking smallness of the number of merchants so rewarded would seem to suggest that the merchant class played only a minor part in the revolutionary movement. This impression would be, however, highly misleading. Traditionally, bourgeois *as individuals* have nowhere taken active part in *revolutionary politics*. Indeed, it is probably one of the outstanding characteristics of the capitalist class and is closely related to its economic and ideological habitat that it customarily operates on the political stage—particularly in times of upheaval— through retainers, agents, and allies, rather than directly through its own members. And surely in Japan, in a political environment entirely dominated by the feudal tradition and with hungry and eager *samurai* and *ronin* in superabundant supply, the merchants of Yedo and Osaka readily discerned the better part of wisdom in substituting their money for their persons in the struggle for freedom. "The descendants of the wealthy shopkeepers of Yedo and Osaka played an important, indeed an indispensable part in the movement which ended by overthrowing the Shogunate in 1868, because it could scarcely have succeeded without their financial backing." G. B. Sansom, *op. cit.*, p. 189.

economic fruits of the Revolution. "Less. dramatic than the political
and military exploits of the *samurai*, but more far-reaching in accom-
plishing both the overthrow of the *Bakufu* and the stabilization of the
new regime, was the financial support of the great *chonin*, especially
of Osaka, where it is said 70 per cent of Japan's wealth was concentrated. . . . the decisive battles in the war for the Restoration . . .
were fought and won with funds supplied by the *chonin*."[35]

It would take us too far afield, and would be unnecessary for our
present purpose, to trace in any detail the changes in Japan that were
brought about by the Meiji Revolution. Suffice it to say that it succeeded in creating the political and economic framework indispensable
for capitalist development. Providing a striking example of how "*governments*, f.i. Henry VII, VIII etc. enter as instrumentalities of the
process of historical dissolution and as creators of conditions for the
existence of capital,"[36] the regime emerging from the Restoration drastically shifted the country's economic gears and provided a tremendous
impetus both to the still incomplete primary accumulation of capital
and to its transfer from purely mercantile to industrial pursuits.

As far as the former is concerned, no effort was spared to squeeze
as much as possible out of the hard-pressed direct producers. The
economy being predominantly agrarian, with between 70 and 75 percent of the population engaged in agriculture, the bulk of the economic
surplus could not but continue to come out of the peasantry.[37] This
was assured by what constituted the outstanding trait of the Japanese
development: the blending of feudal relations in agriculture with a
strong, centralized, capitalist-dominated state furthering by all available means the growth of capitalist enterprise.[38] In fact, the combined
pressure of the reorganized and "streamlined" state and the now dominant new "bourgeois" landowning class of the *jinushi* led to a marked
increase of the burden imposed on the peasantry. If the share of the

[35] E. Herbert Norman, *op. cit.*, p. 49.

[36] Marx, *Grundrisse der Kritik der Politischen Ökonomie* (Rohentwurf)
(Berlin, 1953), p. 406. (Italics and abbreviation of "for instance" in the
original.)

[37]"The Japanese merchant . . . lacked such opportunities for the
accumulation of capital through trade and plunder as were enjoyed by
his counterpart in 16th-17th century Europe." Norman, *op. cit.*, p. 51.

[38] "The Meiji Revolution, far from suppressing them, incorporated in
the new capitalist society of Japan and legally sanctified the essential
relations of feudal property." H. Kohachiro Takahashi, "La Place de la
Révolution de Meiji dans l'histoire agraire du Japon," *Revue Historique*
(October-November 1953), p. 248.

agricultural output retained by the direct producer was 39 percent
during the first half of the nineteenth century, it fell to 32 percent
after the agrarian reform promulgated by the Meiji government, not
to exceed 42 percent until 1933-1935.[39] It is thus no exaggeration to
say that the main source of primary accumulation of capital in Japan
was the village which in the course of its entire modern history played
for Japanese capitalism the role of an internal colony.[40]

The traditional policy of ruthless direct extractions from the peasants was supplemented by a number of other devices calculated to
maximize the aggregate economic surplus. Wages of workers employed
in non-agricultural activities were rigorously held down to rock bottom
—a principle that was easy to enforce in a labor market glutted with
agricultural surplus population. Even more important was the systematic inflationary policy initiated by the Meiji administration, which
resulted not merely in further redistribution of income in favor of
capital accumulation but also in expansion of the economic surplus
through the utilization of previously unemployed resources.[41] The
most significant contribution to the primary accumulation of capital
resulted, however, from the issuance of government debentures in payment of indemnities to the dislodged feudal lords, and the assumption
of their debts by the government. "The feudal lord ceased to be a *terri-
torial* magnate drawing his income from the peasant and became instead, by virtue of the commutation of his pension, a *financial* magnate investing his freshly capitalized wealth in banks, stocks, industries or landed estates, and so joined the small financial oligarchy."[42]
Similarly the settlement of the claims of the *samurai* to a regular government stipend that was effected by their capitalization in the form

[39] *Ibid.*, p. 262, where the work of the well-known Japanese statistician
and historian M. Yamada is referred to as the source of these data.

[40] Ya. A. Pevsner, *Monopolisticheski Kapital Yaponii* (Monopoly Capital
of Japan) (Moscow, 1950), p. 11.

[41] The scope and methods of the deficit financing involved are surveyed
in Thomas C. Smith, *Political Change and Industrial Development in
Japan: Government Enterprise, 1868-1880* (Stanford, California, 1955),
Chapter VII.

[42] Norman, *op. cit.*, p. 94. Takahashi makes an additional important
observation: "These measures taken by the government of the Restoration
on one hand relieved the magnates (*daimyo*) of their ancient debts to
usurers, and on the other hand transformed the capitalists-usurers who
were often compelled to lend them money under feudal coercion into
bearers of debentures redeemable by the nation. What only yesterday
was valueless paper now became capital with a modern function." *Op. cit.*,
p. 252 *n*.

of interest-bearing bonds resulted in further swelling of the stock of available capital. This capital, centralized and administered by the rapidly growing banking system, became the basis for a massive expansion of credit. Direct government borrowing from the banks, indeed the nearly complete amalgamation of the Treasury with some of the leading banking houses of the time—Mitsui, Ono, Simada, Yasuda, and others—and the lavish profits earned by the latter in the process of this cooperation, boosted further the spectacular agglomeration of capital in the hands of a small number of financial establishments.[43]

Yet although the utmost was done in this way to fill the coffers of the bourgeoisie, to create new and vast fortunes, and to increase the capital available to the existing and prospective business class, this effort per se failed to induce a spurt of investment in *industrial* development. Just as during the last stages of the Tokugawa rule, so after the Meiji Restoration the mere concentration of tremendous wealth in the hands of the merchants, combined even as it was with a plethora of cheap manpower, did not suffice to call forth a shift from mercantile to industrial activities on the part of the entrepreneurs. "Many . . . merchant families, most notably Mitsui, did . . . take a leading role in the development of industry, but in the early years of the Meiji period . . . merchants almost to a man stuck resolutely to traditional fields of activity—commodity speculation, trade, and moneylending."[44] The process of primary accumulation of capital was still far from completed; Japan was still going through the mercantile phase of capitalism.

It was stressed before that the mercantile bourgeoisie never accomplished by itself the transition to industrial capitalism. It always required energetic and openhanded support on the part of the state, brought under the control of the rising capitalist class. Such an impetus was indeed provided by the modernized, capitalist state created by the Meiji Revolution, an impetus that moved the Japanese economy off dead center, that launched it on the road of industrial capitalism. What Marx observed in general terms about the genesis of industrial capitalism precisely describes Japanese conditions at the time of the

---

[43] From 1875 to 1880 the aggregate capital of banks expanded from 2,450,000 yen to 43,040,000 yen. "The increase was very largely the result of the issuance of pension funds to *samurai* and *daimyo* in 1876; these bonds could be exchanged at the treasury for bank notes to be used in the establishment of national banks." Thomas C. Smith, *op. cit.*, Chapter IV. Cf. also Pevsner, *op. cit.*, p. 20.

[44] Thomas C. Smith, *op. cit.*, Chapter IV.

Meiji Restoration. "The minimum of the sum of value that the individual possessor of money or commodities must command in order to metamorphose himself into a capitalist, changes with the different stages of development of capitalist production, and is on any given stage different in different spheres of production, depending on their specific technical conditions. Certain spheres of production demand, even at the very outset of capitalist production, a minimum of capital that is not as yet found in the hands of single individuals. This gives rise partly to state subsidies to private persons, as in France in the time of Colbert, and as in many German states up to our own epoch; partly to the formation of societies with legal monopoly for the exploitation of certain branches of industry and commerce."[45]

The Meiji state went much further; it invested heavily in railway construction, in shipbuilding, in the development of a communications system, in basic industries, in production of machinery, and the like. The story of the early industrialization of Japan has been told many times: through it runs like a red thread the dominant part played by the government in accelerating the development of industrial capitalism. How this government policy was carried out is relatively unimportant. Some of the government investment was financed directly with what was no longer required to pay the stipends of the *samurai*—an amount that in earlier days used to absorb nearly all of the government's ordinary revenues. Other ventures were made possible by far-reaching government guarantees to the investors. Still others were promoted by the government's commitments to purchase many years' output of the newly established enterprises. Whichever way was chosen, the result was invariably a tremendous enhancement of the power of industrial capital. The profits earned by the Mitsui, Mitsubishi, Sumitomo, Okura, and other future "Zaibatsu" on various government contracts were truly fabulous. They were perhaps overshadowed only by the gains provided these concerns by the government's eventual policy of "re-privatization" of the state-owned industrial enterprises. "There is no doubt that this policy greatly enhanced the power of the financial oligarchy, especially in view of the ridiculously low prices at which the government sold its model factories."[46]

[45] *Capital* (Kerr ed.), Vol. I, p. 338. (The translation has been slightly changed in the light of the German original.) The first part of this passage, incidentally, is of considerable relevance to our earlier discussion of monopoly capitalism; cf. p. 76 above.

[46] Norman, *Japan's Emergence as a Modern State* (New York, 1946), p. 131. "The factories were sold, as a rule, for 15 to 30 percent of the

Thus in the early history of industrial development in Japan (as for that matter in other countries) there is not much to be seen of the daring and innovating entrepreneur whom our modern rewriters of history present, for only too transparent reasons, as the original creators and promoters of all economic progress.[47] Indeed, if anything is obvious, it is the exorbitant amount of protection and bribery on the part of the state that was required to pull capital away from its favorite speculation and usury to investment in productive enterprise.

And this brings us back to the question which was raised at the outset of the present discussion and which encompasses its central theme. What was it that enabled Japan to take a course so radically different from that of all the other countries in the now underdeveloped world? Or, in other words, what was the historical constellation that left room for a bourgeois revolution in Japan which in turn led to the establishment of a bourgeois-dominated regime serving from its very inception as a vigorous and relentless engine of Japanese capitalism?

The answer to this question is extraordinarily complex and at the same time extraordinarily simple. It is simple because, reduced to its core, it comes down to the fact that Japan is the only country in Asia (and in Africa and in Latin America) that escaped being turned into a colony or dependency of Western European or American capitalism, that had a chance of independent national development. It is complex because it was only a felicitous confluence of a large number of more or less independent factors that gave Japan its lucky break.

Basic among them—reminiscent of the paradox presented by Western Europe and in particular by Great Britain—was the backwardness and poverty of the Japanese people and the paucity of their country's natural resources.[48] "Japan had very little to offer either as a market

---

amounts which they cost the government and so that the buyers were permitted to pay the purchase price over long periods of time, sometimes as long as two to three decades." Pevsner, *op. cit.*, p. 23.

[47] On the currently rampant research in "entrepreneurial history" lavishly supported by corporations and learned foundations the purpose of which is the glorification of the robber baron, cf. Leo Huberman, "The 'New' History or the Crowning of Mammon," *Monthly Review* (August 1952), as well as Herbert Aptheker, *Laureates of Imperialism* (New York, 1954).

[48] Even now, after nearly one hundred years of intensive explorations, the known natural wealth of Japan cannot be compared with that of most other industrial countries. It has no oil, no bauxite, no nonferrous metals, very little coal and iron, the only saving feature being its large capacity

for foreign manufactures or as a granary of raw materials for Western industry."[49] Consequently the lure of Japan to Western European capitalists and governments came nowhere near the irresistible attraction exercised by the gold of Latin America, the flora, fauna, and minerals of Africa, the fabulous riches of the Indies, or the supposedly bottomless markets of China.

No less important was the fact that in the middle of the nineteenth century, when Western penetration of Asia reached the highest degree of intensity, the resources of the leading Western European countries were already severely taxed by other undertakings. Especially Great Britain, the world's leading colonial power, had enough on its hands in Europe, the Near East, India, and China without becoming involved in a militarily most uninviting campaign for the conquest of Japan. This strain on Britain's expansionist capabilities accelerated the far-reaching change in the nature and orientation of its colonial policy that was afoot from the middle of the nineteenth century. Although veiled by a political debate that appeared to be mere shadow boxing—with the Tories fully accepting the essence of Palmerston's foreign policies—it actually implied the transition from old-fashioned piracy characteristic of the mercantile phase of capitalism and of primary accumulation of capital to the more subtle and complex strategy of modern imperialism.[50]

But what decisively affected the position of Japan was another characteristic of modern imperialism: the growing rivalry among the established imperialist whales, and the arrival on the world stage of a new imperialist power, the United States. It was that rivalry, with the resulting checks and balances in international power politics, that had much to do with preventing Britain from meting out to China all of the punishment that was suffered by India; and it was this very

---

for generating hydroelectric power. Cf. E. W. Zimmerman, *World Resources and Industries* (revised edition, New York, 1951), in particular pp. 456, 525, 718.

[49] Norman, *op. cit.,* p. 46.

[50] "The old Imperialism levied tribute; the new Imperialism lends money at interest." H. N. Brailsford, *The War of Steel and Gold* (London, 1914), p. 65. The waning importance of merchant capital and the waxing of industrial and financial interests leading to a marked cooling off of the enthusiasm for additional commitments to the conquest of rather doubtful Far Eastern markets reflected itself in the progressive decline of the influence of the so-called Old China Hands. Cf. the excellent account in N. A. Pelcovits, *Old China Hands and the Foreign Office* (New York, 1948).

same international jealousy that rendered it impossible for any one imperialist power to attempt the conquest of Japan.[51] Although in the case of Japan it was the United States that carried out the initial opening-up and that imposed upon it its first unequal treaty, neither the stage reached in the development of American capitalism nor its international status allowed the United States as yet to try to establish exclusive control over Japan. "The proximity to China gave Japan extraordinary strategic importance. The powers that forced upon Japan the unequal treaties watched jealously lest any one of them gain predominant influence in Japan, let alone be able to convert it into its colony and thus into a staging area for further advance into China."[52]

Both the possibility and the necessity of staving off the Western menace exercised a powerful impact on the speed and direction of Japan's subsequent development. It was not only allowed to invest its economic surplus in its own economy; its being spared the mass invasion of Western fortune hunters, soldiers, sailors, and "civilizers" saved it also from the extremes of xenophobia which so markedly retarded the spread of Western science in other countries of Asia. The exceptional Japanese receptiveness to Western knowledge, so frequently referred to and so warmly commended by Western writers, was largely due to the fortunate circumstance that Western civilization was not brought to Japan at the point of a gun, that Western thought and Western technology were in Japan not directly associated with plunder, arson, and murder as they were in India, China, and other now underdeveloped countries. This permitted the retention in Japan of a sociopsychological "climate" not inimical to the adoption of Western science both through the importation of Western technicians and through dispatching young men to Western centers of learning.

On the other hand the threat of Western penetration acted as an ever-present stimulant to Japan's economic development. Toward the end of the Tokugawa period it appeared as an essentially military danger, and was treated accordingly by the feudal rulers. Considerable

[51] "The peculiar complexity of the international situation from 1850 right through to the end of the American Civil War and the outbreak of the Franco-Prussian War, and the stalemate resulting from the Anglo-French intrigues in Japan . . . gave Japan the vitally necessary breathing-space in which to shake off the restricting fetters of feudalism which had caused the country to rot economically and to be exposed to the dangers of commercial and military domination from abroad." Norman, *op. cit.*, p. 46.

[52] Kh. Eydus, *Yaponia ot Pervoy do Vtoroy Mirovoy Voiny* (Japan from the First to the Second World War) (Moscow, 1946), p. 4.

efforts were undertaken by them to establish strategic industries such as iron, armaments, and shipbuilding.[53] Yet superimposed upon a feudal, backward society, without a basis for growth in its socioeconomic structure, those modern industrial enclaves remained insignificant alien bodies in a pre-capitalist, pre-industrial economy.

Matters took an altogether different turn in the '60s. The foreign threat was no longer "merely" a threat to Japan's national independence. Japan's markets, rendered defenseless by the unequal treaties, were flooded by foreign wares. The very existence of Japan's rising capitalism was gravely endangered. The policy of the government that emerged from the Meiji Revolution was fully attuned to the interests that it represented and to the issues that it had to solve. Neither foreign competition nor foreign aggression could be deterred by building a few armaments factories or by piling up a stock of weapons. What was called for was the rapid development of an integrated industrial economy capable of supporting modern warfare and at the same time able to meet the onslaught of foreign competition.

This correspondence of the vital interests of Japanese capitalism with the military requirements for national survival was of momentous importance in determining the speed of Japan's economic and political development after the Meiji Revolution. It greatly accelerated its economic growth by directing investment into basic industries, shipbuilding, communications, and the like rather than solely to armaments factories. At the same time it enabled the new bourgeois government to harness the patriotic and martial fervor of the *déclassé* military castes to its quest for a modern economy. Less than half a century had to pass before the concentrated, monopolistically controlled industry provided a firm basis for an impressive military potential which, combined with the purposefully nurtured chauvinism of the *samurai* and their descendants, turned Japan from an object of imperialist intrigues into one of Western imperialism's most successful junior partners. In the words of Lenin, "by their colonial looting of Asian countries the Europeans managed to harden one of them—Japan—for great military exploits that assured it of an independent national development."[54]

IV

It is obviously impossible even to conjecture on the speed with which the now backward countries would have gone the way of Japan and would have autonomously generated a process of capitalist development and economic growth, in the absence of Western invasion and exploitation. Indeed, the rapidity of Japan's transformation into a capitalist, industrialized country was due to a large extent to the military and economic threat from the West. Yet whatever might have been the tempo and the specific circumstances of the forward movement, there is ample evidence in the history of all the countries in question to indicate the nature of its general trend. Regardless of their national peculiarities, the pre-capitalist orders in Western Europe and in Japan, in Russia and in Asia were reaching at different times and in different ways their common historical destiny.[55] By the eighteenth and nineteenth centuries they were universally in a state of disintegration and decay. Peasants' revolts and the rise of the bourgeoisie shattered everywhere their very foundations. Depending on specific historical conditions, on the internal strength of their pre-capitalist social orders and on the intensity of the anti-feudal pressures, bourgeois revolutions and the development of capitalism were more or less effectively resisted and retarded. Nowhere would they have been indefinitely prevented. Indeed, if the most advanced countries' contact with the backward world had been different from what it was, if it had consisted of genuine cooperation and assistance rather than of oppression and exploitation, then the progressive development of the now underdeveloped countries would have proceeded with incomparably less delay, less friction, less human sacrifice and suffering. A peaceful transplantation of Western culture, science, and technology to the less advanced countries would have served everywhere as a powerful catalyst of economic progress. The violent, destructive, and predatory opening up of the weaker countries by Western capitalism immeasurably distorted their development. A comparison of the role played by British science and British technology in the development of the United States with the role played by British opium in the development of China fully epitomizes this difference.

Marx

[55] "In the commodity production unfolding in the depths of Chinese feudal society there were nascent already the first beginnings of capitalism. China would have therefore even without the impact of foreign capitalism gradually developed into a capitalist country." Mao Tse-tung, *Isbrannye Proizvedenia* (Selected Works) (Moscow, 1953), Vol. III, p. 142.

SIX

Towards a Morphology of Backwardness, I

TURNING now to the current situation in the underdeveloped capitalist countries, we must try to assemble anew—even at the cost of some inevitable repetition—various strands of the historical development that has been outlined above, so as to place in sharper relief what constitutes its direct and natural outgrowth. Indeed, the forces that have molded the fate of the backward world still exercise a powerful impact on the conditions prevailing at the present time. Their forms have changed, their intensities are different today; their origin and direction have remained unaltered. They control now as they have controlled in the past the destinies of the underdeveloped capitalist countries, and it is the speed with which and the processes by which they will be overcome that will determine these countries' future economic and social development.

The way in which capitalism broke into the historical development of the now underdeveloped countries precluded the materialization of what we have termed the "classical" conditions for growth. Little needs to be said about our first classical requirement. As the term "underdeveloped" suggests, output in underdeveloped countries has been low and their human and material resources have been greatly underutilized, or altogether unemployed. Far from serving as an engine of economic expansion, of technological progress and of social change, the capitalist order in these countries has represented a framework for economic stagnation, for archaic technology, and for social backwardness. Thus to the extent to which it depends on the volume of aggregate output and income, the economic surplus in backward capitalist countries has necessarily been small. Not that it has constituted a small proportion of total income. On the contrary, our second classical condition has been fully satisfied: the consumption of the productive population has been depressed to the lowest possible level, with "lowest possible" corresponding in this case closely to a subsistence minimum or to what in many underdeveloped countries falls notably below that benchmark. The economic surplus therefore while by comparison with the advanced countries small in *absolute* terms has accounted for a large *share* of total output—as large as, if not larger than, in advanced capitalist countries.

So this is not where "the dog is buried," where one may find the principal discrepancy between the situation that prevails in underdeveloped countries and what was envisaged in the classical model of economic growth. The discrepancy is most profound, indeed decisive, when it comes to our third and fourth classical conditions, those relating to the *mode of utilization* of the economic surplus. This has to be considered in some detail.

It is a typical feature of economic backwardness, if not always synonymous with it, that the majority of the population is dependent on agriculture, and that agriculture accounts for a large share of the backward countries' total output. While this ratio differs from country to country, almost everywhere a considerable proportion of agricultural output is produced by subsistence peasants who in turn constitute the bulk of the agricultural population. Their holdings are as a rule small, and their productivity (per man and per acre of land) is extremely low. Indeed, in most underdeveloped countries the peasants' marginal productivity is so negligible that the departure from agriculture of a sizable part of the rural population would not lead to a reduction of aggregate agricultural output.[1] Even if the peasants' holdings were wholly the unencumbered properties of those who operate them, the output secured with their help would barely provide a narrowly circumscribed subsistence minimum for the farm family, and in many countries would fail to reach even this rock-bottom level. In

[1] A good discussion of this structural rural unemployment or, as it has been called, "disguised unemployment," will be found in B. Datta, *The Economics of Industrialization* (Calcutta, 1952), Chapter V, which also refers to some of the relevant literature.

actual fact, however, a large proportion of small holdings in nearly all underdeveloped countries are not owned by the peasants but are rented, predominantly from landowners, occasionally from the state. Yet whether owned or held in tenancy, these holdings have to support not merely the peasants' families but also the payments of rent or taxes (or both). In a great number of cases they must in addition furnish the means required to meet interest payments on the peasants' debts contracted either in connection with the original acquisition of the holding or for consumption purposes—in lean years or in cases of emergencies. The subsistence peasant's obligations on account of rent, taxes, and interest in all underdeveloped countries are very high. They frequently absorb more than half of his meager net product. An additional drain on his disposable income results from the highly unfavorable terms of trade under which he is usually forced to operate. Exploited by middlemen of all kinds, he receives low prices for what little he has to sell, and pays high prices for the few industrial commodities that he is in a position to buy. Thus the economic surplus that is squeezed out of the peasant sector of agriculture is appropriated by the landowners, the moneylenders, and the merchants, and, to a smaller extent, by the state.[2]

In the part of the agricultural economy composed of large estates that are not parceled out in small holdings but operated as plantations with the help of hired labor, output (per acre of land) is frequently higher than on small holdings. The economic surplus accruing to the landowners in the form of profits tends also to be larger, in particular in view of the fact that their terms of trade are usually better than those of the small peasants.[3]

Taking agriculture as a whole, it is highly probable that the economic surplus generated in this sector of the underdeveloped economy comprises at least one half, and in many countries more than one half, of its aggregate output. It is obvious that the use made of this significant share of the national product is of crucial importance for the economic development of the underdeveloped countries. And it is no

[2] There exists furthermore in most underdeveloped countries a narrow, comparatively affluent, rural stratum that constitutes a hybrid of peasants, merchants, and usurers: the "kulaks" in Russian terminology. They employ hired labor, engage in trade and moneylending, function typically as the "bloodsuckers" of their respective villages, and appropriate a sometimes considerable share of the economic surplus.

[3] Information on much of the above is excellently summarized in United Nations, *Land Reform* (1951).

less obvious that in all underdeveloped countries the bulk of it is *not* used to expand and to improve their productive plant and facilities. A considerable share of the economic surplus accruing to the land-owning class is absorbed by its excess consumption. What aroused the ire of Adam Smith, Ricardo, and other classical economists is still the rule in the backward countries. Maintenance of sumptuous residences, lavish living, acquisition of conspicuous luxuries serving as symbols of wealth and status, large numbers of servants, entertainment, and travel—all account for much of what is received and spent by the landowning aristocracy.[4] It finds it highly unattractive to employ its revenue for the improvement of its land or for the introduction of better agricultural implements. This attitude may be to some extent irrational, nurtured by the tradition, style of life, and social conventions peculiar to landed squires. For the most part, however, it is wholly appropriate to the objective economic conditions.

If the land is operated in the form of large estates, the expensiveness of—normally imported—agricultural machinery and the cheapness of agricultural labor militate against investment in plantation enterprise. What is more, returns on capital invested in agriculture tend to materialize slowly, so that the high rates of interest prevailing in underdeveloped countries greatly discourage the sinking of funds in agricultural improvement. At the same time, the usually large fluctuations of agricultural prices render such investment particularly risky. Under these circumstances, the landowner has every reason to avoid being saddled with the obligation to service a fixed debt, while lenders have every reason to discriminate against long-term loans for agricultural purposes.

The situation is even worse if the land is in the hands of small tenants. Most agricultural improvements based on the application of modern technology can be realized only in large-scale farming. Neither tractors nor mechanical harvesters can be adequately utilized on dwarf holdings. Yet even in cases in which improvements could be undertaken regardless of the sizes of the individual plots—irrigation of an

---

[4] To be sure, some of the dissipated economic surplus finds its way back into mass consumption. As in the case of the Church and the feudal lords in the Middle Ages, alms of all kinds, support of relatives, old retainers, and protegés of various descriptions hold an important position in the budgets of the landed proprietors. Needless to say, while more rational on humanitarian grounds, this form of utilization of the economic surplus is no more conducive to economic growth than the outright prodigality of the landowners themselves.

entire area, for instance—the incentive for the landowner to undertake the requisite investment is necessarily weak. With rents very high and the standard of living of the tenants desperately low he would find it difficult, if not impossible, to raise the rent on the improved land. Such increases in productivity as this investment might bring to the rented land might add somewhat to the income of the tenant but could hardly be counted on to reimburse the investing landowner.

Not that the amounts available to the landowners for investment purposes are large. On the contrary, the necessity of maintaining the style of life appropriate to their status in society exercises a powerful drain on their incomes, and forces many of them—particularly in bad years—to get into debt on ruinous conditions, to mortgage and sometimes to lose their estates. Whatever remains in the hands of the more thrifty or more fortunate owners is not devoted to the improvement of their holdings. Attracted by the high rates of interest paid for loans, they use their funds, directly or through intermediaries, for money-lending operations or for the acquisition of the additional land that is continually thrown upon the market by the bankruptcies of peasants and other landowners.

Thus while a large share of the economic surplus produced in agriculture remains *potential* surplus that could be used for investment if excess consumption and unproductive expenditures of all kinds were eliminated, what *actual* surplus there is becomes imbedded in the economic pores of the backward societies making but little contribution to increase of productivity. It would be a fallacy, nevertheless, to believe that an elimination of waste and of misallocation of the economic surplus would represent all that is needed to generate a sustained upward trend in agricultural investment and output. It is this fallacy that underlies the view that an agrarian reform—breaking up the large estates, endowing some landless peasants with plots of their own, and freeing tenants of their oppressive obligations—would put an end to the stagnation of agriculture in backward countries. Undoubtedly the immediate effect of such measures would be a more or less significant increase of the peasantry's disposable income. Yet with the income level as low as it is, and as it would remain even after the large estates had been split up into a multitude of dwarf holdings and after the payments of rent had been entirely abolished, little if anything would be saved out of the income increments. Moreover, whatever improvement in the peasants' standard of living would be accomplished in this way would be bound to be short-lived. It would be rapidly wiped out by increases of population that would necessitate further partitions of holdings and bring the per capita income back to its previous level or below. Worse still, the parceling of land would reduce the possibilities for achieving what is obviously the foremost need of agriculture in backward countries: a rapid and substantial increase of its aggregate output. For an agricultural economy based on tiny farm units would offer little opportunity for an increase of productivity. To be sure, something can be achieved by improvement of seeds, by increased usage of fertilizers, and the like. As noted before, however, a major increase of productivity and output depends on the possibility of introducing specialization, modern machinery and draught power, a possibility present only under conditions of large-scale farming.

This points to what constitutes probably the most vexing perplexity confronting the majority of underdeveloped countries. An agrarian reform, if it takes place in the midst of general backwardness, will retard rather than advance a country's economic development. While temporarily improving the living standards of the peasantry, it will depress aggregate output and eliminate what little economic surplus agriculture used theretofore for productive purposes.[5] More serious still, the now increased consumption of the old and newly created subsistence peasants and the division of large estates that had been producing commercial crops will greatly reduce the share of agricultural output that was available before for urban utilization: for food, for industrial processing, or for exports.

In the past of the advanced capitalist countries this problem was solved by a multipronged process. In the first place, capitalist development swept over agriculture and caused, as it were, an agrarian counter-revolution to cancel the agrarian revolution in provoking which it originally played a decisive part. Raising agriculture thus to a new level, it led to its "capitalization," to a new concentration of production in the hands of capitalist farmers, to the differentiation of subsistence peasants into agricultural laborers and market-oriented agricultural entrepreneurs. Secondly, by offering the carrot of industrial employment, but primarily by wielding the stick of physical coercion, it transferred large numbers of peasants into the industrial labor force, in this way relieving the population pressure on farm households and simultaneously raising the per capita income of those

[5] Cf. W. E. Moore, *Economic Demography of Eastern and Southern Europe* (Geneva, 1945), pp. 55-98.

who remained in agriculture. Thirdly, by expanding industry it came early into a position to offer rural producers manufactured commodities in exchange for what they had to sell, and was thus able both to secure food for the growing urban population and to provide agriculture with implements, fertilizers, and the like, which in turn led to an increase in agricultural productivity.

Thus under conditions of capitalism, if it is to be successful in contributing to overall economic development and not to bog down in the propagation and multiplication of rural slums, agrarian reform must not only go together with accumulation of capital, but must be accompanied by a rapid advance to industrial capitalism. This advance depends on and results in both the agrarian revolution and what we have just called the agrarian counter-revolution. It is only by means of the agrarian revolution that the feudal order is broken and the state subordinated to the requirements of capitalist development. The creation of a bourgeois-dominated state able and willing to promote directly, and to create the conditions favoring indirectly, the growth of industrial enterprise is, however, decisive if the transition to industrial capitalism is to proceed with any degree of rapidity.[6] At the same time it is only through the agrarian counter-revolution that growing industrial capitalism obtains the indispensable agricultural hinterland, and assures itself of a sufficient supply of manpower, food, and industrial raw materials.

It must be immediately added that the above should not be taken as saying that agrarian reforms in underdeveloped countries are redundant or are not moves in the right direction. What it is intended to warn against, however, is the now widely held "liberal" notion that agrarian reform is a panacea for all the ills of economic and social backwardness. Far from it! Its historical role is highly uncertain and depends entirely on the conditions under which it takes place and on

[6] This has to be borne in mind when considering such agrarian reforms as that undertaken by Stolypin in Tsarist Russia, those carried out before the Second World War in Eastern and Southeastern Europe, or those currently enacted (or talked about) in some countries of Latin America, Southeast Asia, and the Near East. These agrarian reforms, proceeding in an "orderly manner," represent handouts on the part of the governments largely controlled by landowning interests, are calculated to appease a restive peasantry, and are usually combined with lavish compensations of the feudal landlords. They frequently serve not to break the feudal grip on the state but rather to strengthen it. They tend therefore to accentuate all the negative repercussions of agrarian reforms without leading the way to industrial development and to the reorganization and rationalization of the agricultural economy resulting therefrom.

the forces by which it is propelled. If promoted by a government dominated by a feudal-comprador coalition, it becomes the temporary stabilizer of an economic, social, and political constellation that by its very nature is inimical to progressive development. And if advancing it in the long run, it tends to delay it more or less significantly in the short run. On the other hand, if it comes about in spite of obstruction on the part of such a government, as a result of overwhelming pressure of the peasantry—in other words, if it assumes the character of an agrarian *revolution*—it represents a major advance along the road to progress. Indeed, it is indispensable in order to eliminate a parasitic landowning class and to break its stranglehold on the life of an underdeveloped country. It is indispensable in order to satisfy the legitimate aspirations of the peasantry and to secure the foremost prerequisite of all economic and social development: the release of the creative energies and potentialities of the rural masses held down and crippled by centuries of degrading oppression and servitude. And it is indispensable because only through a distribution of land among working peasants can the political and psychological conditions be attained under which it is possible to approach a rational solution of the agrarian problem: cooperative, technically advanced farms operated by free and equal producers.

II

As a German writer once remarked, whether there will be meat in the kitchen is never decided in the kitchen. Nor is the fate of agriculture under capitalism ever decided in agriculture. Economic, social, and political processes unfolding outside of agriculture, and in particular the accumulation of capital and the evolution of the capitalist class, while themselves originally largely determined by the processes that have taken place in agriculture, become with the onset of capitalism the prime movers of the historical development. In the underdeveloped capitalist countries—predominantly agrarian—this may be less obvious than in the advanced ones; it is, however, no less true.

Even in the backward capitalist country the non-agricultural sector appropriates a large share of the nation's aggregate economic surplus. It accrues there to *four* distinct, if closely interrelated, types of recipients. There are in the first place the merchants, moneylenders, and intermediaries of all kinds, some of them living in rural areas, but by the nature of their activities not belonging to the agricultural population. The most striking single feature of this socioeconomic stratum is its *size*. No one who has ever set foot in China of old, in Southeast Asia, in the Near East, or in pre-war Eastern Europe can have failed to notice the staggering multitude of merchants, dealers, peddlers, trading-stand operators, and people with nondescript occupations crowding the streets, squares, and coffeehouses of their cities. To some extent their activities are those customary in all capitalist countries—if more conspicuous in underdeveloped countries than where the same type of "work" is carried on by correspondence or over the telephone; for the most part, however, the nature of their transactions is peculiar to the conditions prevailing in the early phases of capitalist development.

We have already mentioned the rural producers' highly unfavorable terms of trade. Ignorant, parochial, and poor, with only small quantities of produce to dispose of, the individual peasant or small landowner is an ideal object for mercantile exploitation. Frequently in financial straits, particularly in years of bad harvests and bad prices or in cases of unexpected emergencies, he is forced to seek advances on future deliveries, to pay usurious rates of interest for such loans, and to accept whatever prices his buyer may be prepared to pay for his output. Realizing very little cash at the end of the crop year, he becomes incapable of extricating himself from further advances, gets enmeshed in unfavorable contracts, undertakes to purchase from the dealer to whom he sells his produce whatever manufactured goods he is able to afford, and slips into complete dependency on "his" merchant and moneylender. It hardly needs to be added that the profits collected by the latter assume exorbitant proportions.

Nor is the trade in agricultural produce and with agricultural producers the only source of large mercantile profits. Where markets are as disorganized and isolated as they are in underdeveloped countries, such profits are sought and found in an amazing variety of ways. Real estate deals, exploitation of temporary and local shortages of various goods, speculation and arbitrage, brokerage fees for establishing contacts between buyers and sellers—all yield sizable gains to the skillful operators engaged in such transactions. The more or less chronic inflation in most underdeveloped countries which gives rise to black markets in foreign currencies, gold, and other valuables offers further opportunities for lucrative commerce, while the ever-present chance of procuring various concessions from government continually invites the resources, the energy, and the ingenuity of well-connected and affluent men of affairs.

By the nature of its pursuits this class of people dwelling in the

sphere of circulation is wholly open to entry and is consequently continually swarming with new arrivals. They are scions of existing merchant and noble families, members of the *déclassé* gentry, more able
and enterprising peasants, craftsmen dislodged by competition, various
people who acquired an education but no opportunity to use it, and
the like. Competition among them is fierce, and their *average* income
accordingly low. Nevertheless the aggregate profit that they are in a
position to secure assumes a considerable magnitude.[7] Making no contribution to speak of to social output, this group constitutes the urban
counterpart of the structurally unemployed in the villages. Viewed
from the standpoint of economic development, however, its role is
quite different and much more important. The consumption of the rural
structural unemployed comes out of the means of subsistence of the
peasant masses. It encroaches upon the economic surplus only insofar
as it raises the subsistence minimum of the peasants and thus con-
stricts the amount of rent that can be extracted by the landowner. To
be sure, to the extent to which it is derived from direct exploitation
of the peasantry, the maintenance of the superabundant mercantile
population is supported from the same source. Yet to a large extent
it is based on transfers of surplus appropriated by other classes:
landowners, foreign enterprises, and domestic industrialists. The diversion of this surplus to the upkeep of a parasitic stratum constitutes a
significant drain on capital accumulation.[8]

[7] "It is unacceptable," says Ricardo Torres Gaitan, one of the leading
Mexican economists, "that commerce should produce a larger income than
agriculture and above all inadmissible that the activity of the merchants
should create an income more than twice as large as that of agriculture."
Quoted in A. Sturmthal, "Economic Development, Income Distribution,
and Capital Formation in Mexico," *Journal of Political Economy* (June
1955), p. 198 *n.*

[8] This group, absorbing some of their societies' most capable and dynamic individuals, at the same time wastes, corrupts, and destroys a vast
quantity of what is perhaps one of the scarcest productive resources of all:
creative human talent. While this is not very different from what takes
place in advanced capitalist countries, the proliferation of "tertiary" occupations in an underdeveloped country is not to be confused with their
expansion under advanced economic and social conditions. Just as obesity
may be an indication of either affluence or squalor, so large numbers of
people engaged in the sphere of circulation (and services) may testify to
both economic advancement and economic backwardness. This point is
clearly made in B. Datta, *The Economics of Industrialization* (Calcutta,
1952), Chapter VI, although it would seem that the significance of the
resource-waste involved is underestimated. This error stems as usual from
viewing this waste in relation to *aggregate income* rather than in relation
to the *economic surplus.*

Important as it is that the *"lumpenbourgeois"* element of the mercantile class eats up a large share of the economic surplus accruing
to the class as a whole, even more portentous is the fact that such
capital as is accumulated by its wealthier members is typically not
turned into the *second* bracket of the non-agricultural economy: industrial production. Existing for the most part in small morsels, it
can find profitable application only in the sphere of circulation where
relatively small amounts of money go a long way, where the returns
on individual transactions are large, and where the turnover of the
funds involved is rapid. And merchants in possession of larger resources find even better opportunities for gain in buying up land
yielding rent revenue,[9] in various undertakings auxiliary to the operation of Western business, in importing, exporting, moneylending, and
speculation. Thus to the extent that a transfer of capital and business
energies from mercantile to industrial pursuits is at all possible, the
transfer price becomes inordinately high.

To be sure, the now underdeveloped countries have this in common
with the early phase of capitalist development in Western Europe or
in Japan where powerful forces also tended to prevent the *exit* of
capital from the sphere of circulation, where nevertheless the transition from mercantile to industrial employment of capital was accomplished in the course of time. However, what distinguishes their situation sharply from the historical past of the advanced capitalist countries is the existence of formidable obstacles barring the *entry* of such
mercantile accumulations as they have into the sphere of industrial
production.

III

Industrial expansion under capitalism depends largely on its gathering its own momentum. "Capital rapidly creates for itself an internal

---

[9] It should be noted that there can be no presumption whether the
amounts paid for land are surplus transfers or whether they represent
deductions from accumulated surplus and are used for consumption purposes. Where the sellers of land are bankrupt landowners, or peasants
ridden by debt—although the debt itself may have originated in consumption—the former is likely to be the case: the proceeds of the sale of land
will be used to pay off the debt and thus swell the capital of the lender.
Where the sellers are peasants or landowners driven to dispose of their
property by the impossibility of meeting their current expenses or by
emergencies, the latter will be true. In any case the sums realized from
the sale of land do not usually turn to industrial investment.

market by destroying all rural handicrafts, that is by spinning, weaving, making clothes etc. for all, in fine by transforming into exchange values commodities that were theretofore produced as direct use values —a process that results spontaneously from the severance of the worker (albeit a serf) from land and ownership of his means of production."[10] Not that this dissolution of the pre-capitalist economy, the disintegration of its natural self-sufficiency, has not taken place in most of the now underdeveloped countries. On the contrary, as was mentioned earlier, in all areas of Western penetration, commercial agriculture to a considerable extent displaced traditional subsistence farming, and manufactured commodities invaded the market of the indigenous craftsman and artisan. Yet although, as Allyn Young put it, "division of labor depends in large part upon the division of labor,"[11] in the now backward areas this sequence did not unfold "according to plan." It took a different course: such division of labor as was bred by the initial division of labor resembled the apportionment of functions between a rider and his horse. Whatever market for manufactured goods emerged in the colonial and dependent countries did not become the "internal market" of these countries. Thrown wide open by colonization and by unequal treaties, it became an appendage of the "internal market" of Western capitalism.

While significantly stimulating industrial growth in the West, this turn of events extinguished the igniting spark without which there could be no industrial expansion in the now underdeveloped countries. At a historical juncture when protection of infant industry might have been prescribed even by the sternest protagonist of free trade, the countries most in need of such protection were forced to go through a regime of what might be called industrial infanticide which influenced all of their subsequent development. With their limited demand for manufactured goods amply (and cheaply) supplied from abroad, there was no opportunity for profitable investment in a native industry that would cater to the available domestic market. In the absence of such investment there was, furthermore, no occasion for further investment. For investment is called forth by investment: one investment act gives rise to another, and the second investment act provides the rationale for the third. In fact, it is this clustering of investments,

[10] Marx, *Grundrisse der Kritik der Politischen Ökonomie* (Rohentwurf) (Berlin, 1953), p. 411.
[11] "Increasing Returns and Economic Progress," *Economic Journal* (December 1928), p. 533.

their synchronization, that sets off the chain reaction which is synonymous with the evolution of industrial capitalism. But just as investment tends to become self-propelling, so lack of investment tends to
become self-perpetuating.

Without the widening impact of investment, the originally narrow
market remained of necessity narrow.[12] Under such circumstances
there could be no spreading of small industrial shops that marked elsewhere the transition from the merchant phase of capitalism to its industrial phase. When in the course of time the possibility arose of
undertaking some industrial production, whether because of the pro-
curability of the necessary tariffs or of other government concessions,
such enterprise was sometimes founded by foreigners (usually in conjunction with domestic interests) who brought to bear their experience
and "know-how" upon the organization of the new venture. Setting out
to supply commodities similar in quality and design to those previously
brought in from abroad, they erected single large-scale modern plants
which were sufficient to meet the existing demand. Although the total
amount of capital needed for such a venture was frequently large, the
part of it spent in the underdeveloped country was small, with the
bulk of the outlays involved taking place abroad on the acquisition of
foreign-made machinery, of foreign patents, and the like. The stimulating effect on the economy as a whole resulting from such investment was accordingly slight. What is more, once an undertaking of
that scope had taken place in an industry, both the limitations of demand and the magnitude of the required investment reduced greatly
or eliminated entirely the chances of another enterprise being launched
in the same field. The amount of capital required to break into the
monopoly's privileged sanctuary, the risks attendant upon the inevitable struggle, the leverages that the established concern could use to
harass and to exclude an intruder—all tended to decimate the inducement for merchant capital to shift to industrial pursuits. The narrow
market became monopolistically controlled, and the monopolistic control became an additional factor preventing the widening of the market.

This is not to say that such industrial development as has taken
place in the backward countries did not represent a tremendous advance from the situation in which their industrial markets were entirely controlled by supplies from abroad. These had ruined native

[12] This was discovered to their sorrow also by Western capitalists who
had anticipated no limits to their ability to export manufactured goods to
the thickly populated areas of Western commercial penetration.

handicrafts, and smothered what little industrial development there was in the affected countries without offering the displaced artisans and craftsmen any alternative employment in industry. The corresponding industrial expansion took place in the West. To this the newly founded industrial enterprises represented, as it were, an antidote. They repatriated at least some of the manufacturing part of the original division of labor, undertook at least some industrial investment at home, provided at least some employment and income to native labor. Yet this antidote was inadequate. It not only did not suffice to offset the damage that had been done earlier; the way in which it was administered was such as to give rise to a cancerous growth no less powerful and no less harmful than the evil which in the beginning it partially cured.

The new firms, rapidly attaining exclusive control over their markets and fencing them in by protective tariffs and/or government concessions of all kinds, blocked further industrial growth while their monopolistic price and output policies minimized the expansion of their own enterprises. Completing swiftly the entire journey from a progressive to a regressive role in the economic system, they became at an early stage barriers to economic development rather similar in their effect to the semi-feudal landownership prevailing in underdeveloped countries. Not only not promoting further division of labor and growth of productivity, they actually cause a movement in the opposite direction. Monopolistic industry on one hand extends the merchant phase of capitalism by obstructing the transition of capital and men from the sphere of circulation to the sphere of industrial production. On the other hand, providing neither a market for agricultural produce nor outlets for agricultural surplus labor and not supplying agriculture with cheap manufactured consumer goods and implements, it forces agriculture back towards self-sufficiency, perpetuates the idleness of the structurally unemployed, and fosters further mushrooming of petty traders, cottage industries, and the like.[13]

[13] There would be no need even to mention the utterly retrograde nature of this return to the "happy" condition of rural self-sufficiency and village industry were it not for the increasing favor and encouragement that it has been gaining in the Western countries. The United States government under the so-called Point Four Program, as well as the Ford Foundation, for instance, has been devoting considerable funds to "sell" this scheme to governments of underdeveloped countries, while economists have been advancing it in recent writings on economic development. (Cf., e.g., W. H. Nicholls, "Investment in Agriculture in Underdeveloped Countries," *American Economic Review* (May 1955), or H. G. Aubrey, "Small Industry

Thus in most underdeveloped countries capitalism had a peculiarly twisted career. Having lived through all the pains and frustrations of childhood, it never experienced the vigor and exuberance of youth, and began displaying at an early age all the grievous features of senility and decadence. To the dead weight of stagnation characteristic of pre-industrial society was added the entire restrictive impact of monopoly capitalism. The economic surplus appropriated in lavish amounts by monopolistic concerns in backward countries is not employed for productive purposes. It is neither plowed back into their own enterprises, nor does it serve to develop others. To the extent that it is not taken abroad by their foreign stockholders, it is used in a manner very much resembling that of the landed aristocracy. It supports luxurious living by its recipients, is spent on construction of urban and rural residences, on servants, excess consumption, and the like. The remainder is invested in the acquisition of rent-bearing land, in financing mercantile activities of all kinds, in usury and speculation. Last but not least, significant sums are removed abroad where they are held as hedges against the depreciation of the domestic currency or as nest eggs assuring their owners of suitable retreats in the case of social and political upheavals at home.

IV

This brings us to the *third* branch of the non-agricultural part of the underdeveloped country's economic system: foreign enterprise.[14]

---

in Economic Development," *Social Research* (September 1951).) We can do no better than repeat the eloquent comments on this method of "helping" the peasantry in the backward countries made more than half a century ago by Karl Kautsky: "In the capitalist-exploited home industry we find the longest and most exhaustive working day, the most pitiful remuneration of the work performed, the largest incidence of female and child labor, the most miserable living and working quarters, in one word: the most outrageous conditions that can be found under our mode of production. This is the most infamous system of capitalist exploitation and the most degrading form of proletarization of the peasantry. All attempts to aid a population of small peasants that is no longer able to eke out a livelihood by purely agricultural labor by fostering a home industry must bring about after a short and very doubtful improvement a crash into the deepest and most hopeless misery." *Die Agrarfrage* (Stuttgart, 1899), pp. 180 ff.

[14] As in the case of mercantile business, much of it is actually located in rural areas, and physically related to agriculture. Its economic status, however, has little if anything to do with agriculture proper.

The totally or partially foreign-owned establishments catering to the *internal* market of the underdeveloped country present no special problem.[15] What was said earlier about its industry as a whole, applies equally to them. While some of the economic surplus that they appropriate is spent locally, as on the maintenance of highly paid executives, most of it (including the personal savings of these executives) is transferred abroad. It thus adds to an even lesser extent to capital formation in the underdeveloped countries than what accrues to the domestically owned firms.

More complex—but also more important—is the role played by foreign concerns in an underdeveloped country producing commodities for export. These not only account for the bulk of foreign interests in backward areas, and embody large investments of capital, but are also responsible for a major share of the host countries' and the world's total output of the products in question. To get some notion of their impact on economic development of the underdeveloped countries in which they are located, it will be useful to consider separately the different aspects of their activities: (1) the significance of the *investment* undertaken by the foreign enterprise; (2) the *direct* effect of its *current* operations; and (3) its more *general* influence on the underdeveloped country as a whole.

Beginning with the first, it should be noted that the foreign concerns embarking upon the production of exportable staples (with the exception of oil) have, as a rule, started their activities with relatively little investment of capital. For the control over the necessary natural resources—primarily land for plantations or for mining—was secured either by forcible expropriation of the native populations or by acquiring it at a more or less nominal price from the rulers, feudal lords, or tribal chiefs dominating the respective areas. Thus the accrual of capital to the underdeveloped countries that resulted from the initiation of foreign exploitation of their natural resources was negligible. Even later on, when the scope of export-oriented business in the underdeveloped countries markedly increased, the amount of capital actually transferred to them from the advanced countries has been much smaller than commonly supposed. Such expansion as businesses producing for exports were interested in undertaking could be easily financed by the profits derived from their highly remunerative opera-

---

[15] "Typical manufacturing industries working chiefly for the domestic market do not appear to attract foreign capital." League of Nations, *Industrialization and Foreign Trade* (1945), p. 66.

tions. Speaking of the British experience, Sir Arthur Salter observes that "it was only in an earlier period, which terminated soon after 1870, that the resources for foreign investment came from an excess of current exports over imports. In the whole period from 1870-1913, when total foreign investment increased from about £1000 million to nearly £4000 million the total new investments made were only about 40% of the income from past investments during the same period."[16] The somewhat similar growth of Dutch, French, and (later on) American holdings abroad followed substantially the same pattern: it was largely attributable to the plowing back of profits earned by operations in foreign countries.[17] Thus the increase of Western assets in the underdeveloped world is only partly due to capital exports in the strict sense of the term; it is primarily the result of the reinvestment abroad of some of the economic surplus secured abroad.[18]

This in itself is of some interest in view of the frequently expressed moral indignation about the violation of the Western capitalists' "sacred" property rights in some underdeveloped countries.[19] What matters in the present context, however, is the question whether the economic surplus generated and invested in the underdeveloped countries has made a significant contribution to those countries' economic development. Even on the most favorable interpretation of the record such a claim can hardly be sustained. A part of the investment undertaken by the concerns in question consisted of whatever price was paid for the property title on the natural resources acquired. As just mentioned, this price was usually very low, frequently not amounting to more than what was required to bribe the officials and potentates involved. With their income disposal habits we have already become

[16] *Foreign Investment* (Princeton, 1951), p. 11.

[17] With reference to postwar American investments abroad, a recent authoritative government publication states that "much of these consisted of reinvested foreign branch earnings, rather than new capital raised in the United States." *Report to the President on Foreign Economic Policies* ("Gray Report") (Washington, 1950), p. 61. And as late as 1954, United States private investments abroad "increased by nearly $3 billion while the earnings on earlier investments amounted to approximately $2.8 billion." S. Pizer and F. Cutler, "International Investments and Earnings," *Survey of Current Business* (August 1955).

[18] Cf. also Erich Schiff, "Direct Investments, Terms of Trade, and Balance of Payments," *Quarterly Journal of Economics* (February 1942).

[19] Needless to say, the problem is seriously complicated by the fact that what has been stated above refers to net global balances, while the individuals and corporations involved today may be, and frequently are, not identical with those that collected the profits at an earlier stage.

acquainted; they certainly have not been conducive to the augmentation of the backward countries' productive wealth.[20]

A much larger part of the necessary investment, indeed its bulk, consists of what has been called "investment in kind." This means that the firms sinking their profits (or, for that matter, additional funds) into the enlargement of their undertakings or the establishment of new ones spend a large proportion of the amounts so employed on equipment produced in their home countries. Nor could it be otherwise, since the required equipment is not available in the areas in which the investment takes place, and the investing firm and its personnel have an understandable bias in favor of the familiar tools manufactured at home. As a consequence, with the orders for investment goods going to the industry of the advanced country, the investment act occasioned by the founding or by the expansion of a foreign enterprise in an underdeveloped country as well as by the eventual replacement of its equipment constitutes an expansion of the advanced country's internal market, rather than a widening of that of the underdeveloped country. To be sure, to the extent that local construction is necessary, and roads, mines, office buildings, residences for imported personnel, camps for native workers, and the like, have to be built with the help of local supplies and local labor, a part of the total investment outlay takes place in the underdeveloped country and leads to a corresponding increase of its aggregate income and demand. The amount involved is, however, usually small because even this part of the investment program relies heavily on imported articles such as construction materials, transportation equipment, office and household appliances, as well as engineers, technicians, and foremen brought in from abroad to supervise or carry out the construction projects.

With the benefits to the underdeveloped countries resulting from the investment associated with the establishment or expansion of foreign export-oriented enterprise thus not amounting to much, we may inquire now into the effects of its *current* operations. These consist of producing agricultural commodities or materials such as minerals and oil and shipping them abroad. It is important for us to trace the mode of utilization of the resources thus obtained. We may

---

[20] Under present, less "romantic" conditions, the payment for the required access to natural resources assumes in a number of underdeveloped countries the form of more or less sizable royalties and taxes on *current output* collected by the local governments. Sometimes it also involves providing them with sporadic grants or loans, making them more pliable in subsequent negotiations. To this we shall come later.

start with that part of them that is used for remuneration of labor. Determined everywhere by native labor's abysmally low rates of pay, and reflecting in some lines of production a high degree of mechanization with a correspondingly small size of labor force employed, the part of the companies' total revenue that is absorbed by wages is generally small. In Venezuela, petroleum accounts for over 90 percent of all exports (and for a large part of total national product), but the oil industry employs only some 2 percent of Venezuela's labor force,[21] and its local-currency expenditures (exclusive of government payments) do not exceed 20 percent of the value of exports;[22] some seven-eighths of these expenditures have gone to meet the wages and salaries bill, with the remainder being used for purchases within the country. In Chile "before the first world war about 8 percent of the active population was engaged in the mines or associated processing plants, but this proportion has fallen fairly steadily."[23] According to an unpublished study of the International Monetary Fund, the proportion of the value of the industry's total product locally spent is also approximately 20 percent; the parts of labor and material costs respectively cannot be determined. In Bolivia about 5 percent of the workers are employed in the tin mines; it has been estimated that during the last half of the 1940s about 25 percent of total receipts were required to meet wage payments, but this is undoubtedly high, because the low official rate of exchange was used to compare dollar sales figures with Bolivian wage figures.[24] In the Middle East all of 0.34 percent of the population are engaged in the oil industry[25] while less than 5 percent of the oil revenues are paid out as wages. In some countries with very small populations and large raw materials developments the proportion of people employed in connection with them is of course larger (for example, about 10 percent in the North-

[21] Ragnar Nurkse, *Problems of Capital Formation in Underdeveloped Countries* (Oxford, 1953), p. 23.

[22] Banco Central de Venezuela, *Memoria* (1950), p. 36, quoted in C. E. Rollins, "Mineral Development and Economic Growth," *Social Research* (Autumn 1956). I am greatly indebted to Dr. Rollins for placing at my disposal the manuscript of this excellent paper from which I have drawn a number of additional references.

[23] United Nations, *Development of Mineral Resources in Asia and the Far East* (1953), p. 39.

[24] Rollins, *op. cit.*, where M. D. Pollner, "Problems of National Income Estimation in Bolivia" (Master's thesis, New York University, 1952), is referred to as the source for this statement.

[25] United Nations, *Review of Economic Conditions in the Middle East* (1951), p. 63.

ern Rhodesian copper mines), but these cases are exceptional. Even there, moreover, the share of total receipts of the industries that is paid out in wages is approximately the same as in other instances just mentioned.

It would be a mistake, however, to believe that this small part of the total revenue secured through raw materials exploitation serves in its entirety to widen the underdeveloped country's internal market. In the first place some of the labor involved consists of foreigners who fill managerial and semi-managerial positions and whose pay is accordingly high. Although they maintain a high standard of living, they are in a position to set aside sizable shares of their incomes. In fact, one of the main attractions of their jobs is the possibility of accumulating considerable savings in a relatively short time. Needless to say, these savings are either currently sent out of the country or are taken back home eventually when their owners leave their posts.[26] Nor are the amounts which they use for consumption purposes entirely spent on local output. While the housekeeping of foreigners in underdeveloped countries typically involves the employment of numerous native servants, and while obviously many consumer goods are obtained from local sources, a large portion of their spending is directed towards accustomed articles that are supplied from abroad. Thus the total amount that foreign wage receivers spend on locally produced goods and services and that forms an increase of the underdeveloped countries' aggregate demand is normally very small.

In the case of native labor the situation is somewhat different. Doing work requiring little skill, they earn wages that are extremely low, frequently barely sufficient to provide for a narrowly defined subsistence minimum. But even where their pay is higher, allowing for a somewhat better standard of living, it hardly leaves room for saving. Thus the wages received by the native workers can be counted on to be spent on consumption.[27] Yet a certain part of what they purchase is supplied by the employing company itself: in particular, housing. What is more, many workers' camps are so located that it is found to be easier and cheaper to import many of the consumer

[26] The infrequent cases of individuals becoming enamored with the countries in which they are employed and deciding to get "economically naturalized" can be safely disregarded.

[27] In some countries such as, for instance, Burma, the outflow of funds sent by semi-migratory labor for the upkeep of their families in the countries of their origin is a matter of considerable importance.

goods that they buy rather than to procure them from the frequently distant local sources.[28]

In sum, the income derived by the inhabitants of the so-called source countries from the activities of the export-oriented foreign enterprises, consisting primarily of wage payments to a relatively small number of wage earners, is everywhere very small. Since variations in the world demand for the commodities in question affect in the main their price rather than the volume of their output—for technical and economic reasons that need not detain us here—the level of native employment tends to vary but little. And since their wages are also rather sticky, their aggregate receipts *in absolute terms* are on the whole quite stable. They obviously represent a changing *share* of the total value of output depending on the prices at which it is sold. Yet taking good years together with the bad, it would seem that the proportion is somewhere around 15 percent, with the percentage being as low as 5 in some areas and some years and as high as 25 in others. While even such an addition is undoubtedly most valuable to the poverty-stricken populations of the underdeveloped countries, in appraising its significance to economic development the nature of its recipients should be clearly realized. Accruing for the most part to low-paid workers, it is directed towards acquisition of most elementary wage goods that are produced in agriculture, by local craftsmen, or imported, and therefore cannot possibly form a market encouraging the development of industrial enterprise.[29]

The balance of the aggregate proceeds from the sale of the output of foreign export-oriented enterprise may be grouped under two headings. Its bulk is accounted for by the companies' gross profits (after taxes and royalties) which include depreciation and depletion charges; the remainder consists of payments of taxes, royalties, and the like, to the government of the countries in which production takes place. We shall come to the latter presently. As far as the former are concerned, their mode of utilization is subject to con-

---

[28] This is very noticeable in the case of the Bolivian tin companies; "for many years the companies maintained stores which were largely stocked from abroad . . ." C. E. Rollins, *op. cit.* Needless to say, the reason for this is in many cases not so much the lower price of imported goods but the usual motivation underlying the so-called truck system. In the case of the export-oriented firms, the cheapness of shipping *from* the West is an important factor encouraging the importation of goods to be sold in company stores.

[29] It gives rise to mercantile profits; these, however, are not what is lacking in underdeveloped countries.

siderable variations. As we have seen earlier, for the most part they have been reinvested abroad. This is, however, a statistical balance referring only to global aggregates and to long periods. For individual countries and particular time stretches, the fluctuations of both profit withdrawals and foreign investments have been quite divergent and quite violent. While at times in some countries withdrawals have exceeded investments, at other times and in other places it has been the other way round. While some firms took home all or most of their profits, others engaged in additional foreign investment. World-wide business organizations have frequently transferred their profits from the country or countries in which they originated to areas where investment opportunities were superior. Nor can it be said that there has been any community of fate of the underdeveloped countries taken together, and that the profits generated in one underdeveloped country, if not plowed back there, are invested in another underdeveloped country. The opposite has actually been the case: profits derived from operations in underdeveloped countries have gone to a large extent to finance investment in highly developed parts of the world. Thus while there have been vast differences among underdeveloped countries with regard to the amounts of profits plowed back in their economies or withdrawn by foreign investors, the underdeveloped world as a whole has continually shipped a large part of its economic surplus to more advanced countries on account of interest and dividends.[30]

V

The worst of it is, however, that it is very hard to say what has been the greater evil as far as the economic development of underdeveloped countries is concerned: the removal of their economic surplus by foreign capital or its reinvestment by foreign enterprise. That such has been actually the somber dilemma stems not merely from the pronounced paucity of the direct benefits derived by the underdeveloped countries from foreign investment; it is even more clearly realized if the overall impact of foreign enterprise on the development of underdeveloped countries is given some consideration. This is not the way in which matters are viewed in more or less

[30] Cf. Jacob Viner, "America's Aims and the Progress of Underdeveloped Countries," in *The Progress of Underdeveloped Areas* (B. F. Hoselitz, ed.) (Chicago, 1952), pp. 182 ff.

official Western writing on the subject. Thus the authors of the previously cited article in the United States Commerce Department's *Survey of Current Business* roundly assert that "the great expansion of foreign productive facilities represented by [the United States corporations'] investment has been of great importance in the improvement of economic conditions abroad."[31] Although apparently less confident, Professor Mason holds that ". . . the expansion of mineral production is, in general, not only compatible with the economic growth of underdeveloped areas but may greatly facilitate industrialization in these areas."[32] And Professor Nurkse, also all but certain, concludes that ". . . the trouble about foreign investment of the 'traditional' sort is not that it is bad, or that it does not tend to promote development generally; it does, although unevenly and indirectly. The trouble is rather that it simply does not happen on any substantial scale. . . ."[33]

This position is based essentially on the following considerations. One is that the transfer abroad of returns on foreign investment is not to be regarded as an encroachment upon the underdeveloped country's economic surplus, for whatever is being transferred would simply not exist in the absence of foreign investment. Thus since in the absence of these transfers there would be no foreign investment, the transfers themselves imply no real cost to the paying country and cannot therefore be considered as adversely influencing its economic development.[34] Secondly, it is argued, the operations of foreign enterprise, by passing a part of its output to the native population in reward for services rendered, increase to *some* extent its aggregate income. Thirdly, it is pointed out that foreign enterprise, whatever may be its *direct* contribution to the welfare of the peoples inhabiting the underdeveloped countries, renders them a major service *indirectly* by stimulating the construction of roads, railways, power stations, and the like, as well as conveying to their capitalists and workers the business know-how and the technical skills of the advanced countries. Finally, stress is laid on the fact that Western enterprise by remitting taxes and royalties to the governments of the source

[31] S. Pizer and F. Cutler, "International Investments and Earnings" (August 1955), p. 10.
[32] "Raw Materials, Rearmament, and Economic Development," *Quarterly Journal of Economics* (August 1952), p. 336.
[33] *Op. cit.*, p. 29.
[34] Cf. S. Herbert Frankel, *The Economic Impact on Under-Developed Societies* (Oxford, 1953), p. 104.

countries places in their hands important funds for financing the development of their national economies.

As is the case with most bourgeois economic reasoning based on "practical intelligence," this is judicious and plausible on the surface. Yet encompassing merely one segment of reality, and dealing with it not historically but by the now very fashionable method that might be called "animated statics," it conveys a conception that is both biased and misleading. Let us take up these arguments in turn.

It is undoubtedly correct that if the natural resources of the under-developed countries were not exploited, there would be no output to provide for the transfers of profits abroad. This is, however, where the firm ground under the first of the above propositions ends. For it is by no means to be taken for granted that the now underdeveloped countries, given an independent development, would not at some point have initiated the utilization of their natural resources on their own and on terms more advantageous than those received from foreign investors. This could be dismissed if foreign investment and the course taken by the development of the underdeveloped countries were independent of each other. However, as we have seen earlier, as the case of Japan convincingly demonstrates, and as will become presently still clearer, such independence cannot possibly be assumed. In fact, to assume it amounts to begging the entire issue and prejudging it from the very outset. But there is still another aspect to the problem. With regard to some agricultural products, it might be thought that since they consist of recurring crops, and since an outlet for them can be found only in exports, their production and shipment abroad constitute no sacrifice whatever to the source countries. This is a grievous, albeit commonly accepted, fallacy. Quite apart from the fact that export-oriented corporations have traditionally engaged in the most predatory exploitation of the plantation land under their control, the establishment and expansion of these plantations have brought about the systematic pauperization, indeed in many instances the physical annihilation, of large parts of the native population. The cases are legion, and citing a few will have to suffice: "The one-crop culture of cane sugar in the Brazilian northeast is a good example. The area once had one of the few really fertile tropical soils. It had a climate favorable to agriculture, and it was originally covered with a forest growth extremely rich in fruit trees. Today, the all-absorbing, self-destructive sugar industry has stripped all the available land and covered it completely with sugar cane; as a result this is one of the starvation areas of the continent. The failure to grow fruits, greens and vegetables, or to raise cattle in the region, has created an extremely difficult food problem in an area where diversified farming could produce an infinite variety of foods."[35] In most of Latin America, what "helped in definitively ruining the native populations was the one-track exploitation to which almost every region was dedicated: some were given over to mining, others to coffee planting, some to tobacco and others to cacao. This specialization brought on the deformed economy which is still found in such countries as Salvador, which produces practically nothing but coffee, and Honduras, which exports nothing but bananas." In Egypt "a large part of the irrigated land was reserved to produce cash export crops . . . particularly cotton and sugar—which further aggravated the nutritional poverty of the fellah." In Africa "the first European innovation which worked to upset native food customs was the large-scale production of cash crops for exports, such as cacao, coffee, sugar and peanuts. We already know how the plantation system works . . . a good example is that of the British colony of Gambia in West Africa, where the culture of food crops for local consumption has been completely abandoned in order to concentrate on the production of peanuts. As a result of this mono-culture . . . the nutritional situation of the colony could hardly be worse." In what has represented for a long time the internal colony of American capitalism—the Southern states—very similar effects were produced by sugar, and in particular by cotton. "In the United States, the cotton-growing states make up the nation's lowest income group. The statistical correlation between cotton growing and poverty is startling. Cotton culture has two harmful effects on the soil: (1) depletion of soil fertility . . . (2) the damage done by erosion. . . . All this is realized clearly now, but it was not understood and appreciated in the nineteenth century—the century that measured success in dollars and cents at the expense of lasting assets."[36]

[35] Josué de Castro, *The Geography of Hunger* (Boston, 1952), p. 97. The three following passages quoted in the text are from pages 105, 215, and 221 of this outstanding work. Professor de Castro notes, incidentally, that while soil erosion and exhaustion are a plague of the entire colonial world, experts "go so far as to assert that, for all practical purposes, there is no such thing as erosion in Japan." (P. 192.)

[36] E. W. Zimmerman, *World Resources and Industries* (revised edition, New York, 1951), p. 326. Needless to say, the author discriminates unfairly against the nineteenth century. In the capitalist world of the twentieth, success is still measured by the same yardstick, the difference being only that large-scale enterprise thinks more about its longer-run returns.

To avoid misunderstanding, the above is not to be taken as arguing against division of labor, intranational and international specialization, and the resulting increase of productivity. What it clearly demonstrates, however, is that an intranational and international specialization that is so organized that one participant of the team specializes in starvation while the other assumes the white man's burden of collecting the profits can hardly be considered a satisfactory arrangement for attainment of the greatest happiness for the greatest number.

Nor is the "no sacrifice" proposition much stronger where the output of the export-oriented foreign enterprise is made up not of recurring agricultural crops but of products of extractive industries: minerals, oil, and the like. Although in this case the displacement of the native population and the destruction of their traditional bases of existence may have assumed somewhat lesser proportions than in connection with plantation agriculture—it has been not by any means negligible—the long-run effect of this type of raw materials exploitation may be no less telling. Indeed, there is no reason to consider the raw materials resources of underdeveloped countries as a free good available in infinite supply. Even if the exhaustion of raw materials for the world as a whole is a bogy that can safely be disregarded, as far as individual countries and specific materials are concerned, the danger is far from minor.[37] Thus to a number of underdeveloped countries what little they receive at the present time for the raw materials with which they are endowed may well turn out to be the mess of pottage for which they are forced to sell their birthright to a better future.

[37] What Professor Mason observes in relation to the United States applies or will apply more or less soon and to a larger or lesser extent also to other countries: "The available evidence concerning oil and various other minerals . . . indicates pretty clearly a rising real cost of discovery. In addition we know that with respect to copper, lead and zinc, the trend has for decades been toward the extraction of lower and lower grade ores. Finally it should be mentioned that there has not been a really important new discovery of some of our most important metals for at least three decades." "Raw Materials, Rearmament, and Economic Development," *Quarterly Journal of Economics* (August 1952), p. 329. This is clearly realized in a number of raw-materials-producing countries, for instance Venezuela, where "sowing petroleum" is the slogan expressing the anxiety over the possible exhaustion (or decline in value) of its oil reserves; Bolivia, where the concern over tin is no less pronounced; and a number of timber-exporting countries, where the end of the timber bonanza is in sight.

That the mess is not large, and the quantity and quality of pottage very modest, was seen above. That this is increasingly realized by the peoples of the affected countries is demonstrated by mounting hostility towards foreign enterprise, and by the extent of cajolery and coercion that are continually being applied to induce native workers to work for Western business. While it may well be true that the natives' reluctance to perform adequately for starvation wages is due to a "cultural lag" and to insufficient insight into what is good for them, the chances are that their resistance is caused by the simple fact that they are much better off in their traditional ways of life, by comparison with what foreign capital is pushing and pulling them into.

Since the decline of slavery as a mode of labor mobilization, the most frequent system of recruitment and retention of reluctant native laborers has been the long-term indenture, supported by a penal sanction for non-fulfillment. This relationship is nominally contractual. . . . Among illiterate peoples, the contract is often a more formal than actual protection for the worker, and there is usually no effective control over the promises made by the recruiter but not a part of the actual contract. Once having entered into the contract and having been transported far from his native village, the worker has little recourse for the false promises or any effective way of breaking off the relationship. . . . Thus whether the "contract" arises out of force and fraud or out of the pressure of poverty, its performance involves a substantial element of direct compulsion. In the Netherlands Indies, particularly in the Outer Provinces, the penal sanction for enforcing employment contracts remained in effect until 1940. It is still widely used in Africa, particularly with respect to workers in the mines. . . . Throughout the colonial and mandated areas of Southeast Asia and the Pacific, the shortage or unwillingness of local workers for plantations, mines, or factories has provided the rationale for the widespread use of indenture. . . . The use of various forms of more or less moderate coercion to secure *hacienda*, mining, and even factory labor is endemic in Latin America. The forms vary from the common peonage, or debt servitude, to the long-term indenture contract similar to that used in many colonial areas. . . .[38]

Thus if apologists of imperialism insist that one ". . . must be able to show that merely geographic investment is actually harmful to the recipient country, which must mean that it results in a lower real income for the inhabitants than they would otherwise have at-

[38] W. E. Moore, *Industrialization and Labor* (Ithaca and New York, 1951), pp. 60-62. Cf. also the literature referred to on those pages, in particular the most informative book by B. Lasker, *Human Bondage in Southeast Asia* (Chapel Hill, North Carolina, 1950).

tained,"[39] such a demonstration can be readily supplied if due allowance is made for the handful of compradors who are the only inhabitants of the underdeveloped countries who derive substantial benefits from the operations of foreign raw materials enterprises.

VI

This brings us to our third question—also the third of the arguments listed above—concerning foreign export-oriented enterprises' *indirect* effect on the economic development of underdeveloped countries. In a number of areas the establishment and operation of foreign enterprise has necessitated investment in installations not forming an integral part of, but entirely indispensable to, the production and exportation of raw materials. Such facilities are railways and harbors, roads and airports, telephone and telegraph, canals and power stations. Generally speaking, those are good things for any underdeveloped country to get. Even if their construction per se does not contribute much to the widening of the backward areas' internal markets—since most of the investment related to it is apt to be "investment in kind" consisting of imported equipment—still the projects, once completed, are usually considered to have a beneficial effect by increasing the possibilities for local investment. This effect is referred to as "external economies" which arise whenever the operation of one enterprise facilitates (cheapens) the establishment or the conduct of another. Thus the construction of a power plant for the purposes of one manufacturing or mining unit may save another manufacturing or mining unit the expense of building a power plant of its own, thus supplying it with cheaper energy than it could otherwise obtain. Similarly the setting up of a sawmill for the requirements of one factory may cheapen the building of another factory in the same area.

It is important to distinguish the amelioration of conditions for economic expansion coming about in this way from what might be called the "investment-snowball-effect"—the process previously referred to in which investment in one enterprise becomes possible in

[39] A. N. McLeod, "Trade and Investment in Underdeveloped Areas: A Comment," *American Economic Review* (June 1951), p. 411. The term "merely geographic investment," aptly coined by H. W. Singer, refers to "foreign investment that is geographically located in the underdeveloped countries but never becomes a part of their economies, remaining really a part of the investing economies instead."

view of the widening of the market caused by investment in other enterprises. This distinction must be stressed because it tends to be blurred in most writings on economic development, with the resulting confusion leading to serious errors. For while the investment-snowball-effect is nearly synonymous with economic development and necessarily implies the appearance of "external economies," the emergence of facilities that *could* give rise to external economies need not by any means result in increased investment and in general economic growth. To put it differently: synchronized acts of domestic investment reflecting increased division of labor and causing a cumulative widening of the internal markets create as a by-product external economies, that is, conditions which in turn facilitate further division of labor and further investment. However, for this improvement of conditions for investment to result actually in further investment, economic and social development must have reached a stage in which there is the possibility for a transition to industrial capitalism. Otherwise such virtual sources of external economies as may appear in the economic system will only strengthen the forces keeping the economic and social structure in whatever mold it happens to be in, or will remain mere potentialities—available but not utilized—and join other productive forces that are not employed, and contribute little if anything to the country's economic development.

What this means is that the part that can be played by external economies in promoting investment is the same as the role that can be played in it by the cheapening of any cost factor, for instance, by the lowering of the rate of interest. And just as it has been recognized to be a mistake to expect that on a given level of income and effective demand a mere lowering of the rate of interest will result in an increase of investment, so it is a fallacy to believe that the sheer presence of potential sources of external economies is bound to generate economic expansion. The similarity goes further. As the earlier insistence of economics on the strategic significance of the rate of interest was by no means "innocent"—implying as it did the desirability of *laissez faire* and of government non-intervention in economic affairs—so likewise the current clamor for providing underdeveloped countries with installations giving rise to external economies (power stations, roads, etc.) is far from being a mere theoretic fad. Its significance becomes transparent as soon as one asks, *to whom* should the facilities that are to be erected furnish the external economies? It is necessary only to take a glance at the statements of official economists and of various big-business-dominated organizations to see clearly that such sources of "external economies" as are to be created in underdeveloped countries are primarily to assist Western enterprise in the exploitation of their natural resources. What is more, the pronounced emphasis on the indispensability of government aid in financing these projects reflects the time-honored notion of business as to what constitutes "harmonious cooperation" between national administrations and monopolistic corporations: the former should shoulder the costs of establishment and conduct of business with as little as possible financial "intervention" of the interested firms, while the latter should reap the profits resulting therefrom with as little as possible financial "intervention" of the public treasury.

Thus while Mr. Nelson Rockefeller and his associates stress that "with critical shortages developing rapidly, a quickened and enlarged production of materials in the underdeveloped countries is of major importance,"[40] Professor Mason points out that "such development can rarely take place without the expansion of auxiliary facilities—railroads, roads, port development, electric power and the like—which have a contribution to make to general economic development."[41] And no bones are made as to who should foot the bill for the necessary investments, and as to what is to enjoy pride of place in judging the urgency of investments in "auxiliary facilities": those that will promote "a quickened and enlarged production of materials in the underdeveloped countries" or those that "have a contribution to make to [their] general economic development." The famous Gray Report answers both questions with all possible clarity. After expressing the historically sound view that "private investment will probably be selective with the bulk of the new funds going into minerals development in a relatively few countries," its authors proceed to explain that "private investment is the most desirable method of development," that "the scope for private investment should be widened as far as possible," and "the need for public investment correspondingly adjusted."[42]

The crux of the matter is that the "auxiliary facilities" in question are for the most part auxiliary to no one but foreign export-oriented

[40] International Development Advisory Board, *Partners in Progress, A Report to the President* (Washington, 1951), p. 8.

[41] "Raw Materials, Rearmament, and Economic Development," *Quarterly Journal of Economics* (August 1952), p. 336.

[42] *Report to the President on Foreign Economic Policies* (Washington, 1950), pp. 52, 61.

business, and that the external economies stemming from them benefit nothing but additional production of raw materials for export. This is due in part to the fact that the installations set up by foreign enterprise or at its behest are naturally so designed and located as to serve its requirements. Whether we consider the railway construction sponsored by foreign enterprise in India, in Africa, or in Latin America, the entire layout of which has been such as to facilitate the movement of raw materials towards ports of exit, and the development of harbors, which has been dictated by the needs of raw materials exporters, or whether we think of power plants located so as to supply energy to foreign mining enterprises, and of irrigation schemes designed to service foreign-owned plantations, the picture is everywhere the same. In the words of Dr. H. W. Singer, "the productive facilities for export from underdeveloped countries, which were so largely a result of foreign investment, never became a part of the internal economic structure of those underdeveloped countries themselves, except in the purely geographical and physical sense."[43]

Yet the physical characteristics of the foreign-enterprise-sponsored auxiliary facilities are not the primary cause of their sterility as far as the economic development of underdeveloped countries is concerned. Much more important is the consideration that even if their design and location are such as to correspond fully to the technical requirements of economic growth in the backward areas, their effect would still remain nil (or negative) as long as they constitute alien bodies in a socioeconomic structure into which they have been artificially injected. For it is not railways, roads, and power stations that give rise to industrial capitalism: it is the emergence of industrial capitalism that leads to the building of railways, to the construction of roads, and to the establishment of power stations. The identical sources of external economies, if appearing in a country going through the mercantile phase of capitalism, will provide, if anything, "external economies" to mer-

[43] "The Distribution of Gains Between Investing and Borrowing Countries," *American Economic Review* (May 1950), p. 475. It is interesting to note that the United Nations Technical Assistance Mission in Bolivia concludes its analysis of the country's mining economy with the statement that "this new trading economy remained divorced to an extraordinary degree from that of the rest of the country." *Report of the UN Mission of Technical Assistance to Bolivia* (1951), p. 85; while the United Nations Economic Commission for Latin America in its *Recent Facts and Trends in the Venezuelan Economy* (1951) observes that petroleum operations in Venezuela could be more properly considered a part of the economy in which the investing companies are domiciled than of Venezuela itself.

chant capital. Thus the modern banks established by the British during the second half of the nineteenth century in India, in Egypt, in Latin America, and elsewhere in the underdeveloped world became not fountains of industrial credit but large-scale clearing houses of mercantile finance vying in their interest charges with the local usurers. In the same way, the harbors and cities that sprang up in many underdeveloped countries in connection with their briskly expanding exports did not turn into centers of industrial activity but snowballed into vast market places providing the necessary "living space" to wealthy compradors and crowded by a motley population of petty traders, agents, and commissionmen. Nor did the railways, trunk roads, and canals built for the purposes of foreign enterprise evolve into pulsing arteries of productive activities; they merely accelerated the disintegration of the peasant economy and provided additional means for a more intensive and more thorough mercantile exploitation of the rural interiors.

Professor Frankel is entirely right in saying that "the history of such 'investments' in Africa and elsewhere affords many examples of railway lines, roads, ports, irrigation works, etc. in the 'wrong places' which not only failed to lead to income-generating development, but actually inhibited more economic developments which might otherwise have taken place."[44] It cannot be stressed strongly enough, however, that the principal harm done by those investments consists not in their being directed towards the "wrong" projects at the "wrong" places and in thus detracting funds from investments in "right" projects at the "right" places. The principal impact of foreign enterprise on the development of the underdeveloped countries lies in hardening and strengthening the sway of merchant capitalism, in slowing down and indeed preventing its transformation into industrial capitalism.

VII

This is the really important "indirect influence" of foreign enterprise on the evolution of the underdeveloped countries. It flows through a multitude of channels, permeates all of their economic, social, political, and cultural life, and decisively determines its entire course. There is first of all the emergence of a group of merchants expanding and thriving within the orbit of foreign capital. Whether they act as whole-

[44] *Some Conceptual Aspects of International Economic Development of Underdeveloped Territories* (Princeton, 1952), p. 14.

salers—assembling, sorting, and standardizing commodities that they purchase from small producers and sell to representatives of foreign concerns—or as suppliers of local materials to foreign enterprises, or as caterers to various other needs of foreign firms and their staffs, many of them manage to assemble vast fortunes and to move up to the very top of the underdeveloped countries' capitalist class. Deriving their profits from the operations of foreign business, vitally interested in its expansion and prosperity, this comprador element of the native bourgeoisie uses its considerable influence to fortify and to perpetuate the *status quo*.

There are secondly the native industrial monopolists, in most cases interlocked and interwoven with domestic merchant capital and with foreign enterprise, who entirely depend on the maintenance of the existing economic structure, and whose monopolistic status would be swept away by the rise of industrial capitalism. Concerned with preventing the emergence of competitors in their markets, they look with favor upon absorption of capital in the sphere of circulation, and have nothing to fear from foreign export-oriented enterprise. They too are stalwart defenders of the established order.

The interests of these two groups run entirely parallel with those of the feudal landowners powerfully entrenched in the societies of the backward areas. Indeed, these have no reason for complaints about the activities of foreign enterprise in their countries. In fact, these activities yield them considerable profits. Frequently they provide outlets for the produce of landed estates, in many places they raise the value of land, often they offer lucrative employment opportunities to members of the landed gentry.

What results is a political and social coalition of wealthy compradors, powerful monopolists, and large landowners dedicated to the defense of the existing feudal-mercantile order. Ruling the realm by no matter what political means—as a monarchy, as a military-fascist dictatorship, or as a republic of the Kuomintang variety—this coalition has nothing to hope for from the rise of industrial capitalism which would dislodge it from its positions of privilege and power. Blocking all economic and social progress in its country, this regime has no real political basis in city or village, lives in continual fear of the starving and restive popular masses, and relies for its stability on Praetorian guards of relatively well kept mercenaries.

In most underdeveloped countries social and political developments of the last few decades would have toppled regimes of that sort.

That they have been able to stay in business—for business is, indeed, their sole concern—in most of Latin America and in the Near East, in several "free" countries of Southeast Asia and in some similarly "free" countries of Europe, is due mainly if not exclusively to the aid and support that was given to them "freely" by Western capital and by Western governments acting on its behalf. For the maintenance of these regimes and the operations of foreign enterprise in the underdeveloped countries have become mutually interdependent. It is the economic strangulation of the colonial and dependent countries by the imperialist powers that stymied the development of indigenous industrial capitalism, thus preventing the overthrow of the feudal-mercantile order and assuring the rule of the comprador administrations. It is the preservation of these subservient governments, stifling economic and social development and suppressing all popular movements for social and national liberation, that makes possible at the present time the continued foreign exploitation of underdeveloped countries and their domination by the imperialist powers.

Foreign capital and the governments by which it is represented have steadily kept their part of the bargain to this very day. Although official opinion at the present time, while admitting that "colonial powers added the weight of government proscription and discouragement to the economic forces handicapping industrial expansion in raw materials producing areas," feels strongly that "those days . . . are gone forever,"[45] unhappily nothing could be a more egregious misreading of current history. Whether we look at the British proceedings in Kenya, in Malaya, or in the West Indies, at French operations in Indo-China and North Africa, at the United States' activities in Guatemala and the Philippines, or whether we consider the somewhat "subtler" United States transactions in Latin America and the Far East and the still more complex Anglo-American machinations in the Near East, very little of the *essence* of the imperialism "of those days" can be said to have "gone forever."

To be sure, neither imperialism itself nor its *modus operandi* and ideological trimmings are today what they were fifty or a hundred years ago. Just as outright looting of the outside world has yielded to organized trade with the underdeveloped countries, in which plunder has been rationalized and routinized by a mechanism of impeccably "correct" contractual relations, so has the rationality of smoothly

[45] E. S. Mason, "Nationalism and Raw Materials," *The Atlantic* (March 1953), p. 62.

functioning commerce grown into the modern, still more advanced, still more rational system of imperialist exploitation. Like all other historically changing phenomena, the contemporary form of imperialism contains and preserves all its earlier modalities, but raises them to a new level. Its central feature is that it is now directed not solely towards the rapid extraction of large sporadic gains from the objects of its domination, it is no longer content with merely assuring a more or less steady flow of those gains over a somewhat extended period. Propelled by well-organized, rationally conducted monopolistic enterprise, it seeks today to rationalize the flow of these receipts so as to be able to count on it in perpetuity. And this points to the main task of imperialism in our time: to prevent, or, if that is impossible, to slow down and to control the economic development of underdeveloped countries.

That such development is profoundly inimical to the interests of foreign corporations producing raw materials for export can be readily seen. There is of course the mortal threat of nationalization of raw materials producing enterprises that is associated with the ascent to power of governments in backward countries that are determined to move their nations off dead center; but, even in the absence of nationalization, economic development in the source countries bodes nothing but evil to Western capital. For whichever aspect of economic development we may consider, it is manifestly detrimental to the prosperity of the raw materials producing corporations.[46] As under conditions of economic growth employment opportunities and productivity expand in other parts of the economy, and the class consciousness and bargaining power of labor increase, wages tend to rise in the raw materials producing sector. While in some lines of output—on plantations primarily—those increased costs can be offset by the adoption of improved techniques, such mechanization involves capital outlays that are obviously repugnant to the corporations involved. And in mining and petroleum operations even this solution is hardly possible. These in general employ the same methods of production that are in use in the advanced countries, so that the technological gap that could be filled

[46] The only possibly favorable effect of income growth in the source countries—the rise of their own demand for raw materials—can be safely neglected. It is nowhere likely to come to much, and certainly not before a very advanced stage of development is reached. Thus in the case in which the internal consumption of the source country absorbs the largest observed proportion of its total output, in Venezuela, less than 4 percent of Venezuelan oil is sold in the domestic market.

is accordingly very small. With the prices of their products in the
world markets representing a fixed datum to the individual companies
—at least in the short run—increased labor costs combined with various fringe benefits resulting from growing unionization, as well as
rising costs of other local supplies, must lead necessarily to a reduction
of profits. If thus the longer-run effects of economic development cannot but be damaging to the raw materials exporting corporations, the
immediate concomitants of economic development are apt to be even
more disturbing. They will be, as a rule, higher taxes and royalties
imposed on the foreign enterprises by the local government seeking
revenue to finance its developmental ventures, foreign exchange controls designed to curtail the removal of profits abroad, tariffs rendering
the importation of foreign-made equipment more expensive or raising
the prices of imported wage goods, and others—all inevitably interfering with the freedom of action of foreign enterprise and encroaching
upon its profitability.[47]

Small wonder that under such circumstances Western big business
heavily engaged in raw materials exploitation leaves no stone unturned
to obstruct the evolution of social and political conditions in underdeveloped countries that might be conducive to their economic development. It uses its tremendous power to prop up the backward areas'
comprador administrations, to disrupt and corrupt the social and
political movements that oppose them, and to overthrow whatever
progressive governments may rise to power and refuse to do the bid-
ding of their imperialist overlords. Where and when its own impressive
resources do not suffice to keep matters under control, or where and
when the costs of the operations involved can be shifted to their home
countries' national governments—or nowadays to international agencies such as the International Bank for Reconstruction and Development—the diplomatic, financial and, if need be, military facilities of
the imperialist power are rapidly and efficiently mobilized to help
private enterprise in distress to do the required job.[48]

[47] The preceding paragraph is essentially a reformulation of a statement
by Dr. C. E. Rollins in his previously cited paper, "Mineral Development
and Economic Growth," *Social Research* (Autumn 1956).

[48] It is unfortunately not possible to enlarge here on this tremendously
important subject. A comprehensive study of contemporary imperialism
is lacking, and the total picture has to be pieced together from scattered
information. In addition to what has been referred to in an earlier chapter,
see the interesting account of imperialist activities centering on oil in
Harvey O'Connor, *The Empire of Oil* (New York, 1955); the well-
documented description of what probably constitutes the outstanding case

VIII

The gearing of policies and opinion in the West to the support of big business in its concerted effort to preserve its positions in the backward countries, and to sabotage their economic development, reflects itself in official pronouncements no less than in economic writings. Thus President Eisenhower defined the aims of American foreign policy as "doing whatever our Government can properly do to encourage the flow of private investment abroad. This involves, as a serious and explicit purpose of our foreign policy, the encouragement of a hospitable climate for such investment in foreign countries."[49] This view was echoed by Mr. C. B. Randall, the Chairman of the Commission on Foreign Economic Policy, who insists that "a new and better climate for American investment must be created"—rejoicing at the same time over the fact that "happily this is being recognized and such countries as Turkey, Greece, and Panama have led the way in modernizing their corporate laws and creating the right sort of atmosphere for our investment."[50] And with what might be called truly "disarming brutality" the big business position was expressed by August Maffry, Vice-president of the Irving Trust Company and one of Wall Street's most influential economists. In a special report prepared for the United States Department of State, he calls for "total diplomacy" in the service of the American foreign investment drive. "The improvement in investment climate in friendly countries by more direct measures should be the objective of a total and sustained diplomatic effort by the United States. . . . All agencies of the U. S. Government concerned with foreign economic development should exercise constant vigilance for discriminatory or other actions by foreign governments adversely affecting the interests of American investors and employ all possible diplomatic pressures to forestall or remedy

---

of imperialist intervention in the postwar period in N. Keddie, *The Impact of the West on Iranian Social History* (unpublished dissertation, University of California at Berkeley, 1955); the useful report on United States interventions in Latin America in O. E. Smith, Jr., *Yankee Diplomacy* (Dallas, 1953)—to name only a few.

[49] State of the Union Message, 1953.

[50] *A Foreign Economic Policy for the United States* (Chicago, 1954), Chapter II; the list of the countries that rated this special commendation is rather noteworthy. It could be extended to include Franco's Spain, Syngman Rhee's Korea, Chiang Kai-shek's Formosa, Castillo's Guatemala, and a few other similarly development-minded parts of the "free world."

them." Not too choosy about methods, he further suggests: "There is still another and a very promising way in which the U. S. Government can assist in achieving better conditions for investment in foreign countries. This is by aiding and abetting by all available means the efforts of private investors to obtain concessions from foreign countries in connection with specific proposed investments. . . . Once concessions have been won through combined private and official efforts in a particular case, then the way is open to generalize them for the benefit of all other private investors."[51]

Since "American private investment abroad is largely concentrated in mining investments, notably in the petroleum field," and since "it is probably substantially true that in the absence of very special circumstances no American private capital will now venture abroad unless the prospects are good that . . . the returns will amortize the investments within five years or so,"[52] it can be readily visualized what kind of governments in the underdeveloped countries are needed for such investments to be assured of the required hospitality. And it is no more difficult to perceive what type of regime and what variety of social and political forces in the underdeveloped countries have to be furthered by "total diplomacy" and by the application of "more direct measures" if the "right sort of atmosphere" for foreign investment is to be created in the raw-materials-rich parts of the backward world.

[51] "Program for Increasing Private Investment in Foreign Countries" (mimeographed, New York, 1952), pp. 10-12.
[52] Jacob Viner, "America's Aims and the Progress of Underdeveloped Countries," in *The Progress of Underdeveloped Areas* (B. F. Hoselitz, ed.) (Chicago, 1952), p. 184.

SEVEN

Towards a Morphology of Backwardness, II

WE may now try to complete our rapid survey of the mode of utilization of the underdeveloped countries' economic surplus, dealing simultaneously with the last of the earlier listed arguments in favor of foreign enterprise. For this we must inquire briefly into the use made of such economic surplus as is appropriated by its *fourth* claimant outside of agriculture: the state. The amounts involved obviously vary from country to country. In some countries they are as small as, say, in most of Latin America or in the Philippines; in others they are as large as, for instance, in Venezuela and some of the Near Eastern petroleum areas. The variations are no less pronounced with regard to what we have called the economic *locus* of the government revenues, and to the (closely related to it) methods of their collection. In a number of countries—again typically in the petroleum-producing areas—the government receipts constitute easily identifiable *transfers* of economic surplus; elsewhere they form *additions* to the economic surplus based on a corresponding curtailment of the share of total output available for mass consumption. In the former cases they stem for the most part from taxes, export duties, and royalties paid largely by foreign enterprise; in the latter, their sources are various, mainly indirect levies imposed upon the population either via tariffs on imports and excises on mass consumption goods or via inflationary issuance of currency.[1]

While there are also considerable differences in the manner in which revenues are spent by the individual governments, the diversity in this respect is very much smaller. In fact, the countries in question can be easily grouped under three broad headings: first, the vast colonial territories that are directly administered by the imperialist powers (nearly all of Africa, parts of Asia, and a few, relatively small, areas in America); secondly, the overwhelming majority of the backward countries ruled by regimes of a clearly pronounced comprador character; and thirdly, a few underdeveloped countries having governments of what might be called a "New Deal" orientation—principally India, Indonesia, and Burma.[2]

As far as the first group is concerned, there has been since the end of the war a great deal of publicity to the effect that the current administration of the colonies on the part of the imperialist powers is altogether different in spirit, purpose, and outcome from what it used to be in the now allegedly liquidated past. Indeed, as President Truman in announcing the celebrated Point Four of his 1949 Inaugural Address promised "to supply the vitalizing force to stir the peoples of the world into triumphant action, not only against their human oppressors, but also against their ancient enemies—hunger, misery and despair," so the governments of Britain, France, Belgium, and Portugal were advertising ten-year plans of colonial development the professed purpose of which was the advancement of the health and welfare of the peoples inhabiting the territories under their control.

Yet, the strategies of the United States' activities under the Point Four program and of the Western European powers' efforts under the colonial development schemes were inspired by kindred spirits. In the Point Four program "particular emphasis . . . is given . . . to the stimulation of a greatly expanded flow of private investment."[3]

---

[1] In those (relatively few) countries where high duties and sales taxes affect luxury goods, the resulting fiscal receipts may also represent transfers of the economic surplus rather than an increment to it.

[2] There were in the past a few additional countries belonging to this group in Latin America—notably Mexico under Lázaro Cárdenas as well as Guatemala and Chile. But these "special situations" have meanwhile been "adjusted" and the countries in question safely brought back into our second group.

[3] United States Department of State, *Point Four, Cooperative Program for Aid in the Development of the Economically Underdeveloped Areas* (Washington, 1949), p. 4.

Similarly the Western European governments pledged that "every effort is being made, and will continue to be made, to encourage the inflow of private capital. It is to be hoped that private investors will fully realize the advantages that investment in the territories can offer."[4] In fact, it would seem that the maximization of those advantages is what has been primarily on the mind of the architects of Point Four and of the Western European colonial planners. Apparently still interested—to use Cecil Rhodes's famous saying—"in land, not niggers," the blueprints of "triumphant action" in the colonies place their main accent on the development of raw materials. That such is the case with regard to the Point Four program is clearly stated by the agency entrusted with its administration: "Location, development and economical processing of mineral and fuel resources is a major aspect of the program of technical cooperation for economic development of underdeveloped countries"—presumably because "many underdeveloped mineral resources in the areas which will participate in the cooperative effort are of considerable importance to the more highly developed nations of the world, including the United States."[5] And that nothing different is intended by the Western European benefactors of the colonies is certified by the Organization for European Economic Co-operation: "Within the present programme of development, the territories can make an important contribution to the defence of the free world to which they belong [sic!] particularly by increasing their production of raw materials."[6]

Yet the required profitability of private exploitation of raw materials is predicated upon the presence of various "auxiliary facilities": railways, trunk roads, harbors, power stations, and the like. Their construction, however, has but rarely attracted private capital.[7] As we

[4] Organization for European Economic Co-operation, *Investments in Overseas Territories in Africa South of the Sahara* (Paris, 1951), p. 79.

[5] U. S. Department of State, *op. cit.*, p. 20.

[6] Organization for European Economic Co-operation, *loc. cit.*

[7] This is due to low returns on investments in public utilities in underdeveloped countries as compared with those in raw materials enterprise. In the four years 1945–1948 the average annual return on the book values of American investment in backward areas was 3.2 percent in public utilities as against 13.4 percent in all types of business including public utilities, and as much as 26.7 percent in petroleum. H. J. Dernburg, "Prospects for Long-Term Foreign Investment," *Harvard Business Review* (July 1950), p. 44. The reason for such low yield in public utilities in the underdeveloped countries is not far to seek: it is primarily due to the high average costs of a unit of output resulting from their inability to make

know, "free enterprise" has never begrudged that part of the job to the public treasury, and accordingly more than three fourths of all projected expenditures in the French territories are earmarked for the creation of such sources of "external economies" to raw materials enterprise, while the corresponding proportion of the Belgian outlays is approximately two thirds, and of the British about one half.[8]

To be sure, the balance is to be spent on so-called "social services," that is, improved nutrition, medical care, education, and the like. But even this spending is essentially governed by considerations of Western capital's "enlightened self-interest," and is oriented towards providing raw materials business with improved human sources of external economies. What Professor de Castro says about this matter deserves to be quoted at length:

> The European colonizer, when he offers the Negro a larger quantity of food than is normally available in the native village, is merely trying to attract workers, and to provide them with a quantity of energy which he expects to get back in the form of productive work. What he is really providing is not better nutrition, but merely an abundance of fuel. The same thing is happening in Africa, right now, that happened in tropical America in connection with the feeding of Negro slaves. The slave owners, anxious to get as much production as possible, always took care to provide them with . . . a diet that kept the slaves in apparent good health, and made possible the hard agricultural labor demanded of them. This policy of the plantation owners of Brazil and the Antilles . . . led to the mistaken conclusion that the Negro slaves were one of the best-fed groups in the colonial population. This was never true. The slave's diet was bulky, but it was always bad. The so-called full-belly policy greatly worsened the nutritional situation of the Negro in Equatorial Africa. . . . the Negro showed much more frequent signs of dietary deficiency . . . after entering the service of the colonizers than he had before. . . . The nutritional situation is especially precarious in the mining districts, where fresh foods are practically unknown.[9]

Nor can there be any doubt that it is still the full-belly policy that guides at the present time the spending on social services on the part of the colonial administrations of the imperialist powers. The British Secretary of State for the Colonies said in the House of Commons on May 27, 1949, that "a large part of the outlays falling under

---

full use of economies of scale which in turn is caused by lack of sufficient simultaneous investment in enterprises that would be users of their services.

[8] Cf. United Nations, *Review of Economic Conditions in Africa* (1951), pp. 111 ff.

[9] *The Geography of Hunger* (Boston, 1952), p. 223.

the heading 'social services' are regarded as an 'economic expenditure for promoting the greater efficiency of the worker and preventing a great deal of waste.' "[10] And that the same motivations inspire the American well-wishers of the colonial peoples can be gleaned from the following passage in the previously mentioned Report by Messrs. Nelson Rockefeller and associates: "Absenteeism on the Vitória-Minas railroad was cut dramatically by effective malaria control. This has made it possible to reduce maintenance crews by one-third, which, in turn, has cut the cost of extracting and transporting iron ore and mica from the Rio Doce Valley."[11]

That this "renewed drive to find cheap raw materials, new sources of mineral wealth, fresh supplies of food for export from countries which themselves are desperately underfed"[12] represents a flagrant disregard for the developmental requirements of the colonial areas calls for no elaboration. This is obvious in the light of the entire historical record as well as in view of all the theoretical considerations pertaining to economic and social development of underdeveloped countries via foreign exploitation of their raw materials. It is expressed with admirable precision in the United Nations report referred to above: "Investment in the developed sector of the economy is concentrated on the production of primary products for export. . . . Practically all of the capital upon which this production has been developed had to be imported from outside Africa, and, with the exception of the Union of South Africa and parts of North Africa, this investment has had a relatively small effect in generating secondary incomes and investment. Gross exports receipts, in considerable proportion, are transferred as incomes abroad in the form of loan charges and dividends on invested capital."[13]

II

Nor is the situation in any better shape when we consider the second group of the underdeveloped countries, those that are no longer outright colonies of the capitalist powers but are managed for them by local comprador administrations. The most important among them

[10] United Nations, *loc. cit.*
[11] International Development Advisory Board, *Partners in Progress,* A Report to the President (Washington, 1951), p. 54.
[12] Basil Davidson, *Report on Southern Africa* (London, 1952), p. 271.
[13] *Review of Economic Conditions in Africa* (1951), p. 17.

are the oil-producing lands in the Middle East and Latin America as
well as a number of Latin American countries yielding valuable minerals and foodstuffs. The difference between these two groups that
most concerns us in the present context is that the raw materials
exploitation in the first group—the colonial territories—has not
reached as yet a very advanced stage, while the output of raw materials in the second group of countries has already attained a tremendous
volume. To be sure, this difference is of recent origin, and even where
it has been pronounced for a longer period of time it has not much
affected the situation of the respective countries. With the exception
of Iran it was not until the interwar period that oil production assumed
major proportions, and it was not until the end of the Second World
War that the governments of the source countries were able to lay
their hands on significant sums of money resulting from oil proceeds.[14]

Since then, however, the administrations of nearly all oil-producing countries have succeeded in securing greatly improved contractual
arrangements with the companies exploiting their oil resources.[15]
Although the actual remittances from the foreign corporations in question do not necessarily correspond to the proportion of their revenues
due to the local governments under the now prevailing terms of the
concessions,[16] the amounts currently obtained by the national authorities, while varying from country to country, are very large in nearly
all oil-producing parts of the world. Indeed, they are stupendous however one looks at them, whether in terms of aggregates or in terms of
receipts per capita of the population.

[14] For a graphic synopsis of the history of the Middle Eastern petroleum
concessions, cf. United Nations, *Review of Economic Conditions in the
Middle East* (1951), pp. 58, 59; a good short account of the earlier history
of the royalties agreements between various local governments and oil-
producing companies will be found in R. F. Mikesell and H. B. Chenery,
Arabian Oil (Chapel Hill, North Carolina, 1949), Chapter IV. That review
is brought up to date in "Oil and Social Change in the Middle East," *The
Economist* (July 2, 1955).

[15] This was partly due to the vast expansion of demand for oil during
and after the war and the resulting intensification of the rivalry among
the oil companies—particularly between those domiciled in the United
States and Britain respectively—partly due to the mounting popular pressures in the underdeveloped countries threatening the political stability of
the local administrations and thus limiting the extent of their possible subservience to foreign interests.

[16] "Since most of the concession companies are controlled by or integrated with marketing companies, the amounts of their profits attributable
to operations within the concession country can be manipulated so as to
keep such payments to a minimum." Mikesell and Chenery, *op. cit.*, p. 39.

In the Middle East, six areas—"country" would hardly be an appropriate designation for some of them—inhabited by 30 million people contain 64 percent of the world's known oil resources and account for approximately 20 percent of the total world production of petroleum. In the 1954 order of output they are Kuwait, Saudi Arabia, Iraq, Qatar, Iran, and Bahrein. In the nine years after the end of the Second World War the governments of those six regions received by way of direct payments on the part of foreign petroleum companies the equivalent of 3 billion United States dollars.[17]

The transfer in a short time of such an amount of money to the governments of the source countries might well be pointed to as a major "indirect" contribution of foreign enterprise—so large, in fact, as to overshadow entirely whatever considerations have led us to be most skeptical about the favorable nature of its impact on the economic development of the underdeveloped countries. Unfortunately, however, there could be hardly any claim less founded on observable facts. For its validity depends entirely on what use has been made of the moneys that were turned over to the local administrations, on the part that the payments played in advancing the peoples inhabiting these countries along the road of economic and social progress. As Al Smith was fond of saying: "Let's look at the record!"

"On the Persian Gulf," says *The Economist*, ". . . states and sheikhdoms are still run on a feudal basis, and little distinction is drawn between national revenue and the privy purse of the ruler." Considering these "states and sheikhdoms" in turn, we may start with Kuwait. This realm, inhabited by less than 200,000 people, yielded in one year alone (1954) nearly 220 million dollars paid by the British-American-owned Kuwait Oil Company. There is no accurate information on the mode of utilization of these staggering receipts. What is known, however, leaves no doubt that they are not even partly used to raise the productivity or the living standards of the Kuwait population. They are, in fact, among the poorest people in the world—with an annual income of about 50 dollars per capita—more than 90 percent of whom are suffering from chronic starvation and tuberculosis. At the same time one third of the Sheik's revenues is reported to go into his privy purse, another third to be regularly invested in

[17] For the years 1946–1949 the estimate is on the basis of data contained in International Monetary Fund, *Balance of Payments Yearbook* (Washington, 1949) and *Balance of Payments Yearbook*, Vol. 5 (Washington, 1954); the estimates for the years 1950–1954 are supplied in *The Economist, loc. cit.*

foreign securities, with the balance devoted to public uses. These uses have been primarily modernization of the city and its harbor, the building of a water distillation plant (to avoid the importation of brackish water of the Shatt-al-Arab from Iraq), and the erection of an "out-of-this-world" new palace[18]—all enterprises more conducive to the happiness of the Sheik's family and of the foreign staff of the Kuwait Oil Company than to the welfare of the Kuwait Arabs.

Although the oil revenues of the King of Saudi Arabia, reckoned per capita of his 6 million subjects, come nowhere near the bonanza that descended upon the Sheik of Kuwait, his aggregate receipts are now, and have been during the entire postwar period, considerably higher than those of the ruler of Kuwait. In 1954, for instance, they reached 260 million dollars. What is done with this money seems to be something of a mystery. "The only experiment made in recent years (1947) to conduct the administration on the basis of a published, and much publicized, budget was such a fiasco that no further attempt has been made to take the people into the confidence of the Government."[19] This reticence in disclosing much about the use made of the "ever-increasing flood of gold [pouring] into the Government's coffers" has very good reasons. Already in wartime, when under Anglo-American Lend-Lease programs considerable sums were paid to Ibn Saud, "the Arabian response was a further orgy of extravagance and mismanagement, accompanied by the growth of corruption on a large scale and in the highest quarters":

The oil made it possible for Arabia to indulge in extravagance out of its own resources. And it did it literally on a princely scale: leading off with the dispatch of a dozen princes to the New World to inaugurate the new era of the United Nations, and to ransack America for motor-cars and other aids to the enjoyment of life. Other such expeditions followed, one led by the Crown Prince and another by Abdullah Sulaiman himself: each bringing back to Arabia substantial mementoes of its invasion of the richest country in the world, among whose wonders one member of one of these expeditions singled out as the most wonderful of them all a submarine night-club with walls of glass, through which the circumambient fish could watch the dancing. With American motor-cars and other industrial products, including cine-cameras and projectors, air-conditioning sets and sports

[18] Harvey O'Connor, *The Empire of Oil* (New York, 1955), Chapter 28.
[19] H. St. J. B. Philby, *Arabian Jubilee* (London, 1952), p. 228. It may be worth noting that the author of this informative book cannot possibly be suspected of a bias against the Saudi Arabian regime. Indeed, the volume was dedicated to Ibn Saud, and its motto is: "Praise him for his mighty acts; praise him according to his excellent greatness."

paraphernalia, came many American notions and even a taste for American food. I have sat down to *al fresco* dinners in the Crown Prince's garden estate at Riyadh, to which every item on the menu had come fresh from America in refrigerator planes.[20]

The Economist sizes up the situation quite succinctly: "Actual expenditure [in Saudi Arabia] . . . despite the astronomic growth of its income has in recent years regularly and considerably exceeded revenue. Judging by appearances, one reason for this deficit is that a large proportion of the revenue furnishes a cushioned existence, and palatial private investment in real property abroad, to princes, ministers, rivals for power and other palace connections."[21] And what remains is spent on the maintenance of a vast military establishment eating up almost 35 percent of total expenditures and on a sprawling Ecclesiastic Department. The former represents according to competent observers the principal physical instrument for the maintenance of the regime while the latter constitutes its no less indispensable ideological pillar.[22]

That both are urgently needed can be readily seen. The per capita income of the population is of the same order as that in Kuwait. Although malaria, tuberculosis, and venereal disease are rampant, and the bulk of the population is illiterate, the budget for 1953-1954 provided for 5.3 percent of total expenditure for education, health, and social services.[23] At the same time, while 80 percent of the population live on dates, a large part of which have to be imported, an official of a United States Agricultural Commission that visited Saudi Arabia in the '40s expressed the belief that the arable acreage "could

[20] *Ibid.*, pp. 227, 231. Abdullah Sulaiman, referred to in the passage above, is Saudi Arabia's Minister of Finance, in charge of the budget, which "apart from the untouchable provision made for the royal exchequer and unpremeditated raids from the same direction on the resources of the State, would be administered at the sole discretion of the Finance Department, which could always withhold funds provided in the budget from any other department soever, and did normally withhold the pay of the lower grades of officials for periods varying from eight months (at the worst) to four months (at the best)." (P. 228.)

[21] "Oil and Change in the Middle East" (July 2, 1955).

[22] Henry A. Atkinson and associates, *Security and the Middle East, The Problem and Its Solution,* Proposals Submitted to the President of the United States (New York, 1954), p. 81. Mr. Philby reports that Ibn Saud, whose political acumen he much admires, held that "the Ecclesiastical Commissioners did more good to the country than all the other departments put together, in catering for the spiritual welfare of the people."

[23] *Security and the Middle East,* p. 82. Needless to say, it is not even certain that this allotment has been actually spent for the stated purpose.

be increased at least ten-fold by the utilization of ground-waters alone."[24] And that the potentialities for the expansion of manufacturing are tremendous goes without saying.

The conditions prevailing in the other Middle Eastern oil countries are so similar to what happens in Saudi Arabia and Kuwait that one might almost substitute the name of one country for that of another. In Iraq, inhabited by 5 million people, the government collected in 1954 over 191 million dollars from the oil companies. While the per capita annual income of the Iraqis is reported to be higher than that of most other Arabs (something in the order of 90 dollars), only 20 percent of the potentially cultivable land is used, and only a negligible area is irrigated. The state of health of the population is abominable, about 90 percent of the people are illiterate, and unemployment is widespread. The oil revenues sink into the bottomless pit of a corrupt administration controlled by absentee landlords which "by . . . applying its oil royalties to the ordinary budget . . . has been able to curtail the taxes on the capitalist class, and at the same time to enlarge its administrative apparatus. It has strengthened the government but has worsened the living standards for the population."[25]

Although both "Iraq and Iran have a wide range of alternative natural resources,"[26] and therefore large potentialities of economic development, the latter country is no further advanced than the former. To be sure, Iran's oil revenues are considerably smaller than those of Iraq; they have been coming in, however, for a much longer period of time. Yet their fate has been the same as elsewhere: they went down the drain of corruption, extravagance, and waste.

Thus there can be hardly any difference of opinion on the applicability to all of the oil-bearing Middle East of what Mr. Philby concluded about Saudi Arabia: "It only needed a little restraint and judicious administration to place the country beyond the reach of want for ever, and to raise it to a high level of permanent prosperity."[27] Indeed, by a simple calculation one can get a rough notion of the opportunities lost. Suppose that the 3 billion dollars that accrued to the six oil-producing countries in the course of the nine postwar years up to 1954 had been used for productive investment. Assume furthermore that the ratio of the quantity of plant and equipment to the

[24] *Ibid.*, p. 83.
[25] *Ibid.*, p. 72.
[26] *The Economist, loc. cit.*
[27] *Op. cit.*, p. 231.

quantity of output produced with its help (however measured) were in the Middle East 3:1, that is, similar to what it is, say, in the United States.[28] Under such circumstances the current income of the 30 million people inhabiting the Middle Eastern oil area (apart from oil!) would be higher than it is now by 1 billion dollars per year, that means, by about 50 percent. What is more, if the annual oil revenues had been productively invested as they came in, the aggregate increase of income for the nine-year period would have reached nearly 3 billion dollars! And this does not take into account the investment-snowball-effect, that is, the entire income increase that would have resulted from other investment stimulated in turn by the investment of the oil receipts. Nor does it involve any "subversive" assumptions on what might have happened if the oil resources of the countries in question were exploited for their own benefit rather than for the benefit of Western oil companies.

A comparison of what could have been accomplished in Venezuela —the official display window exhibit of the benefits derived by an underdeveloped country from foreign exploitation of its raw materials[29]—with what has actually been attained with the help of the oil revenues accruing to its government is no less striking than in the Middle East. Having surpassed 500 million dollars in 1954, the Venezuelan government's total receipts from the oil companies are by far the largest in the oil-producing world. With a population of 5 million, these receipts in per capita terms are exceeded only by those of Kuwait, Qatar, and Bahrein. To be sure, a part of these tremendous revenues has been spent by the government on promotion of economic

---

[28] This assumption is not so far-fetched as might at first be thought. While on one hand in the earlier phases of industrialization this ratio may be raised by the inadequacy of the labor force and a more rapid wear and tear of machinery resulting therefrom, there are on the other hand forces that tend to lower the ratio in underdeveloped countries by comparison with advanced capitalist countries. For one thing, underdeveloped countries have the advantage of being able to introduce right away most modern and productive equipment without having to carry along much of a backlog of antiquated facilities; secondly, under conditions of rationally planned industrialization they can make full use of such capital goods as they have in contradistinction to the excess capacity continually present under monopoly capitalism. For an interesting, if incomplete, discussion of this problem, cf. V. V. Bhatt, "Capital-Output Ratios of Certain Industries: A Comparative Study of Certain Countries," *Review of Economics and Statistics* (August 1954), pp. 309 ff.

[29] See, for instance, The President's Raw Materials Policy Commission, *Resources for Freedom* ("Paley Report") (Washington, 1952), Vol. I, p. 61.

development, but, to borrow the words of *The Economist,* "the oil sowing policy has been painfully slow in bearing fruits . . . broadly speaking only the fringes of the nation's economic resources have been touched."[30]

It is important to realize the reasons for both phenomena, the achievement of at least *some* improvement in the country's economic position that has taken place on the basis of the oil receipts, and the tantalizing slowness of the advance. As far as the former is concerned, the first and foremost factor to be taken into account is that the socio-political circumstances in Venezuela have been such as to preclude a regime quite as outrageous as those, say, in Saudi Arabia, Iraq, or Kuwait. For one thing, Venezuela was somewhat more advanced than the Middle Eastern countries even before the advent of the oil industry. What was crucial, however, was that under the impact of the Great Depression, the New Deal atmosphere in the United States, and the mounting resistance to imperialism in all of Latin America, there was a powerful democratic upsurge in Venezuela.

So long as the dictator Gomez ruled, there was little trouble. Execu-tioners and jailers silenced the critical. But after his death in 1935, Vene-zuela emerged from a dark century of civil war, anarchy, and military despotism. . . . As parties formed after 1935, the press became inquisitive, the oil workers and others organized unions, and the country emerged into a genuine New Deal of its own. The companies were finally obliged, in 1943, to agree to share their profits 50-50 with the government. . . . Behind the companies' yielding stood the menacing growth of nationalism in Latin America as well as the world over. Mexico, but a few years before, had expelled . . . foreign companies, and nationalized its oil. . . . The example of self-reliance was exhilarating. . . . Making the most of the situation, the companies for their part said humbly that the 50-50 split was their contri-bution to the "good neighbor" policy.[31]

Seeking to retain their broad popular support, the relatively inde-pendent—if ever so circumspect and vacillating—governments that were in office in Venezuela for over an entire decade, and in particular that of the Democratic Action party which came to power in 1945, forced not merely an increase of Venezuela's oil revenues, but began devoting a share of them to economic development, and initiated eco-nomic and social policies as distasteful to the oil companies as to

[30] Issue of January 7, 1950. While some advances have been made since, the rate of progress has been very small. Cf. United Nations, *Economic Survey of Latin America 1953* (1954), pp. 177, 223.

[31] Harvey O'Connor, *The Empire of Oil* (New York, 1955), Chapter 25.

native capitalist interests. What was worst, they could not be relied upon to resist the mounting popular demand for the nationalization of the oil industry. This was a matter, however, to which Washington was—in the words of the correspondent Mr. Milton Bracker—"highly sensitive."[32] Accordingly, in 1948 a military junta overthrew the government of President Rómulo Gallegos—"a democratically elected government that is obviously supported by a great majority of the people" —and promptly undertook to "protect and respect foreign investment." President Gallegos, "a man who has a high standing as a liberal writer and educator outside his country as well as within it," stated a few days later: "United States petroleum companies and local reactionary groups were responsible for the recent army coup in Venezuela. The army clique was encouraged to take over the country by the oil companies and local capital. The military attaché of a large power had been at army headquarters when the coup was staged."[33] Thus Venezuela was made "safe for democracy," the nightmare of nationalization was banished, and the oil companies were assured the loyal services of a local administration subservient to their interests.

And this provides the answer to the second half of our original question. Under the rein of the present companies-supported dictatorship, what is spent on economic development is considerably less than what is at its disposal, and the purposes of such spending are determined not by the best interests of the Venezuelan people but by the requirements of foreign capital. Thus, apart from the inordinately high proportion of government receipts devoted to the maintenance of the military establishment, very little is allotted to the improvement of agriculture, and the bulk of the expenditures are absorbed by the construction of roads, airports, and harbor facilities, by the spectacular expansion and modernization of the city of Caracas, and by similar undertakings highly desirable from the standpoint of foreign capital operating in Venezuela, but contributing little to the emergence of a balanced national economy.[34] As the government, true to the directives

[32] *New York Times*, December 8, 1948.

[33] *New York Times*, November 25, November 27, and December 6, 1948. The military attaché referred to by Mr. Gallegos was later identified as Colonel Adams of the United States Embassy in Caracas.

[34] On the pattern of government expenditures in Venezuela in 1936–1937 and 1950–1951, cf. United Nations, *Public Finance Surveys: Venezuela* (1951), p. 82; information for the subsequent years is assembled in C. E. Rollins, "Raw Materials and Economic Development" (unpublished dissertation, Stanford University, 1955).

of its American sponsors, abstains from encroaching upon the area
ordained to be reserved for private investment, it confines its outlays
to providing sources of "external economies" to free enterprise. But
since Venezuela, like all the other underdeveloped capitalist countries,
is still going through what is essentially the mercantile phase of capitalism, and since for all the reasons that we have encountered earlier
there is little inducement (and possibility) for industrial investment
on the part of domestic capitalists, such investment as is facilitated by
the lavish external economies made available by the comprador government is primarily *foreign* investment. Yet foreign investment—even
if catering to the domestic market—consists in the main of assembly
plants or factories producing consumer goods to satisfy the demand
increases resulting from government spending. Being chiefly investment in kind, it expands but little the host country's internal market,
and does not lead to the emergence of basic industries indispensable
to rapid and lasting economic growth. Accordingly, apart from the
cement industry that has grown rapidly in response to government
demand, what industrial development has taken place in Venezuela
has affected primarily such commodities as tinned milk, edible oils,
biscuits, chocolates, while the "production of cigarettes and beer
reached unprecedented levels."[35]

It goes without saying that this increase in the production of consumer goods (supplemented as it is by a rising volume of imports)
reflects in itself an improvement in the country's economic condition.
Yet an improvement attained in this way not only does not tend to
generate a momentum of its own, it cannot even be counted on to
survive its original stimulus: the government spending of the oil revenues. A decline in the price of petroleum, and a resulting drop in the
government receipts—let alone an exhaustion of the oil resources—
would destroy the artificial prosperity just as rapidly as the postwar
oil boom has brought it about.[36]

[35] United Nations, *Economic Survey of Latin America 1951-1952* (1954),
p. 195, and *Economic Survey of Latin America 1953* (1954), p. 224.
[36] Not to mention the fact that this prosperity itself affects a relatively small segment of the country, both as to area and population. It is
"merely a matter of wonderment for nine-tenths of the people, who live
outside the charmed world of oil. Disease-ridden and hunger-wracked, their
lot on their tiny *conucos* on the mountainsides or in the peasants' huts of
the *latifundias* is much the same now as before oil was discovered. At
least 200,000 have fled the countryside for gilded Caracas where they live
under the bridges, along the gullies, or far up the mountainside in
ironically named 'ranchos' built of the city's refuse. The handsome publi-

The astronomic magnitude of their revenues from foreign enterprise renders the oil-producing countries an elite in the group of underdeveloped areas administered by comprador governments. The rest of them, those exporting minerals and agricultural staples of all kinds, do not, as a rule, participate in the profits of the foreign concerns but collect taxes on their output (or their income), with the resulting receipts very much lower than those of the oil countries be it in terms of absolute amounts involved or in terms of payments per capita of the population. Still, the revenues of Chile, with about 6 million population, on account of remittances by the foreign-owned mining industry came to over 60 million dollars in 1951, and the tin revenue of Bolivia, with about 4 million population, was over 20 million dollars in 1949 and about 15 million dollars in 1950. With receipts of such magnitudes coming in for a considerable period of time, their prudent utilization for the advancement of the national economy might have enabled the receiving countries to make at least a start on the road of economic development. How little has been actually accomplished is well known to anyone who has taken the trouble to get acquainted with the history of these and similarly situated countries. Waste, corruption, squandering of vast sums on the maintenance of sprawling bureaucracies and military establishments the sole function of which is to keep the comprador regimes in power, characterize all of the countries in question.[37]

We have dealt thus far with the use made by the imperialist-controlled administrations of the receipts from foreign enterprise. Very little needs to be added concerning the economic surplus which they extract directly from the underlying populations. This represents a varying part of their aggregate revenues, not by any means insignifi-

---

cations of the government extolling the glories of the capital city naturally ignore these abodes of the forgotten." Harvey O'Connor, *The Empire of Oil* (New York, 1955), p. 267.

[37] The use made of the government revenues in Bolivia is described in C. E. Rollins, "Raw Materials and Economic Development" (1955) (cited at note 34 above). In Colombia "much has been spent on debatable economic ventures . . . above and beyond this is the heavy spending on the military. These expenditures, which the government officially estimates at 18% of the current budget, but which is probably closer to 35% help prop up Colombia's dictatorship. . . . To strengthen his regime against popular discontent, Rojas has pushed inexperienced army officers into all kinds of civilian posts. Graft is flagrant . . . Bogotanos daily turn up with new jokes about corruption in high places—not excluding the presidency." *Business Week*, August 27, 1955, pp. 116 ff. For what is done with

cant even in the cases of the oil countries. Its main sources are highly
regressive taxes: on sales, on imported goods, as well as head and land
taxes borne primarily by the peasantry. Although in a number of
underdeveloped countries progressive income taxes appear on the
statute books, they exist for the most part largely on paper. Tax
evasion is a craft highly developed in these areas, and the number of
devices available to wealthy landlords and merchants to avoid the
payment even of what little taxation is nominally imposed on them is
legion. Nor does this task represent a major challenge to their ingenuity. Dealing with regimes dominated by them and staffed from top
to bottom by members of their own class or by their corrupt and
servile hirelings, they have no trouble either in preventing the legal
imposition of onerous levies, or, where this is politically inexpedient,
in avoiding their payment. That the burden of taxation in underdeveloped countries does not fall on their feudal and capitalist classes
but is borne by the broad masses is not a problem in tax administration. It is determined by the structure of their societies and by the
class character of their governments. As Professor Mason correctly
observes, "the elimination of tax avoidance on the part of some very
large income receivers may require changes that run considerably
beyond an improvement in administration."[38] And, needless to say,
the mode of utilization of the domestically raised surplus cannot be
distinguished from that of the surplus transfers from foreign business.

Before leaving this topic, material on which abounds, we must
deal briefly with two further, closely interrelated, points. One relates
to the much publicized fact that foreign enterprises in many underdeveloped countries engage in more or less considerable amounts of
spending on various undertakings designed to improve the living conditions of the people in the areas of their operations. Thus in many
places oil companies and mining concerns have provided relatively
superior housing for their employees, have built schools, hospitals,
movie theaters, and the like. Yet as far as the welfare of the native
populations is concerned, the importance of this type of company
spending tends to be grossly exaggerated. For one thing, it is simply

---

government revenues in other countries of this group, cf. Anthony H.
Galatoli, *Egypt in Midpassage* (Cairo, 1950), and Economic Survey Mis-
sion to the Philippines, *Report to the President of the United States*
(Washington, 1950)—to name but two further sources.

[38] *Promoting Economic Development* (Claremont, California, 1955), p.
60.

an aspect of the previously mentioned full-belly policy indispensable in order to secure the necessary labor force and to increase its efficiency.[39] Secondly, that even so the trees do not grow into the skies can be seen from the continual difficulties encountered by oil and mining enterprises in securing the required number of men,[40] as well as from the recurrent and violent strikes that have affected foreign enterprise in almost all underdeveloped countries. And, in any case, the number of people allegedly basking in the sun of corporate generosity constitutes, as we have seen earlier, a tiny proportion of the countries' total population. Thus "the Anglo-Iranian Oil Company, with its long start over all rivals in production, was in the early postwar years also ahead in welfare. Even now, no other company can match its record of 16,000 Iranian families housed."[41] This, indeed, is quite a number for a country inhabited by over 18 million people from whom Anglo-Iranian has derived billions of dollars of profits!

The other point has to do with the frequently encountered observation that what the government of a source country does with its receipts from foreign enterprise has after all nothing to do with the "purely economic" appraisal of the foreign enterprise's contribution to the economic development of the underdeveloped countries. This view affords a veritable textbook example of the inherent incapacity of bourgeois economics to penetrate the subject matter of its investigation. Crudely tearing asunder a historical phenomenon, turning away from the complex whole in order to see better its much simpler parts, it arrives at statements which, even if partaking of truth with regard

[39] "It is not enough for the company simply to train workers and to pay good wages. . . . The worker must be sociologically conditioned to a different mode of living if he is not to be spoiled in the process. It is also a fact that one of the most important contributions to productivity which flows from a higher standard of living lies in the improved health of the worker. . . . Therefore it is essential from the standpoint of the effectiveness of the worker that his increased money income provide the physical conditions of healthful living for himself and his family." R. F. Mikesell and H. B. Chenery, *Arabian Oil* (Chapel Hill, North Carolina, 1949), pp. 81 ff. Or, as *The Economist* tersely puts it, "paternalism towards local employees became part of the science of the oil business." "Oil and Change in the Middle East," July 2, 1955.

[40] The local employer, although frequently paying lower wages and providing none of the amenities offered by foreign companies, "seems to get all the men he wants either because working for him carries the advantage of less time spent in daily travel to and from the desert, or because he shows less expectation of solid plod the whole day through." *The Economist, loc. cit.*

[41] *Ibid.*

to the parts, constitute falsehoods with regard to the whole. For a historical phenomenon is inseparable from what represents its inevitable outgrowth. As we have stressed before, the exploitation of raw materials in underdeveloped countries by foreign capital, and the existence of wasteful, corrupt, and reactionary comprador regimes in these countries, are not fortuitous coincidences but merely different if closely interconnected aspects of what can be only adequately understood as the totality of imperialism.

"Today it is plain," says *The Economist,* "that government and company are caught in an interlocking embrace, and that for many years to come neither partner will be able to do without the other."[42] And it is to intensify and to perpetuate this embrace that the companies' home governments help destroy such progressive movements as may rise to power in backward areas, that they give diplomatic, military, and financial support to properly behaved comprador administrations, that they assist and abet the reactionary social and political forces upon which these administrations rest. Similarly, it is to intensify and to perpetuate this embrace that the companies themselves try to create "by their thrift plans, home ownership schemes, training programmes and other methods . . . a class with a vested interest in a tranquil life for the whole community. An ideal is reached when the local speaker refers not to 'the company' but to 'our company.' "[43] Whether this "ideal" will ever be reached is fortunately very doubtful. Although the United States State Department's Point Four specialists are unquestionably right in saying of the peoples inhabiting the underdeveloped countries that "by leaving them unable to fulfill their reasonable aspirations, their misery makes them fertile ground for any ideology which will hold out to them promise, however false, of means toward a better life,"[44] the events of the last decade in the entire underdeveloped world give ample reason to expect that the ideology of "our company"—even where it should take root—will be an obfuscation only short-lived.

[42] *Ibid.* What applies to the Middle East applies with no lesser force to Latin American countries, to the Philippines, and to certain parts of Southeast Asia.
[43] *Ibid.*
[44] *Point Four, Cooperative Program for Aid in the Development of the Economically Underdeveloped Areas* (Washington, 1949), p. 2.

III

In the third group of the underdeveloped countries, those that have recently attained their national sovereignty and are administered by what we have termed New-Deal-type regimes, matters have a different complexion. Their governments were brought to power by broad popular movements the primary and unifying purpose of which was the overthrow of colonial rule and the establishment of national independence. Struggling against imperialism and its domestic ally, the feudal-comprador coalition, the national movements assumed the character of united fronts of the progressive bourgeoisie striving to find a road towards industrial capitalism, of intellectuals seeking a better future for their country, and of active elements of the urban and rural proletariat rising against the misery and oppression of imperialist-comprador domination. In some countries even essentially reactionary segments of the feudal aristocracy joined the nationalist camp, interested primarily in deflecting popular energies from the struggle for social change into a fight against foreign subjugation.[45]

The unity of the nationalist movement has been subject throughout to severe stresses and strains. Its right wing, fearful that the national struggle, by mobilizing and organizing the popular masses, might create conditions for a social revolution, sought to minimize the role of workers and peasants in the anti-imperialist front, sought to proceed cautiously by negotiations and compromises with the established powers, and was continually tempted to sell out and accept some *modus vivendi* with the colonial rulers. Its left wing, anxious, indeed, to combine national freedom with social liberation, was relentlessly pressing for a broad participation of the masses in the national struggle, for intransigent, revolutionary action. Yet as long as the primary objective, national independence, was not reached, the centripetal forces were on the whole stronger than the centrifugal; the fight for national independence overshadowed and absorbed the struggle for social progress.

All this began to change as soon as the basic goal of the national movements was finally attained. Weakened by the Second World War, and no longer able to withstand the pressure for national liberation in the colonies, the imperialist powers were compelled to bow to the inevitable and to grant political independence to those countries in

[45] Dr. Mossadegh's followers in Iran may serve best to illustrate this.

which the anti-imperialist forces were strongest, in which they could not possibly expect to maintain further their colonial rule. In the words of John Foster Dulles, "when the fighting in World War II drew to a close, the greatest single political issue was the colonial issue. If the West had attempted to perpetuate the *status quo* of colonialism, it would have made violent revolution inevitable and defeat inevitable. The only policy that might succeed was that of bringing independence peacefully to the more advanced of the 700,000,000 dependent persons."[46]

However, with the problem of national independence—political, if not by any means economic—out of the way, the basic class conflict of an antagonistic society necessarily becomes intensified and clarified. While a number of important, indeed central, issues of economic and social development in colonial and dependent countries are actually closely linked with the question of national independence, there are at least as many the relation of which to the national problem consists primarily of their being confused and obscured by it. Neither the oppression and exploitation of the peasantry by the landed aristocracy nor the strangulation of industrial development by monopolistic business are merely *national* questions; they are just as much, if not more, *social* problems, to be faced and to be dealt with as such. Thus the nationalist movements, after acquiring power in the newly established national states, cannot but enter a process of disintegration. The socially heterogeneous elements, ever so tenuously united during the period of the anti-imperialist struggle, become more or less rapidly polarized and identified with the opposing class forces within the framework of the new society.

The rapidity of this breakdown of national unity and the accentuation of the internal class struggle depend on the specific historical circumstances in the individual country. Where the advanced urban proletariat has played a major role in the nationalist movement, and where it was sufficiently strong and organized to assume the leadership of the peasantry's struggle for an agrarian revolution, the split in the nationalist camp proceeds fast; its capitalist, bourgeois component,

---

[46] *War or Peace* (New York, 1950), p. 76. The above is a much sounder analysis of the factors which forced the granting of independence to colonies that would otherwise have evicted their Western rulers than Mr. Dulles' subsequent hypothesis that "the religion of the West and the economic and social philosophies of the West combined to promote a peaceful withering away of political rule by the West and its replacement by self-government." (P. 87.)

confronted at an early stage with the specter of social revolution, turns swiftly and resolutely against its fellow traveler of yesterday, its mortal enemy of tomorrow. In fact, it does not hesitate to make common cause with the feudal elements representing the main obstacle to its own development, with the imperialist rulers just dislodged by the national liberation, and with the comprador groups threatened by the political retreat of their foreign principals. As Lord Acton wisely remarked, "the bonds of class are stronger than those of nationality."[47] Under such conditions, the political independence barely won turns into a sham, the new ruling group merges with the old ruling group, and the amalgam of property-owning classes supported by imperialist interests uses its entire power to suppress the popular movement for genuine national and social liberation and re-establishes the *ancien régime* not *de jure* but *de facto*. China under the Kuomintang, Pakistan, the Philippines, South Korea, South Vietnam typify this process.

Where the popular pressure for social liberation is less pronounced at the time of the attainment of national independence—be it because of the numerical and political weakness of the working class or because of the passivity of the peasantry caused by age-old servitude and by deeply rooted religious superstitions—the national bourgeoisie may feel more secure, and may try to prevent the future upsurge of strong revolutionary forces by making an all-out effort to lay the foundations for the evolution of an indigenous industrial capitalism, to create a modern capitalist state. The fate of such an undertaking hinges on a number of factors: on the economic and political strength of the national bourgeoisie, on the quality of its leadership, on its determination to dislodge the feudal and comprador elements from their position of dominance, on the intensity of the resistance on their part, and on the extent to which the international constellation permits the elimination or considerable weakening of the support given to these strata by the world's imperialist powers.

It may well be that conditions are at the present time most propitious in the case of Egypt for the country's entering upon the road of "Japanese development." That the officers' corps and the army are apparently backing Egypt's national bourgeoisie, that its leaders seem to be determined to overcome the opposition of the feudal and comprador interests, and that the international situation is such as to enable them to conduct an independent policy—all this greatly en-

[47] *Essays on Freedom and Power* (Meridian Edition, New York, 1955), p. 224.

hances the chances of success of their current campaign to move the country in the direction of industrial capitalism. Yet Egypt is obviously a relatively small member of our third group of underdeveloped countries. The situation is much more complex when it comes to the most important country in that bracket: India.

There the united front of anti-imperialist forces is still—if only precariously—intact, and provides the broad political basis for the government of the national bourgeoisie. Yet this breadth of the national coalition which accounted for the enormous strength of the Congress Party in the days of its struggle for national independence at present nearly paralyzes the administration that it supports. Although still enjoying the approval of the overwhelming majority of the articulate part of the nation, it encounters unsurmountable difficulties in attempting to formulate and to carry out a program of economic and social regeneration. Setting out to promote the development of industrial capitalism, it does not dare to offend the landed interests. Seeking to mitigate the most outrageous inequalities of incomes, it refrains from interfering with the merchants and moneylenders. Looking for an improvement of the wretched position of labor, it is afraid to antagonize business. Anti-imperialist by background, it is courting favors from foreign capital. Espousing the principles of private property, it promises the nation a "socialist pattern of society." Fancying itself to be *au-dessus de la mêlée,* standing above the struggle of the antagonistic classes, it merely reflects the stage which the class struggle has reached in Indian society. Anxious to reconcile irreconcilable needs, to compose radical differences, to find compromises where decisions are inevitable, losing much valuable time and energy in bridging recurrent conflicts within its own fold, this government substitutes minor reforms for radical changes, revolutionary words for revolutionary deeds, and thus endangers not only the very possibility of realizing its hopes and aspirations but even its very tenure in office. Handicapped by the heterogeneity and brittleness of its social foundations and by the ideological limitations resulting therefrom, the essentially petty-bourgeois regime is incapable of providing genuine leadership in the battle for industrialization, is powerless to mobilize what is most important: the enthusiasm and the creative energies of the broad popular masses for a decisive assault on their country's backwardness, poverty, and lethargy.

We have surveyed earlier the forces impeding capital formation and productive investment in both the rural and the urban sectors of the economy of a backward country. These forces are as powerful in India as anywhere in the underdeveloped world. Therefore in India, as in the other underdeveloped countries, it is only the state that is in a position to mobilize the surplus potentially present in the economic system and to employ it for the expansion of the nation's productive facilities. But if in the present colonial areas the surplus extracted by their administrations is used not for the benefit of their peoples but primarily to further the interests of the imperialist powers, and if in the countries of our second group the vast volume of surplus appropriated by the comprador governments is similarly used or entirely wasted, in the case of India the problem is differently structured. There the amount of resources seized by the state is much *smaller* than the potential economic surplus; and what is no less serious, the use made of it, in spite of all good intentions, is not such as to provide for most rapid and balanced economic growth. Although, as *The Economist* puts it, "like the Red Queen, India has to run fast even to stand still,"[48] half-measures and drift are the outstanding characteristics of its policies—all high-sounding declarations to the contrary notwithstanding. "From time to time Socialism is proclaimed to be the ultimate aim of Congress policy and India's plans. In a statement on industrial policy, issued in 1948, it was laid down that the state would be responsible for basic development and would exercise control over all key sectors of the economy. But the Ministers who have been directly responsible for India's economic development—the Finance Minister and the Minister of Commerce—are well aware of the limits of state action. . . . In the first three or four years realism and pragmatism have become to some degree the basis of official policy."[49] This "realism and pragmatism" found expression in the utterly inadequate goals of the first Five-Year Plan which "even in its final form as published in December 1952 . . . appears rather modest in the scale of expenditure it contemplates, both absolutely and in relation to national income. An outlay of Rs 20,000 million over a five-year period represents little more than 5 percent of national income which is not much more than the rate of investment prevailing before the plan came into effect."[50]

This prudence may appear to have been borne out by the conditions in the country prevailing at the end of the first Five-Year Plan.

[48] "India—Progress and Plan" (January 22, 1955).
[49] *Ibid.*
[50] United Nations, *Economic Survey of Asia and the Far East 1953* (1954), p. 59.

Indeed, there has been a conspicuous improvement in the general economic situation, expressing itself in the marked rise in the volume of the available food supplies, as well as in a certain increase of industrial output. It would be extremely rash, however, to conclude on the basis of this "boom" of the last few years that the country has entered the road to economic development, to rapid and steady progress. For it is the consensus of all careful students of the Indian economy that its comparatively successful performance during the latter part of the first Five-Year Plan is primarily due to two altogether exceptional harvests and to their favorable repercussions upon the balance of payments, raw material availability, and so forth. Neither the modest increase in the area under irrigation that has taken place under the first Five-Year Plan nor any other government measures thus far can be fairly credited with this stroke of good fortune. To be sure, what the first Five-Year Plan *did* supply is a most impressive testimonial to India's tremendous developmental potential. The construction of large multipurpose projects, the implementation of a number of impressive irrigation schemes, the establishment of several new modern plants—all demonstrate beyond conceivable doubt the prodigious capacities of Indian technicians and workers.

Yet the second Five-Year Plan that is to cover the 1956–1961 period is by no means so designed as to provide them with the necessary opportunities. Even the farthest-reaching document thus far to appear in connection with it—Professor P. C. Mahalanobis' *Draft Plan-Frame*[51]—suffers from the failure to attack frontally the principal obstacles blocking India's economic progress. Postulating as a target a 5 percent annual increase of national income—a modest rate of growth representing, however, a considerable acceleration compared with the performance of the past—it accepts the existing rate of investment as its point of departure, and seeks to attain this objective by a partial shift of the currently forthcoming investment from consumer goods industries to producer goods industries. Since private capital cannot be expected to carry out this shift, it assigns the government the responsibility for both the initial investment in producer goods industries as well as future investment needed to absorb their output. It leaves entirely open, however, the issue of the ways and means by which the government is to secure the requisite resources. In this way it supplies an elegant demonstration of what *could* be

[51] Indian Statistical Institute, *The Second Five Year Plan 1956/57-1960/61, Recommendations for the Formulation of the Second Five Year Plan* (Calcutta, 1955).

accomplished if society had the possibility of determining the mode of utilization merely of its actual economic surplus, but fails to provide a concrete blueprint for economic policy.

In the hands of the "realistic" and "pragmatic" Planning Commission which has processed the *Draft Plan-Frame* into what is apparently to become the definitive Plan,[52] even this progressive feature of the earlier document has become lost. If in most realistic industrialization schemes the share of investment going to producer goods industries is at least 40 percent, and if the *Draft Plan-Frame* assigned to these industries about 20 percent of total investment, the Planning Commission has whittled it down to 11 percent. And the envisaged government outlay is not to be financed by an energetic effort at the mobilization of the existing economic surplus but by its *increase:* via inflation and sales taxes on mass consumption goods. With the living standards of the Indian population as low as they are, the possibility of squeezing mass consumption is obviously very limited. Unless major changes should occur in this respect in the course of the quinquennium, the second Five-Year Plan will turn out to be a second edition of the first Five-Year Plan—attaining rates of growth providing for only an insignificant increase of per capita income.

The only policy that can be considered adequate at the present stage of India's economic development is to adopt as the basis of the development program the investment of as large as possible a share of national income. According to a number of independently undertaken calculations, there can be hardly any doubt that 15 percent of national income could be invested without any reduction of mass consumption. What is required for this purpose is the fullest attainable mobilization of the potential economic surplus that is currently generated by the country's economic system. This is to be found in the more than 25 percent of India's national income which that poverty-ridden society places at the disposal of its unproductive strata. It is visible to the naked eye as the share of agricultural output withdrawn from the direct producers by the landowners in the form of rent and by the moneylenders in the form of usury interest. It can be seen in the profits of business, the bulk of which is not plowed back into productive enterprise but spent on consumption by its proprietors.[53]

[52] Government of India, Planning Commission, *Second Five Year Plan, A Draft Outline* (1956).
[53] While a large share of total profits still goes to foreign owners, of what profits remain in the country almost one half is distributed in the form of dividends. United Nations, *Economic Survey of Asia and the Far*

It is needless to stress that such a mobilization of the potential economic surplus is bound to meet with determined opposition from the property-owning strata, and can only be accomplished as a result of a relentless struggle against the "small class, whose main interest is the preservation of its wealth and privileges."[54] The present Indian government, however, is neither able nor willing to accept that challenge and to provide the leadership in breaking the resistance of urban and rural vested interests. By attempting to evade this inevitable conflict, by dodging its responsibility for realizing a genuine program of economic and social progress, this government jeopardizes its great historical chance: the peaceful transformation of a great country from a state of squalor and oppression to that of a rapidly advancing socialist democracy. For economic and social development—like an airplane—has to proceed with high minimum speed if it is to proceed at all. If the necessary momentum of growth is not attained, the danger is great that the reactionary forces may succeed once more in warding off a "disaster" and in blocking—if only temporarily—the only possible exit from the impasse of exploitation, oppression, and stagnation. They may be able to make use of the exasperation of the masses and of their disillusionment with vacuous socialist phraseology to stage a fascist overturn and to impose upon them a dictatorship that would give a new lease on life to the rule of capitalism in city and village. Whether the Indian people's tortuous road will have to go through a phase of fascism or whether they will be spared that ordeal, only history can show.

IV

There are three important corollaries from the preceding analysis. First, contrary to the commonly held view that receives a great deal of emphasis in Western writings on underdeveloped countries, the principal obstacle to their development is *not* shortage of capital. What *is* short in all of these countries is what we termed *actual* economic surplus invested in the expansion of productive facilities. The *potential* economic surplus that could be made available for such investment

---

East 1953 (1954), p. 63, as well as B. Datta, *The Economics of Industrialization* (Calcutta, 1952), p. 229. More recent calculations referring to the latest available data indicate that reinvestment of profits does not come to more than 25-30 percent.

[54] United Nations, *Measures for the Economic Development of Under-Developed Countries* (1951), par. 37.

is large in all of them. To be sure, it is not large in absolute terms, that is, in terms of the absolute magnitudes we deal with in advanced countries such as, say, the United States or Great Britain, although there are some underdeveloped countries where it is considerable even by this standard. It is large, however, as a *proportion* of their national incomes, and accordingly it is sufficiently large if not necessarily to permit large absolute increments to their output, yet to enable them to attain high, and indeed very high, *rates of growth*. It must be stressed that what we are speaking about is not their planned economic surplus—the realization of which, it will be recalled, involves among other things the rational employment of currently unemployed resources—but merely their potential economic surplus, that is, what would be available for investment given a purposeful utilization of the national output produced with such resources as are presently employed. In an as yet unpublished monograph, Dr. Harry Oshima has made careful calculations with regard to a number of countries for which more or less adequate information can be obtained, and has come to the following tentative conclusions. In Malaya as of 1947, the potential economic surplus amounted to 33 percent of gross domestic product while gross investment accounted for 10 percent of gross domestic product. For Ceylon (1951) these ratios are 30 percent and 10 percent respectively; for the Philippines (1948), 25 percent and 9 percent; for India, 15 percent and 5 percent; for Thailand, 32 percent and 6 percent. In Mexico from 1940 to 1950 the share of profits to net national product rose from 28.6 percent to 41.4 percent.[55] In Northern Rhodesia (1949) property income (not counting the income of unincorporated enterprise) amounted to 42.9 percent; in Chile (1948) to 26.1 percent; in Peru (1947) to 24.1 percent.[56] Nothing needs to be added to what has already been said about the overflow—in the most literal sense—of the potential economic surplus in the oil-producing countries. And for the countries of Eastern and Southeastern Europe, both Rosenstein-Rodan and Mandelbaum estimated—and as we now know, underestimated—their capacity to invest at about 15 percent of their national income.[57]

[55] A. Sturmthal, "Economic Development, Income Distribution and Capital Formation in Mexico," *Journal of Political Economy* (June 1955), p. 187.
[56] United Nations, *National Income and Its Distribution in Under-Developed Countries* (1951), p. 17.
[57] P. N. Rosenstein-Rodan, "The Industrialization of Eastern and South-Eastern Europe," *Economic Journal* (June-September 1943); K. Mandelbaum, *The Industrialization of Backward Areas* (Oxford, 1945), p. 34.

The principal obstacle to rapid economic growth in the backward countries is the way in which their potential economic surplus is utilized. It is absorbed by various forms of excess consumption of the upper class,[58] by increments to hoards at home and abroad, by the maintenance of vast unproductive bureaucracies and of even more expensive and no less redundant military establishments.[59] A very large share of it—on the magnitude of which more is known than on that of others—is withdrawn by foreign capital. That the profits earned by foreign interests in the underdeveloped countries are very high, indeed considerably higher than the returns on home investments, is well known. A recently published, extraordinarily interesting study provides an excellent survey of the profits realized by British business in underdeveloped countries.[60] While the material there assembled abounds with examples of firms having for periods of more than forty years average profits in the order of 50 percent per annum and more, "the facts presented may be summarized in a few words: (1) of the more than 120 companies . . . whose dividend records have been presented in the various tables, only 10 failed to make average annual returns of more than 10 percent over periods of from one to several decades on the face value of their ordinary shares, and only 17 failed during their most prosperous five years to pay aggregate dividends at least equivalent to their capital; (2) 70 companies made aggregate payments during their most flourishing half-decade amounting to more than twice their capital, and . . . more than a fourth of the group recouped their

[58] This is a horse of a different color from "an increase in the tension, impatience and restlessness which cause an upward shift in the consumption function, and which acts as an impediment to savings," attributed by Professor Nurkse to the operation of the "demonstration effect" of higher living standards in the advanced countries. In the face of mass starvation of the overwhelming majority of the people inhabiting the backward areas, and of the waste and extravagance of their capitalist stratum visible to the naked eye, it is nothing short of mockery to "hesitate"—as Professor Nurkse does—"to make any class distinction in this connection," and to speak of some "national" propensity to consume. *Problems of Capital Formation in Underdeveloped Countries* (Oxford, 1953), pp. 65, 68, 95.

[59] The nature of the statistical information gathered and made available by the governments of underdeveloped capitalist countries is—not surprisingly—such as to render the assessment of these quantities extremely difficult. Dr. Oshima's previously cited study attempts—to my knowledge, for the first time—at least partly to fill this gap for those countries for which the data can be pieced together.

[60] J. F. Rippy, "Background for Point Four: Samples of Profitable British Investments in the Underdeveloped Countries," *Journal of Business of the University of Chicago* (April 1953).

entire capital in a single year or less; (3) the returns 1945-1950 suggest
that the years of lush dividends have not vanished."

A comparison of the dividends paid by (1) Dutch corporations
mainly operating in the Netherlands with those paid by (2) Dutch
corporations mainly operating through branches or subsidiary companies in the Netherlands East Indies is no less suggestive.[61]

Year	Dividends of Group 1 (percent)	Dividends of Group 2 (percent)
1922	4.8	10.0
1923	4.2	15.7
1924	4.5	22.5
1925	5.0	27.1
1926	5.2	25.3
1927	5.6	24.8
1928	5.6	22.2
1929	5.4	16.3
1930	4.9	7.1
1931	2.2	3.0
1932	2.1	2.5
1933	2.2	2.7
1934	2.1	3.3
1935	2.0	3.9
1936	3.3	6.7
1937	4.5	10.3

Similarly Belgian investments in the Belgian Congo yielded returns
considerably in excess of those earned by Belgian companies at home.
"Net profits of corporations operating mainly in the Congo averaged
16.2 per cent of their combined share and reserve capital during the
years 1947-1951, as against 7.2 per cent for corporations operating
in Belgium."[62]

Nor is the impression different if we compare the earnings of

[61] J. Tinbergen and J. J. J. Dalmulder in *De Nederlandsche Konjunk-
tuur* (August 1939), p. 122, cited in Erich Schiff, "Direct Investments,
Terms of Trade, and Balance of Payments," *Quarterly Journal of Economics* (February 1942), p. 310.
[62] United Nations, *The International Flow of Private Capital, 1946-1952*
(1954), p. 26.

United States' enterprises operating in underdeveloped countries with those recorded on domestic investment.[63]

Year	Ratio of Earnings to Book Value in Underdeveloped Countries (percent)	Ratio of Earnings to Book Value in the United States (percent)
1945	11.5	7.7
1946	14.3	9.1
1947	18.1	12.0
1948	19.8	13.8

Correspondingly remittances to foreign capital claim considerable parts of the underdeveloped countries' aggregate foreign receipts. Thus in 1949 investment income payments as percent of current foreign receipts were 5.0 in India, 8.5 in Indonesia, 6.5 in Egypt, 10.0 in Mexico, 8.6 in Brazil, 17.1 in Chile, 17.7 in Bolivia, 34.3 in Northern Rhodesia, 53.1 in Iran—to name only some of the most important countries.[64]

Where the situation is nothing short of outrageous—matched perhaps only by what happens to the economic surplus of the oil-producing countries—is in the British colonial empire. These areas, the population of which has undoubtedly the world's lowest per capita income, have been made by Britain's "paternalistic" government (Labor as well as Conservative) to *support* throughout the entire postwar period the United Kingdom's incomparably higher standard of living. In the years 1945 through 1951 the colonies were forced under innumerable pretexts to accumulate no less than 1 billion pounds of sterling

[63] H. J. Dernburg, "Prospects for Long-Term Foreign Investments," *Harvard Business Review* (July 1950), p. 44. A rough calculation on the basis of data supplied in S. Pizer and F. Cutler, "International Investments and Earnings," *Survey of Current Business* (August 1955), leads to the conclusion that since 1949 this discrepancy has significantly increased.

[64] D. Finch, "Investment Services of Underdeveloped Countries," International Monetary Fund, *Staff Papers* (September 1951), p. 84. It should be noted that in a number of countries these percentages are considerably lower in 1949 than they were before the Second World War. This is due to postwar exchange controls that have in a number of countries prevented the outflow of investment income. How much of the amounts thus blocked will be reinvested by their owners in the blocking countries, and how much will be taken out as soon as regulations permit, is obviously impossible to say.

balances. Since these represent the difference between the colonies' receipts from abroad and their payments to other countries, this billion pounds constitutes the colonies' capital *export* to Britain! In the measured words of the author on whose excellent paper the above is based, the colonies' "investment of £1,000 million in Britain does not accord well with commonly held ideas on the desirable direction of capital flow between countries at different levels of economic development. There is a belief that British colonial policy has been pursued with great financial generosity. The colonies' needs were great 'so the British taxpayer came to the rescue.' It is thought that the United Kingdom, since the war, has given large sums of money to help the colonies. One purpose of this paper has been 'to test the order of thought by the order of things.' "[65]

As was stressed before in a different connection, the importance of the underdeveloped countries' payments abroad to their economic development is not adequately measured by whatever proportion of their national income those payments may represent. The paramount significance of the transfers becomes clear only if it is realized what share of the underdeveloped countries' *economic surplus* is removed in this way. Small wonder that "many under-developed countries feel that this is too high a price to pay for capital"[66]—particularly once it is seen how small a contribution, if any, foreign capital makes to economic growth in the host countries.

Related to the misconception that shortage of capital is the most important factor preventing economic development in the backward countries is another rather generally encountered notion, that the deterioration of terms of trade in the raw materials producing areas has been seriously retarding their economic development.[67] While the

[65] A. D. Hazlewood, "Colonial External Finance Since the War," *Review of Economic Studies* (December 1953), pp. 49 ff. Mr. Hazlewood's first quotation is from the official government publication *Introducing the Colonies* (1949), p. 58.

[66] United Nations, *Measures for the Economic Development of Under-Developed Countries* (1951), par. 225.

[67] "Such general statistical data as are available indicate that from the latter part of the nineteenth century to the eve of the Second World War, a period of well over half a century, there was a secular downward trend in the prices of primary goods relative to the prices of manufactured goods. On the average, a given quantity of primary exports would pay, at the end of this period, for only 60 per cent of the quantity of manufactured goods which it could buy at the beginning of the period." United Nations, *Relative Prices of Exports and Imports of Under-Developed Countries* (1949), p. 7. This has been greatly emphasized by H. W. Singer in his

reality of this tendency is not to be denied—although on this score some doubt has been voiced[68]—and while its importance to some countries is not to be gainsaid, its general significance to the economic development of underdeveloped countries is highly questionable, to say the least. For this there are two reasons. In the first place, with reference to many underdeveloped countries little meaning can be attached to the category "terms of trade." We have noted earlier that oil companies can manipulate their profits and therefore the f.o.b. prices of their products so as to minimize the amount of royalties due to the governments of the source countries. And what is true about the oil-producing firms is no less true about other raw-materials-producing and -exporting foreign enterprises. Many of these concerns are of imposing size, themselves own the processing and marketing facilities for their exports—located as a rule abroad—and frequently operate on their own account (or are closely linked with) organizations supplying the requisite transportation services. Under such circumstances the f.o.b. price of the raw materials exported by the underdeveloped countries is determined in the light of numerous and complicated considerations pertaining to differences in national taxation systems and in royalty agreements with local governments, as well as to intracompany financial arrangements, with individual concerns free to allocate their profits to one or to another of their affiliates and subsidiaries. Thus depending on what is most advantageous at any particular time, high or low prices (and large or small profits) may appear on the books of the raw-materials-producing-and-exporting firm, of the processing enterprise, or even of the shipping company—all of which may be controlled by the same proprietary interests.[69]

This leads to the other, more important, aspect of the matter. For most underdeveloped countries exporting raw materials, especially for the majority of them where the production and exportation of the raw materials are carried on by foreign enterprise, changes in the

---

"The Distribution of Gains Between Investing and Borrowing Countries," *American Economic Review* (May 1950), in particular pp. 477 ff.

[68] A. N. McLeod, "Trade and Investment in Underdeveloped Areas: A Comment," *American Economic Review* (June 1951). Cf. also H. W. Singer's "Reply" in the same issue.

[69] The existence of foreign exchange controls, for instance, provides a strong stimulus to understate the profits earned in the underdeveloped countries by shifting them as much as possible to the home branches of the corporations involved. Needless to say, this policy could give a peculiar twist to the "terms of trade" of a country like, say, Guatemala.

terms of trade, to the extent that they depend on changes in the prices of the raw materials rather than on those of the imported goods, *make actually very little difference.* To be sure, higher f.o.b. prices of the exported raw materials may strengthen somewhat the bargaining power of native labor or of the native peasant-producers in their dealings with the producing or wholesaling company. Similarly lower f.o.b. prices may cause shutdowns of operations and increased unemployment. As mentioned earlier, however, the nature of the raw materials economy is for the most part such that the supply is fairly inelastic, and that changes of demand affect primarily the level of prices and *profits.* Yet it cannot be stressed too strongly that the relevance of the magnitude of profits to the welfare of the peoples inhabiting the under-developed countries or to their countries' economic development depends entirely on to whom these profits accrue and on the use which is made of them by their recipients.[70] A decline of profits may merely involve lower remittances abroad, possibly painful to the foreign stockholders of the companies involved or even disturbing to the countries the balance of payments of which are thus adversely affected; but this may be of no major consequence to the economy of the area the raw materials of which are being exported. Conversely, a rise of the profits earned by the raw materials enterprises may imply larger remittances on account of dividends or some investment in the expansion of raw materials production—also, as we have seen, of no particular import-ance to the underdeveloped areas. In fact, since an increase of prices of raw materials and a corresponding swelling of profits of the raw materials enterprises does usually lead to larger payments to foreign capital, the higher prices of their exports do not result in an increased capacity of the underdeveloped countries to import foreign goods but rather in an expansion of their "unrequited" exports. In the words of Dr. Schiff, who was the first—to my knowledge—to stress this very important consideration: "The fact that, as a consequence of a rise in exports and thereby in gross and net business profits, additional funds are being drained out of the country, means that the outside world, merely by intensifying the demand for the country's export articles, secures part of the means with which to pay for the additional articles

[70] This is pointed out in a somewhat different frame of reference in the important paper by H. Myint, "The Gains from International Trade and the Backward Countries," *Review of Economic Studies* (1954-1955), No. 58, pp. 129 ff.

it buys. It need not ultimately ship to the country additional goods or services equivalent to the total additional quantity of goods bought there. To some extent the system is self-financing."[71] And, needless to add, if the increased profits accrue not to foreign business but to native wholesale merchants and exporters, what *they* do with that bonanza is decisive on the role that the improved terms of trade play in the economic life of the benefited country.[72]

V

The *second* corollary has to do with another fad rampant in current writing on economic development which characteristically never tires of explaining the backwardness of underdeveloped countries either by the working of some "eternal forces" or by a random assortment of profound-sounding but highly superficial reflections. To the latter belongs the lamentation bewailing the lack of "entrepreneurial talent" in the underdeveloped countries, the ample supply of which purportedly must be credited with the economic advancement of the Western countries. Inspired by the work of Weber and Schumpeter—both of whom, incidentally, stand miles above such platitudes—economists identified with this view stress the crucial role played by the "creative entrepreneur" in promoting economic progress. Thus Professor Yale Brozen holds that "efficient technological advance, i.e., the development and use of techniques which will do most to raise productivity and increase income, requires a supply of innovating entrepreneurs checked or

[71] "Direct Investments, Terms of Trade, and Balance of Payments," *Quarterly Journal of Economics* (February 1952), p. 310.

[72] Thus as changes in the price of oil can be followed with equanimity by the peoples of Saudi Arabia or Iran, so there is ample evidence that the postwar boom in various raw materials and foodstuffs produced and exported by a number of Latin American countries has had little effect on the life of their populations or on the speed of their economic development. It should be borne in mind, incidentally, that aggregative national income statistics are of no relevance in this connection, for an increase in the prices of exported raw materials will be reflected in them as an increase of national income regardless of whether this increase has appeared as an increase in the wages of the working population or as an increase of profits accruing to foreign capital. This is why Venezuela—judging by official national income estimates—has a per capita income of the same order as, for instance, France, Holland, or Belgium! Cf. United Nations, *National Income and Its Distribution in Under-Developed Countries* (1951), p. 3.

goaded by a free market."[73] Professor Moses Abramovitz in turn finds that "a substantial part of the explanation of the differences in the level of investment between developed and undeveloped countries, among advanced economies, and between different stages in the progress of any single country, is to be found in the size, energy, and scope of operations of the entrepreneurial or business class."[74] And Professor Arthur Cole is so carried away as to proclaim that "to study the 'entrepreneur' is to study the central figure in modern economic history, and . . . the central figure in economics."[75]

The trouble with the theory centering on this "central figure" is, however, that it either boils down to a tautology, or that its contents are simply fallacious. If it is to be given the former, more merciful interpretation, the doctrine is reducible to the finding that in the absence of industrial capitalism there are no industrial capitalists, and vice versa—which is indubitably a correct proposition but also one that is singularly unexciting. For in all parts of the world and at all times in history there have been ambitious, ruthless, and enterprising men who had an opportunity and were willing to "innovate," to move to the fore, to seize power, and to exercise authority. Yet at some times and places this elite supplied the headmen of tribes, at others it provided knights, courtiers, and ecclesiastical dignitaries, while in a certain phase of the historical process it produced merchant-princes, adventurers, explorers, and pioneers of science. Finally, during the latest period of historical development—in the age of modern capitalism—it has given rise to the capitalist entrepreneur organizing industrial production or mastering the art of finance so as to be able to bring under his control vast concentrations of capital. It should be obvious that what the theorist of entrepreneurship has to explain is not the sudden appearance of men of genius—such men have been with us since the beginning of time!—but the fact that these men in a certain historical constellation have turned their "genius" to the accumulation of capital, and that they found the best way to accomplish this end

[73] "Entrepreneurship and Technological Change," in H. F. Williamson and J. A. Buttrick (eds.), *Economic Development, Principles and Patterns* (New York, 1954), p. 224.
[74] "Economics of Growth," in B. F. Haley (ed.), *A Survey of Contemporary Economics* (Homewood, Illinois, 1952), Vol. II, p. 158.
[75] "An Approach to the Study of Entrepreneurship," in F. C. Lane and J. C. Riemersma (eds.), *Enterprise and Secular Change* (Homewood, Illinois, 1953), p. 187.

to be investment in industrial enterprises. Failing to do this and invoking instead a *deus ex machina* is not unlike "explaining" squalor by the existence of poverty, and renders the theory of the strategic importance of the entrepreneur entirely worthless. But the now so fashionable explorer of entrepreneurial history "when dealing with an economic relation the historical genesis of which he does not know, naturally finds it comfortable to explain its emergence in terms of a philosophy of history, and he resorts to mythology: Adam or Prometheus happened on this idea all set up and ready, whereupon it was launched, etc. Nothing is more boringly arid than this kind of fanciful *locus communis*."[76]

Since a historical and sociological comprehension of the alleged insufficiency of entrepreneurial talent is not even attempted in the literature attributing economic backwardness to an inadequate supply of this "factor of production," it may be supposed that what the writers in question aim at is not so much a general theory of development as rather the registration of a specific fact observable in underdeveloped countries. This fact is presumably a lack of the character traits which constitute the entrepreneur among the individuals inhabiting the backward areas, with this lack then being explicable only by some biotic or psychic peculiarities of the thus underprivileged nations. We need not waste time on such explanations, the racist overtones and implications of which remain probably hidden even to the most enthusiastic apologists of what is frequently made to appear as a particular asset of the Anglo-Saxon peoples—the risk-taking, daring, imaginative, and frugal businessman—for the simple but sufficient reason that the shortage of entrepreneurial, or for that matter any other, talent exists nowhere except in Western disquisitions on the subject of economic development. For, to put it bluntly, there is an abundance, if not indeed a superabundance, of entrepreneurial ability in the underdeveloped countries. Whether we look at India, or at the Near East, at Latin America or at the backward European countries such as Greece and Portugal, all of them swarm with scheming, contriving, risking, and sharply calculating entrepreneurs bent on "combining resources" to their best advantage, determined to maximize their profits within the framework of existing opportunities. The problem of entrepreneurial ability in underdeveloped countries is very much akin to that of the economic surplus. It consists not so much in the inadequacy of its supply as in the use that is made of what is available under the prevailing social

[76] Marx, *Grundrisse der Kritik der Politischen Ökonomie* (Rohentwurf) (Berlin, 1953), p. 6.

and economic order. We may let one distinguished observer speak for many: "While southern Asia does not lack a class of entrepreneurs, business enterprise tends to be concentrated in the distributive trades, exporting and importing, real estate speculation and money lending."[77] And this could be said equally well about most of the underdeveloped world.[78]

VI

Yet, as a Russian saying has it, these are merely blossoms—the berries are still to come. Indeed, the supreme effort of bourgeois social science to attribute the backwardness and stagnation in the greater part of the capitalist world to factors that may be thought of as unrelated to the economic and social order under which it lives, is undertaken in the theorizing on population with which the current literature on underdeveloped countries is replete. There despondency is the order of the day, and a gloomy view is taken of the possibility of improving the lot of the "teeming millions" in the underdeveloped countries. The continual and possibly accelerating increase of population resulting from a high and rising birth rate and a decline of the death rate due to advancing hygienic conditions is seen as precluding a rapid growth of per capita income. The heavy overcast of the Malthusian menace thus darkens the prospects of the peoples inhabiting the backward areas, with the only ray of hope lying in their speedily adopting some more or less drastic measures to curb the expansion of their popula-

[77] E. S. Mason, *Promoting Economic Development* (Claremont, California, 1955), p. 46.

[78] The matter can be particularly well elucidated by the example of Portugal. There "the now large class of persons with substantial capital show a marked preference for either keeping it in liquid forms or buying land. . . . Some of them seem able to rouse themselves only when fighting off an attempt by a more vigorous Portuguese firm to break into a field of production which they have managed to monopolize." "Portugal," *The Economist* (April 17, 1954). It is safe to assume that, once thus "roused," they display all the talents of entrepreneurship that presumably enabled them in the first place to amass their "substantial capital" and to build up their monopolistic positions. It is in the existence of these monopolistic conditions, as well as of all the other relations that were previously discussed, that one has to look for an explanation of the slowness or absence of industrial growth in underdeveloped countries, rather than in sterile speculations on "inherent lethargy," "preference for the maintenance of family concerns," and "lack of enterprise" supposedly characteristic of the capitalists in backward countries.

tions. Academic economists express this profound pessimism in measured terms befitting scholarly writing: "If birth-rates cannot be reduced in some fairly close relation to the prospective fall in death-rates not only will there be no increase in per capita incomes, there may well be a decrease."[79] Popular writers catering to a wider audience use more colorful language. "Never before, in history," exclaims one of the most successful among them, "have so many hundreds of millions teetered at the edge of the precipice." This is caused by the fact, he explains, that the "two curves—of population and the means of survival—have . . . crossed. Ever more rapidly they are drawing apart. The farther they are separated the more difficult will it be to draw them together again."[80] And another author, whose book is adorned by an introduction by Julian Huxley, warns grimly that "in time the inevitable will happen, and the world's total number of people . . . will be too great for the food produced."[81] Indeed, if the "untrammeled copulation" of "spawning millions" is not brought to an end, there is nothing that can be done about the prevailing condition in the underdeveloped world: "unless population increases can be stopped, we might as well give up the struggle."[82]

To be sure, the "we" in this context is merely a manner of speech. Those who "might as well give up the struggle" are not "us"—whoever that may be—but the starving, disease-ridden, and desperate masses in the backward countries. They "might as well" get rid of the "sort of thinking . . . that leads to the writing and acceptance of documents like the Communist Manifesto and the Atlantic Charter. It tricks man into seeking political and/or economic solutions for problems that are political, economic, social, geographic, psychological, genetic, physiologial, etc." While this awe-inspiring list of factors responsible for the present state of affairs is presumably to indicate how much pondering the people in underdeveloped countries ought to undertake before saying—let alone doing—anything about the existing misery, all this deep thought will actually lead to naught. For "our education must be reshaped, as the story of our existence in an environment as *completely* subjected to physical laws as is a ball we let drop from our hands."[83]

[79] E. S. Mason, *Promoting Economic Development* (Claremont, California, 1955), p. 53.

[80] W. Vogt, *Road to Survival* (New York, 1948), pp. 265, 287. This book was given a lift by an introduction by Mr. Bernard M. Baruch.

[81] R. C. Cook, *Human Fertility: The Modern Dilemma* (New York, 1951), p. 322.

[82] Vogt, *op. cit.*, p. 279.

[83] *Ibid.*, pp. 53, 286. (Italics supplied.)

Although it is "of course, far more convenient, and much more in conformity with the interests of the ruling class . . . to explain . . . 'overpopulation' by the eternal laws of Nature, rather than by the historical laws of capitalist production,"[84] this "explanation" has no more to do with science today than it had in the case of Malthus, for the scientific facts in the matter are altogether different from what the neo-Malthusians would wish us to believe. To mention them in "desperate brevity": it is, first of all, *not* true that miserable living standards, famine, and epidemics necessarily go together with dense populations or with their rapid increases. Professor Grundfest has worked out the following little table which presents (in rounded figures) population densities in some "poor" (backward) and some "rich" (advanced) countries.

"Poor"		*"Rich"*	
Surinam (Dutch W. Indies)	4	Belgium	800
Bolivia	10	England and Wales	750
Belgian Congo	13	United Kingdom	500
Colombia	26	Holland	610
Iran, Iraq	30	Italy	400
Philippines	175	France	200
India	250	Scotland	170
Martinique (French W. Indies)	615	Spain	140

"These figures," he observes, "bring out a number of facts: (a) 'Poor' countries are so, independently of their population densities, and despite possession of rich agricultural and/or mineral resources. (b) Colonies may have much lower population densities than their 'mother' countries, and much richer resources (for example, Surinam and the Belgian Congo), and yet be very much poorer. (c) There is no correlation between the population density and the living standards of the 'rich' countries, which rank in the latter respect about as follows: England, Scotland, France, the Low Countries, Italy and (far behind) the least populated, Spain. (d) There is, however, a direct correlation between living standards as just ranked and industrialization. . . . (e) All the 'poor' countries also have one common factor: they are industrially underdeveloped, and their resources are exploited extractively for the (capitalist) world market."[85] The last two conclusions—those pointing to the degree of industrialization rather than to the

[84] Marx, *Capital* (Kerr ed.), Vol. I, p. 580n.
[85] "Malthusiasm," *Monthly Review* (December 1951), p. 251.

density of the population as the crucial determinant of per capita income—are fully corroborated by the prevailing relation between power consumed and national product.[86] It is as follows:

	Consumption of Energy per capita (Coal equivalent in millions of tons)	National Income per capita (in U.S. dollars)
United States	16,100	1,810
Canada	15,600	970
Great Britain	9,500	954
Belgium	7,770	582
Sweden	7,175	780
Germany (Western)	5,785	604
France	4,755	764
Switzerland	4,685	849
Poland	4,600	300
Hungary	2,155	269
Japan	1,670	100
Italy	1,385	394
Portugal	570	250
Turkey	570	125
India	155	57
Burma	45	36

But if it is sheer fabrication that the poverty of a country is caused by population pressure, it is nothing short of fantastic to attribute it to the "physical" impossibility of providing enough food for a growing population.[87] The absurdity of this view is equally obvious whether

[86] These figures refer to the year 1950 and were compiled from data in J. F. Dewhurst and associates, *America's Needs and Resources* (New York, 1955), p. 1099, and in M. Gilbert and I. B. Kravis, *An International Comparison of National Products and the Purchasing Power of Currencies* (Paris, N.D.), p. 30. Needless to stress, the estimates of per capita incomes are rather uncertain. Those for Great Britain, France, Germany, and Italy are based upon a study of relative prices. The others are translated into U.S. dollars from their own currencies at official exchange rates. Nevertheless they convey at least approximately the *relative* positions of individual countries.

[87] Thus a report released by no less an organization than the Rockefeller Foundation (*Public Health and Demography in the Far East*, 1950) announces that "sooner or later the increasing pressure of people on subsistence will lead to the reestablishment of the forces of death, whether by general debility of the people or by famine and pestilence," while

we consider the problem in its relevant time dimension or follow the prophets of doom into their science-fiction calculations concerning the year 2100 or 2200. As far as the former is concerned, the answer is provided in an excellent paper by Dr. C. Taeuber, head of the Statistics Branch of the Food and Agriculture Organization of the United Nations. These are reported conclusions reached by researchers in this field: "It is feasible to bring into production some one billion acres of land in the tropical areas, and some 300 million acres of land outside the tropics. The assumed production level per crop acre in the tropics is equivalent to that already achieved in the Philippines, for the nontropical soils the equivalent is that already achieved in Finland. Adding the assumed production under these conditions to that considered attainable from present crop land would more than adequately provide all of the required foodstuffs, and for cereals, roots and tubers, sugar and fats and oils, the total 'attainable' under these conditions would be more than double the goals used in these computations."[88] Colin Clark goes even further. He believes that, apart from the new lands that could be brought into cultivation, enough could be produced by scientific management of those already in use. "World population may be expected to increase at the rate of 1% per annum, while improvements in the technique of agriculture may be expected to raise output per man-year at the rate of 1½% per annum (or 2% per annum in some countries). Any profound Malthusian pessimism is thereby completely discredited—scientific improvements alone are capable of taking care of the increase of world population."[89]

When it comes to the Jules Verne calculations of the neo-Malthusians, all that needs to be said about them is admirably expressed in the lucid monograph by the Director of Stanford University's Food Research Institute, Professor M. K. Bennett: "No one ought to be impressed by calculations of land-man ratios, such as will show in arithmetical perfection that *if* world population should increase at its current rate of about one per cent annually, a specific year in the future could be named when only one square inch of the earth's surface would be

Mr. R. C. Cook rhetorically inquires: "Even if science could find a way to synthesize bread and beefsteaks from sea water, could such a multitude be fed?" *Human Fertility: The Modern Dilemma* (New York, 1951), p. 323.

[88] "Utilization of Human Resources in Agriculture," *The Milbank Memorial Fund Quarterly* (January 1950), p. 74.

[89] "The World's Capacity to Feed and Clothe Itself," *Way Ahead* (The Hague, 1949), Vol. II, No. 2, quoted in Josué de Castro, *The Geography of Hunger* (Boston, 1952), p. 286.

available per person. This is purely an arithmetical exercise. It is also a sterile one. . . . Society may be counted upon to act in such a way that the impeccable arithmetical calculation fails to work out; society has the power to act. The arithmetic carries in itself no element of prediction, no element of compulsion. Equally sterile and uninteresting are all efforts to calculate how many people could ultimately be fed by the produce of the earth's surface. . . . Serious students, however, tend nowadays to turn their analytical powers and tools on parts of the world rather than upon all of it; on history and observed tendencies more than on prophecy, on prospects for a few decades rather than for centuries or eons to come."[90] And a British scholar concludes an illuminating "survey of man's productive capabilities" with the statement: "This planet is not limitless, but it is sufficient for the support of all who are likely to live on it. What is perhaps more to the point, human beings have reached a stage of technological development when they can produce from the available resources not merely subsistence, but abundance."[91]

Therefore—and this is the third basic fallacy of Malthusianism old and new—it is wholly meaningless to talk about "overpopulation" in any general sense. In order for the notion "overpopulation" to have any significance, it has to be unequivocally stipulated *in relation to what* the population is supposed to be excessive. However, once this is made clear, it will be realized that there are few places, if any, of which it could be fairly said that they suffer from overpopulation *in relation to natural resources*. This surely cannot even be so much as suggested with regard to the world as a whole. Such overpopulation as exists at the present stage of historical development is overpopulation *not* in relation to natural resources but *in relation to productive plant and equipment*. In the penetrating words of Engels, "the pressure of population is not upon the means of subsistence but upon the means of *employment*."[92]

The supply of the necessary "means of employment" is, however, not a natural datum but a *social* phenomenon which can only be under-

[90] *Population, Food, and Economic Progress,* Rice Institute Pamphlet (July 1952), p. 58.
[91] R. Brittain, *Let There Be Bread* (New York, 1952), p. 223. John Boyd Orr says in the introduction to this fascinating work: "This book gives the most complete account I have seen of what can be done with modern science to create a world of plenty." It should be read by anyone who is not entirely immune to the neo-Malthusian bacillus.
[92] Letter to F. A. Lange, March 29, 1865, in Marx and Engels, *Selected Correspondence* (New York, 1934), p. 198.

stood and acted upon as such. As was shown above, the difference between the actual economic surplus invested in the expansion of mankind's productive wealth and the potential economic surplus that *could* be used for that purpose in a rationally organized society has grown so vast—both in advanced *and* in underdeveloped countries—that an enormous increase of productive facilities could be accomplished in relatively short order.[93] As Dr. Taeuber puts it, "given that knowledge, the question . . . remains, whether the necessary changes will be made in economic, social, and political institutions to bring about the improvements that are within reach."[94]

Thus, "what is so often called 'the race between population and food supply' might better be looked upon—if there is a race at all—as a race between population and economic development."[95] For economic development, and only economic development, can solve both aspects of the so-called overpopulation problem. It increases the supply of food and at the same time reduces the growth of the population. To quote Professor Bennett once more, "In general terms I think it has become safe to say: with rising consumption levels, the long-run tendency is for birth rates to fall—marriage to be somewhat deferred, family size to be limited through exercise of forethought and contraceptive practice; and when consumption level rises sufficiently high, birth rates may stabilize."[96] What is more, economic growth, by improving medical facilities and by spreading prophylactic care, tends greatly to reduce the death rate—the most salutary and the most urgently needed development everywhere, and in particular in the backward countries. For a reduction of the death rate implies not only a rise in the health, vitality, and productive efficiency of the population, but also—and this is especially important—a decline in child mortality. The significance of this

[93] It should be noted that even the stand-by categories of bourgeois economics, "scarcity of resources" and "shortage of capital," which were meaningful during capitalism's competitive youth, that is, as long as the capitalist order was still progressive in relation to the preceding age of feudalism, become fictitious in the phase of monopoly capitalism and imperialism. They are just as vacuous as the notion "optimal allocation of resources" under conditions of unemployment and waste, and serve merely to perpetuate the ideological fog in which "overpopulation," backwardness, and misery are made to appear as inexorable consequences of eternal laws of Nature, of "immutable economic relations," rather than of the irrationality of the economic and social order of capitalism and imperialism.

[94] *Op. cit.*, p. 83.

[95] Bennett, *op. cit.*, p. 27.

[96] *Ibid.*, p. 54.

in purely economic terms can be fully appreciated if it is realized that something like 22.5 percent of the Indian national income is absorbed by the maintenance of children who die before they reach the age of fifteen and thus never get an opportunity of leading a productive life.[97]

To be sure, it cannot be gainsaid that it is "conceivable" that after the conditions for rapid and rational economic advancement have been created, after its impact on the birth and death rates has made itself felt, and after all the possibilities of scientific utilization of the earth's resources have been exhausted, there still could emerge a shortage of food or other products indispensable for the maintenance of the human race. This is, however, at the present stage of historical development so patently a red herring across the trail that one may safely join Professor Bennett in "confessing to a complete lack of interest" in the problem. As Engels pointed out in the letter to F. A. Lange quoted above, if "science . . . will . . . at last be applied in agriculture on a large scale and with the same consistency as in industry," and if all the unutilized or underutilized "regions have been ploughed up and after that a shortage sets in, then will be the time to say *caveant consules.*"

Meanwhile, indeed, it is desperately urgent to sound the alarm—but not because eternal laws of Nature make it impossible to feed the globe's population. The alarm must be sounded because the economic and social system of capitalism and imperialism condemns untold multitudes to privation, degradation, and premature death. The alarm must be sounded because it is the economic and social system of capitalism and imperialism that prevents the urgently needed full mobilization of the potential economic surplus and the attainment of rates of economic advancement that can be secured with its help. As we have seen before, the potential economic surplus in most underdeveloped countries is in the proximity of (or above) 20 percent of their national incomes. Whichever capital-output ratios might be reasonably assumed, its productive investment would yield income increases of 7 to 8 (and frequently more) percent per annum.[98] Such increases as

[97] D. Ghosh, *Pressure of Population and Economic Efficiency in India* (New Delhi, 1946), p. 22, quoted in J. J. Spengler, "The Population Obstacle to Economic Betterment," *American Economic Review* (May 1951), p. 351.

[98] This obviously does not take into account the possibility of a tremendous acceleration of the process of economic growth if the backward areas were to be aided generously and unselfishly by the more advanced nations. Yet such aid, needless to say, cannot be forthcoming within the framework of the capitalist order.

take place at the present time, where they take place at all, are either barely sufficient to keep up with the 1 to 2 percent rate of population growth, or exceed it only insignificantly.

It is, verily, "a race between population and economic development" —a race rendered doubly dramatic by the cold grimace of misanthropy and cruelty staring from each page of imperialist writings on the population problem in underdeveloped countries. What matters is not that "humanitarianism is not an important national interest; governments simply do not act on the basis of such unadulterated considerations."[99] What matters is the systematic dissemination of an ideology that is contemptuous of human happiness and disdainful of human life—if the happiness and the life involved are those of "gooks," "chinks," "niggers," and other "lower races." For no other significance can be attached to pronouncements such as the following: "The modern medical profession, still framing its ethics on the dubious statements of an ignorant man who lived more than two thousand years ago— ignorant that is, in terms of the modern world—continues to believe it has a duty to keep alive as many people as possible."[100] The medical profession would derive more adequate guidance from the finding that "there is little hope that the world will escape the horrors of extensive famines in China within the next few years. But from the world point of view, these may be not only desirable but indispensable. A Chinese population that continues to increase at a geometric rate could only be a global calamity." That at least some members of the medical profession begin to "frame their ethics" more in keeping with the "terms of the modern world" is indicated by an assertion of this sort: "It is obvious that the first objective of the medical-health program must *not* be the simple, natural one of saving lives: instead, it must be the development of means whereby the Chinese people will reduce their birth rate."[101]

Professor Norbert Wiener fully understands the implications of this neo-barbarism: "If this denial of medical aid is done with conscious purpose, or even if it is done without purpose, and the facts penetrate home to those Englishmen and Americans who are what the Englishmen

[99] E. S. Mason, *Promoting Economic Development* (Claremont, California, 1955), p. 13.

[100] W. Vogt, *Road to Survival* (New York, 1948), p. 48; the following quotation is from p. 238.

[101] G. F. Winfield, *China: The Land and the People* (New York, 1948), p. 344. It is important to note that the author is a medical doctor dispatched to China by the Board of Foreign Missions of the Presbyterian Church in the United States.

and the Americans of the present day like to think they are, it will be so damning of all claims to a high moral status that it will be simply intolerable. Even the loss of the position of the white man will be a calamity much more to be accepted."[102] Professor Wiener obviously has not yet "framed his ethics" in accordance with the requirements of the "modern world." These "requirements" are wholly grasped by our "modern" friends of the peoples inhabiting the underdeveloped countries. "Wiping out a series of communicable diseases in a population which does not have enough to eat, and bringing a torrent of new babies into an economy that cannot support even the people already born, are invitations to disaster." The worst part of it would be "a steady decrease of the percentage of the earth's population which subscribes to the ideas and culture patterns [sic!] evolved in the Western world since 1600." What would make the disaster confounded is that unless a plan is adopted "for enhancing the inborn qualities of future generations . . . [by] raising the birth rate of the competent and the gifted . . . badly distributed fertility will result in . . . speeding the erosion of our biological and cultural heritage."[103] And this—worries Mr. Vogt—will mean a "high cost of policing parts of overpopulated Europe and Asia."[104]

It could be objected that, while it is true that the "pursuit of these lines of thought for the purpose of insuring white supremacy is but a consent to the war of all against all,"[105] such lines of thought are fortunately characteristic merely of the "lunatic fringe" of our society. This—alas!—is not so. Neither Mr. Baruch endorsing the book of Mr. Vogt, nor Mr. Julian Huxley praising the book by Mr. Cook, are known to inhabit our society's intellectual outskirts. Nor can it be held

[102] The Human Use of Human Beings (Boston, 1950), p. 52.

[103] R. C. Cook, Human Fertility: The Modern Dilemma (New York, 1951), pp. 282, 295, 255, 315. While there is obviously no reason for suggesting the possibility of plagiarism on the part of Mr. Cook, it may be interesting to note how "different thinkers" independently arrive at similar conclusions—given similar socioeconomic and ideological premises. "Since the inferior is always numerically superior to the best, the worse would multiply itself so much faster—given the same opportunity to survive and to procreate—that the best would be necessarily pushed into the background. Therefore a correction in favor of the better must be undertaken. Nature provides one by subjecting the worse ones to difficult living conditions which in themselves reduce their numbers. As to the rest, finally, it does not permit indiscriminately its multiplication but effects a ruthless choice according to strength and health." Adolf Hitler, Mein Kampf (Munich, 1934), p. 313.

[104] Op. cit., p. 79.

[105] Wiener, op. cit., p. 53.

that it is unfair to impute to such public figures views which they might not hesitate to repudiate were they to realize their implications. For the subjective good will or wickedness of individuals is not at issue—although, as J. S. Furnivall somewhere wisely remarks, "in policy, as in law, men must be held to intend the natural consequences of their acts"—at issue is exclusively the part played in the objective world by the mentality that they reflect and continually promote. This is the mentality of a social and economic system that is cornered by its own monstrous inadequacy, that stands squarely in the way of further growth and indeed of the survival of the human race.

Economic development is at the present time the most urgent, most vital need of the overwhelming majority of mankind. Every year lost means the loss of millions of human lives. Every year spent in inaction means further weakening, further exasperation of the peoples vegetating in the backward countries. John Foster Dulles has for once put his finger on the nub of the matter: "We can talk eloquently about liberty and freedom, and about human rights and fundamental freedoms, and about the dignity and worth of the human personality, but most of our vocabulary derives from a period when our own society was individualistic. Consequently, it has little meaning to those who live under conditions where individualism means premature death."[106] Those conditions are, indeed, not the conditions of an individualistic society, they are the conditions of monopoly capitalism and imperialism.

This state of affairs becomes daily more absurd and—more unnecessary. It *must* be abolished, it *can* be abolished. A new social order is possible in which the present class differences will have disappeared and in which—perhaps after a short transitional period involving some privation, but at any rate of great value morally—through the planned utilization and extension of the already existing enormous productive forces of all members of society, and with uniform obligation to work, the means for existence, for enjoying life, for the development of all bodily and mental faculties will be available in an equal measure and in ever-increasing fulness.[107]

The "state of affairs" that was "unnecessary" in 1891, at the time of Engels' writing, has become even more so in our day. The then "already existing enormous productive forces" have since reached prodigious power. The problem of underdevelopment, of overpopulation, of want and of disease could now be solved by a concerted,

[106] *War or Peace* (New York, 1950), p. 257.
[107] Engels, Introduction to Marx, *Wage Labor and Capital*, in Marx and Engels, *Selected Works* (Moscow, 1949-1950), Vol. I, p. 73.

planned effort of the world as a whole within the lifespan of one generation. From this one cannot conclude, however, that such will be in fact the course of historical events. "It would be erroneous to believe," said Lenin, "that revolutionary classes always have sufficient strength for the accomplishment of the overturn at the time at which the conditions of the socioeconomic development have rendered the need for that overturn entirely ripe. No, human society is not arranged so rationally and so 'conveniently' for its progressive elements. The need for the overturn may become ripe, but the strength of the revolutionary creators of that overturn may turn out to be inadequate for carrying it out. Under such conditions society rots and this rotting sometimes lasts entire decades."[108]

It is such a period of rotting that a large part of the world is going through at the present time. As Mr. Vogt put it at the conclusion of his book, "the human race is caught in a situation as concrete as a pair of shoes two sizes too small." The image is exact. But the pair of shoes are monopoly capitalism and imperialism. The dilemma that the majority of mankind faces today is either to liberate itself from both or to be cut down by them to the size of the crippling clogs.

[108] *Sochinenya* (Works) (Moscow, 1947), Vol. 9, p. 338.

EIGHT

The Steep Ascent

IT is in the underdeveloped world that the central, overriding fact of our epoch becomes manifest to the naked eye: the capitalist system, once a mighty engine of economic development, has turned into a no less formidable hurdle to human advancement. What Alexis de Tocqueville remarked with reference to political institutions applies on a scale broader than he himself could have visualized: "The physiognomy of a government may best be judged in its colonies, for there its features are magnified and rendered more conspicuous. When I wish to study the merits of the administration of Louis XIV, I must go to Canada; its deformity is there seen as through a microscope."[1] Indeed, in the advanced countries the discrepancy between what *could* be accomplished with the forces of production at the disposal of society and what is in fact being attained on the basis of them is incomparably larger than in the backward areas.[2] But while in the advanced countries this discrepancy is obscured by the high *absolute* level of productivity and output that has been reached during the capitalist age, in the underdeveloped countries the gap between the actual and the possible is glaring, and its implications are catastrophic. There the difference is not, as in the advanced

[1] Quoted in S. Herbert Frankel, *The Economic Impact on Under-Developed Societies* (Oxford, 1953), p. 17.

[2] In that sense Professor Mason is undoubtedly right when he says that "perhaps the United States is the underdeveloped area rather than the Middle East." *Promoting Economic Development* (Claremont, California, 1955), p. 9.

249

countries, between higher and lower degrees of development, between the now reachable final solution of the entire problem of want and the continuation of drudgery, poverty, and cultural degradation; there the difference is between abysmal squalor and decent existence, between the misery of hopelessness and the exhilaration of progress, between life and death for hundreds of millions of people. Therefore, even bourgeois writers occasionally admit that in the underdeveloped countries the transition to a rational economic and social organization is vitally urgent—while holding at the same time that the advanced countries can "well afford" to remain under the domination of monopoly capitalism and imperialism.[3] Nothing, however, could be more egregiously erroneous. For, as we have seen, the rule of monopoly capitalism and imperialism in the advanced countries and economic and social backwardness in the underdeveloped countries are intimately related, represent merely different aspects of what is in reality a global problem. A socialist transformation of the advanced West would not only open to its own peoples the road to unprecedented economic, social, and cultural progress, it would at the same time enable the peoples of the underdeveloped countries to overcome rapidly their present condition of poverty and stagnation. It would not only put an end to the exploitation of the backward countries; a rational organization and full utilization of the West's enormous productive resources would readily permit the advanced nations to repay at least a part of their historical debt to the backward peoples and to render them generous and unselfish help in their effort to in-crease speedily their desperately inadequate "means of employment."

Yet for reasons that were touched upon earlier,[4] and that would take us beyond the scope of the present discussion to analyze further, this is not the way in which the historical process has unfolded. Far from being aided by the advanced countries, the backward nations' transition to an economic and social order assuring them of a progres-sive development is taking place against the embittered resistance of the imperialist powers. What Lenin wrote in 1913 about the Euro-pean countries could well be written today about the entire advanced West: "In civilized and advanced Europe, with its brilliantly de-

[3] Thus the authors of the previously cited United Nations report, *Measures for the Economic Development of Under-Developed Countries* (1951), discount for "a number of under-developed countries . . . the pros-pect of much economic progress until a social revolution has affected a shift in the distribution of income and power." (Par. 37.)

[4] Cf. above, p. 141.

veloped machine industry, its rich all-around culture and constitution, a historical moment has been reached when the commanding bourgeoisie, out of fear for the growth and increasing strength of the proletariat, is supporting everything backward, moribund and medieval. The obsolescent bourgeoisie is combining with all obsolete and obsolescent forces in an endeavour to preserve tottering wage slavery."[5] This support for "everything backward, moribund and medieval" can be observed everywhere: whether we look at China and Southeast Asia, at the Near East and Latin America, at Eastern and Southeastern Europe, or at Italy, Spain, and Portugal. Its aim is to prevent social revolutions wherever possible, and to obstruct the stabilization and progress of socialist societies wherever such revolutions have taken place.

Little needs to be said at this juncture about the more purely military aspects of the matter. What few traces of genuine humanism still remained in the consciousness of the bourgeoisie from the days of its glorious youth all but vanished under the impact of the intensified class struggle. If the second half of the nineteenth century and the first quarter of the twentieth century were still marked by a series of international agreements directed towards the "humanization" of warfare, in imperialism's present struggle against the national and social liberation of the peoples inhabiting the underdeveloped countries no holds are barred. "Operation Killer" is considered to be as legitimate as "Operation Strangle," and the burning of entire towns and villages as unobjectionable as pouring napalm on civilian populations. This position was epitomized in a statement of President Eisenhower: "The use of the atom bomb would be on this basis, Does it advantage me or does it not. . . ? If I thought the net was on my side I would use it instantly."[6] Needless to add, this formula does not reflect an exceptional ferocity of particular individuals but the utter moral bankruptcy of a decaying social order.[7]

[5] "Backward Europe and Advanced Asia," *Selected Works in Two Volumes* (Moscow, 1950), Vol. I, Part 2, p. 314.

[6] Quoted in the brilliant article by Helen M. Lynd, "Realism and the Intellectual in a Time of Crisis," *The American Scholar* (Winter 1951-1952), p. 26.

[7] As Marx observed, speaking of the Paris Commune, "all this . . . only proves that the bourgeois of our days considers himself the legitimate successor to the baron of old, who thought every weapon in his own hand fair against the plebeian, while in the hands of the plebeian a weapon of any kind constituted in itself a crime." *The Civil War in France*, in Marx and Engels, *Selected Works* (Moscow, 1949-1950), Vol. I, p. 489.

But since it is far from certain that the "net" would be on the side of the imperialist camp, the ultimate expedient of war has to be dealt with with the utmost caution and employed only where the very existence of capitalism and imperialism appears to be threatened. Meanwhile everything short of war is used to sabotage the development of the socialist countries. Not that it is not recognized that a great deal is being accomplished and can be accomplished by the nations that have adopted a system of socialist planning. Indeed, the authors of the United Nations report on *Measures for the Economic Development of Under-Developed Countries* correctly state that "if the leaders win the confidence of the country, and prove themselves to be vigorous in eradicating privilege and gross inequalities, they can inspire the masses with an enthusiasm for progress which carries all before it";[8] and John Foster Dulles acknowledges that "Soviet Communists . . . can and do implement policies with the portrayal of a 'great Soviet Communist experiment' with which, during this century, they are catching the imagination of the people of the world, just as we did in the nineteenth century with our 'great American experiment.' "[9] And while it is generally recognized that the first and foremost need of the underdeveloped countries is a rapid increase of their national income, Professor Mason certifies that "to the promotion of economic development Communism can bring formidable advantages. . . . Over the long run, given a measure of administrative competence in the investment and use of new capital resources national income is likely to increase at an extremely rapid rate."[10]

One might expect that under such circumstances the backward nations that have at last managed to emerge from their age-long state of stagnation would receive congratulations and encouragement, if nothing more tangible, from those who are purportedly deeply concerned with their advancement. Such an expectation would reflect, however, a wholly naive conception of the existing situation. As Lenin asks, "where, except in the imagination of the sentimental reformists are there any trusts capable of interesting themselves in the condition of the masses instead of the conquest of colonies?"[11] In fact, the progress made in the underdeveloped countries by means of socialist

---

[8] Par. 38.
[9] *War or Peace* (New York, 1950), p. 256.
[10] *Promoting Economic Development* (Claremont, California, 1955), p. 6.
[11] E. Varga and L. Mendelsohn (eds.), *New Data for Lenin's Imperialism—The Highest Stage of Capitalism* (New York, 1940), p. 184.

planning is greatly disconcerting to Western official opinion. Although Mr. Dulles notes that Communists "in China have had some success in arousing a sense of social responsibility and in imposing discipline on its supporters"—which is obviously a major step forward in the struggle for economic development—he piously hopes that this advance may come to naught in view of the Chinese "national character" which he describes, in apparent admiration, as follows: "The Chinese through their religious and traditional habits of thought have become an individualistic people. The family has been the highest unit of value, and individual loyalty has been to ancestors and descendants. There has been only a little of the broader loyalty to fellow men or to some social or class group or to nation."[12] Such a "national character" is, no doubt, a Godsend to imperialists whose sole concern is to dominate the people blessed with it. Accordingly Mr. Dulles feels that "the religions of the East are deeply rooted and have many precious values. Their spiritual beliefs cannot be reconciled with Communist atheism and materialism. That creates a common bond between us, and our task is to find it and develop it."[13] This sentiment is echoed by Professor Mason who expects religion to be a major obstacle in the way of progress in socialist countries, and who holds that in "southern Asia as elsewhere religion is a strong bulwark against Communism."[14] It is hardly surprising that "everything backward, moribund and medieval" in the underdeveloped countries themselves sees eye to eye with its friends and protectors in the West. Vitally concerned with having the underlying populations form a "spiritual society of individuals who love God . . . who work hard as a matter of duty and self-satisfaction . . . and for whom life is not merely physical growth and enjoyment, but intellectual and spiritual development,"[15] the ruling classes in the underdeveloped countries spare no energy and receive a great deal of American support in their effort to strengthen the sway of religious superstitions over the minds of their starving subjects. What do they or the imperialists care that these superstitions represent a major roadblock on the way to progress? What do they and their Western accomplices care that the cost of maintaining religious obfuscation is increased starvation, multiplied death! As Dr. Balogh observed on his

---

[12] *Op cit.*, p. 245.
[13] *Ibid.*, p. 229.
[14] *Op. cit.*, p. 29.
[15] Dulles, *op. cit.*, p. 260.

trip to India, "the religious revival fostered by the richer classes . . . prevents a rational policy to improve livestock. India has 200,000,000, cattle, many of them quite useless, existing on an extremely scanty food supply. Yet the slaughtering of cattle is banned by law in many sections and has been stopped *de facto* in most areas. Even monkeys are sacrosanct, though they destroy or eat an estimated one and a quarter million tons of grain annually."[16] Like the aristocrats at the end of the feudal age, the economic royalists in these latter days of monopoly capitalism and imperialism are not themselves under the sway of obscurantism of this sort. Yet they consider it quite wholesome for their wood-hewers and water-carriers at home and abroad.[17] John Foster Dulles has put the matter in a nutshell: "We have no affirmative policies beyond, for we cannot go further with material things."[18]

Indeed, it is capitalism's inability to "go further with material things," to serve as a framework for economic and social development, that forces its apologists and politicians to rely for its stability on circuses rather than on bread, on ideological claptrap rather than on reason. Thus the campaign for the preservation of capitalism is advertised today more energetically than ever as a crusade for democracy and freedom. In the days of the early struggle against feudalism, when capitalism was a powerful vehicle of progress and when enlightenment and reason were written on the banner of the rising capitalist class, this claim had at least partial historical validity. It had all but lost it in the second half of the nineteenth century, when bourgeois rule was increasingly menaced by the rising socialist movement, and when it became ever more transparent that "by freedom is meant under the present bourgeois conditions of production free trade, free selling and buying."[19] And it has turned into an altogether hypocritical sham in the age of imperialism, when capitalism, having lost control over one third of the globe, is fighting for its very existence. As Engels brilliantly foresaw, "on the day of the crisis and on the day after the crisis . . . *the whole collective reaction . . . will group*

---

[16] "How Strong Is India?" *The Nation* (March 12, 1955), p. 216.

[17] Thus while the Rockefeller Foundation has devoted a growing part of its present disbursements to the promotion of divinity schools and other religious pursuits in the United States, the Ford Foundation has been lavishly financing Moslem, Buddhist, and similar enterprises in the underdeveloped countries.

[18] *Op. cit.*, p. 254.

[19] Marx and Engels, *Manifesto of the Communist Party*, in *Selected Works* (Moscow, 1949-1950), Vol. I, p. 46.

itself around pure democracy."[20] That the "whole collective reaction"
it is, and that the "pure democracy" for which it allegedly fights is
nothing but pure freedom of exploitation can readily be seen from
the membership roster of the so-called free world. Spain and Portugal,
Greece and Turkey, South Korea and South Vietnam, Thailand, Pakistan and the sheikdoms of the Middle East, the military dictatorships
of Latin America and the Union of South Africa—all have been promoted by the imperialist crusaders to the status of "democratic states."
And if Professor Mason, in a passage omitted in a previous quotation,
objects to the "extraordinarily rapid rate" of increase of national
income that can be attained in a socialist society because it would
depend on a "totalitarian regime exercising the weapons of terror
[and] . . . squeezing standards of living . . . that no democratic
state could possibly accomplish,"[21] he does not there note the fact
that such terror as has taken place in the course of all social revolutions—frequently excessive, always painful and deplorable—represented the inevitable birth pains of a new society, and that such
squeezing of living standards as has occurred has affected primarily,
if not solely, the ruling class whose excess consumption, squandering
of resources and capital flight had to be "sacrificed" to economic development. Nor is bourgeois economics in the habit of expressing any
such misgivings about the comprador and colonial regimes "exercising
the weapons of terror [and] . . . squeezing standards of living" for
the sake of the preservation of the wealth and profits of their supporters and in order to perpetuate misery and stagnation in their countries—as in Formosa or in Greece, in Malaya or in Kenya, in Mada-
gascar or in Algiers, in the Philippines or in Guatemala.

   The crude apologetics which identify freedom with freedom of
capital, equate the interests of a parasitic minority with the vital
needs of the people, and treat imperialism as synonymous with democracy would hardly call for attention were it not for two considerations
relating them directly to the problem of future development. The first
has to do with the profound impact of this ideology and of the historical circumstances underlying it on the social, political, and cultural evolution of the imperialist nations themselves. This impact is
epitomized in Marx' and Engels' trenchant remark that "no nation
can be free if it oppresses other nations"; its tragic importance is

<hr/>

[20] Letter to Bebel, December 11, 1884, in Marx and Engels, *Selected
Correspondence* (New York, 1934), p. 434. (Italics in the original.)
   [21] *Op. cit.*, p. 6.

manifest beyond possibility of error whether we look at the early history of the "oppressor nations" or at their most recent record, whether we think of Western Europe or of Czarist Russia, of Asia or of America. Yet all that is possible at this point is to take note of this terribly important matter; to enlarge upon it would take us too far afield.[22]

II

The other consideration more directly germane to our present problem is the direct effect of the imperialist activities reflected and inspired by this "neo-jingoism" on the course of events in the underdeveloped countries. This effect is most telling; and its magnitude can be studied with the needed concreteness. As far as those underdeveloped countries are concerned that still constitute parts of the "free world," it assumes two principal forms. In the first place, their dominant comprador elements, always supported by the imperialist powers, are now aided more energetically, more systematically, more openly. They not only receive subsidies for the promotion of religion, for the conduct of their political activities, they are also given direct military assistance in their struggle against their increasingly restive people. In an ever-growing number of these countries the regimes based on the reactionary forces owe their existence solely to this help received from the imperialist West.[23]

Secondly, a large number of these governments—if not all of them—are not merely supplied with armaments, they are also compelled to devote considerable parts of their countries' national income to the building up and maintenance of large military establishments. The proportion of national income spent on military purposes is over 5 percent in Pakistan, nearly as large in Turkey, over 3 percent in Thailand, and much larger in the Philippines, Greece, and some other countries—not to speak of South Vietnam, South Korea, and Formosa, where the percentage is still greater. It should be recalled that the significance of this burden can be fully appreciated only if it is considered *not* in relation to total national income but as a share of the economic surplus. Indeed, in most if not all of these countries military spending is equal to or exceeds their total productive investment!

[22] Cf. above, p. 129.
[23] This applies to the Philippines no less than to Formosa, to Iran no less than to South Korea, and to Spain no less than to Guatemala.

This wholesale destruction of resources that could by themselves serve as the basis of a massive growth of "means of employment" is justified by Western imperialists and their agents in the underdeveloped countries by adducing the supposed danger of Soviet aggression. Yet some who clamor most loudly about the aggressiveness of the Soviet Union do not themselves really believe their own propaganda. They are fully aware that the Soviet Union has no intention of attacking capitalist countries. The accuracy of this is confirmed by many students of Soviet policies not suspect of socialist sympathies. One of the leading United States experts on Soviet problems leaves not the slightest doubt on this question: "The theory of the inevitability of the eventual fall of capitalism has the fortunate connotation that there is no hurry about it. The forces of progress can take their time in preparing the final *coup de grace*. . . . The Kremlin . . . has no right to risk the existing achievements of the revolution for the sake of vain baubles of the future. . . . There is no trace of any feeling in Soviet psychology that . . . the goal must be reached at any given time."[24] Essentially the same view is held by the man obviously most concerned with the problem, the United States Secretary of Defense, Mr. Charles E. Wilson, who "told a Senate Appropriations subcommittee . . . that the American people should be reassured by Soviet concentration on fighter aircraft production as a sign that the Russians intend to build an Air Force of principally defensive capability."[25] Innumerable other observers in the United States as well as in Western Europe have expressed their conviction that the socialist camp, preoccupied with internal construction, is utterly unlikely to initiate a war.[26]

Thus what the danger of "Soviet aggression" really amounts to is the danger of so-called "subversion"—the now fashionable designation of social revolution. This was clearly expressed by John Foster Dulles: "The imposition on Southeast Asia of the political system of Communist Russia and its Chinese Communist ally, *by whatever means*, would be a grave threat to the whole free community. The United States feels that that possibility should not be passively accepted, but should be met by united action."[27] It is, however, either a most fatuous

---

[24] George F. Kennan, *American Diplomacy 1900-1950* (Chicago, 1951), pp. 116, 118.

[25] *New York Times*, May 20, 1953.

[26] This conviction partly accounts for the pronounced tendency in Western Europe as well as in India—even among people who are most critical of the Soviet Union—to blame the foreign policy of the United States for artificially generating an atmosphere of war danger.

[27] Speech to the Overseas Press Club on March 29, 1954, as quoted in *Monthly Review* (May 1954), p. 2. (Italics supplied.)

misunderstanding of history or its deliberate misrepresentation to treat social revolutions in individual countries as resulting from "outside subversion" or as "imposed" by foreign plots and machinations. Indeed, as the great English historian of the Soviet Union remarks, "the revolution of 1917, itself the product of the upheaval of 1914, was a turning-point in world history certainly comparable in magnitude with the French revolution a century and a quarter earlier, and perhaps surpassing it."[28] Was this "turning-point in world history" the result of skillfully organized "subversion"? Or was the Chinese revolution, another event of tremendous historical significance engineered by Soviet specialists in "subversion"? The answer to this question is provided by the United States Department of State as well as by Mr. Kennan, for a long time one of the Department's leading officials. "The unfortunate but inescapable fact is that the ominous result of the civil war in China was beyond the control of the government of the United States. Nothing that this country did or could have done within the reasonable limits of its capabilities could have changed the result; nothing that was left undone by this country has contributed to it. It was the product of internal Chinese forces, forces which this country tried to influence but could not."[29] And Mr. Kennan "understates" that "to attribute the revolution which has taken place in China in these recent years primarily to Soviet propaganda or instigation is to underestimate grievously, to say the least, a number of other highly important factors."[30] The matter is aptly summed up in a remark of Lenin: "The dominance of capitalism becomes subverted not because someone wants to seize power. Such seizure of power would be nonsense. The termination of the dominance of capitalism would be impossible, if the entire economic development of capitalist countries had not led to it. The war has accelerated this process and rendered capitalism impossible. No force would destroy capitalism if it were not undermined and subverted by history."[31]

The conclusion is inescapable that the prodigious waste of the underdeveloped countries' resources on vast military establishments is *not* dictated by the existence of an *external* danger. The atmosphere of such danger is merely created and re-created in order to facilitate the existence of the comprador regimes in these countries, and the

---

[28] E. H. Carr, *Studies in Revolution* (London, 1950), p. 226.
[29] United States Department of State, *United States Relations with China* (Washington, 1949), p. xvi.
[30] *Op. cit.*, p. 152.
[31] *Sochinenya* (Works) (Moscow, 1947), Vol. 24, p. 381.

armed forces that they maintain are needed primarily, if not exclusively, for the suppression of *internal* popular movements for national and social liberation. The tragedy of the situation has the dimensions of a Greek drama. In Hitler's extermination camps the victims were forced to dig their own graves before being massacred by their Nazi torturers. In the underdeveloped countries of the "free world," peoples are forced to use a large share of what would enable them to emerge from their present state of squalor and disease to maintain mercenaries whose function it is to provide cannon fodder for their imperialist overlords and to support regimes perpetuating this very state of squalor and disease.[32]

The counter-revolutionary crusade has not merely a crippling effect on the underdeveloped areas under imperialist control; its repercussions are also strongly felt in the countries that belong to the socialist camp. Foremost among them is the inescapable necessity to devote a considerable share of national resources to the maintenance of military establishments. But in the case of the socialist countries those establishments are *defense* establishments. Confronted with implacable hatred on the part of the capitalist class, threatened with programs of "liberation" and "preventive wars," the socialist countries are continually forced to fear an attack from the imperialist powers. David Sarnoff, one of America's leading monopolists, goes a long way towards clarifying the entire issue. "Though the Soviets want a nuclear war no more than we do," he writes, "they accept the risk of it in pushing their political offensive. We, too, cannot avoid risks. (It might become necessary, Mr. Dulles said recently, 'to forego peace in order to secure the blessings of liberty'!)"[33] Yet—in remarkable contrast to the anti-socialist propagandists on the highest level—Sarnoff

[32] "Brigadier-General W. L. Roberts, U.S. Army, the commander of the Korean Military Advisory Group, told the New York Herald Tribune correspondent on June 5, 1950 . . . 'KMAG is a living demonstration of how an intelligent and intensive investment of 500 combat-hardened American men and officers can train 100,000 guys who will do the shooting for you. . . . In Korea the American taxpayer has an army that is a fine watchdog over investments placed in this country and a force that represents the maximum results at the minimum cost." Quoted in Gunther Stein, *The World the Dollar Built* (London, 1952), p. 253.

[33] "A New Plan to Defeat Communism," *U.S. News & World Report* (May 27, 1955), p. 139. It should be noted, incidentally, that the views of General Sarnoff, then chairman of the Radio Corporation of America, cannot possibly be considered those of an eccentric. As the editors of *U.S. News & World Report* remark in their introductory statement, they were "discussed thoroughly with President Eisenhower who commended . . . the approach in his press conference."

grasps incisively that "we must realize that world Communism is *not*
a tool in the hands of Russia—Russia is a tool in the hands of world
Communism. Repeatedly Moscow has sacrificed national interests in
deference to world revolutionary needs." Thus it is obvious that the
"political offensive" General Sarnoff is concerned with has no connection with the absurd notion of "Russian imperialism" but is simply
the spread of social revolution. Indeed, "that the challenge is global
must be kept clearly in view. Red guerrillas in Burma, Communists
in France or the U.S., the Huks in the Philippines, Red agents in Central America—these are as much 'the enemy' as the Kremlin itself."
As we have seen before, however, it cannot possibly be held that social
revolutions are the handiwork of crafty agents or must be attributed
to "Soviet propaganda or instigation." They are the result of class
struggles within capitalist societies that no one can abolish or suspend.
What follows from this is that a social revolution in a country that
is capitalist today may induce the imperialists to "forego peace" and
plunge the world into a nuclear war. What follows, furthermore, is
that the socialist camp may be faced with such a catastrophe at any
time. For it can neither "regulate" social revolutions so as not unduly
to upset the imperialist beneficiaries of the "blessings of liberty,"
nor can it actually foresee which social revolution will be considered
by the imperialist powers as a *casus belli*, as the signal for starting a
general holocaust.

To be sure, this does not mean that a global war may break out
"any minute," that the world lives permanently on the crater of a
volcano, and that future developments are altogether unpredictable.
What it does mean, however, is that in our age of imperialism and
social revolutions the danger of war is continually present, and that
the socialist countries have no alternative but to sacrifice considerable
parts of their resources to the maintenance of adequate defense.[34] The
resulting slowing down of their advance, the consequent pressure on
their standards of living, represent the principal cost of imperialism
to the peoples in the socialist countries. The effects of the propaganda
campaigns that the imperialist camp launches against them cause an
additional strain. These are calculated to create "a spirit of mutiny, to
keep the Kremlin off balance, to deepen existing rifts, to sharpen eco-

----

[34] It is here that the political and ideological struggle against imperialism within the advanced capitalist countries, which reduces their willingness to start wars, links up directly with the effort to accelerate and
facilitate economic and social progress in the underdeveloped countries,
capitalist and socialist alike.

nomic and empire problems," and often consist of "programs of spiritual and religious character . . . [which] preach faith in the Divine, abhorrence of Communist godlessness, resistance to atheism."[35] And they do provide some succor to the remnants of the former ruling classes in the socialist countries, they strengthen the hold of superstitions on the minds of backward peasants and workers, they increase the difficulties encountered in educating and organizing people for a collective effort to overcome their poverty. Thus they aggravate the internal conditions in those countries, strengthen the hand of those who are most suspicious of Western intentions, and in this way hamper the countries' progress toward democracy and socialism. But to follow General Sarnoff's advice and rename the "Voice of America" the "Voice of America—for Freedom and Peace" would not make much difference. "Facts are stubborn things," and John Foster Dulles has pointed them out with all the necessary accuracy: "There is no use having more and louder Voices of America unless we have something to say that is more persuasive than anything yet said."[36]

III

The establishment of a socialist planned economy is an essential, indeed indispensable, condition for the attainment of economic and social progress in underdeveloped countries. Yet, as Lenin put it, "for the bourgeois revolution, which arises out of feudalism, the new economic organizations are gradually created in the womb of the old order, gradually changing all the aspects of feudal society. Bourgeois revolution was confronted by only one task—to sweep away, to cast aside, to destroy all the fetters of the present society. By fulfilling this task every bourgeois revolution fulfills all that is required of it; it accelerates the growth of capitalism."[37] The task confronting a socialist revolution in a backward country is much more complex. It must not merely generate a vast development of the country's productive forces. It must also—in order to accomplish this—create the altogether new economic and social order of socialism. "The bourgeois revolution *terminates* usually with the conquest of power, while for the proletarian revolution the conquest of power represents merely its

[35] Sarnoff, *op. cit.*, pp. 138, 140.
[36] *War or Peace* (New York, 1950), p. 261.
[37] *Selected Works in Two Volumes* (Moscow, 1950) Vol. II, Part 1, pp. 418 ff.

beginning, with power employed as a leverage for the reconstruction of the old economy and the organization of the new."[38]

In this "reconstruction of the old economy and the organization of the new," the mobilization of the country's potential economic surplus represents the first, and, on many counts, decisive step. To some extent it is relatively simple. The expropriation of foreign and domestic capitalists and landowners, and the consequent elimination of the drain on current income resulting from excess consumption, capital removals abroad, and the like, lead to an instantaneous increase of the actual economic surplus. The only economic question that arises in this connection is the physical nature of the resources that are thus freed for alternative utilization. For the most part, however, they actually exist in a form that permits their immediate transfer to productive employment. Whether they appear as labor and materials used for the construction of residential dwellings or for the manufacture of luxury articles for the upper classes, or whether they become available as foreign exchange previously spent on nonessential imports or on transfers of funds abroad, this part of the potential economic surplus can be directly shifted to productive use.[39]

More complicated is the mobilization of such potential economic surplus as exists in the form of unproductive labor of all kinds. While the economic and social structure disappears that had supported the existence of merchants, brokers, moneylenders, and the like, and while therefore also the night clubs, hotels, stores, and other establishments catering to their requirements are forced out of business, the individuals affected are not necessarily readily transferable to alternative employment. Although in somewhat longer run the reallocation works itself out, during the period of transition the difficulties and the individual hardships involved may assume considerable proportions. The

[38] Stalin, *Sochinenya* (Works), Vol. 8 (Moscow, 1948), p. 21. (Italics in the original.)

[39] An important modification of the above arises, obviously, in the case of an economic blockade imposed on a socialist country by the capitalist world. In that case, the normal sale of exports may become impossible, and the immediate consequences for the blockaded country dire. Although under the given circumstances there was no question of socialism, the boycott of Iranian oil after the temporary nationalization of the enterprises of the Anglo-Iranian Company is a good case in point. On the whole, however, such blockades are not likely to be of long duration; the competition among buyers of the export commodities may be counted upon to be sufficiently keen to puncture a blockade at an early date. This applies particularly to situations in which the commodities involved are raw materials and foodstuffs with a world-wide market.

problem obviously diminishes to the extent to which some of the thus dislodged individuals emigrate, as has happened in a number of countries. If they remain within the country, they become a burden either on their relatives or on public relief, or else they find some form of productive employment in which they are frequently—for charitable reasons—paid a wage in excess of their actual contribution to social output. Needless to say, the crisis is most acute in the case of aged people; a reorientation toward a new mode of existence is accomplished relatively easily by the younger ones. In any case, the aggregate volume of consumption on the part of the unproductive classes becomes significantly reduced.

Yet this decline of unproductive consumption cannot by any means be counted upon to result in a corresponding increase of the actual economic surplus. To a considerable extent it is bound to lead to an expansion of mass consumption. If the expropriation of industrial and mining enterprises, railways, large raw materials establishments, and the like, will normally transfer to society the control over such surplus as they used to generate, the agrarian revolution—bound to form an integral part of the social revolution in most underdeveloped countries —splitting up large estates and abolishing rent payments by the peasantry, as well as the elimination of traders, usurers, and the like terminating the exploitation of the people by merchant capital, do *not* transfer economic surplus from private to public disposal. By destroying its social foundations, they wipe it out in its entirety, and correspondingly increase the real income of the rural population.[40]

This is not to say that such an increase of consumption *and* actual economic surplus will take place *immediately* after the revolution. The decline of total output that is most likely to result from the general

[40] In Russia before the First World War landlords and kulaks, accounting between them for 50 percent of the total bread grains output, marketed 47 and 34 percent of their respective productions. The middle and small peasants responsible for the other half of total output marketed 14.7 percent of their crops. In 1926-1927 kulaks producing 13 percent of the aggregate bread grains output marketed 20 percent of it, while middle and small peasants, now accounting for 85.3 percent of the total production, marketed merely 11.2 percent. As a result the city received approximately half as much marketed grain as before the Revolution. The striking fact that somewhat similar developments have taken place in post-revolutionary China has been observed in the interesting study of M. Ganguli, "Reorganization of Chinese Agriculture after Land Reform," *Indian Economic Review* (August 1953), and Doreen Warriner notes much the same in Eastern and Southeastern Europe after the revolutions. Cf. her *Revolution in Eastern Europe* (London, 1950).

upheaval and disorganization that are bound to accompany and to follow the revolutionary crisis may not only preclude a rise in investment and an improvement in living standards but may actually cause a more or less sharp reduction of both. Indeed, not merely may the economic surplus disappear, but even the maintenance of essential consumption—particularly in urban areas—may run into serious difficulties. It goes without saying that nothing general can be postulated about the likely duration or depth of such a breakdown. It depends on the intensity of the political struggle associated with the revolutionary transition, on the scope of the resistance of the ruling class to the new revolutionary government, and so on. It depends no less on the enthusiasm, civic consciousness, and discipline of the people, as well as on the maturity of the socialist forces coming into power and their ability to find the right policies and to create rapidly the machinery of the new administration. "The difference between socialist revolution and bourgeois revolution lies precisely in the fact that the latter finds ready forms of capitalist relationships; while the Soviet power—the proletarian power—does not inherit such ready-made relationships. . . . The organization of accounting, of the control of large enterprises, the transformation of the whole of the state economic mechanism into a single huge machine, into an economic organism that will work in such a way as to enable hundreds of millions of people to be guided by a single plan—such was the enormous organizational problem that rested on our shoulders."[41] In this respect, as in many others, every new socialist government faces a task much easier than that which confronted a socialist government that came to power at an earlier date in another country. Historical experience is cumulative to those who understand it, and Hegel's famous dictum that "people and governments never have learned anything from history" is in itself a generalization that has been rendered obsolete by the very course of history. The socialist parties that come to power in different countries in the future will be able to draw on the wealth of experience—both positive and negative—gathered in the Soviet Union, and will thus be saved, at least partly, the ordeal of groping for every single step that was the lot of the first socialist government in the history of man.

Yet neither this, nor the technical assistance and material help that a new arrival in the socialist camp will receive from older members can be relied upon to spare it entirely the frictions and difficulties

[41] Lenin, *op. cit.*, p. 420.

of the initial period. These frictions and difficulties, which are more or less seriously aggravated by foreign military, economic, and political interventions, cause the "squeezing of standards of living" so deplored and condemned in bourgeois writings on the subject. Yet, as Lenin stressed, "for the sake of the success of . . . [the] revolution, the proletariat has no right to shrink from a temporary decline in production, any more than the bourgeois enemies of slavery in North America shrank from a temporary decline in cotton production as a consequence of the Civil War of 1863-65."[42]

What is of crucial importance, however, is that the revolutionary turmoil during which a decline of output, consumption, and investment may become inevitable is a *transitory* phenomenon, the duration of which is usually greatly exaggerated by counter-revolutionary propaganda. In Russia, where the economic breakdown was caused as much by World War I as by the subsequent revolution and civil war, it took only a few years to restore the *pre-war* level of agricultural output, and approximately eight years to regain the *pre-war* industrial position. In China, as well as in most socialist countries of Eastern and Southeastern Europe where war-caused destruction also greatly damaged productive capacities, *pre-war* levels of output were exceeded within two to three years after the revolutions.[43]

Once the revolutionary crisis is over, the pre-revolutionary volume of output restored, and the new order politically and administratively stabilized, economic expansion is by no means predicated upon a reduction of mass consumption below its *pre-revolutionary* level. What its ignition may crucially depend on, however, in all countries where the agrarian revolution has accompanied the social revolution, is the recapturing of the potential economic surplus now largely absorbed by the increase of peasant consumption. The importance of this problem obviously differs from country to country, depending on its economic structure prior to the revolution. In a number of countries— for instance, in the oil-producing Middle East, or in the minerals-producing areas of Africa or Latin America—the amount of economic

[42] *Selected Works in Two Volumes* (Moscow, 1950), Vol. II, Part 2, p. 457. (The dates 1863-65 are as in the Lenin text.)

[43] In most planned economies of Eastern and Southeastern Europe the pre-war volume of output was attained by 1949; cf. United Nations, *Economic Survey of Europe in 1949* (1950). In China total production in 1952, three years after the formation of the People's Republic, was higher than in any preceding year of Chinese history; cf. United Nations, *Economic Bulletin for Asia and the Far East* (November 1953).

surplus that the social revolution places in the hands of society may be so large that employment of part of it for an immediate increase of mass consumption may still leave enough so that the government can initiate an ambitious program of productive investment. Elsewhere, where the bulk of output (and therefore of the economic surplus) was produced in agriculture, and is accounted for after the revolution by the middle and small peasantry, the mobilization of this surplus constitutes the indispensable condition for any developmental endeavor.

Yet it is precisely here, where such mobilization of the surplus is inevitable, that the difficulties by which it is beset are most formidable. The increase of mass consumption brought about by the agrarian revolution, while absorbing a large part of the aggregate potential surplus, permits a relatively minor improvement in per capita terms, and does not constitute a *qualitative* change in the peasants' standard of living. It alleviates their state of starvation, it does not terminate their state of abysmal poverty. Therefore all efforts on the part of the government to seize this increment of their real income for investment purposes encounter embittered resistance.

The Soviet experience in this respect during the '20s is typical of what happens in the wake of an agrarian revolution. Although an income tax might seem to be a simple solution of this problem, this device is all but useless in the framework of a dwarf peasant economy. Neither the assessment of income accruing to nor the collection of the tax from the now multiplied number of subsistence farmers[44] is a manageable task. The fiscal authorities run into strong opposition on the part of the peasants just freed from the tax and rent burdens of the pre-revolutionary days, but, what is even more important, the very nature of a subsistence farm's output renders the payment of the tax well-nigh impossible. Consisting of a wide variety of agricultural products and marketed to a minimal extent, it leaves the subsistence peasant with insignificant money receipts. The gathering of taxes in kind, however, is an administratively hopeless undertaking. Not much more promising is another conceivable method for "siphoning off" some of the output of agriculture: the so-called "opening the scissors," i.e. a shift in relative prices in favor of nationalized industry. This strategy too is frustrated by the poverty of the subsistence farmer whose semi-natural economy reduces to a minimum the quantity of produce that he exchanges for the most essential manufactured

[44] Before the war there were 15-16 million peasant households in Russia. In 1927 this number was 24-25 million.

goods (kerosene, salt, matches, and the like). The wealthier farmers, on the other hand—the kulaks—who are in possession of some quantities of marketable produce, tend to increase their own consumption or to use their surpluses for the purchase of livestock or other assets from other peasants (or private city dwellers) rather than to trade with the government on terms below what they consider to be the "parity" ratio. At the same time, state and cooperative enterprises that take over the distribution and credit functions cannot possibly engage in the extortionist activities of the merchants and moneylenders of old.

Thus the mobilization of the potential economic surplus that was dormant in the structure of the pre-revolutionary capitalist society becomes the first and foremost problem that has to be solved by the socialist government if it is to be able to embark upon a planned program of economic development. Indeed, until such a mobilization has become possible the scope of planning remains limited in one of its principal aspects: the apportionment of total output as between current consumption and the economic surplus. For here lies one of the decisive differences between the capitalist and the socialist order. Under capitalism the structure of total output, its distribution as between mass consumption and economic surplus, and the allocation of the economic surplus itself as between capitalists' consumption and various types of investment, are determined by the prevailing relations of production, by profit maximization on the part of the capitalist class, and by the existing distribution of the means of production and income. In a socialist planned economy, both the structure of the social product and the disposal over it are subject to conscious, rational determination on the part of the socialist society. "The conditions of existence forming man's environment, which up to now have dominated man, at this point pass under the dominion and control of man, who now for the first time becomes the real conscious master of Nature, because and in so far as he has become master of his own social organization. The laws of his own social activity, which have hitherto confronted him as external, dominating laws of Nature, will then be applied by man with complete understanding, and hence will be dominated by man."[45]

Yet such a situation does not exist as long as a large, and crucially important, part of the national output, that of agriculture, remains inaccessible to planning by the socialist government. The only way to

[45] Engels, *Anti-Dühring* (New York, 1939), p. 309.

include it in the general nexus of the national economy is by liquidat-ing subsistence farming as the principal form of agricultural activity and transforming agriculture into a specializing, labor-dividing, and market-oriented industry in which the structure of output as well as its distribution between the consumption of those who work in it and the surplus accruing to society as a whole can be determined by the planning authority, as in the case of other industries. Under condi-tions of socialism this transformation cannot be accomplished except by means of productive cooperation of the peasants, through collectivi-zation of peasant farming—a subject to which we shall return pres-ently. And although this aspect of the matter should not be overem-phasized at the expense of other no less important ones, it must be stressed at this point that if there were no other powerful reasons for the desirability of collectivization of agriculture, the vital need for the mobilization of the economic surplus generated in agriculture would in itself render collectivization finally indispensable. By transferring the disposal of agricultural output from individual peasants to gov-ernment-supervised collective farm managements, collectivization de-stroys the basis for the peasants' resistance to the "siphoning off" of the economic surplus. Given collectivization, the share of agricultural output consumed on the farm can be fixed by direct allotment to col-lective farm members, while farm consumption of nonagricultural commodities can be regulated by fixing the prices paid by the govern-ment for the marketed share of agricultural output and charged by the nationalized sector of the economy for goods supplied to the farm population.

That the socialist government is thus placed in the position of deciding on the share of aggregate output to be withdrawn from con-sumption and devoted to purposes of investment (and/or collective utilization) does not per se imply anything about the contents of that decision. Although the objective of economic planning under socialism is, in Stalin's formulation, "the securing of the maximum satisfaction of the constantly rising material and cultural requirements of the whole of society through the continuous expansion and perfection of socialist production on the basis of higher techniques,"[46] the distribu-tion of resources as between material and cultural requirements as well as the speed of expansion and perfection of socialist production have to be determined in the light of the concrete conditions prevail-

[46] *Economic Problems of Socialism in the USSR* (New York, 1952), p. 33.

ing at any particular phase of a country's historical development. Thus an economically advanced socialist country may at a certain stage of its evolution consider it unnecessary to strive for a particularly rapid increase of its per capita material output. The elimination of the irrationalities and waste characteristic of the capitalist order, and the reorganization of the social production concomitant with it, may be regarded as all that is necessary to assure society of a satisfactory supply of material goods. The current replacement of the normal wear and tear of productive equipment on the basis of advancing technology combined with productive investment of comparatively small proportions of net output may suffice to provide for rates of growth allowing not only adequate standards of living for the expanding population but permitting both generous help to less developed countries and a marked shortening of the working day. With the expansion of cultural requirements calling possibly for relatively little investment and perhaps in the main for additional leisure, the planning authority could under such circumstances keep the actual economic surplus within narrow bounds. On the other hand, an economically backward socialist country like the Soviet Union surrounded by hostile capitalist powers has been confronted with an altogether different situation. There maximal attainable rates of growth of *material* output were dictated not merely by the necessity of radically lifting the desperately low per capita supply of food, clothing, housing, and the like, but also by the urgency of speedily creating a military potential sufficient to deter a foreign aggressor.[47] Clearly, in that setting the planning authority will seek to divide aggregate output in such a way as to be able to provide for maximum possible investment in the production of material output—which is the indispensable basis for advance. Similarly, in some of the new arrivals in the socialist camp massive assignment of resources to defense may be thought of as unnecessary in view of the countries' geographic location or other considerations, while rapid construction of transportation facilities may be deemed to be of vital urgency. And in another country the highest attention to educational requirements may be indicated, with other targets given

[47] "We are 50-100 years behind the advanced countries. We have to traverse this distance in ten years. We shall either accomplish it or else we shall be crushed." Stalin, *Sochinenya* (Works), Vol. 13 (Moscow, 1951), p. 39. It is interesting to note that this statement was made on February 4, 1931, i.e. almost exactly ten years prior to Germany's invasion of the Soviet Union.

a lower priority. In all these cases different proportions of aggregate output will have to be withdrawn for investment.

It is therefore impossible to generalize even on the magnitude of aggregate material output that a socialist society will wish to strive for, once a certain level of advancement has been reached. Nor is it possible to formulate abstract principles concerning the division of the aggregate output as between consumption and investment. What is more, while the maximization of the rates of growth—if such be the requirement of the concrete situation—is tantamount to a minimization of current consumption (or, conversely, maximization of the economic surplus), it would be erroneous to equate such minimization of consumption conducive to speediest growth with its reduction to some rock-bottom levels. In view of the obvious relation between consumption standards and the ability and willingness to work on the part of the population, minimum consumption compatible with maximum output (and growth) may, and in most underdeveloped countries will, require a more or less substantial *increase* of the existing consumption standards. Given a small initial output and accordingly limited possibilities for such an increase, it will have to be differentiated, with the largest increases provided where their incentive effects can be expected to be most telling. Accordingly, while it might be thought at first that maximization of the rates of growth calls for plowing back into the economy all increments in output resulting from current investment, in actual fact some splitting of these increments so as to increase *both* investment and consumption may be a more effective, or even the only possible, method of attaining the largest possible increase in production.

The problem was fully grasped in the famous resolution of the Fifteenth Congress of the Communist Party of the Soviet Union, "On the Directives Concerning the Formulation of the Five-Year Plan of Economic Development": "As far as the relation of accumulation to consumption is concerned, it is necessary to bear in mind that it is impossible to approach it with the view to a *simultaneous* maximum magnitude for both . . . for this is an unsolvable problem. Neither is it possible to approach it with one-sided concern for accumulation in any given period of time, or with one-sided concern for consumption. Taking into account both the relative contradiction between these elements and their interaction and interdependence, and considering that in terms of long-run development both concerns in general coincide, it is necessary to approach the problem as one of optimal combination of both factors. With regard to the speed of development it is also necessary to keep in mind the extreme complexity of the task. Here it is necessary not to strive for maximal tempo of accumulation for the next year or for the next few years, but for such a coordination of the components of the national economy as will assure the fastest development over a long period."[48]

The share of aggregate output that becomes actual economic surplus is thus determined under socialism in the light of the specific possibilities, requirements, and tasks characteristic of a given socialist society at any given stage of its historical development. With regard to its magnitude, to the processes by which it is generated, and to the purposes that it is to serve, it has nothing in common with the actual economic surplus under capitalism. As *planned economic surplus* it is kept within limits drawn by the needs of society as a whole; as *planned economic surplus* it is so mobilized as to be borne equitably by the entire population; and as *planned economic surplus* it is so utilized as to provide for the optimal development of society's human and material resources over the long run.

IV

With the volume of the surplus to be invested in any given period thus decided upon, its most purposeful allocation is the central task of the planning organs of a socialist society. Since we do not intend here to invade the neighboring province of the theory of economic planning, we will merely attempt to outline briefly what would seem to be the central issues involved.

There is first of all the question—given a great deal of attention in Western literature—whether economic development should be striven for via industrialization or whether progress should be sought by raising the productivity of agriculture. Raised thus as a generality, the question is entirely intractable. But if it is approached concretely, either the dilemma implied in it disappears or the answer is almost self-evident. We may clarify the problem by visualizing it in relation to *capitalist* underdeveloped countries, and by assuming that what is looked for is the most desirable policy of some planning authority—

[48] *VKP(B) v Resolutziakh i Resheniakh S'ezdov, Konferentzii i Plenumov TsK* (Communist Party of the Soviet Union in Resolutions and Decisions of Congresses, Conferences and Plenary Sessions of the Central Committee) (Moscow, 1941), Part 2, p. 236.

for otherwise the inquiry is altogether pointless. This may be best approached by considering agriculture in its two prevalent forms: large-scale plantation enterprise and subsistence farming. As far as the former is concerned, nothing needs to be added to what was said about it earlier. Mechanization and increased productivity on plantations producing predominantly for export would hardly improve the conditions in the countries in question. In fact, the effect might be downright detrimental, since the additional machines would displace a number of native plantation workers and deprive them of the meager livelihood they were able to earn before. Since the implements used for the mechanization of plantation operations would usually be imported, their manufacture would not offer offsetting employment opportunities. Nor could the increased productivity of the remaining labor force be counted on to result in higher wage rates; the excess supply of labor is likely to nip in the bud any such development. All that would happen would be an expansion of profits earned by the foreign and/or domestic plantation owners, with these increased profits going abroad and utilized no differently from those earned before. To the extent to which the larger profits in the plantation business would stimulate its expansion, the result would be also far from beneficial. Additional plantations would spell further displacement of subsistence farmers, further pauperization of the rural population, and further accentuation of the underdeveloped country's lopsided economic development.

When it comes to subsistence farming, the problem is somewhat more complicated. There can be no doubt that a number of useful things can be done for the subsistence peasants in underdeveloped countries. Whether through the supply of better seeds and better livestock, or by providing agronomic advice and cheaper credit, there is the possibility of raising their real income. The rate of improvement that can be attained in this way is, however, so small that the population growth is likely to prevent any appreciable increase in per capita output. It surely cannot be expected to give rise to surpluses. Yet all such ameliorative measures, if they result in no surpluses, become quasi-philanthropic actions, assume the nature of sporadic "shots in the arm," develop no momentum of their own, and furnish no bases for further expansion. Indeed, a significant increase of agricultural productivity is predicated upon the utilization of modern farming techniques—mechanical draught-power, complex equipment, and chemicals—most of which are applicable only under conditions of large-scale farming. The subsistence peasant in backward areas (and, for that matter, elsewhere) has neither the means for acquiring the necessary implements, nor—and this is even more important—would he be able to employ them on his dwarf plots.

To be sure, large-scale farming can, and in some advanced countries did, emerge in the course of capitalist development. It was the result of what was earlier called the "agrarian counter-revolution," of the massive penetration of capitalism in agriculture, of far-reaching differentiation of the rural population, and of the consequent evolution of rural capitalists and of rural proletariat. But quite apart from the fact that this process was exceedingly painful, accompanied as it was by enclosures and by wholesale ruination of the peasantry, it was possible only on the basis of the transition from the merchant phase of capitalism to industrial capitalism. For it was only this transition that led to the capitalist invasion of agriculture and to the technological revolution in farming, providing at the same time both a market for the produce of large-scale agricultural enterprise and at least a partial outlet for the displaced and the dispossessed rural masses. Thus it should be clear, even to those who at the present time wish to advocate this avenue of development for the backward countries, that it is only through industrialization of these countries that a major increase in the productivity of their agricultures can be attained. Nevertheless, bourgeois writings on the subject abound with warnings against "overemphasis" on industrialization, against "fanatical nationalism leading to excessive haste in industrial development," and the like. Indeed, in official Western opinion, emphasis on the priority of agriculture—with the desirability of some consumer goods industries admitted for good grace—has become the earmark of a "prudent" and "statesmanlike" attitude towards the economic development of underdeveloped countries. While there may occasionally be some merit in this position with regard to some *capitalist* underdeveloped countries that undertake more or less isolated industrial projects that are neither adequately planned nor properly coordinated with other economic policies, it reflects primarily not a preoccupation with the interests of the peoples inhabiting the underdeveloped countries but a solicitude for the interests of Western monopoly capital. This has been stated so frankly in an important government document referred to earlier that the relevant passage should be cited at some length. "The potentialities and problems of the underdeveloped countries and *the nature of our interest in their economic development* indicate the character of development programs that we should support. . . . For countries with resources that can be developed to meet a profitable world demand, this may be the most efficient way of obtaining additional goods. . . . The main requirement, in most cases, is for development which will improve agricultural production. Development along these lines must be balanced with expanded facilities for industrial production, at the outset especially in light industries producing consumers' goods. . . . The United States will have an increasing need for raw materials, particularly minerals, as domestic resources are progressively exhausted."[49]

It is quite obvious that a socialist government in an underdeveloped country can have nothing in common with such a "development" policy calculated to preserve the underdeveloped countries as sources of raw materials for the imperialist West and thus to perpetuate their state of economic, social, and political backwardness. In a socialist society the dilemma—industrialization *or* improvement of agriculture—becomes entirely meaningless, since progress is indivisible, with the maintenance of harmony between the two sectors of society being one of the crucial conditions for rapid and healthy development. As a social revolution in the underdeveloped countries cannot and does not "wait . . . until capitalist production has developed everywhere to its utmost consequences, until the last small handicraftsman and the last small peasant have fallen victim to capitalist large-scale production,"[50] so the backwardness prevailing in the majority of countries and the almost medieval state of their agriculture represent *the* largest legacy of capitalism to be overcome by the socialist society. The method by which this should be accomplished was indicated by Engels. Sparing the small peasants the spontaneous, destructive experience of uprooting and proletarianization to which they are subjected by the capitalist transformation of agriculture, it should give them "the opportunity of introducing large-scale production themselves, not for account of the capitalists but for their own, common account," and should enable the peasant to effect "a transition of his private enterprise and private possession to cooperative ones."[51]

This program was developed and lent concreteness and specificity in the Soviet Union by Lenin. Writing in 1918, he formulated it with

[49] *Report to the President on Foreign Economic Policies* ("Gray Report") (Washington, 1950), p. 59. (Italics added.)
[50] Engels, "The Peasant Question in France and Germany," in Marx and Engels, *Selected Works* (Moscow, 1949-1950), Vol. II, p. 395.
[51] *Ibid.*, pp. 393, 394.

utmost clarity: "Such despoliation of human energies and labor as takes place in the small, individual peasant economy cannot last any longer. If a transition were to take place from this splinter economy to a socialized economy, productivity of labor could double and treble, human labor could be saved twofold and threefold both for agriculture and for the human economy at large. . . . Our commitment and our duty is to direct [all forces of technology] . . . so that the most backward branch of production, agriculture . . . should be placed upon a new road, so that it should be transformed, and so that agriculture should be changed from a trade conducted irrationally, obsoletely into an activity based on science and the achievements of technology."[52]

Little reflection is needed to see that this recognition of the urgency of agricultural development is nothing like the notion that agriculture should be assigned priority over industry, or that improvement of agriculture should be considered the "main requirement" of underdeveloped countries. On innumerable occasions Lenin emphasized the paramount importance of industrialization. "The salvation of Russia lies not only in a good harvest on the peasant farms—that is not enough; and not only in the good condition of light industry, which provides the peasantry with consumers' goods—this, too, is not enough; we also need *heavy* industry. And to put it in good condition will require many years of work."[53] And taking both a longer and a more general view, he stressed that "if Russia becomes covered with a tight network of power stations and of mighty technical installations, then our communist economic construction will serve as an example for socialist Europe and Asia that are to come."[54] For, indeed, modernization of agriculture and massive industrialization are as closely connected as Siamese twins. It is the growth of industry that supplies agriculture with the technical wherewithal for its development and with manufactured consumer goods for the rural population, and it is the expansion of agriculture that provides food for the increasing industrial labor force, and many raw materials for the rising industrial production. What is more, "it is precisely . . . [the] saving of labor that represents one of the main advantages of large-scale farming,"[55] that constitutes the indispensable prerequisite of industrialization, and it is the evolution

---

[52] *Sochinenya* (Works) (Moscow, 1947), Vol. 28, p. 319.
[53] *Selected Works in Two Volumes* (Moscow, 1950), Vol. II, Part 2, p. 697. (Italics in the original.)
[54] *Sochinenya* (Works) (Moscow, 1947), Vol. 31, p. 486.
[55] Engels, *loc. cit.*

of modern industry that furnishes the market for the enlarged agricultural output.

To be sure, insight into this interdependence would not seem to indicate directly the point of Archimedes from which the entire structure could be moved off dead center. Should the available economic surplus be used first for investment in agriculture, or should it be devoted to industrial construction? The former course runs into the just registered fact that under conditions of a peasant "splinter economy" there is neither much room for fruitful investment nor much prospect that such investment as could be undertaken would yield at a reasonably early date an appreciable surplus to be used for industrial development. At the same time, however, the creation of cooperative farms representing the socioeconomic framework in which both could be accomplished—a significant increase of agricultural output *and* the mobilization of such surplus as is generated in agriculture—depends on the availability of agricultural implements and other resources with which the newly created large-scale farms need to be equipped. For as Marx and Engels noted, "the setting up of a collective economy is predicated upon the development of machinery, upon the utilization of natural resources, and of many other productive forces. . . . In the absence of those conditions, the collective economy would not itself represent a new productive force, would be lacking all material basis, and would rest upon merely theoretical foundations. This means, it would be nothing but a freak amounting to no more than the household of a monastery."[56] Indeed, in the absence of these conditions collectivization might make it feasible to mobilize the economic surplus generated in agriculture but not to raise the level of agricultural productivity, and thus not to transform agriculture into an "activity based on science and the achievements of technology." The collective farms might become large-scale latifundia manned by a starved peasantry rather than prosperous agricultural enterprises providing high living standards to their members and large agricultural surpluses for society as a whole. What is more, how in that case could the peasants be induced to join (and to stay in) the productive cooperatives, to turn to (and to stay in) collective farming? For clearly, the possibility of enlisting the peasants' support for collectivization, and of arousing their enthusiasm for the building of a modern agricultural economy, is predicated upon making them "understand

[56] "Marx und Engels über Feuerbach," *Marx-Engels Archiv* (Frankfurt, N.D.), Vol. I, p. 284.

that this is in their own interest, that this is the sole means of their salvation." It cannot be accomplished "forcibly but by dint of example and the proffer of social assistance for this purpose."[57] Yet the establishment of exemplary large-scale farms in a number sufficient to be impressive, and "proffering social assistance" on an adequate scale, is precisely what is impossible in the absence of a developed industry. Worse still, even a major effort at swaying the peasantry both by "dint of example" and by massive assistance is likely to encounter suspicion and opposition on the part of the peasants. Overcoming these, however, "presupposes such a standard of culture among the peasants . . . that this cannot be achieved without a complete cultural revolution." And the cultural revolution in turn "bristles with immense difficulties of a purely educational (for we are illiterates) and material character (for to be cultural we must achieve a certain development of the material means of production, we must have some material base)."[58]

This would suggest that the correct policy would be to make the beginning in industry, that industrial development should be given all support that is feasible, and that the social, technical, and cultural revolution in agriculture must be postponed until society has gathered sufficient industrial strength to erect the material foundations for the reconstruction of agriculture. The practicability of such a program depends, however, on the availability of resources for a significant expansion of industry, in other words, on the capacity of agriculture to provide a surplus large enough to support a sufficient volume of industrial construction.

It would seem that what we are faced with is a vicious circle. There can be no modernization of agriculture without industrialization, and there can be no industrialization without an increase of agricultural output and surplus. Yet, as is usual in the universe of social and economic relations, the interlocking of factors appears thus stringent, and the circularity of a constellation thus compelling, only so long as it is considered merely abstractly—merely "speculatively," as Marx would have said. In a concrete historical situation there are a number of elements that enter the process and permit a breakthrough where in the "grayness of theory" an exit appears impossible. In the early history of capitalism the solution was provided by large-scale transfusion of economic surplus from abroad (by looting of colonies or by orderly

[57] Both citations from Engels, *op. cit.*, pp. 393, 394.
[58] Lenin, *Selected Works in Two Volumes* (Moscow, 1950), Vol. II, Part 2, pp. 722, 723.

processes of capital import) as well as by severe pressure on the living standards of the urban and rural masses. As Professor Mason puts it, "in adjusting the balance between so-called 'property rights' and so-called 'human rights' it was certainly not the property rights that suffered."[59] As a result, "a great deal of the capital aggregations that we are at present enjoying are the result of the wages that our fathers went without."[60]

Socialist Russia had to look for a different escape from this impasse. Not only could it not rely on exploitation of colonies or on loans from abroad, it had to devote a considerable part of its meager resources to the maintenance of the indispensable defense establishment. Nevertheless, it undertook to cut the Gordian knot by creating a powerful industry and *simultaneously* providing agriculture with the technical instrumentalities for its modernization and collectivization. The solution of this gigantic task was attained at a stupendously high cost. As Stalin said, "it was necessary to accept sacrifices, and to impose the severest economy in everything. It was necessary to economize on food, on schools, on manufactured goods so as to accumulate the indispensable means for the creation of industry. This was the only way for overcoming the famine with regard to technical equipment."[61] Nor were the costs merely economic. The voluntary principle in enrolling the peasants in the collective farms was consistently flouted. While the official pronouncements stressed the voluntary nature of the collectivization movement, thus attempting to help conjure the desired result, in fact compulsion and terror were decisive in achieving this "profound revolutionary overturn, a leap from an old qualitative state into a new qualitative state equal in its consequences to the revolutionary overturn in October 1917."[62]

There can be no doubt that such a revolutionary break with the centuries-old backwardness of the antediluvian Russian village could not have been achieved with the consent of the irrational, illiterate, and ignorant peasantry. As in all situations in which the objective requirements of social development collide with the individuals' appraisal of

[59] *Promoting Economic Development* (Claremont, California, 1955), p. 44.

[60] Aneurin Bevan, *Democratic Values*, Fabian Tract No. 282 (London, 1950), p. 12.

[61] *Voprosy Leninisma* (Questions of Leninism) (Moscow, 1939), p. 487.

[62] *Istorya Vsesoyuznoy Kommunisticheskoy Partii (Bolshevikov)—Kratki Kurs* (History of the Communist Party of the Soviet Union (Bolsheviks)—Short Course) (Moscow, 1938), p. 291.

those requirements, the latter may obstruct and delay the historical process; they cannot stop it forever. Moreover, the individuals' attitudes towards any given course of events, being far from immutable and unmoldable, come eventually into harmony with the objective changes —sometimes slowly and sometimes rapidly. What is decisive, and what determines whether such a harmony emerges in the course of time, is whether the changes that do take place actually correspond to society's objectively extant and objectively ascertainable needs. The fact that the collectivization of agriculture in Russia—all the suffering associated with its initial phase notwithstanding—was the only possible approach to a broad avenue of economic, social, and cultural progress assured it of eventual success. That force had to be used in carrying out the revolutionary transformation of agriculture "does not imply," as Oskar Lange says, "that the Soviet government was not concerned with obtaining the assent of the population to its objectives, as well as to the methods of carrying them out. This assent, however, was obtained *ex post facto,* through the propaganda and educational activities of the State and of the Communist Party."[63] What is even more important, this assent was obtained by the overriding fact that the *material performance* was such as to demonstrate to an ever-increasing number of people that collectivization was a tremendous, and, indeed, an indispensable step towards economic and social advancement. Although "the main contribution that collective forms of agriculture made in . . . [the] hard years of the first quinquennium to the progress of industrialization was the substantial increase they afforded in the marketable surplus of agricultural produce,"[64] within four years it was possible to overcome most of the adverse effects that the collectivization upheaval had upon agricultural production. And in the final year of the Second Five-Year Plan, the grain harvest reached an all-time record, while the output of so-called technical crops (flax-fiber, cotton, sugar beet) more than doubled by comparison with 1928.[65]

Thus was solved not only the food problem, both in the collectivized village and the rapidly expanding city, but consumers' goods industries

[63] *The Working Principles of the Soviet Economy* (New York, 1943), p. 7.
[64] Maurice Dobb, *Soviet Economic Development Since 1917* (London, 1948), p. 247, where it is stated that "in the harvest year 1932-3 . . . [it] was almost double what it had been six years before in the case of grain and potatoes, and more than double in the case of cotton, flax and wool."
[65] Cf. A. Baykov, *The Development of the Soviet Economic System* (Cambridge and New York, 1947), p. 325.

obtained the raw materials base indispensable for their growth, and the
government came into a position of accumulating substantial food
reserves for possible emergencies. The role that those reserves played
during the war a few years later is well known. This is, however, far
from being the entire story. What is equally important is that the increased agricultural production was accompanied by a release of over
20 million people from agriculture—a migration from village to city
that was indispensable for the growth of industry. It reflected a per
capita increase of productivity in agriculture of as much as 60 percent
between 1928 and the end of the 1930s.[66] And this in turn was the
result of a "proffer of social assistance" to agriculture on a tremendous
scale. Having received in the course of the First Five-Year Plan nearly
a quarter of a million tractors, and almost twice as many by the end
of the Second Five-Year Plan, Russian agriculture, "previously one of
the most backward . . . [was able] to accumulate in the space of a few
years an enormous production capital—in agricultural machinery and
buildings—and to mechanize the main branches of cultivation to a much
greater extent than other countries had done in the course of a long
period of history."[67] In sum—to borrow the words of the author of
a monumental study of Soviet agriculture, whose critical attitude towards the Soviet Union is well known—"the socialization drive in
agriculture achieved to a large extent its major economic purpose of
serving as a basis for the industrialization drive. But this is about all
it did achieve . . . "[68]

Indeed, this *is* "about all"! The story of Soviet industrialization has
been told many times, and there is no need to repeat it. Suffice it to
realize that the rates of growth of industrial production from the beginning of the industrialization campaign—leaving out the years of the
Second World War— were over 18 percent per year, while aggregate
output increased at the rate of approximately 16 percent per year. "Such
a rate of growth represents a doubling each quinquennium; and is
nearly twice as great as that found during exceptional boom periods
in the capitalist world, such as the United States in the second half of the
1880's (8.6 percent), Russia in the 1890's (8 percent), or Japan between 1907 and 1913 (8.6 percent). With this may be compared a
5 percent rate of growth for manufacturing production in the United

[66] Dobb, *op. cit.*, pp. 253, 285.
[67] Baykov, *op. cit.*, p. 323.
[68] Naum Jasny, *The Socialized Agriculture of the USSR* (Stanford,
California, 1949), p. 33.

States between 1899 and 1929 and 3 percent in Britain between 1885 and 1913."[69]

The "revolution from above" that consolidated the socialist order in Russia and that marked the actual beginning of comprehensive socialist planning led to a sharp deterioration in the immediate economic situation, to a grievous disruption of the normal flow of agricultural (and consumers' goods) production, and caused a painful drop in the standard of living. In this it was very much like most revolu-

[69] Maurice Dobb, "Soviet Economy: Fact and Fiction," *Science & Society* (Spring 1954). "Inspired" by the requirements of the cold war and by the obvious implications of this performance of socialist planning for the underdeveloped countries, a large number of Soviet experts, especially in the United States, have endeavored to deflate this historically unprecedented performance. Yet even the farthest-going among them, Mr. Jasny, could not help recognizing 8-9 percent annual growth of income from 1928 to 1937. *The Soviet Economy During the Plan Era* (Stanford, California, 1951), p. 85. Other investigators, although setting out to "revise" and "correct" Soviet statistics, have substantially corroborated them. Professor D. R. Hodgman, in *Soviet Economic Growth* (A. Bergson, ed.) (New York, 1953), presents an index of industrial production showing annual growth-rates of 15-16 percent for the period 1927-1928 to 1937, and an annual rate of increase of over 20 percent for the years 1946-1950. Professor Alexander Gerschenkron, on the other hand, has proven by laborious compilations that there is no more basis for suspecting an "upward bias" in the Soviet statistical series than in any other time series of index numbers. Although stating that "the exact extent of the—alas, so elusive— bias in the 1926-27 index must still remain a matter of conjecture" (*A Dollar Index of Soviet Machinery Output, 1927-28 to 1937* (The Rand Corporation, 1951), p. 58), he has not considered it appropriate to draw the conclusion from his own investigations, and to repudiate the obviously tendentious regurgitations on the "bias" in Soviet statistics. Some time ago I too was of the opinion that such bias marred the reliability of Soviet national income statistics (cf. my "National Income and Product of the U.S.S.R. in 1940," *Review of Economic Statistics* (November 1947)). Upon further study and reflection I have come to the conclusion, however, that to the extent that such an exaggeration actually exists, it is a fault that is common to all index number comparisons over time, and that, on the other hand, there is ample evidence in data referring to unaggregated physical outputs that fully corroborates the overall impression conveyed by aggregative Soviet statistics. In any case, the current preoccupation with Soviet statistical information, and the efforts of Messrs. Jasny, Gerschenkron, Schwartz, and others are anything but exercises in "pure science": they are part of a more general campaign of denigration of socialist planning the historical accomplishment of which is, however, miles above all of these meaningless quibbles. In the words of Mr. P. J. D. Wiles, "deflate them how we will, these [Soviet] statistics continue to show a rate of growth of industrial production permanently greater than that *ever* achieved by *any* 'capitalist' country. I have yet to read an expert, however sceptical or politically hostile, who proves the contrary." Letter to *The Economist*, September 19, 1953. (Italics in the original.)

tionary breaks in history. Yet while the illness that it provoked was acute and painful, it was manifestly an illness of growth: it reached its crisis with enormous speed and yielded to convalescence within a few years. By the end of the First Five-Year Plan the worst "squeezing" of the consumer was over, by 1935 rationing could be abolished, and "living standards in 1937 probably were higher than in any year since 1928 (the year when the First Five-Year Plan was launched), and according to some indications may even have surpassed those of the earlier year."[70] While this rise in living standards was interrupted by the threat of war, and in particular by the war itself, the postwar decade witnessed their rapid and consistent improvement. By the end of 1954 they were approximately 75 percent above those of the last year before the war.[71]

Two important conclusions emerge from the above: (1) Under conditions of socialist planning there can be no question as to whether development should proceed through industrialization *or* through improvement of agriculture. It can take place only by a *simultaneous* effort in both directions. To be sure, the difficulties that are involved are enormous, although their nature and their intensity change incessantly in the course of the historical development. They assume divers forms —the foreign threat to the security of the socialist country, irrationality on the part of popular strata still under the influence of the ideologies of the capitalist past, all-pervasive scarcity of resources. Intimately interrelated as they are, they cannot be overcome in isolation. As poverty, illiteracy, and disease breed mythology, religious superstitions, and obscurantism, so does the sway of obfuscation retard the development of productive forces. As the danger of capitalist aggression prevents the use of resources for rational purposes, so does backwardness and the resulting military weakness whet the appetite of imperialism. Yet if this interdependence renders the task of the socialist government particularly arduous in its early phases, if it results in an exasperating necessity to attack simultaneously on innumerable fronts, it is this very concatenation of the factors determining the possibilities of advancement at any given time that yields an acceleration of achievement at every

[70] A. Bergson, *Soviet National Income and Product in 1937* (New York, 1953), p. 10. In a note on the same page, Professor Bergson refers to the fact that even Mr. Jasny's computations show the living standards in 1937 to exceed by about 10 percent those in 1928.

[71] Cf. Malenkov's Report to the Nineteenth Party Congress on October 5, 1952, and the Report on the Fulfillment of the 1954 Economic Plan, in *Pravda,* January 21, 1955.

succeeding stage. (2) What the experience of the Soviet Union and of other socialist countries clearly demonstrates is that the actual economic surplus need not be *maximized* in order to secure tremendously high rates of investment and economic expansion. These are fully compatible with a consistent and sizable rise of people's standards of living.[72] They are possible on the condition of a correct *allocation* and rational *utilization* of such economic surplus as is made available for productive investment. While the former has to be governed by the long-term requirements of economic growth rather than by the desire for immediate rapid increases of consumable output, the latter consists of maximal exploitation of all available productive capital. Accordingly the investment policy has to place its main accent on the development of industry —lifting agriculture at the same time high enough to support the industrialization process—so as to be able eventually to turn around and give agriculture a major boost with the help of the expanded resources of industrial production. Consequently, the capital-output ratio has to be made as favorable as possible by squeezing all available equipment in industry, transportation, and agriculture to the limits of its serviceability.[73]

V

The *second* question arising in connection with the task of the optimal allocation of the economic surplus is whether economic development should be sought through the expansion of producers' goods (heavy) industries, or through an increase of consumers' goods (light) industries. What this question actually involves is the distribution of national income as between consumption and the economic surplus, or—what is essentially the same—the extent of growth that is to be achieved during such a planning period as may be under consideration.

[72] This has been rightly stressed on a number of occasions by Maurice Dobb. Cf. his *Soviet Economic Development Since 1917* (London, 1948), in particular Chapter 10, as well as *Some Aspects of Economic Development* (Delhi, 1951), p. 37 and *passim*.

[73] It is estimated that the capital-output ratio in the USSR is approximately half of what it is in the Western countries. In view of the lesser skill of the Russian workers in many branches of the economy this suggests a more than double intensity of the utilization of the productive assets. Academy of Sciences of the USSR, Institute of Economics, *Politicheskaya Ekonomya--Uchebnik* (Political Economy—A Textbook) (Moscow, 1954), p. 470.

In analyzing expanded reproduction, Marx formulated clearly the basic condition for economic growth: the current gross product of Department I (producers' goods industries) has to exceed the current replacement demand for producers' goods on the part of Department I and of Department II (consumers' goods industries).[74] Or, as Lenin put it, "in order to expand production . . . it is necessary to produce first the means of production, and this requires, consequently, the expansion of that branch of social production which manufactures means of production."[75] Clearly, the quantity of the additional means of production that is to be produced in any given year depends on the degree of expansion of aggregate output that is aimed at in the subsequent years.

For the newly created producers' goods industries will produce during the period of their functioning *investment goods,* and these investment goods will be appropriately utilized only if the volume of investment during that period is such as to absorb their output. In other words, the economic surplus in that time has to be such as to match the physical output of the growing investment goods industries. Conversely, if the newly erected industries should produce *consumers' goods,* they will be adequately utilized only if consumption is so expanded (and the surplus so contracted) as to provide an adequate market for their output. The decision on the *speed* of economic growth determines therefore both the share of national income that is to constitute economic surplus, and also the physical nature of the required investment. Large investment in producers' goods industries is tantamount to high rates of growth sustained during the entire planning period, and, correspondingly, a program directed towards economic development via consumers' goods industries implies automatically not only smaller initial investment but also much lower rates of ensuing growth.[76] Not that investment can be oriented toward one objective to the exclusion of the other. The expansion of Department I is predicated upon an increase of the supply of consumers' goods for the workers newly employed in the producers' goods industries; investment in Department II requires an increase in the supply of producers' goods to equip the new plants producing consumers' goods.[77] The maintenance

[74] *Capital* (Kerr ed.), Vol. II, Chapter 21.

[75] *Sochinenya* (Works) (Moscow, 1947), Vol. 2, p. 137.

[76] Cf. on this the excellent paper by Maurice Dobb, "Rates of Growth Under the Five-Year Plans," *Soviet Studies* (April 1953), reprinted in his *On Economic Theory and Socialism* (London, 1955).

[77] Accessibility of foreign trade does not change the essence of the argument. In that case export industries regardless of the physical nature of their

of the proportions required for a smooth unfolding of the development process is the principal task of the planning authorities. Errors committed in this respect, in particular in regard to sufficient increase of consumers' goods output, may cause serious economic and political stress and endanger the realization of the development plans.[78]

As mentioned above, a socialist country that has reached a stage in which further net investment is no longer considered necessary would reduce the economic surplus currently withdrawn to what is required to provide for certain collective outlays, administration, and the like, and would rely on replacement of worn-out machinery by technically more advanced equipment for such expansion of output as might be called for by the growth of the population. In that case, the facilities of Department I would have to be compressed to the level of the replacement requirements, with this compression being accomplished partly by conversion of the existing plants to consumers' goods production, and, where this is impossible, by cessation of their replacement. It goes without saying, none of the planned economies is today anywhere near this state, and the continual emphasis in these countries on investment in heavy industries reflects the brutal but undeniable fact that for a considerable period ahead rapid expansion of aggregate output will remain the order of the day.

VI

Closely related to this range of issues is the *third* problem of planning for economic development that has to be briefly mentioned. It is the hoary question as to whether capital-intensive or labor-intensive methods of production should be chosen for the development programs of the underdeveloped countries. In the conventional literature on the subject the answer to this question is treated as a foregone conclusion.

---

output become "producers' goods" industries since their product—foreign exchange—can be converted into capital goods. Whether such a course is advisable depends on the natural resources of the country in question, on the comparative possibilities of productivity increases in producers' goods industries and those working for export, as well as on the terms of trade which the developing country may expect to face after the expansion of its exports.

[78] Such errors were made in the Soviet Union as well as in some of the socialist countries of Eastern and Southeastern Europe, and created considerable difficulties in the provisioning of the cities. Cf. the interesting study "The Economy of Hungary, 1950 to 1954," United Nations, *Economic Bulletin for Europe* (August 1955).

For instance, Professor Nurkse writes that in underdeveloped countries "the same capital intensity as in economically advanced countries should be neither desired nor permitted."[79] This view is usually based on the existence of a large rural surplus population in most underdeveloped countries whose transfer from the state of "disguised" unemployment to some alternative occupation would result in an increase of aggregate output. Disregarding the far-fetched suggestion—clearly not intended to be taken seriously—that "the investment workers, before they start building a piece of fixed capital such as a road, could, after all, sit down and make the most necessary primitive tools with their own hands, starting, if need be, from scratch," a worker transferred from the village to industrial occupation has to be given a quantity of productive equipment at least sufficient to enable him to produce the equivalent of his own subsistence. Unless this can be done, his transfer from the village would involve a simple consumption subsidy to the new worker, reducing accordingly the surplus that is available to society for investment purposes. What is more, the transfer of a "disguised" unemployed person from the village to the industrial center calls for a certain outlay on housing, communal services, hospitals, schools, and the like, which reckoned per capita may easily double the amount needed for the setting up of an additional industrial worker. If *this* outlay is taken into account, the labor-intensive techniques may well involve a *larger* outlay of capital per unit of output than the capital-intensive alternatives.[80]

No less important is an additional consideration. The new industrial workers have to be paid the going industrial wage, which means that

[79] *Problems of Capital Formation in Underdeveloped Countries* (Oxford, 1953), p. 45. The next quotation is from *ibid.*, p. 44.

[80] A qualification to the above may be in order to the extent that some of the potential industrial labor force may consist not of rural "disguised" unemployed, but of a somewhat different variety of unemployed: those who already live in the cities. They should not be confused with what has been called "Keynesian unemployed": individuals who *lost* their jobs in view of the curtailment of output caused by general or partial depression. They are people who have come to the cities looking for work, and having found none remained in the cities filling the ranks of the "undisguised" unemployed, vegetating on the margin of society by means of occasional earnings, begging, thievery, and so forth. The numbers of such "Lumpenproletarians" are quite large in some countries. Their importance for the argument in the text is greatly reduced by the fact that most of them are demoralized to the point of being for the time essentially unemployable. And where their employment is possible, they cannot be expected to develop into useful workers if permitted to remain in the hovels in which they usually "reside."

they have to be assured of the quantity of food, clothing, and the like that constitutes the socially necessary standard of living in the country in question. Quite apart from the difficulty of obtaining the requisite food from the village—for the crucially important fact about the rural "disguised" unemployed is that he does *not* bring his food with him—the need of providing consumers' goods for the workers employed on the new investment projects implies that, if labor-intensive techniques are used, the expansion of Department I calls for a larger expansion of Department II than if capital-intensive techniques are chosen. Thus labor-intensive techniques spell a slowing down of the expansion process, a lowering of the rates of economic growth. This is very well formulated by Maurice Dobb, and we can do no better than state his conclusions in his own words: "The choice between more or less capital-intensive forms of investment has nothing to do with existing factor-proportions. . . . It depends, not on the existing ratio of available labour to capital (treated as a stock), but on precisely the same considerations as those which determine the choice between a high and a low rate of investment . . . namely the importance to be attached to raising consumption in the immediate future compared with the potential increase of consumption in the more distant future which a particular rate of investment and form of investment will make possible. In other words, the same grounds which would justify a high rate of investment . . . would justify also a high degree of capital intensity in the choice of investment-forms; and *vice versa*."[81]

Further, in deciding on the utilization of capital-intensive versus labor-intensive techniques, the planning authority has to bear in mind that the abundance and "cheapness" of currently available labor may well be only a temporarily prevailing condition *preceding* the realization of any given stretch of the developmental program. Aware of the aggregate demand for labor entailed by its own plans, the authority has to consider therefore that relatively soon, during the lifespan of the equipment that is to be installed, labor may turn from a relatively ample to a relatively scarce factor, particularly when this involves skilled labor.

Nor is this all. Economic development, as we have seen, is predicated upon the expansion of producers' goods industries. And it so happens that there are hardly any producers' goods that can be produced by the investment worker's "sitting down" and "starting from scratch." In

[81] "A Note on the So-Called Degree of Capital-Intensity of Investment in Under-Developed Countries," *Économie Appliquée* (Paris, 1954), No. 3, reprinted in *On Economic Theory and Socialism* (London, 1955), from which the above is quoted (p. 149).

fact, the techniques required for the output of tractors or machine tools, of electrical equipment or aluminum, leave relatively little room for choice between capital-intensive and labor-intensive processes. In most cases, the choice that *is* left is whether to produce or not to produce a particular commodity. Thus the underdeveloped countries can either industrialize, and in doing so make use of the sole advantage that historical development has bestowed upon them—the ability to draw upon the scientific and technological achievements of the more advanced countries—or forego industrialization and remain content with snatching a few crumbs from the rich table of technical progress by importing some second-hand equipment from the industrial countries thus raising their "welfare" at a snail's pace. Therefore the economists' injunction to give preference to labor-intensive techniques in formulating programs of economic development is far from being an "innocent" theoretic fallacy, as might appear at first blush. It represents an important link in the now fashionable campaign to prove "scientifically" that the backward countries should "go slow" (or, better still, not go at all) in the direction of industrialization and economic development.

VII

Throughout this discussion it has been implicitly assumed that a socialist country, planning for its development, represents a closed economy in a hostile capitalist surrounding. Even for Russia this assumption is rather unrealistic. For although Russia's foreign economic relations after the Revolution were at no time overly intense, economic intercourse with the capitalist world played an important role in the process of its industrialization, particularly in the years of the First Five-Year Plan. At that time it enabled Russia not only to secure sizable short-term credits from the capitalist countries that were severely hit by the depression and anxious to obtain outlets for their exports; it made an even larger contribution to Russian economic development by permitting the Soviet Union to acquire a substantial quantity of industrial equipment that it was technically incapable of producing at home.[82] Had the importation of such machinery been impossible, the

[82] For a brief survey and analysis of the foreign economic relations of the Soviet Union, cf. my "The U.S.S.R. in the World Economy," in *Foreign Economic Policy for the United States* (S. E. Harris, ed.) (Cambridge, Massachusetts, 1948).

initial difficulties of the industrialization process would have been still larger, and the sacrifices connected with it even more protracted and grievous. It was not until the completion of the First Five-Year Plan that Russia's trade with foreign countries markedly declined and that the country achieved nearly complete self-sufficiency, economically as well as technically.[83]

Yet in this respect, Russia's position was rather atypical; there are few other countries in the world today to which Lenin's dictum could apply that they by themselves have "all that is necessary and sufficient for the building of a socialist society." In most other countries, in particular in the underdeveloped ones, the economic structure and the resource endowments are such that economic relations with the outside world represent not merely a highly desirable mitigation of otherwise not insuperable difficulties but indeed a condition of their very survival. Even a country as large and as rich in natural resources as China would be hard pressed to lay the foundations of an industrial economy in the absence of the possibility of importing most essential industrial (and agricultural) equipment. And what is true of China applies a fortiori to other very much less self-sufficient backward countries.

Little need be said about the benefits that an underdeveloped socialist country can derive from foreign loans. They may greatly reduce the need for mobilizing all attainable economic surplus at the very beginning

[83] What should actually be understood without saying, but must be stressed in view of frequent confusion and misrepresentation, is that at no time was the effort to attain economic independence from the capitalist world dictated by a "philosophy of autarchy" or similarly irrational notions. It was governed exclusively by the realization of the continual danger of foreign economic and military aggression, as well as by the necessity of insulating the economic development of Russia from the vagaries of international markets. If the former consideration had ample support in the experience of Western intervention following the Revolution, the latter concern was wholly justified by the development of the terms of trade of the raw materials exporting countries. As early as October 1927, the Resolution of the Central Committee of the Communist Party formulating the principles to be followed in the preparation of the First Five-Year Plan stated explicitly: "Taking into account the possibility of military aggression of capitalist countries against the first proletarian state in history, it is necessary to work out the Five-Year Plan in such a way as to give maximum attention to those branches of the national economy in general, and of industry in particular, that will play the main part in assuring the defense and economic stability of the country in time of war." *VKP(B) v Resolutziakh i Resheniakh S'ezdov, Konferentzii i Plenumov TsK* (Communist Party of the Soviet Union in Resolutions and Decisions of Congresses, Conferences and Plenary Sessions of the Central Committee) (Moscow, 1941), Part 2, p. 202.

of the industrialization process, thus alleviating the stresses and strains inevitably associated with that phase of economic development. They may facilitate the overcoming of the hurdles presented by the inter-dependence of industrial and agricultural development, and make it possible to solve some of the problems of transition by the importation of agricultural machinery, of industrial equipment, or of food. They may even save the beneficiary country the necessity of hasty collectiviza-tion of the small peasant and allow it to "do everything at all per-missible to make his lot more bearable, to facilitate his transition to the cooperative should he decide to do so, and even to make it possible for him to remain on his small holding for a protracted length of time to think the matter over, should he still be unable to bring himself to this decision."[84] It is quite clear, however, that while advanced capitalist countries could readily provide such loans, they can hardly be counted on to do so on a significant scale. They either tie such credits to political and economic conditions unacceptable to socialist countries, or supply them merely on a short-term basis in times of depression when the need for additional sales temporarily overcomes the basic unwilling-ness to help socialist countries. Actually, only socialist countries can be expected to lend on adequate terms to other socialist countries; here, however, the possibilities are as yet rather limited in view of the still pronounced poverty even of the most advanced or, rather, least back-ward socialist countries.

But the opportunity of securing loans from abroad is only one advantage, and by no means the most important one, stemming from economic contacts with foreign countries. What may be a great deal more significant—in fact, vital—to a number of countries is the possi-bility of trading more or less large parts of their national outputs so as to be able to obtain the *physical assortment* of goods required for their consumption and industrial and agricultural investment. To be sure, most if not all countries of the world could shift their productive re-sources so as to attain a self-sufficient economy, and such a policy may even be unavoidable under conditions of war or of political and eco-nomic siege. But this does not mean that—such emergency conditions aside—there is any interest on the part of the socialist countries in pushing the diversification of their outputs to the point of comprising a complete basket of all products required for economic development

[84] Engels, "The Peasant Question in France and Germany," in Marx and Engels, *Selected Works* (Moscow, 1949-1950), Vol. II, p. 394.

and for the welfare of their populations. In some countries such a degree of diversification would be even technically impossible; in others the costs involved would be so high as greatly to reduce productivity and aggregate output. Although such a reduction of productivity and output would not necessarily depress the living standards of the peoples inhabiting the underdeveloped countries—in a number of cases, paradoxically enough, even the opposite might be the case, with profits being the only diminished part of national income—it would sharply cut down, if not entirely wipe out, the potential economic surplus that could be turned to purposes of economic development. It is only necessary to think of the oil-producing Middle East or Venezuela, of rubber-producing Malaya, or of sugar-producing Cuba to visualize the effect of self-sufficiency upon the magnitude of their potential economic surplus. Therefore all socialist countries—large and small, more and less advanced—are interested in maintaining trading relations with foreign countries, capitalist and socialist alike. In actual fact, however, the maintenance and development of such relations with capitalist countries have been beset by considerable difficulties in the history of all socialist countries. Apart from the fact that the realization of their industrialization programs inevitably reduces their ability to continue exporting food and raw materials that were usually purchased from them by the industrial countries, political obstacles to trade have assumed paramount importance. After the end of the Second World War the socialist countries of Eastern and Southeastern Europe and China were subjected by the capitalist powers to what is virtually an economic blockade, and thus deprived of the possibility of acquiring precisely those goods that they need most for their industrialization. It was undoubtedly accurate of the United Nations Economic Commission for Europe to point out in a recent bulletin that "the costs of development in a small country, poorly endowed with energy and material resources, will be increased and growth held back, unless it is prepared to take fairly full advantage of the international division of labor."[85] But it is not wholly within the small country's power to follow this good advice! In fact, if it were not for the possibility of trading with other socialist countries, a policy of self-sufficiency would have been *de facto* forced upon the socialist countries by the hostility of the Western powers. In that case the small socialist countries and those the resources of which are (at the present time) either poor or highly specialized might have been

[85] *Economic Bulletin for Europe* (August 1955), p. 94.

actually incapable of surviving and might have succumbed to the combined forces of economic dependence and political pressure.

The situation changes, however, quite drastically with the appearance and industrialization of a large group of socialist countries that are able to establish economic cooperation and mutual assistance. This permits not only the extension of credits to each other if and when such possibilities exist, it permits also the placing of their trading relations on a firm basis of long-term agreements that free the parties of uncertainties with regard to the volume and prices of their exports and imports. It leads furthermore to a far-reaching coordination of their plans for economic development, assuring them of the possibility of taking full advantage of economies of scale, to avoid unnecessary duplication of productive facilities, to exchange technical information, and so forth. As Oskar Lange points out, it is only in the framework of international collaboration among socialist countries that international division of labor and the principle of comparative costs come into their own and are transformed from ideological phrases masking the exploitation of the weak countries by the strong ones into operating principles of economic activity.[86]

What is most important, the meaning of the principles of international division of labor and of resource allocation according to comparative advantages of different countries undergoes a radical change. Governing economic relations among socialist countries, these maxims are no longer interpreted so as to freeze the *existing* division of labor and to preserve the *prevailing* specialization among individual nations. On the contrary, the aim of both national and international economic planning within the socialist camp seeks a rapid departure from the underdeveloped countries' lopsided economic structures which frequently rest upon one or two export commodities. Such a departure toward a diversification of their productive activities is not only highly desirable but altogether indispensable. Without it there is neither a chance for long-term economic growth nor a possibility for the liquidation of their social and cultural backwardness, for the termination of what Marx used to call the "idiocy of rural life."[87]

---

[86] *Zagadnenia Ekonomii Politycznei* (Problems of Political Economy) (Warsaw, 1953), pp. 127 ff. Cf. also D. Granick, "The Pattern of Foreign Trade in Eastern Europe and Its Relation to Economic Development Policy," *Quarterly Journal of Economics* (August 1954).

[87] It is thus likewise a crucially important condition for a gradual reduction of the striking economic and cultural disparity between urban and rural areas that is observable in all capitalist countries.

The mandatory reorganization of the economies of the underdeveloped countries with a view toward diversification and rapid increase
of aggregate output calls, however, neither for a precipitous reallocation
of their productive resources nor for an indiscriminate taking up of new
lines of production. The decision on both the speed and the nature
of the desired shifts has to take into account a large number of economic,
social, locational, and technical considerations all of which determine
the attractiveness of available alternatives. Taken together, they yield
a schedule of comparative advantages of possible lines of investment,
a schedule that is—needless to say—different for different countries. It
cannot be based on conditions prevailing at any given time, but has
to encompass such changes as can be expected to occur in the course
of the planning period both within the planning country and abroad.[88]
And it is quite clear that the more possible it is to draw it up with
the maximal help of other countries and with full knowledge on the
nature and rate of their planned development, the more rational will
be the resulting allocation of resources.

Such collaboration between socialist countries represents a truly
epoch-making advance compared with the structure of international
economic relations among imperialist powers and underdeveloped
countries in which "an initial power supremacy enables the imperial
power to shape the direction and composition of the colony's trade,

---

[88] It might be even more appropriate to call it a "schedule of comparative disadvantages," when what is at issue is the differential between the
costs of producing a new article and the costs of acquiring it in exchange
for what is currently produced in the underdeveloped country. In some
cases this differential may be quite prohibitive, in others it may be sizable
at the time but promise to decline as the domestic output of new products
increases and/or as other branches of the economy are developed, in still
others it may be caused merely by the existing shortage of skilled manpower and may therefore disappear entirely as the result of a few years
of experience and training. The entire magnitude of this differential
(calculated on the basis of the output anticipated during the planning
period and considering the changes in costs of the relevant products at
home and abroad that may also be expected to take place during the
period in question) must be added to the cost of the direct investment
in the respective plant and facilities. Undertakings requiring the lowest
aggregate outlays will be preferable to those requiring larger allocations
of resources—everything else being equal. Clearly, in most cases "everything else" is not likely to be equal. The setting up of a printing shop
may involve higher outlays than the building of a liquor factory; preference
may still be given to the former. What this schedule permits, however, is
the realization of the costs involved in making choices, regardless of the
considerations on the basis of which those choices may have to be made.

and the trade relations which are thus established in turn strengthen markedly the original power position held by the imperial power."[89] Yet this represents merely a first step towards a fully rational organization of the world economy. Its present, as yet "underdeveloped," nature is necessitated not merely by the fact that it affects only a relatively small number of countries, but even more by the circumstance that all of these are still to a lesser or larger degree economically backward. The former limitation greatly reduces the benefits that could be reaped from a global division of labor and specialization, the latter curtails the scope of mutual aid that the individual countries are in a position to provide.

In an advanced socialist commonwealth this collaboration among its individual components will go very much farther—indeed, assume a new quality. As the age of capitalism will have increasingly receded into the "prehistory of mankind," one of its outstanding legacies will commence its departure from the historical stage. The political and economic phenomenon of the *nation* will slowly but certainly follow the demise of the economic and social order to which it owes its genesis and crystallization. For capitalism, having in its rise created and developed the national entity with all of its progressive and barbaric features, has also produced the conditions for its ultimate disintegration and disappearance. And capitalism, while having "given a cosmopolitan character to production and consumption in every country" and having substituted for "old local and national seclusion and self-sufficiency . . . intercourse in every direction, universal interdependence of nations,"[90] achieved this "cosmopolitan character" and this "universal interdependence" in an antagonistic, intrinsically explosive fashion. It brought them about through subjugation of the weak countries to the strong, through imperialism, colonialism, and exploitation. Having transferred the notions of bourgeois democracy to international relations, it proclaimed the "world community" to be composed of equal and sovereign countries—recognizing, by this very insistence on the equal status and equal rights of the imperialist powers and their dependencies, of the large and the small, of the rulers and the ruled, the profound inequality of the peoples inhabiting the advanced and the underdeveloped countries respectively. What Marx noted with respect

[89] A. O. Hirschman, *National Power and the Structure of Foreign Trade* (Berkeley and Los Angeles, 1945), p. 13.

[90] *The Communist Manifesto*, in Marx and Engels, *Selected Works* (Moscow, 1949-1950), Vol. I, p. 36.

to the individuals comprising capitalist society applies equally to individual nations within the world system of imperialism: *"Equal right is an unequal right for unequal labor.* It recognizes no class differences, because everyone is only a worker like everyone else; but it tacitly recognizes unequal individual endowment and thus productive capacity as natural privileges. *It is therefore, a right of inequality, in its content, like every right."*[91]

It is this inequality in which the majority of mankind perishes in continual misery while a tiny minority, that has built its advanced status upon this very misery, sits idly by—it is this state of "equal rights of all nations" that gives rise to the powerful popular movement against imperialism and colonialism and for national and social liberation. But while this movement has already partly succeeded and will eventually succeed entirely in overthrowing the rule of imperialism and putting an end to the dominance of one nation over another, it can merely create the indispensable *conditions* for the elimination of inequality among nations rather than eliminate this inequality itself. As the social revolution leads to, but does not itself result in, the abolition of classes, so the national revolution leads to, but does not itself result in, the abolition of nations. For both to materialize, far-reaching developments have to change entirely the structure and content of social existence. Economic growth has to make powerful strides bringing the development of productive forces to a level permitting decent standards of living and health not only to a few "chosen" nations but to all parts and members of the socialist world. What is more, these standards have to be substantially equalized—naturally taking into account cultural and climatic peculiarities of different regions. This will undoubtedly require "subsidization" of some areas by those that happen to enjoy "differential rents" due to their having more fertile soils, more ample mineral resources, or a longer tradition of industrial activity. There is no more to be said against such "subsidization" than there is against one part of the country "subsidizing" another part of the country, or against food and clothing and lodging being distributed among members of one family without regard to their *individual* contributions to the family's total income. It requires, in other words, the dethronement of the relation governing all aspects of existence under capitalism, the relation of *quid pro quo*, the law of value. Needless to

[91] *Critique of the Gotha Program, ibid.*, Vol. II, p. 22. (Italics in the original.)

say, this is not something that will be attained by the revolution itself. To reach this state, the only state worthy of the dignity and potentialities of man, will take decades—decades in which new generations of human beings will be educated as members of a socialist cooperative society, rather than as competitive wolves in the jungle of the capitalist market. It is and will be an uphill struggle, for deeply seated are the modes of thinking and reacting implanted in humanity by a "culture" of buying and selling, by centuries of dominating and being dominated, by ages of exploiting and being exploited. The difficulties of conquering this tradition will be large on the national scale; they will be even larger on the international. "The more backward a country is, the stronger is the hold within it of small agricultural production, patriarchalism and ignorance, which inevitably lend particular strength and tenacity to the deepest of petty-bourgeois prejudices, viz., national egoism and national narrowness. These prejudices cannot but die out very slowly, for they can disappear only after imperialism and capitalism have disappeared in the advanced countries, and after the whole foundation of the economic life of the backward countries has radically changed."[92] And Stalin correctly formulated some of the immediate requirements for decisive progress towards this more distant goal: "It is necessary . . . to ensure such a cultural advancement of society as will secure for all members of society the all-round development of their physical and mental abilities. . . . For this, it is necessary, first of all, to shorten the working day at least to six, and subsequently to five hours. This is needed in order that the members of society might have the necessary free time to receive an all-round education. . . . It is likewise necessary that housing conditions should be radically improved, and that real wages of workers and employees should be at least doubled, if not more."[93] For it is only on the basis of a cultural revolution, a tremendous increase of educational standards, an "unconditional surrender" of superstition, ignorance, and obfuscation to realism, reason, and science that the abolition of classes and a socialist commonwealth can be attained *intra-nationally*. And it is only on the basis of a high standard of living, of abundance of material goods, that the *international* equalization can take place in which all parts of society contribute to the advancement of the whole, in which the "haves"

[92] Lenin, *Selected Works in Two Volumes* (Moscow, 1950), Vol. II, Part 2, p. 469.

[93] *Economic Problems of Socialism in the USSR* (New York, 1952), p. 53.

what is function of a cultural revolution in socialist theory?

are as able and willing to help the "have-nots" as the "have-nots" are progressively freed of the necessity of being helped by the "haves." It will be
said by the skeptic and the cynic that all this is at best a "symphony of
the future." Undoubtedly it is. It is a symphony, however, the first movement of which can be heard by all who succeed in freeing themselves
from the mental and psychic stupor into which they are continually
drugged—systematically, implacably, and purposefully—by all the manifold and elaborate agencies of capitalist ideology.

incredibly belief in rationality of man * * * *note: rationality "ever-increasing"*

The attainment of a social order in which economic and cultural
growth will be possible on the basis of <u>ever-increasing rational domina-
tion</u> by man of the inexhaustible forces of nature is a task exceeding
in scope and challenge everything thus far accomplished in the course
of history. If the wealth of mankind consists essentially, as Marx said,
of the totality of its abilities and its aspirations, then its poverty is
likewise nothing other than its ignorance and its timidity. Striving to
place reason in the place of superstition and to substitute confidence
in human capacities for submissive acceptance of a pernicious reality
has always been an arduous and hazardous undertaking. It encounters
not only the embittered resistance of all the "furies of private property,"
it also runs headlong into Dostoevski's Underground Man who "vomits
up reason" and who asks "What do I care for the laws of nature and
arithmetic, when for some cause or other I dislike those laws as well
as the fact that two times two makes four?" This Underground Man
has been pampered and cultivated by the entire apparatus of bourgeois
civilization. The economists make their contribution by presenting the
capitalist system as basically the only possible, indeed "natural," framework of economic activity—if perhaps subject to some improvement.
The psychologists chip in by pronouncing the unconscious to be the
dark, unfathomable force bringing inevitably to naught all efforts to
further the cause of reason, at the same time attributing the observable
structure of the "Id" to perennial, biotic forces rather than to the
frustrations and anxieties continually produced and reproduced by an
inhumanly organized society.[94] Literati like Aldous Huxley, Orwell,
Koestler do their share by drawing surrealistic pictures of what they
understand to be a rational society and by trying to provoke in this

[94] This is the chief weakness of Freud, which leads him, particularly
in his later works, into a perilous proximity to mysticism.

way a revulsion against reason among the multitudes of those who are incapable of perceiving the difference between caricature and reality.[95] Others, like Ernest Hemingway—disappointed in history not "behaving" according to their preferences—preach aimlessness, hopelessness, and futility. Artists play their part by creating escapist works, obscuring and distorting all understanding of the real world; and to cap it all, the film industry, the press, radio, and television provide stupefying entertainment and systematically and relentlessly destroy all intelligent thought among young and old, among the ignorant and the educated, in the advanced countries no less than in the backward.

The Underground Man, molded and reared in the treadmill of capitalist culture, will not disappear on the morrow of the social revolution. The destruction of the social basis from which he continually draws his lifeblood greatly weakens his power of resistance; it does not eliminate him overnight. Overcoming this heritage of what will eventually be looked upon as the end of humanity's dark ages will be a protracted campaign filling the lifespan of generations. As Hegel well knew, the ascent of reason has never followed a straight line. It has continually been obstructed and slowed down—by inquisitions and by concentration camps, by gas chambers and by witch hunts. It has been marked by brilliant victories and stopped by grievous defeats, it has gone through exhilarating advances and been bogged down in disheartening retreats. The obstacles that block the way of reason are not merely the hatred and tenacity of the forces clinging desperately to the *status quo*, and the darkness of the people that are held in their grip. The obstacles include also the frequently exasperating inadequacies and mistakes of those who devotedly struggle for its triumph. These aberrations have discouraged and disoriented many who might have found the strength and courage to brave the penalties and ostracism imposed by bourgeois society and to ally themselves with the cause of progress. Yet it is the usual stratagem of opportunists to seize upon errors committed in the advancement of the cause of reason so as to abandon that cause itself and to lapse into agnosticism and passivity.

Errors are, however, unavoidable in all human endeavors; their occurrence forms, indeed, an aspect of the very progress of reason in the furtherance of which they may be committed—and corrected. Of

[95] This has been incisively analyzed in a masterful essay by T. W. Adorno, "Der Entzauberte Traum," in *Die Neue Rundschau* (2nd issue, 1951), reprinted in his *Prismen, Kulturkritik und Gesellschaft* (Berlin and Frankfurt, 1955).

all failings of thought none is probably so dangerous and destructive as the inability to distinguish between irrationality and error. The difference is the same as that between the incoherences of a psychotic and the mistaken statements of a sane person. The former stem from a profound illness, the latter from an inadequacy of knowledge and insight. On a social scale, as on the individual scale, neither can be eliminated except by removing the underlying causes. As a social phenomenon, irrationality will not be overcome so long as its basis, the capitalist system, continues to exist. What is more, just as the psychotic cannot be impressed by argument and persuasion, a social order the very organizational principle of which is irrationality cannot be rendered rational by the progress of science and education. In fact, all the additional knowledge gained by an irrationally constituted society may but enlarge and enhance the powers of death and destruction.

In a society in which reason has been made the governing principle of social relations the situation is radically different. Once more, the evolution of that society will be a long and painful process. "What we have to deal with here is a communist society, not as it has *developed* on its own foundations, but, on the contrary, as it *emerges* from capitalist society; which is thus in every respect, economically, morally and intellectually, still stamped with the birthmarks of the old society from whose womb it emerges."[96] Indeed, for a considerable time both irrationality and error will mar also the socialist order. Crimes will be committed, abuses will be perpetrated, cruelty and injustice will be inevitable. Nor can it be expected that no mistakes will be made in the management of its affairs. Plans will be wrongly drawn up, resources will be wasted, bridges will be built where none are needed, factories constructed where more wheat should have been planted. What is decisive, however, is that irrationality will henceforth not be—as it is under capitalism—*inherent* in the structure of society. It will not be the unavoidable outgrowth of a social system based on exploitation, national prejudice, and incessantly cultivated superstition. It will become a residue of a historical past, deprived of its socioeconomic foundation, rendered rootless by the disappearance of classes, by the end of exploitation of men by men. As the socialist society matures, as it commences to "develop on its own foundations," it will progressively free itself of the legacies of the capitalist past. Its own functional disturbances and errors will be based on misjudgments of rational men resulting from insufficiencies of

[96] Marx, *Critique of the Gotha Program,* in Marx and Engels, *Selected Works* (Moscow, 1949-1950), Vol. II, p. 21. (Italics in the original.)

their intellectual and psychic endowments or from shortcomings in the prevailing state of knowledge. To remedy both, to advance the proficiency of men in the control of nature and in the improvement of their relations among themselves, then becomes the great and proud challenge to all scientific endeavor. With the progress of knowledge transformed into a powerful tool of human advancement, it will become the concern of men and women in all walks of life. Drawing its energies from the immeasurable resources of free people, it will not only irrevocably conquer hunger, disease, and obscurantism, but in the very process of its victorious advance will radically recreate man's intellectual and psychic structure.

To contribute to the emergence of a society in which development will supplant stagnation, in which growth will take the place of decay, and in which culture will put an end to barbarism is the noblest, and, indeed, the only true function of intellectual endeavor. The need for the triumph of reason over myth, for the victory of life over death cannot be proved by means of logical inference. As a great physicist once said, "logic alone is incapable of carrying anyone beyond the realm of his own perception; it cannot even compel him to recognize the existence of his fellow men."[97] This need must rest on the proposition that humanity's claim to life, to development, to happiness requires no justification. With this proposition it stands and falls. This proposition is, however, its sole unprovable and irrefutable premise.

[97] Max Planck, *Das Weltbild der Neuen Physik* (Leipzig, 1929), p. 9.

Index

301